#15

Welcome to America, Mr. Sherlock Holmes

Other books by Christopher Redmond:
In Bed With Sherlock Holmes: Toronto, Simon & Pierre, 1984

Welcome to America, Mr. Sherlock Holmes

Victorian America meets Arthur Conan Doyle

Christopher Redmond

> A. Conan Doyle, manly and taking in person, manner and intellect, won steadily by his genialness, upon the favor his stories had gained in advance. . . . So the authors from another land who have read or discoursed to us, have so far justified in the main their appearance in such role, by preserving the "supreme moment" to the memory of their hearers.
>
> *Major J. B. Pond*

We would like to express our gratitude to The Canada Council and the Ontario Arts Council for their support.

Marian M. Wilson, Publisher

This book has been published with the assistance of a grant from the Canadian Federation for the Humanities, using funds provided by the Social Sciences and Humanities Research Council of Canada.

Copyright © 1987 Christopher Redmond
All rights reserved

No part of this book may be reproduced or transmitted in any form or by any means, electronic or mechanical, including photocopying and recording, information storage and retrieval systems, without permission in writing from the pubilsher, except by a reviewer who may quote brief passages in a review.

ISBN 0-88924-184-8

1 2 3 4 5 ● 91 90 89 88 87

Canadian Cataloguing in Publication Data

       Redmond, Christopher
           Welcome to America, Mr. Sherlock Holmes

       Includes index.
       ISBN 0-88924-184-8

       1. Doyle, Arthur Conan, Sir, 1859-1930 - Journeys - United States.
       2. Doyle, Arthur Conan, Sir, 1859-1930 - Journeys - Canada.
       3. Authors, English - 19th century - Journeys - United States.
       4. Authors, English - 19th century - Journeys - Canada. 5. United States - Description and travel - 1865-1900. 6. Canada - Description and travel - 1868-1900.* I. Title.

       PR4623.R43 1987   823'.8   C87-095195-5

Cover Design: Christopher W. Sears
Photograph: Courtesy Metropolitan Toronto Library, Arthur Conan Doyle Collection.

General Editor: Marian M. Wilson
Editor: Sarah Robertson
Assitant Editor: Jean Paton
Typesetting: University of Waterloo
Printer: Les éditions graphiques Marc Veilleux Inc.

Printed and Bound in Canada

Simon & Pierre Publishing Company Limited
Order Department
P.O. Box 280, Adelaide Street Postal Station
Toronto, Ontario
Canada M5C 2J4

This book is dedicated
to my father Donald A. Redmond
and to those
who share his noble profession
of reference librarian

Sources and Acknowledgements

I could not have written this study without the help of the hundreds of librarians, colleagues and friends around the United States and Canada, and abroad, who helped me find the information. Indeed, it occurred to me from time to time that I was not so much examining a period of Arthur Conan Doyle's life as demonstrating what can be mined from libraries if one has the patience to look and write and ask.

One might expect that the chief source for a study of Arthur Conan Doyle's 1894 American tour would be Doyle's own writings from that period, especially his frequent letters to his mother (in which, if anywhere, he poured out his heart) and his pocket diary. I have no doubt that such documents would have been very valuable to me. But they were not available; presumably they are among a large body of Doyle's papers, used by some early biographers, which have for some two decades been sealed as the result of complicated legal disputes over Doyle's estate. I have therefore conducted my work without access to them. Also unavailable has been a cache of letters from Doyle to his agent during the tour, Major Pond, held by a private collector in Boston. Nor have the surviving papers of Doyle's brother, Innes Hay Doyle, been available; they might have shed some light on the tour from a tangential point of view, that of the young officer who accompanied his literary brother to America.

Sources which were available did include a few Doyle letters in other collections, as well as other contemporary documents. More substantially, they included the reminiscences and letters of people who met Doyle along the way; books of history, with nuggets of information or long passages which helped to set the stage; and, above all, newspaper reports of Doyle's visits to town after town. Accumulation of information from such directions has enabled me to write this study, which is doubtless in places more speculative than I might have hoped. I simply do not know whether, as has been alleged, Doyle disliked Major Pond and found his tour a terrible ordeal. Certainly the detailed reconstruction which I have done – and which, apparently, no previous biographer has attempted – does not seem to justify a description of the whole two-month trip as an unbroken grind. I choose to provide the available facts and pay little attention to previous biographers' generalizations.

For it would not be quite true to say that Doyle's 1894 tour was virgin territory until I came to it; apart from what is in the standard biographies, for example, John Nieminski has privately published an exhaustive compendium of material about the aspects of it which touched on Chicago. But previous research has been sparse. It was immensely fortunate for me that, shortly after I began my work, there was published (in *The Baker Street Journal*) an itinerary of the trip which Richard Lancelyn Green transcribed from a record-book of the tour manager, Major Pond, which is now held in the New York Public Library.

If this book reads as a continuous narrative, I shall feel that I have triumphed, for it was made, not from a few substantial and continuous sources, but out of shreds and patches, and the joy and challenge of writing has been assembling those bits from the books and libraries in which they were hiding. Over the months I lost track of how many letters I had written and how many people had helped me; but I have, I hope, the names of all those who contributed their morsels. It was cheering to receive letters, time after time, from overworked librarians, and others, who answered the inquiries of a stranger promptly and fully and with friendly suggestions. It was notable that small institutions were particularly ready to help, perhaps because they are not daily overloaded by scholars' demands and perhaps also because they saw value in letting the world learn about a great man's visit to their home town. (Inevitably, there were a few people and libraries who were unhelpful, silent or unusually bureaucratic in the face of my requests for assistance.) I am glad to note that the majority of my benefactors are at public institutions; the new knowledge I am able to present is thus a small dividend to the taxpayers in several dozen jurisdictions who have wisely invested over the years in books and records, buildings to hold them and people to maintain them.

In the Notes which follow the text, I attempt to give credit to all those who helped; to indicate the published or manuscript sources which provided the information; and to make a few additional remarks about the significance of what I have reported, or collateral matters which may be of interest. When the text consists of speculation made on my own authority, I trust I have made its nature sufficiently clear. General information of the kind found in standard biographical and historical sources is not cited; I have assumed that the reader can look things up as easily as I can.

For credit and thanks, the name which must head the list is that of my father, Donald A. Redmond, whose example turned me from a Sherlockian into a Doylean scholar; who showed me the way to write books on Doyle, by writing one; who smoothed my path with all sorts of advice; and who time after time has helped me answer knotty questions of fact, finding information in his memory, his own collections, and the library of Queen's University at Kingston, where he carries on the noble work of a reference librarian. He also read the chapters of the book as they were drafted, and made a number of helpful comments.

Sources and Acknowledgements

Reference librarians at the University of Waterloo have been enormously helpful as well; I am grateful to Gary Draper, David Binkley and Jo Beglo for patience with bizarre questions. The University of Waterloo, as my employer, inevitably provided an infrastructure for my work, and that has included the invaluable help of staff in the interlibrary loans office and other departments of the library.

For matters connected with Arthur Conan Doyle himself I have relied heavily on the patient assistance of Cameron Hollyer and Janice McNabb at the Metropolitan Toronto Library, whose Doyle collection is a valuable and still under-used resource. Other departments of the same library have valiantly helped from time to time. I have briefly used the collections of several other libraries:

> The Seeley G. Mudd Manuscript Library, Princeton University; the Ohio Historical Society library and archives; the Long Island Historical Society, Brooklyn; the New-York Historical Society; the Berg Collection of the New York Public Library; the Public Library of the City of Boston; the Smith Memorial Library at Chautauqua, New York; the library of the State Historical Society, Madison, Wisconsin; the McLaughlin Library of the University of Guelph; the Business Library of the Brooklyn Public Library; the public libraries of Niagara Falls (New York), Niagara Falls (Ontario), Glens Falls, and Niagara-on-the-Lake.

When I speak of dozens, indeed hundreds, of people elsewhere who have assisted me, I am not engaging in hyperbole. The names of many of those people appear in the notes and comments. Particular gratitude is due to John Nieminski of Chicago, who encouraged this study, advised me from his considerable knowledge of Doyle and the scholarship about him, and made information available which his own extensive efforts had unearthed. I regret that he did not live to see these results or to read these thanks.

Information which was directly used in the text is acknowledged in the corresponding chapters of notes. I must also acknowledge the names of a large number of people who provided negative evidence (just as valuable as positive evidence, any historian will agree), referred me to sources, or gave other support:

> Marlene Aig of New York; James R. Hobin of the Albany Public Library; Daria D'Arienzo, archivist of Amherst College; Dr. John Jones of Balliol College, Oxford; Peter E. Blau of Washington, D. C.; Cynthia English of the Library of the Boston Athenaeum; the Librarian of *The Boston Globe;* John R. Cronin, librarian of the *Boston Herald;* Henry Scannell of the microtext room, Boston Public Library; Charles Niles, Jr., of the Mugar Memorial Library, Boston University; Mrs. V. E. M. Hartles of the British Embassy, Washington;
>
> Ray Zwick, librarian of the *Cincinnati Enquirer*; Kevin Grace and Alice M. Vestal of the University of Cincinnati libraries; Stuart W. Campbell, archivist of Clark University; Dr. Werner Packull of Conrad Grebel College; Ann Walaskay of the Univer-

Welcome to America, Mr. Sherlock Holmes

sity of Detroit main library; Marie Booth Ferré of Dickinson College, Carlisle, Pennsylvania; Ellen G. Gartrell of the William R. Perkins Library, Duke University; Charles William Eliot II of Cambridge, Massachusetts; Sr. Mary E. Carrigan of Elizabeth Seton College, Yonkers; Mrs. J. Strong of the *Elmira Star-Gazette*; Irene R. Norton of the Essex Institute, Salem, Massachusetts; Paulette Greene, bookseller of Rockville Centre, New York; Irene Montague of the Hampshire Gazette;

Harriot T. McGraw of the development office, Harvard University; Harley P. Holden, curator of the Harvard University Archives; Jeanne T. Newlin of the Harvard College theatre collection; Paul D. Herbert of Cincinnati; Jessica Travis of The Historic New Orleans Collection; Sara S. Hodson of the Huntington Library, San Marino, California; Laurel G. Bowen of the Illinois State Historical Library; Robert A. McCown, manuscripts librarian, the University of Iowa; Vincent Seifried of Jamaica, New York;

the late Dr. Karl Krejci-Graf of Frankfurt; Charles B. Elston, archivist of Marquette University; John D. Cushing of the Massachusetts Historical Society; LeRoy Barrett of the State Archives of Michigan; Kathleen A. Koehler of the Bentley Historical Library, and Richard W. Ryan of the William L. Clements Library, both at the University of Michigan; Charles W. Cooney, jr., of the Milwaukee County Historical Society; "Gail" at the library of the *Milwaukee Journal* and *Sentinel*; Thomas Tomczak of the Milwaukee Public Library; Andrew Malec of the University of Minnesota library; Hartley R. Nathan of Toronto; the Judicial, Fiscal and Social Branch of the National Archives of the United States; Lloyd Johnson of the National Baseball Library; Carlene E. Stephens of the National Museum of American History;

David C. Dearborn of the New England Historic Genealogical Society; Rosemary Lewis of the library at the College of New Rochelle; Lola L. Szladits of the Berg Collection, New York Public Library; Bertram L. O'Neill of Philadelphia; Leon Warmski of the Archives of Ontario;

Helen M. Wilson of the Historical Society of Western Pennsylvania; David K. King of the Free Library of Philadelphia; James Green of the Library Company of Philadelphia; Laurel McGough of the *Pittsburgh Post-Gazette*; Patricia A. Cose of the Port Authority of New York and New Jersey; Carol Woodger of the Port Chester Public Library; B. R. Brown of the Princeton Public Library; Dr. James G. Ravin of Toledo; James C. Andrews of Rensselaer Polytechnic Institute; Rev. Canon Paul Welsby of Rochester Cathedral, Kent; the librarian of the *Rochester Democrat and Chronicle*; Karl Kabelac and Mary M. Huth of the University of Rochester library; Dr. John McCormick of Rutgers, The State University, New Jersey; Rev. Lawrence K. Miech of Saint Francis Seminary, Milwaukee;

Dr. Kevin O'Brien of St. Francis Xavier University; William L. Keogan of St. John's University, Jamaica, New York; Richard D. Tetreau of Saint Peter's College, Jersey City; Karen Preslock of the Smithsonian Institution Libraries; Jeanne Kolva of the Statue

Sources and Acknowledgements

of Liberty National Monument; Thomas M. Whitehead of the Temple University library; Cathy Henderson of Humanities Research Center, University of Texas; Joel Wurl, archivist of the University of Toledo; Fred P. Nickless, Jr., of the alumni office, Tufts University; Wilbur E. Meneray, rare books librarian of Tulane University; Ellen Gladger, archivist of Union College; Robert A. Hull of the Alderman Library, University of Virginia;

Susan Bellingham, rare books librarian; Sally Haag, department of classical studies; Dr. Jan Narveson, philosophy department; Dr. Lionel Needleman, economics department; Dr. Gilman Ostrander, history department; Dr. Manfred Richter, Germanic and Slavic languages and literatures department; and Dr. Gordon Slethaug, department of English, all at the University of Waterloo;

Robert Kunnath of Purdy Library, Wayne State University; Elizabeth G. Fuller of the Westchester County Historical Society; Barrie Cabena of Wilfrid Laurier University, Waterloo; the libraries of the University of Wisconsin at Madison; Denis Kavemeier of the office of university publications, University of Wisconsin at Milwaukee; Lora Brueck of the Gordon Library, Worcester Polytechnic Institute; Dr. A. E. Rodin of Wright State University; Robin Bullock of the Archives-American Heritage Center, University of Wyoming; Tim McCabe of Xavier University, Cincinnati.

I should also like to thank the authorities and staff of the libraries at the following institutions, which provided various material to me through interlibrary loan to Waterloo:

Ball State University; Brooks Memorial Library, Brattleboro, Vermont; the University of Calgary; the Cambridge University Library; Carleton University; the Center for Research Libraries; Cornell University; Duke University; the Legislative Library of British Columbia; Michigan State University; the University of Missouri at Columbia; the National Library of Canada; the University of Oregon; the Pennsylvania State Library; the University of South Carolina; the University of Toronto; Victoria University, Toronto; the University of Western Ontario.

My draft has been read by Dr. Warren Ober, of the Department of English at the University of Waterloo, whose advice I have found extremely useful in making revisions, and by that paragon of knowledge, Janice McNabb. Portions of the manuscript have been read by Ursula Moran and Karen Campbell, who both made helpful comments. I am grateful to two anonymous reviewers who read the manuscript on behalf of the Canadian Federation for the Humanities and made a number of welcome suggestions. The manuscript was much improved by the editing of Sarah Robertson.

Finally and importantly I must thank my wife, Katherine Karlson Redmond, who has provided not only the encouragement, moral support and assistance one might expect from a liberated and loving wife, but also a considerable knowledge of Doyle and the Sherlock Holmes canon, on which I have been able to draw to my constant advantage.

Contents

7   **Sources and Acknowledgements**

14 **Map of Tour**

15 **Author's Note**

16 **Photograph of Arthur Conan Doyle**

17 **Introduction**

27 **October 1894**
    Arrival in New York 27; The Metropolis of the United States 30; Luncheon at the Lotos Club 33; A Chat with Arthur Conan Doyle 35; Parkman Land 37; The Sage of Boston 39; Hunting in the Adirondacks 40; The Stars and Stripes 41; Lecture at Calvary 43; The Limited Train 45; Chicago's Elite 48; A Literary Luncheon 51; Aladdin, Jr. 54; With Riley in Indianapolis 55; Ticket to Cincinnati 57; The Culture of the Queen City 59; Harvest Home 61; The Toledo Cycling Club 64; Dinner in Detroit 66; Spiritualism Past and Present 68; Lecture in Detroit 70; George Meredith 71; Hotels on Wheels 75; Evening in Milwaukee 76; Return to Chicago 78; Heading Back East 81; Literary Tidings 82; Lecture in Brooklyn 85; A Tree Grows in Northampton 88; A Cabman in the Athens of America 91

94 **November 1894**
    Smoke Talk in Worcester 94; Lecture at Amherst College 95; Lecture at Norwich 96; "My Own Theory of Reading" 98; Lecture in Washington 100; Baltimore on Election Day 101; **Round the Red Lamp** *104; Dinner in Philadelphia 106; Next Stop Newark 108; Siss, Boom,*

Ah! 109; *Impressions of America* 111; *A Visit with John Kendrick Bangs* 113; *Audience in Orange* 116; *New Readings at Daly's* 117; *Philadelphia and Princeton* 117; *North to New Rochelle* 119; *Dinner at the Lotos Club* 120; *A Cheque for S. S. McClure* 123; *Return to Boston* 125; *Reading from "The Cardboard Box"* 126; *Interview in Rochester* 127; *The Female College at Elmira* 129; *Pilgrimage to Glens Falls* 130; *Lecture at Schenectady* 132; *Tourist at Niagara Falls* 133; *An Old Friend in Toronto* 134; *Lecture in Buffalo* 139; *Mark Twain's New Book* 139; *Thanksgiving with the Kiplings* 140; *Lecture in Morristown* 142

143 **December 1894**
Rain in Paterson 143; *The Napoleon Fad* 144; *Evening in Flushing* 146; *Fire, Blood, and Corruption* 147; *The Town Hall, Jamaica* 148; *Last Lecture* 148; *A Toast to Arthur Conan Doyle* 149; *Aboard the* Etruria 151

153 **Afterword**

156 **Appendix I – "Readings and Reminiscences"**
Text of Doyle's lecture as he delivered it during his 1894 tour of North America, reconstructed by Christopher Redmond 156
Notes to "Readings and Reminiscences" 166

168 **Appendix II – Notes and Comments**
Epigraph 168
Introduction 168
October 1894 171
November 1894 199
December 1894 219
Afterword 222

224 **Index**

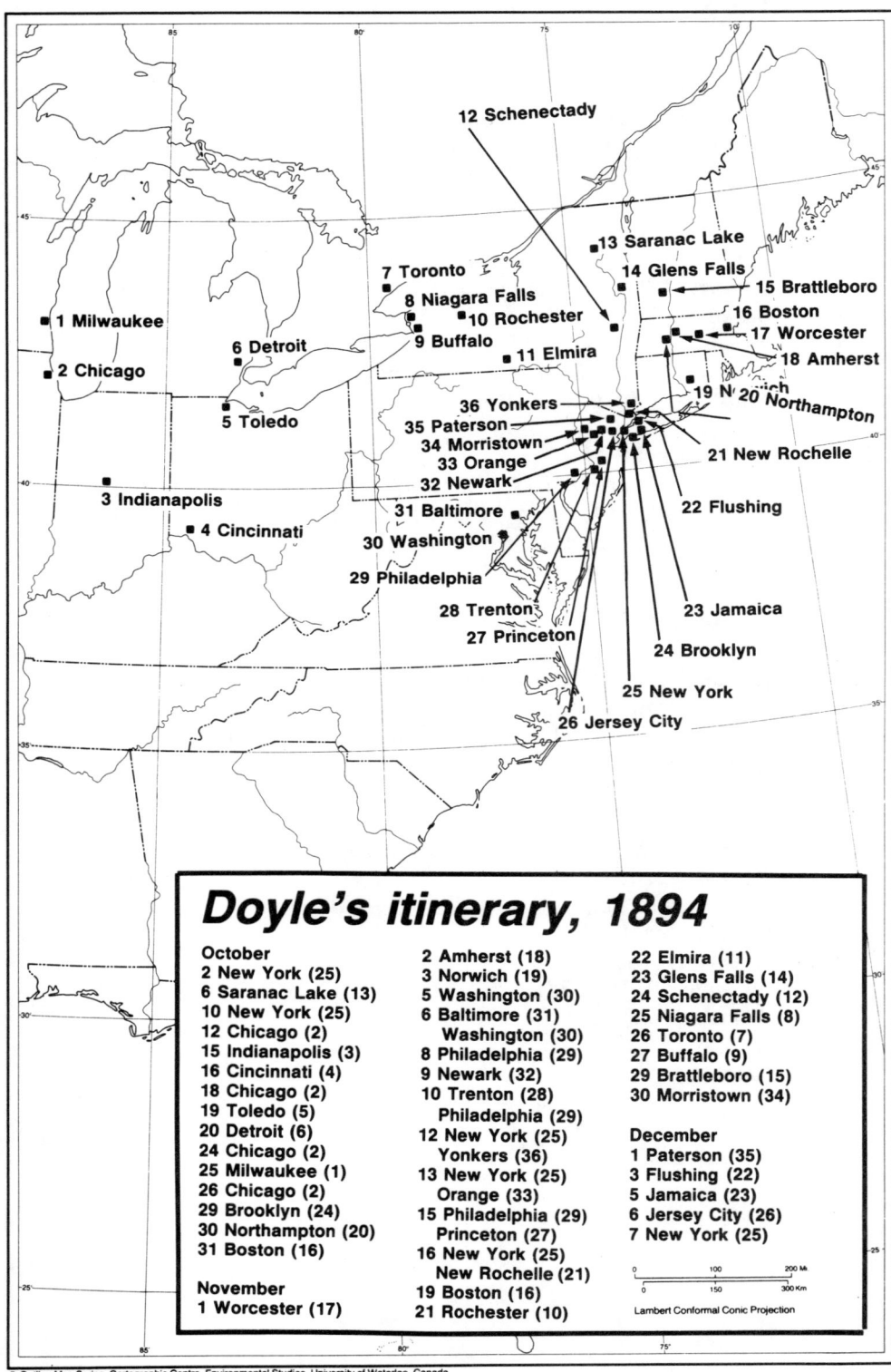

Author's Note

Doyle's 1894 trip, made when he was a young man and known only for his literary work, has been eclipsed in his biographies by the later North American trips of 1914 (when he was described as the best-known living Englishman) and of 1922 and 1923 (when he came to preach his new-found creed of Spiritualism). This book, tracing the 1894 trip in detail, thus presents almost entirely new material.

The bulk of the book is a series of chapters in which Doyle's itinerary, activities, and possible thoughts are traced day by day. His movements on certain days during his tour apparently cannot be reconstructed; I have taken advantage of such gaps to present background and supplementary information. Lacking access to Doyle's notes and letters, for reasons which are mentioned in the Acknowledgements, I have written less than I might otherwise have done about the traveller's own experiences and feelings, and more about the people he met and the impression he made and the kind of America he found. This book is a study of both sides of an encounter.

An Appendix provides the reconstructed text of "Readings and Reminiscences," the lecture which Doyle gave thirty-four times during his tour. Notes following the narrative include sources, tangential comments and references to material in the text that is conjectural rather than firmly documented.

ARTHUR CONAN DOYLE: *Courtesy of Metropolitan Toronto Library*

Introduction

Like every year, 1894 was a mixture of change and stability. There was, of course, no change at Windsor, where Victoria had been queen for fifty-seven years, and now ruled as great-grandmother of a vaster empire than had ever been. Nor, despite the illness and death of Alexander III, did there seem much danger that the Romanov dynasty would lose its control of Russia's throne. But there were rumbles of change from distant lands: in a remote place whose name was then spelt "Corea," a war was breaking out between the little-known empires of Japan and China; battles at places with such anglicized names as Port Arthur and Prince Jerome Gulf were, unknown to newspaper readers of 1894, the beginning of a fifty-year struggle which would lead to battles at Corregidor, Singapore, and Midway.

In 1894, too, anarchists in France assassinated a president, and the civilized world shuddered – but England had almost forgotten Napoleon, and America was a generation removed from its civil war. In Imperial Britain, the Liberal Party under Lord Rosebery was staggering into the political wilderness, and though something called the Parliamentary Labour Party had been formed in 1893, it was the Conservative Party which would replace the Liberals. In America, the President was a Democrat, Grover Cleveland, serving his second term after a four-year Republican hiatus.

For ordinary people, in America as in England, daily life seemed settled and orderly, and starvation was banished to distant villages or city slums. Railways brought towns together and made possible every convenience of modern life, from plentiful and varied food to national magazines and, in Britain at least, national newspapers. Few were rich, but many were well off, and both in England and in America it was possible to begin as an office-boy or bootblack and hope to become the plump, waistcoated proprietor of a healthy business. For women, of course, prospects were narrower, and marriage the chief road to financial advancement, but in Britain efforts were being made to humanize divorce laws on their behalf, and in America there were a few places where women had the vote.

To a contemporary reader, the middle-class newspapers of 1894 show a world which seems at once old-fashioned, touchingly human, and amusingly modern:

Shortly after 11 o'clock a cross-town car whizzed along on its way from Hunter's Point to the City Hall. A crowd of well-dressed, highly respectable people, all in various stages of drowsiness, filled all but four seats.

At Park and North Portland avenues the car stopped, and a party of young people boarded it. There were just eight of them, four girls and four young men. They were laughing and chatting, evidently in high spirits. When the girls started for the empty seats they were stopped by one of the young men, who said:

"Look here, girls; if you sit down we'll have to stand up. Say, what's the matter with your sitting on our laps?"

The girls hesitated a minute, then one of them, a pretty blonde, said:

"If you'll do it, Jennie, I will."

Jennie was not going to be dared, so, without more ado, she plumped herself down in one of the waiting laps, and the other girls, with much laughing and talking, followed her example. . . .

A stern-looking woman who sat opposite drew herself up as stiff as a poker, and tried to freeze the lap sitters with a stony glare, while two youths in another part of the car blushed and giggled alternately. . . .

Finally Father Wagner of St. Bernard's Church, who was in the car, jumped from his seat and said sternly to one of the girls:

"Here, young woman, take this seat and leave that shocking position."

The girl, looking a little alarmed at the priest's stern tone, took the empty seat. Then three other men got up rather sheepishly and offered their seats to the other girls. Two of them accepted, but Jennie, who had been the first one to sit in her escort's lap, sat there with a far away look in her eyes as if she heard or saw nothing of what was going on. . . .

Finally, when the car got to Atlantic avenue and Clinton street, [motorman] Bray decided to summon reënforcements, so he stopped the car, called in Motorman Reardon, and the two gently picked up Jennie, carried her out of the car, and put her on the sidewalk.

English and American civic leaders and editorialists had little doubt that they lived at the pinnacle of civilization, even though there were few great writers and artists then working. Just as well, some of them felt – it was better for ingenuity and talent to be channelled into something useful, such as the creation of more powerful machines, taller buildings, or new household implements to make daily life easier.

Education was supposed to be universal in America, and nearly so in Britain, and if there was a preference for the practical, there was still a desire for the beautiful, the novel and the interesting in the hours of leisure which all but the most desperately exploited workers were starting to enjoy. Thus an entrepreneur and retired army officer named J. B. Pond was meeting a strongly felt need when he brought prominent travellers, reformers, and literary men to lecture on platforms across the United States. Only a few of those who read the newspapers care-

Introduction

fully might realize that early in 1894 Mr. Thomas Edison had given a public demonstration of a new gadget which projected moving pictures onto a blank wall, and foresaw that such an invention would mean the end of the lecture as a community event.

Major Pond, 56 years old in 1894, was at the top of his profession. Having begun his career as a journalist with such newspapers as the Lawrence (Kansas) *Herald of Freedom* in abolitionist days, he went on to serve with the Union Army during the Civil War; and afterwards, abolitionist causes no longer needing promotion, he turned to sending ex-Mormons and anti-Mormons on the lecture trail. In the 1870's he served with the Redpath Lyceum Bureau in Boston, the last gasp of the old lyceum circuit which made the likes of Ralph Waldo Emerson known across America. From 1879 he was in New York as the proprietor of his own lecture service, the chief one in the field.

Pond managed political and literary figures, explorers, humourists, anybody who could draw audiences. The old educational lyceum system was weakening by the time of Oscar Wilde's spectacular tour in 1882, and almost gone by the 1890's, replaced by something closer to sheer entertainment, even if reformers and advocates of special causes, such as women's suffrage, were still often seen on the lecture circuit. The lecturer who held the record in Pond's stable – some two hundred nights in a row, except for Sundays – was George Kennan, who travelled the continent in 1890 talking about Siberia, anarchism, and the wickedness of the Czarist government: not so bad as its reputation, he told his audiences. Under Pond's auspices, Henry Ward Beecher travelled many thousand miles, James Whitcomb Riley took many platforms (when his travelling companions could keep him sober), and Mark Twain gave readings and lectures.

In the fall of 1894, Pond had a great attraction to offer: the young British novelist Arthur Conan Doyle, well known as the creator of the popular Sherlock Holmes. That summer Pond circulated a brochure inviting literary societies and similar groups to book Doyle as a speaker. In it, he cajoled them with favourable paragraphs from reviews of four of Doyle's works, all from American papers. They ranged from the *Christian Inquirer*, calling Doyle's novel *The Refugees* "a sterling historical novel" and even better than his earlier work *Micah Clarke*, to the *Chicago Inter-Ocean*, which observed that Doyle's "style, vigorous, terse, and thoughtful, united to a nice knowledge of the human mind, makes every character a profoundly interesting psychological study. The reader who enters upon one of his studies is loath to drop the book until it is concluded." And that was not a comment on the historical novels, nor yet on the domestic short stories: this reviewer was talking about the tales of Sherlock Holmes. Before the tour was over, the chief personages of the *Chicago Inter-Ocean* would have a chance to form an opinion not only of Doyle the author but of Doyle the man.

Doyle was actually supposed to offer three different lectures during his tour, according to the brochure, which proclaimed him "The latest platform attraction for the season of 1894-5." It showed a solemn portrait of him, leaning on the back of a chair, which originally appeared in *Harper's Weekly*. It bore the imprint of "J. B. Pond, Everett House, 218 Fourth Avenue, New York City, to whom all communications should be addressed." It noted that Doyle's books "attracted public attention at once, and have had an immense sale in this country," and it listed his three offerings thus:

> I. Facts About Fiction
> Synopsis: Tendency of Fiction in England; Hardy's Country Pictures; Stevenson's Influence; A Master of Phrases; A Great Book; Olive Schreiner; Barrie and Scotland; The Short Tale; Rudyard Kipling; The Neurotic Woman; Recent Humor.
>
> •
>
> II. The Novels of George Meredith
> Synopsis: Meredith, the Novelist's Novelist; Permanent Influence on Literature; Early Work; Richard Feverel; Style and Its Uses; The Egoist; Meredith's Humor; His Phrase-Making; His Women; A Renovating Force in Literature.
>
> •
>
> III. Readings and Reminiscences
> Synopsis: Some Early Recollections; A Premature Book; Short Stories; The Detective in Fiction; Romance and Reality; Poe's Influence; Sherlock Holmes; Reading; The Philosophy of Trifles; The Historical Novel; Early American Material; The Refugees; Reading; Fiction as a Profession; The Lord of Chateau Noir.

And it added this promise:

> During the past season Dr. Doyle lectured with great success in England, and everywhere received flattering attention from both the public and the press.
> The interest this announcement has already produced insures a large public for Dr. Doyle on this side of the Atlantic.
> Applications should be made at once, as they will be considered in the order of their receipt.

Dated July 10, 1894, the brochure added a page of praise for Doyle's books, quoted from newspapers and magazines around America, and included a final page on which Harper & Brothers offered to sell *The Refugees* (Post 8vo, Cloth, Ornamental) for $1.75, or *Memoirs of Sherlock Holmes* for $1.50 – the latter commended by the *Brooklyn Eagle* as "A series of excellent detective sketches, written in the terse, vigorous, thought-charged English of a master psychologist and a delineator of character."

In short, Dr. Doyle would be an ornament to any American lecture-platform that year. Groups ranging from the Montefiore Society of Indianapolis to St. Bartholomew's School of Morristown, New Jersey, took up Major Pond's offer. And they all preferred that third lecture, the "Readings and Reminiscences." In the end, Doyle gave "Facts About

Introduction

Fiction" once, the talk on Meredith not at all, his prepared "Readings and Reminiscences" some thirty-four times, and other selections from his own works on four occasions.

The success or failure of the tour depended on Pond, and Doyle had no guarantee that he would come home from it wealthy. Indeed, his financial comments at the end of it had a touch of bitterness. He received either a stated fee or a percentage of the gate from each lecture, and he paid his own travelling expenses. If Pond chose good halls and the advertising was right, profits might be high. If there were too many evenings without an audience, profits might quickly be eaten up. And of course Doyle, not Pond, had to ride the Pullman cars all night, eat in unfamiliar hotels in strange cities, be greeted by strangers who might or might not share his tastes. Between agent and lecturer there was bound to be some tension, as journalist Eugene Field – whom Doyle would meet during his tour – hinted in a letter to Pond in April 1893:

> I am willing to devote fifty nights to you and your diabolical purposes next season, provided we can "get together," as your brother Democrats say. I want one-hundred-and-fifty dollars a night; and by humping yourself, as you can, you'll make good money out of me.

In his autobiography, Doyle would describe Pond as "a quaint character . . . the very personification of his country, huge, loose limbed, straggling, with a goat's beard and a nasal voice . . . a good, kind fellow." Some of the other figures he managed would not recall him so kindly, hinting that he cut financial corners when he could; and everyone would be appalled when he decided to start giving lectures himself. Twain would recall that "I hadn't more than sailed out of Vancouver harbor, one Sunday afternoon, before Pond was at it in a Vancouver church."

Doyle arrived in the United States at the beginning of October, and faced a preliminary itinerary drawn up to conform to his strict intention of being home by Christmas. (Originally he told Pond there were to be no lectures after December 1, but that limit was extended a few days.) The itinerary would be changed, though, as the tour went on. Uncertainty and exhaustion were to be his lot for those two months. He doubtless felt rather as the humourist Bill Nye would feel a year later when he wrote this note to William Webster Ellsworth: "I am professionally in Brooklyn October 31st, but the manager has not yet told me where I'll be on the 1st. That at present is between him and his God."

Doyle's name was well known in America and in England – and in Scotland, country of his birth, though his ancestry was Irish and English. But better known then, as today, was a man who never lived, that man born in Doyle's agile mind and raised to fame with his fingers and pen: Sherlock Holmes. He had written two novels about his detective, one of them the best-selling *The Sign of the Four*. There were also twenty-three short stories – twenty-four if one counts "The Cardboard Box," which appeared in the first American edition of *The Memoirs of Sherlock Holmes*, but not in the British, and which was suppressed in both countries thereafter. One thing ACD presumably did in New York was have a look at the new edition of *The Memoirs* from Harper & Brothers, containing only eleven stories to complement the twelve in *The Adventures of Sherlock Holmes*.

He intended never to write another word about Holmes. There were serious novels in his future, but he assumed he had finished with adventure stories. In his lecture, Doyle hinted that he had a pretty good lifetime's work behind him already. That he was able to support himself by writing, rather than by practising medicine, was proof that he had arrived. He had experienced childhood with a strict and proud mother but a weak, drunken father; medical studies at the bleak University of Edinburgh; a practice which drew barely enough patients to provide meals and a roof; a young wife who contracted tuberculosis; years of writing stories no one wanted to read, and then within a few years success and acclaim.

At the age of 35 years and four months, he was a serious novelist, the author of *The White Company* and *Micah Clarke* (a school edition of which had just appeared) and *The Refugees*. And he was confident about his talent. He was, however, a little nervous about the lectures he was to give, having written to Greenhough Smith, his editor at the *Strand Magazine*, in July that "I go to America in September and I have not got my lectures done yet." Nor had he only then learned that the fall trip would be taking place. As early as May it was all settled and Pond, trying to get the brochure put together, wrote to Doyle asking for press reports and reviews to quote from. Doyle replied that he had none: "I do not, as a rule, read them, far less preserve them. I am speaking on literature at the Authors' Society Dinner tonight, and if any paper says anything kind I'll send it on."

He did, accompanied by his sister, attend the May 31, 1894, dinner of the Society of Authors, held at the Holborn Restaurant, an event where everyone from Moncure Conway to Israel Zangwill, the Comtesse Hugo and Lord Kelvin was present. And he did speak there, in response to a toast proposed by the chairman of the society, Sir Frederick Pollock, Bt., professor of jurisprudence at the University of Oxford and author not only of legal texts but of a chapter on mountaineering, one interest definitely shared with Doyle. *The Times* reported it thus: "He afterwards proposed 'Literature,' coupling with the toast the names of the Bishop of Oxford and Mr. Conan Doyle, to whose eminent position in literature he referred. The Bishop of Oxford and Mr. Conan Doyle responded." There was not much in those two sentences to ornament Major Pond's brochure. But the evening must have been a pleasant one, the company good. The Bishop of Oxford was William Stubbs, almost seventy, formerly regius professor of modern history at Oxford, and an authority on early English charters; Doyle, depicter of old England in *The White Company*, perhaps knew something of his dry,

Introduction

scholarly work on mediaeval documents. (Stubbs told the editors of *Who's Who* that his "recreations" were "making out pedigrees and correcting proof-sheets.") In the chair at the May 31 dinner was Sir Leslie Stephen, the former editor of the *Cornhill*, a clergyman before he lost his faith, and now editor of the *Dictionary of National Biography*. His first wife, Harriet, daughter of William Makepeace Thackeray, died in 1875; he was privately educating the children from his second marriage, among them Virginia, who would one day marry Leonard Woolf; by way of literary work he was about to start writing the life of his late brother, the judge, Sir James Fitzjames Stephen.

Major Pond might have found it difficult to translate this rarefied world of British letters into terms which would interest American sponsors and American audiences. Fortunately, as the text of his brochure illustrates, he did not have to do so; he had to do little, in fact, but mention the name of the great detective, who had died at the Reichenbach Falls in the previous December's issue of the *Strand*.

At the beginning of October 1894, Doyle could not know that within a decade he would have brought Sherlock Holmes back to life, and that there were more than thirty Holmes short stories yet to be written, as well as two great novels of the hawklike detective. He could not know that fifty years after his death it was as the creator of Sherlock Holmes that he would be remembered, not for his historical novels, his domestic and medical tales, the science fiction he would one day write, or even his Spiritualist preachings.

He could not know, either, that within a decade he would be knighted – Sir Arthur Conan Doyle – not in recognition of his literary talents, but to reward his work as a war propagandist. He could not know that in twenty years the brother who accompanied him on the tour, young Lieutenant Innes Hay Doyle, would be a brigadier-general risking his life in something called a World War. He could not know that in the final decade of his life he would travel the world (making two great journeys across this still unknown America) to preach the cause of Spiritualism.

As he worried about his wife, Louise, who was seeking relief for her tubercular lungs in the chill dry air of Switzerland, he could not know that within three years he would meet another woman, Jean Leckie, who would become the great love of his life, and that after Louise's death in 1906 he would marry Jean and begin an all too brief period of bliss. War experience was yet to come; unimagined were the deaths of brother Innes and of Kingsley, the younger of the children he left behind as he made this trans-Atlantic voyage. Still less could Doyle imagine the passion with which he would preach Spiritualism when he came back to New York harbour in 1922 and 1923, or the vituperative criticism which would greet him. In 1894, he was simply a young novelist facing a strange land, hitherto known to him only through books and through his own imagination.

During the tour, he met most of the important literary people in America, from old William Dean Howells to irrepressible young Eugene Field. He planted a tree in Massachusetts, he hoisted a few glasses with a club of young bicyclists, he drew sighs and shy glances from the young ladies of Elmira College. He impressed one observer as looking like a boxing champion; others argued whether he looked like a doctor of medicine and whether his accent was English or Scots or just impossible.

Doyle gave his lecture more than thirty times, in a frontier opera house and in an elegant New York City church. He also gave dozens of interviews, answering the same few questions over and over again: What do you think of America? What do you think of American literature? What do you think of Cincinnati, Amherst, Niagara Falls? Above all, when are you going to write some more about Sherlock Holmes? The thousands of people who came to hear him lecture, too, were chiefly interested in seeing the creator of Holmes and hearing, perhaps, a hitherto untold adventure of the great detective. One of the lectures he prepared for them did provide a new fragment of Holmes, but Doyle was determined to put the emphasis on his more serious work.

A century ago, trans-Atlantic voyages lasted a week or more; jet lag was unknown, yet passengers considered it a wonder of the modern world that they could traverse the ocean so quickly. Though determinedly British, Doyle and his brother chose to make their journey to America on a German ship. Built in Glasgow in 1881, the *Elbe* had four masts, two funnels and three decks. It was operated by the same North-German Lloyd line which by the 1890's had had a sad chain of shipwrecks and other troubles. The wreck of the *Deutschland* in 1875 had killed more than a hundred people. (A poet named Gerard Manley Hopkins, aged 50 and still virtually unknown in 1894, had not yet published the poem which would immortalize that wreck, but he had shown it to a sensitive priest at Stonyhurst College, the Rev. Cyprian Splaine, a former teacher of both him and Doyle.) More recently, in January 1892, the *Eider* had struck the Isle of Wight, though lifeboatmen were able to rescue everyone. The *Elbe* itself would sink in a collision off Lowestoft less than three months later – on January 30 – with the loss of 316 lives, including that of the man who steered it on Doyle's voyage, Captain F. von Gössel.

Still, the *Elbe* was known for comfort. It was not one of the bigger liners on the trans-Atlantic route, but it fit the description which an author applied to one of its rivals: "merely a rather low-roofed hotel, with sea-sickness superadded to all the comforts of home." The company advertised "high-class cuisine," "spacious staterooms for two in both first and second saloon," and cabins adorned with works by renowned artists. And the *Elbe* boasted a speed of sixteen to nineteen knots on trans-Atlantic voyages. Doyle left Southampton on Sunday, September 23, and arrived in New York on the morning of October 2.

Introduction

The choice of the *Elbe* led to an incident in the dining salon one evening when the Doyle brothers, seeing nothing but German and American flags decorating the cabin to mark a special occasion, appropriated a tablecloth and hung up a makeshift Union Jack. There were bad feelings on both sides. Most of the 270 cabin-class passengers were German, for the ship started its voyage from Bremen. The passenger list bore such German names as Geheimrath Gutsch and Frau Gutsch, Mathias Pfatischer, Hans Scheinert and Miss Minna Staigen. And the Doyle brothers were so *very* British. Innes, indeed, at the brave age of twenty-one years and six months, held Her Majesty's commission as a second lieutenant in the Western Division of the Royal Artillery – the army branch which provided fire support in battle for combat forces. The Royal Artillery consisted of eighty field batteries, some stationed at home and some in the colonies. Innes's commanding officer, Major Hickman, authorized a few months' leave from his post at Fort Efford, Plymouth, so he could accompany his brother on the American tour, collecting souvenirs and making diary entries of their experiences. (In 1897 a promotion to lieutenant would start Innes on the ladder which would take him to service in South Africa and France, the rank of lieutenant-colonel, and in 1917 an acting brigadier-generalship. Influenza would kill him in February 1919.)

Aboard the ship were a few other Britishers (as well as Americans) who boarded at Southampton. One Englishman was John Harington Gubbins, diplomat, linguist and scholar, who though only a few years older than Doyle had had an eventful career in the diplomatic service; before he was twenty he was posted to Japan, and now he was Second Secretary of Her Britannic Majesty's Legation in Tokio. His stories and his political knowledge had not yet found their way into the books he would write on *The Progress of Japan, 1853-1871* and *The Making of Modern Japan*. Perhaps in conversation he mentioned the martial arts of Japan: another Englishman, by the name of Barton-Wright, had been trying to codify them for European use, under the name of bartitsu. Accompanying Gubbins on this journey was his wife of barely a year, the former Helen Brodie.

Returning from Germany with his wife, Lila, was an American, Dr. Charles Sumner Tainter, 40 years old and the inventor of the graphophone. He could talk at length about his marvellous invention. It was thirteen years since a sealed box was deposited at the Smithsonian Institution, containing a device created by Tainter and his colleague Alexander Graham Bell. When the box was opened in 1937, curious listeners would hear a scratchy voice declaiming lines from *Hamlet*. But in 1894 it was not at all clear who had invented any of the competing sound-recording devices which were on the market. The American Graphophone Co., which Tainter helped to found (though he was not with that firm in 1894), had been in court charging infringement of its patents by the Edison Phonograph Works. The litigation would go on for decades. Doyle was interested in mechanical recording devices, and probably interested enough to question Tainter about the relative merits of wax (his choice) and tinfoil (Edison's) for such purposes. Doyle had a limitless curiosity, and a retentive memory for detail which he might use in his writings years later. The phonograph would turn up in 1899 in "The Japanned Box," and thirty years later he would write a Sherlock Holmes tale (originally a play), "The Mazarin Stone," in which the plot hinges on the use of such a machine.

Another fellow-passenger was Dr. Charles E. West, an old man with much to talk about. Qualified as both a doctor and a lawyer, he had devoted his life to education and the arts. Arguing that "there should be no limit placed on the educational facilities offered to women in every branch of knowledge, so that their possible achievements may not be bounded by any limitations but those of their own powers," he introduced mathematics, then chemistry, and eventually calculus to the ladies' colleges which he headed: Rutgers Female Institute in New York, the Buffalo Female Academy, and finally the Brooklyn Heights Seminary for young ladies, where he lectured on sculpture, painting, drawing, architecture and everything else, and from which he had retired five years earlier at the age of 80. He had been a Fellow of the Royal Antiquarian Society of Denmark for nearly fifty years, and of course was a member of many other learned societies, as well as the author of such writings and addresses as "Fluxionary and Differential Calculus of Newton and Leibnitz." Long a widower, he was accompanied on this trip by his two daughters, Bertha and Marion, and his son, Charles.

West's obituary six years later would mention just a few of his special interests: "Anglo-Saxon works," etchings and engravings, Japanese ware (he and Gubbins perhaps were able to chat along those lines), Peruvian art, and Greek and Roman coins. It was for him that the State University of New York in 1890 created the honorary degree of Doctor of Paedagogy. Best of all, as an American he may have been able to tell Doyle something about the land he would be touring. This Brooklyn place, for example: he knew he was scheduled to lecture there in December, but what was it like?

October 1894

Tuesday, October 2: Arrival in New York
The *Elbe* docks at eight o'clock at one of New York's busy Hudson River piers. The name of Sherlock Holmes does not appear on its passenger list, but it is Sherlock Holmes whom the city's sharpest young reporters are at the dock to meet. The burly, moustached man who prepares to answer their questions is named Arthur Conan Doyle.

Hundreds of bewildered Germans, Irish and British have crowded in the ship's steerage quarters, hoping to be accepted as new Americans. (It is estimated that America has received a thousand immigrants a day for the past twenty years.) These latest newcomers will shortly be taken by barge to Ellis Island, where they can be herded through the great immigration centre and screened for health and prospects, but for this precious moment they are standing on the free ground of America itself. Cabin passengers such as ACD and his brother will go nowhere near Ellis Island; they have been respectfully and quickly examined as the *Elbe* steamed through New York harbour, past Bedloe's Island, where the 225-ton statue of Liberty Enlightening the World was completed eight years ago. Health and immigration officials reserve their attention chiefly for the passengers in the second cabin, which might include a few would-be immigrants of moderate means. The first cabin surely brings only travelling businessmen, wealthy tourists, and celebrities; for the government's purposes, a quick glance at the passenger list is probably enough. Of course, customs formalities remain: America's high tariffs are well known and require close inspection of arriving luggage.

Major Pond heads a small group which has come down to the dock to meet ACD this morning. Also present are those inevitable reporters. They size him up at once and provide a detailed description, essential in an age without newspaper photographs:

> He is tall, straight, athletic, and his head that his blue eyes make radiant with affability must have been modeled by Energy herself, so profoundly impressed it is with her mark. His forehead is not colossal, yet it is as if it were built of the same marble as the

Titans. His look is merry, quick, curious, inventive, and resolutely fixed on the things that happen, and not on an invisible star.

Reporters pursue him for the rest of the day. They ask his plans – as if Major Pond had not already given them all the details of his lecture tour, knowing that no publicity is cheaper, or more extensive, than what newspaper reporters choose to write. ACD heartily tells them that he can stay only till early December. "I mean to see all I can in that time, though I pledge you my word I'll not venture to write any impressions afterwards. . . . I intend to return next year." Louise will come with him then, he promises.

One of the Messrs. Appleton, who within a month will join the ranks of ACD's American publishers, is a member of the Aldine Club and has arranged for it to be ACD's base while he is in New York. He actually rooms at the Hotel Kensington next door. The Aldine is a congenial place, a society of "printers, publishers, authors and artists," and its president is the writer Frank Stockton, whose short story "The Lady or the Tiger" was published in 1882. Just last March the club moved a few blocks from its earlier premises in Lafayette Place to newer ones at 75 Fifth Avenue, "a brownstone dwelling two doors north of 15th Street, on the east side of the avenue."

Later in the day, reporters of both sexes descend on ACD there, and he finally must say something about Sherlock Holmes. Next day's newspapers will have his answer to the inevitable question:

> Of course, in the last published chronicle concerning Sherlock Holmes, it was made known that he had slipped from the brink of a precipice in the embrace of an arch villain, but it was, at the same time, made known that there was deep water at the foot of the precipice. So there has always been a doubt whether the great detective was drowned or made his escape.
>
> A. Conan Doyle, with an unlighted cigar between his teeth and his round, sunburnt face illuminated by a genial smile, yesterday assured a World reporter that Sherlock Holmes did not escape by means of a passing vessel, and that he – A. Conan Doyle – had not come to America to discover Holmes alive on this side of the Atlantic.

But he is happier to say something about his serious work:

> "I wrote short stories from the age of eighteen to that of twenty-seven. Then the people liked 'Micah Clarke,' and so I wrote novels."
>
> "But how could you ever become so thoroughly in sympathy with the time of Micah Clarke?" asked a young woman, whose eyes had the clearness of crystal.
>
> "Oh, I don't know," Dr. Doyle replied. "It came naturally, I suppose. I always liked history. Then, it was a labor of love."
>
> "Which one of your books do you like best?" asked the reporter.
>
> "I like best 'The White Company,' Dr. Doyle replied, without a moment of hesitation. "I suppose the reason is that it is the one which gave me the most trouble to build."

October 1894

"Now, weren't you influenced by Edgar Allan Poe when you wrote 'Sherlock Holmes'?" asked the reporter.

A hush fell in the room. It could be heard as distinctly as if the string of a violin had snapped, but Dr. Doyle liked the question and replied to it, at once, impulsively:

"Oh, immensely! His detective is the best detective in fiction."

"Except Sherlock Holmes," said somebody.

"I make no exception," said Dr. Doyle, very earnestly. "Dupin is unrivaled. It was Poe who taught the possibility of making a detective story a work of literature."

"But Dupin was not your model," suggested the young woman, whose eyes had the clearness of crystal.

ACD and the reporters go on to talk about Dr. Joseph Bell, the medical professor who was one of the models for Sherlock Holmes, and about "The Story of Waterloo" – ACD's play, currently being acted by Henry Irving. The woman reporter adds "a note to her notes, fine as flies' legs, written in a book bound in bleu-de-France morocco, with silver corners, exquisitely curved." It will not be the last time that Doyle's powerful effect on ladies is noticed.

The inevitable questions about Sherlock Holmes out of the way, ACD says something about more serious literature:

> Of course I know lots of your writers by reputation, but I've never met many of them. Met Bret Harte once at dinner, but have never had the good fortune to run across Mark Twain. Think Miss Wilkins is a genius. I'd read all her short stories, but didn't think she was equal to such a work as 'Pembroke.' I tell you it will live in literature. I'd like to meet her. Major Pond says I've got to lecture about myself and my own books. I'd rather lecture on George Meredith or somebody else, but the Major says it won't do, and I'm bound to follow what he wants. Yes, I'm a doctor. . . .

He answers the same questions more than once. It will be good practice for the rest of the two-month trip.

By now he has seen a little of New York, and cheerfully tells his interviewers that he likes it

> immensely. Never saw such an atmosphere before. You can see twenty miles further here than you can in England, and your city looks all so bright and fresh. I'm pleased and no mistake. I've already been down to Wall street and up to the top of The World building. I like to see things from a good height.

In the evening he is off to the theatre to see *Shenandoah* performed at the Academy of Music. It is Bronson Howard's familiar play of Sheridan's ride and other Civil War incidents, in a production notable for the number of horses it brings onto the broad stage:

> General Haverhill and his staff now ride to the dooryard of the Ellingham mansion on steeds that are restive enough to make folks in the orchestra stalls nervous. . . . Young Haverhill now

> departs upon his fatal mission on horseback, followed by twelve mounted troopers. . . .
> The horse is a noble animal. On the stage, however, he invariably develops a characteristic that has often been noted in flat-bottomed rowboats – a tendency to go sideways instead of front end first. This, on the Academy stage, is bad for the side scenes and the bunch lights in the wings.

The reviewer of the show's first night, five weeks ago, went on to say that some "members of Mr. Charles Frohman's specially-organized acting company are equal to their new tasks," but that the horses and general spectacle, not the acting, are the thing in this production.

Wednesday, October 3: The Metropolis of the United States

New York is "not only the metropolis of the United States," ACD can read in a leading guidebook, "but in population, in wealth, in influence, in enterprise, in all that best distinguishes modern civilization, it is the rival of the great capitals of the Old World." In this magnificent city he has a day for sightseeing, meeting a few literary folk, doing any necessary business about royalties and copyrights, and doubtless arranging a conference with Major Pond about the arrangements for the coming weeks.

Indeed, New York is a great city, with a population which has grown enormously since the 1890 census reckoned it at 1,513,501. The city stretches sixteen miles northward from the Battery to include all of Manhattan Island and something of the mainland beyond it, where the University of the City of New York has just this week opened its new campus. The population would be nearly doubled if one took into account the people of the neighbouring city of Brooklyn, as well as those in the villages of Richmond County to the southwest and Queens County to the east. There is now a proposal to unite all those communities into a greater New York which will stand as a major city of the world, eclipsing Paris and second only to ACD's London.

As a Britisher visiting America ACD is in a long tradition, which virtually requires him to form quick impressions of Americans and be prepared to recite them. (As early as yesterday the reporters were eager to hear them, and no doubt they will be in still heavier demand when he gets home in December.) He has sworn not to write a book about America, but scores of other travellers have been less restrained, and will continue to be. Five years hence, the drama critic William Archer will have his admiring say in print:

> [America] stands for the meeting-place of the past and the future. What the land of Cooper and Mayne Reid was to my boyish fancy, the land of Washington and Lincoln, Hawthorne and Emerson, is to my adult thoughts. . . .
> At no point [in New York] can one as yet say, "This prospect is finer than anything Europe can show." But everywhere there are purple patches of architectural splendour; and one can easily foresee the time when Fifth Avenue, the whole circuit of Central

October 1894

Park, and the up-town riverside region will be magnificent beyond compare. . . .

At night, again, under the purple, star-lit sky, street life in the central region of New York is indescribably exhilarating. From Union Square to Herald Square, and even further up, Broadway and many of the cross streets flash out at dusk into the most brilliant illumination. Theatres, restaurants, stores, are outlined in incandescent lamps; the huge electric trolleys come sailing along in an endless stream, profusely jewelled with electricity; and down the thickly-gemmed vista of every cross street one can see the elevated trains, like luminous winged serpents, skimming through the air. . . .

The New Yorker is far more cosmopolitan than the Londoner; of that there is no doubt. He knows all that we know about current English literature. He knows all that we do *not* know about current American literature. . . .

[T]he differences between American and English manners are really microscopic; and manners, I take it, are the outward and visible signs of temperament. A Scotchman by birth, a Londoner by habit, I walk the streets of New York undetected, to the best of my belief, until I begin to speak.

According to the guidebook, New York has 115,000 buildings, 575 miles of streets, a daily water supply of 75,000,000 gallons flowing through the Croton Aqueduct, thirteen ferry lines to Brooklyn (besides the bridge, still a wonder of the world) and thirteen to New Jersey, steam railways and steamboats, five lines of elevated railroads and seventeen streetcar companies. It also boasts forty-three daily newspapers (thirty-one in English, the rest in German, French, Italian, "Bohemian," Spanish and "Jewish"), four hundred churches, and the Mercantile Library, with some 240,000 volumes.

The guidebook will draw ACD to architectural points of interest as well: the Italian Renaissance city hall, the handsome Italian Gothic courthouse at Jefferson Market, the "substantial and grim-appearing" Tombs prison and the new courthouse beside it, Trinity Church, the Saint-Gaudens statue of Admiral Farragut, the new Metropolitan Museum of Art and the handsome Netherland hotel. "Amusements numerous and varied enough to suit all tastes and all purses range in character from the Metropolitan Opera House to the low concert-saloons of the Bowery and Eighth Avenue," the guidebook adds.

From one of those thirty-one English-language newspapers, the *Tribune*, ACD may have learned yesterday that Buffalo Bill's Wild West Show will run until Saturday at Ambrose Park in South Brooklyn, and that the cornerstone was laid yesterday for the new Clearing House building in Cedar Street. But what really interests New Yorkers, as ACD can quickly discover from a study of the newspapers, is politics. There is barely a month until the Tuesday after the first Monday in November, on which day voters will not only choose congressmen and a host of other officials but express their opinion on the vexing issue of union with Brooklyn and the neighbouring counties. In New York, politics chiefly means Democratic politics, and the perennial conflict between machine politicians and civic reformers. The burning question of the day is whether the Democratic factions in the state can unite behind Senator David Bennett Hill and return him to the governor's mansion he once occupied, or whether there will be a split and a third ticket. The *Tribune* was full of the matter, and full of such news as the injury suffered by bookseller Charles Scribner on Saturday when he was thrown from a wagon by a runaway horse. (Perhaps he could appeal to Clara Barton, founder of the American Red Cross, who is in town and staying at the Waldorf.) In other literary news the *Tribune* has a review of Bartlett's new concordance of the works of Shakespeare. (ACD, who will vaguely remember that Falstaff babbled o' green fields and put some such phrase in Holmes's mouth ten years hence, might be glad of such a book.)

This morning's *New York Times* has police matters on its front page, and ACD surely reads the top story with astonishment, thinking of Scotland Yard's gentlemanly officers. "Clubbing a Minor Offense," it is headed. "Policemen Expect at the Most Only a Light Fine." Charges of graft and brutality in the force are being investigated by a New York state senate committee, and yesterday some of the convicted offenders, in full uniform, were summoned to a downtown hearing room:

> They were the types of the men who complained, when Superintendent Byrnes took away their night sticks, that they were being left to the mercy of the criminal classes.
>
> Some of the clubbers "looked the part," but there were many mild-mannered appearing policemen among them. . . .
>
> Several astonishing clubbing records were made public. In every case the man got off with a fine of not more than thirty days' pay.

ACD may also notice that the *Times* has far more advertisements from people seeking situations than from employers wanting to hire them; last year's recession is still being felt. (Among those advertisements are eleven from young ladies who wish to be governesses.) He can read of the misdeeds of Prince Ruspoli, who is visiting the swell resort of Newport, Rhode Island, and who "did not visit Harvard College Monday, as he intended, though the Faculty had made great preparations for his coming." It seems he missed his train – something ACD surely resolves he will not do during his travels of the next few weeks.

He can read, too, of the cyclone at Little Rock which yesterday wrecked the state penitentiary and insane asylum; of the man in Jersey City who has been convicted of killing his wife; of Anthony Comstock's crusade against vice; of the reorganization of the Union Pacific Railroad (railroads in general have been in trouble since the recession); of the fatal illness of the prominent Chicago lecturer, Professor David Swing; of the decline of Czar Alexander III, confirmed to be suffering from Bright's disease; and of the controversy over who is to operate the lucrative ferry between New York and Staten Island. And if he turns

October 1894

his eye to the editorials, he will see a long and fanciful piece describing a supposed new electric machine, which takes words and assembles them into whatever sort of literary work may be desired.

> Authors, who, after all, are impecunious and undesirable persons, will, of course, find their occupation gone when the Automatic Writer is placed on the market, but they will be no great loss to the world. The work of many of them already shows qualities which resemble the work of machinery, and the sooner they are entirely superseded by machinery the better.

Thursday, October 4: Luncheon at the Lotos Club
Today ACD begins in a serious way to meet the sort of people who will be introduced to him by the hundreds as he travels around America: literary gentlemen, worldly doctors, travellers, explorers, soldiers, scientists whose ideas he will be fascinated to hear. He meets such a group today at a luncheon at the Lotos Club, a foundation unusually far uptown (at 556-558 Fifth Avenue, nearly to 46th Street) where Major Pond has been a member for almost a decade, and where his fellow-members include Samuel Clemens – Mark Twain – and the artist Frederic Remington.

The Lotos Club is best known for its celebrity dinners, and will give one of those in Doyle's honour before his tour is over, but today the event is a modest luncheon, presumably hosted by Major Pond, at which there are a mere eight guests apart from the Doyle brothers. Such club luncheons seem to be a typical form of hospitality enjoyed by British visitors, as that traveller of 1899, William Archer, will gratefully describe:

> I must have met at these luncheon parties, and actually conversed with, at least a hundred different men of all ages and occupations, and I do not remember among them a single dull, pompous, morose, or pedantic person. The parties did not usually exceed six or eight in number, so that there was no necessity for breaking up into groups. The shuttlecock of conversation was lightly bandied to and fro across the round table. Each took his share and none took more. All topics – even the burning question of "expansion" – were touched upon gaily, humorously, and in perfect good temper.

One of today's guests is the scandalous Edgar Saltus, 39, a moustached, olive-skinned lady-killer whom women have dubbed "the Pocket Apollo." His divorce a few years ago did little to improve the reputation his writings had already begun to create. Erotic and violent, with such titles as his newest, *Enthralled*, they do have a whiff of sulphur and patchouli about them. "Do you sell the books of Edgar Saltus?" a customer is said to have asked a bookseller, and the response was indignant: "Sir, I keep Guy de Maupassant's, The Heptameron, and Zola's, but Saltus – never." One Saltus work, *A Transaction in Hearts*, indirectly helped ACD's career: when it was published in *Lippincott's* magazine in 1889, there was such outrage that the editor was fired – and replaced by J. M. Stoddart, who promptly commissioned *The Sign of the Four*. Saltus and ACD probably do not realize that connection between them – nor that they share an infant interest in religious and cosmic questions which will lead ACD to Spiritualism, Saltus to Theosophy.

Another literary man in the group is Chandos Fulton, author of *A Brown-Stone Front* (1873), and a third is Nugent Robinson, who can enlighten ACD on subjects from mercantile law to fruit cultivation as a result of his work as editor of *Collier's Cyclopaedia of Commercial and Social Information* a dozen years ago. Then there is John Brisben Walker, founder and editor of the *Cosmopolitan* Magazine, who took up journalism only after several other careers, including a period as an alfalfa farmer. Educated at Georgetown College and West Point, Walker resigned from the United States Army in 1868 in order to serve in the Chinese military for two years; he is bound to have a story or two to tell about that.

Also military, and perhaps more impressive to young Lieutenant Innes Doyle than Major Pond, is Major David Porter Heap of the United States Army Corps of Engineers. Born in Turkey, Major Heap served in the Army of the Potomac and was cited for gallantry during the Civil War. In peacetime he is an authority on lighthouses and electricity, having served as an American representative at the Paris congress of electricians in 1881, travelled extensively to learn and to advise, and written several books on such matters. He will be promoted to lieutenant-colonel within a few months.

Able to talk on a subject close to ACD's heart is Lloyd Bryce, a former member of Congress and former paymaster-general of the State of New York, who has turned to literature. Jesuit-schooled like ACD, Bryce continued his education at Christ Church College, Oxford, and then returned to America to become a lawyer and begin a political career. During his one term in Congress, 1887 to 1889, he took a keen interest in copyright matters, helping to get the Copyright Act of 1891 enacted. Shortly after he left Congress, he had a story published in *Lippincott's Magazine* – anticipating ACD in that accomplishment by nearly a year. He has written several books since then, and now edits the *North American Review*.

Another guest is Louis Benziger, who will retire from Benziger Brothers a few weeks from now, leaving it the leading Catholic publishing house in the United States. He is noted, too, for his work on behalf of German immigrants – he was one himself, having come to America from Switzerland in 1860 at the age of twenty. Rounding out the guest list is John Lawson Stoddard, one of those celebrity lecturers whose claim to renown is that they are celebrity lecturers and travellers. He has made the name of Stoddard Lectures known in cities around the country, and this fall he will be in his fifteenth season, speaking about the past summer's travels to Rome, Paris, Switzerland, Norway and Ober-Ammergau. A book of his photographs of America and the world

October 1894

will be published one day, and eventually his lecture texts will also see print, in no fewer than ten volumes. No one could be better qualified than this 44-year-old veteran to tell ACD just what it will be like on the lecture circuit.

Friday, October 5: A Chat with Conan Doyle

> One way or another all the light, energy, and available virtue which we have does come out of us, and goes very infallibly into God's treasury, living and working through eternities there. We are not lost – not a single atom of us – of any of us.

They are not ACD's words, though they appear, reproduced in his handwriting and accompanied by the usual pensive photograph of him, in the first issue, published yesterday, of a new penny magazine appropriately called *New Age*. It promises to be "a bright, fresh, interesting weekly paper" which will present "Christian Culture, Social Service, Literary Life," and the editors have prevailed on a number of distinguished people to present a favourite quotation. ACD has chosen this brief passage from the work of Thomas Carlyle, which prefigures his later Spiritualist beliefs and reflects an already keen interest in the survival of personality after death. (He will use it again in the twelfth chapter of *The Stark Munro Letters*, to be published in February 1895.)

Readers are becoming interested in ACD and his favourite quotations, as well as in his personal habits and his taste in tobacco. These interests will be catered to by an article which is about to appear in the British journal *The Idler* – the magazine of a group of bright young men including many of ACD's friends, such as Jerome K. Jerome, who once wanted to marry his sister – and which will be reprinted with additions next month on this side of the Atlantic, in *McClure's*. The author is a former Canadian, Robert Barr, one of the *Idler* coterie and a personal friend of Doyle, and the title is "A Chat with Conan Doyle."

Barr maintains that Doyle did not want to be interviewed about any of the things that would interest readers:

> "What has the public to do with an author's personality?" he asked. "I vowed more than two years ago that I would never see an interviewer again."
> "But you are going to America – "
> "Ah, in America it is a different thing. One should adapt one's self to the ways of a country."
> "But apart from personality, suppose we chat about literature."
> "Well, let us stick to literature then." . . .
> We had looted two comfortable wicker chairs from the house, and were seated at the farther end of the long lawn that stretches from the Doyle residence towards the city of London. . . .

Barr goes on to make fun of his subject's golf prowess and of conventional techniques of interviewing, and then ACD gets a chance to say how splendid he considers the authors of today, rhyming off the names of "at least a dozen men and women who have made a deep mark and are still young," including Rudyard Kipling, Gilbert Parker, Arthur Quiller-Couch, Jerome K. Jerome, Clark Russell and H. Rider Haggard. "I have not read a book for a long time that has stirred me as much as Miss Wilkins' *Pembroke*. I think she is a very great writer." He does not need to add that one of her attractions is the violence, the darkness, the interest in twisted and tormented women, which occupies much of her writing – and of his own.

> I know Cable's work, and Eugene Field's, and Hamlin Garland's, and Edgar Fawcett's, and Richard Harding Davis'. I think Harold Frederic's 'In the Valley' is one of the best of recent historical romances. The danger for American fiction is, I think, that it should run in many brooks instead of one broad stream. There is a tendency to over-accentuate local peculiarities[.]

They – for the interview is a dialogue, in which Barr has at least as much to say as ACD – go on to mention Henry James, William Dean Howells, and the theological novel: "To get an idea to penetrate to the masses of the people you must put fiction round it, like sugar round a pill." There speaks the physician turned writer, the writer who will one day turn preacher for an unpopular cause. And Barr concludes, as a thunderstorm chases interviewer and subject indoors:

> Conan Doyle's study, workshop, and smoking-room is a nice place in a downpour, and I can recommend the novelist's brand of cigarettes. Show me the room in which a man works and I'll show you – how to smoke his cigarettes.

Works written in that Norwood room are coming into print monthly, if not weekly – sometimes authorized by the author, sometimes ventured in the face of a new and still unfamiliar copyright law. In this month's *McClure's* Magazine is the short story "The Meeting of the Sweethearts," which under an earlier title appeared back in June in *The Idler* and several American newspapers, and which will be collected in a new book of stories, *Round the Red Lamp*, in a few weeks. *The Stark Munro Letters* will not begin in America until December, but Rand McNally is publishing a twenty-five-cent paperback of *The Great Keinplatz Experiment*, and early in November there will be cheap Ogilvie paperbacks of *Beyond the City* and *Micah Clarke*. Then will come such tales as "A Foreign Office Romance" in several newspapers and "The Parasite" in *Harper's Weekly* (and at home in *Lloyd's*), and, before Christmas, the first in a series which will be among the most successful things he will ever write, the first tale of Brigadier Gérard.

With all this there are still steady sales of *The Refugees*, *The White Company*, and most of all the four volumes of Sherlock Holmes. From time to time, too, the tales of Holmes appear in newspapers or magazines again; the *Glasgow Weekly Mail* is publishing the *Memoirs* on Saturdays this fall.

October 1894

Saturday, October 6: Parkman Land
Today ACD is in Parkman Land, perhaps trying to imagine how the 350 French and Canadians led by Langy and Trepezec felt when one day in 1758 they got lost on a reconnaissance mission from Ticonderoga and

> could see nothing but brown trunks and green boughs. Could any of them have climbed one of the great pines that here and there reared their shaggy spires high above the surrounding forest, they would have discovered where they were, but would have gained not the faintest knowledge of the enemy.

Most of this vast tract of land is still virgin forest, stretching north from just past Albany as far as the border of Canada – further, indeed, since that border is little more than a line on a map.

The Adirondack region, some five million acres, is a state park, created two years ago, though considerably less than half of it is actually state-owned forest preserve. Under a new constitution which the state of New York is in the process of adopting, it must remain "forever wild." The always trustworthy Baedeker describes the Adirondack region thus to travellers like ACD:

> The whole of the district . . . , except the highest peaks, is densely covered with forest, much of which is still virgin and almost unexplored. Lumbering is carried on very extensively. . . . The *Hudson River* rises in the Tear of the Clouds . . . , and the *Raquette, Saranac, Ausable*, and numerous other rivers and streams connect the labyrinth of lakes. This combination of mountain, lake, and forest is, perhaps, unrivalled elsewhere, and the scenery is of great and varied attraction. . . .
>
> The most frequented and fashionable region is the district of the *Saranac* and *St. Regis Lakes* . . . , which are closely environed by hotels and summer-camps. *Lake Placid* . . . is now almost as frequented, while *Keene Valley* . . . , perhaps the gem of the district, is daily growing in favour. The *Blue Mt.* and *Raquette Lake* region . . . is somewhat more remote from the ordinary run of travel; while the less mountainous districts in the W. are rarely penetrated by visitors except in search of sport.

ACD had a choice of several routes for the day-long journey up to the Adirondacks; Baedeker is inclined to recommend the steamer from New York up the Hudson to Albany (though the New York Central and Hudson River Railroad is an alternative) and from there it is a matter of the Delaware and Hudson Railroad, followed perhaps by a steamer on Lake George. Whatever the route, ACD has a chance to see the beautiful Hudson Valley, and later the Falls of the Mohawk at Cohoes just above Troy, and then the water and the caves at Glens Falls, which he will be back to explore in a few weeks. In this region nearly every name is magical to a reader of Parkman and Cooper: Fort Edward, the Bloody Pond, Fort Ann, Ticonderoga, Lake Champlain. Over these miles of forests, and especially over the north-south water route, wars were fought for more than a century.

Francis Parkman, the great historian of these wars, died almost a year ago, his nine-volume history of New France complete. Writing *The Refugees*, especially, drew ACD to soak himself in the stories of colonial politics, forest exploration, and frontier battles in which English and French butchered each other and were still more savagely butchered by Indian tribes with unpredictable allegiances. In his autobiography, he will lavish praise on Parkman, who might have been his model as a balancer of literary work with the outdoor life:

> I wonder whether any man of letters has ever devoted himself to a task with such whole-hearted devotion as Parkman. He knew the old bloody frontier as Scott knew the border marches. He was soaked in New England tradition. He prepared himself for writing about Indians by living for months in their wigwams. He was intimate with old French life, and he spent some time in a religious house that he might catch something of the spirit which played so great a part in the early history of Canada. On the top of all this he had the well-balanced, unprejudiced mind of the great chronicler, and he cultivated a style which was equally removed from insipidity and from affectation. As to his industry and resolution, they are shown by the fact that he completed his volumes after he had been stricken by blindness.

He will also recall exploring Parkman Land again in 1914, at the beginning of the journey which will take him across Canada in a private railway carriage:

> We explored not only the beautiful, tragic Lake George, but also its beautiful neighbour Lake Champlain, almost as full of historical reminiscence. . . . Up at the head of the lake we saw Plattsburg, where the Americans gained a victory in the war of 1812. The sight of these battle-fields, whether they mark British or American successes, always fills me with horror.

These words will send him off on another paean to the essential unity of Britain and America, another hymn of regret for the wars which divided the English-speaking peoples. No doubt he feels the same emotions during this visit of 1894, and sees as many as he can of the places where there took place the battles Parkman carefully chronicles, and the events James Fenimore Cooper less reliably depicts. In his mind, too, are his own pictures of Indian skirmishes, frontier settlements and Jesuits' long treks, as he compares the landscape of which he wrote with the landscape he now can see. He might well share Parkman's contemplation that

> perhaps, standing at sunset on the peaceful strand, Champlain saw what a roving student of this generation has seen on those same shores, at that same hour, – the glow of the vanished sun behind the western mountains, darkly piled in mist and shadow along the sky. . . .

October 1894

Sunday, October 7: The Sage of Boston

The news cannot reach ACD today, but it will be the chief item in the papers tomorrow morning. *The New York Times* will pay that distinctive newspaperman's tribute, letting a name stand without immediate identification:

> Boston, Oct. 7 – Oliver Wendell Holmes is dead. He passed away without the semblance of a struggle or a pain.
>
> The end came at 12:10 o'clock this afternoon at the venerable poet's town house, 296 Beacon Street. He was surrounded by his children, and visibly conscious of their presence up to within a few minutes of the last, though unable to speak.

The dying man is 85 years old, known not only in his beloved Cambridge, Massachusetts, but everywhere in the English-speaking world as the Autocrat, Professor, and Poet of the breakfast-table, not to mention as the model for all stern yet kindly doctors that ever were. Those "children" at his bedside include a judge of the Massachusetts supreme court – not yet of the Supreme Court of the United States – named Oliver Wendell Holmes, Jr., a legal scholar who on March 3, 1881, inscribed a copy of his first book to his father "from his affectionate son." A few years later ACD wrote his own first book, coincidentally set its most dramatic scenes on March 4, 1881, and named its hero Holmes. It has been his hope to meet the senior Holmes during this trip to America, to shake his hand. In a day or two, emerging from the Adirondack woods, he will learn that he will never have that privilege.

He did not discuss Oliver Wendell Holmes's work in the series "Before My Book-Case" which was published in *Great Thoughts* earlier this year, but he will add several pages about him when he makes those articles into a book in 1907:

> What work it is, how wise, how witty, how large-hearted and tolerant! Could one choose one's philosopher in the Elysian fields, as once in Athens, I would surely join the smiling group who listened to the human, kindly words of the Sage of Boston. I suppose it is just that continual leaven of science, especially of medical science, which has from my early student days given those books so strong an attraction for me. Never have I so known and loved a man whom I had never seen. . . .
>
> Read his books again, and see if you are not especially struck by the up-to-dateness of them. Like Tennyson's "In Memoriam" it seems to me to be work which sprang into full flower fifty years before its time. One can hardly open a page haphazard without lighting upon some passage which illustrates the breadth of view, the felicity of phrase, and the singular power of playful but most suggestive analogy. . . .
>
> Wendell Holmes is for ever touching some note which awakens an answering vibration within my own mind.

Monday, October 8: Hunting in the Adirondacks

ACD has not come to the Adirondacks for the glittering society he might find at Paul Smith's hotel, or for the mixture of nature and riches to be found at the establishments of the Adirondack League Club in the southwestern corner of the region. He may not even be aware of such establishments, though the camp where he is spending these days, ten miles from the railhead at Tupper Lake Junction, is handsome enough. Its name is Bungalow Bay; Eric Pierson Swenson, now 40, built it on the western side of Upper Saranac Lake with some of his Texas banking and cattle wealth, and ACD was invited here through the good graces of Edward Dale Appleton, a classmate of Swenson from Trinity College, Hartford. The Doyle brothers signed the guest-book on October 6, and W. H. Addicks of Philadelphia will sign it on October 10, just before the end of his six-day visit. (Addicks will add a sketch of a dumb-looking deer, missed by a tenderfoot's repeated shots, and will note that the temperature is 40 degrees Fahrenheit.) The camp is an elegant establishment, boasting six master bedrooms with bathrooms – and each of these with a fireplace. Over the lounge fireplace hangs a woodcut of Indians resting beside a pond.

ACD may be aware of the nearby village of Saranac Lake, where Dr. Edward Livingston Trudeau ten years ago founded a non-profit tuberculosis sanatorium, modelled on the sanatorium at Davos, Switzerland, the resort where ACD's wife Louise is trying to recover her health and cure her consumptive lungs. In another part of the Adirondacks, near the village of Oxbow, is buried Caroline, niece of Napoleon Bonaparte, who had hoped to establish a new France in backwoods America after the debacle of Waterloo. But ACD is visiting none of these places; he is camping in the woods and getting up early to hunt.

> For short trips [says Baedeker] one guide and boat can take two persons, but for longer expeditions there should be a guide to each traveller. The boats are small and light, so that they are easily transported over the 'carries' between the lakes on the guide's shoulders. When horses are used for the carries the employer pays for the transportation. . . .
>
> The expenses of a rapid tour through the Adirondacks are apt to be somewhat high, as the guide's fee ($3) and keep ($1–1^1/_2$) have to be added to the traveller's personal expenses ($3 – 5). Camping and sporting parties live, of course, much more cheaply than hotel-guests.

ACD gets up at four o'clock, as he does every morning during this Adirondack excursion, to try his luck at what he calls "buck shooting." Baedeker naturally mentions historical sites, Paul Smith's and the sanatorium in his pages about the Adirondacks, but what brings most visitors to this great wooded region is hunting. A manual to be published four years hence, describing the game to be found in all the forty-four states, says this about New York:

October 1894

> The game animals consist of deer, bear, and elk (introduced into private preserves). Cougar or panther are extremely rare; the same may be said of moose, though it is believed they are extinct. Canada lynx are occasionally found. Red lynx or bob cat, raccoon, fox, rabbit, squirrel, mink, and muskrat are common. Beaver are nearly extinct, a few colonies remaining in the Adirondack region.

That must break ACD's heart if he remembers the comic scene in *The Last of the Mohicans* in which the greenhorn Britisher sees a beaver colony at a distance and mistakes it for a village of savage humans still further off. How he would enjoy seeing that in real life!

> Otter are found only occasionally; the same may be said of fisher. There are, besides, rabbit, hare, woodchuck, marten, skunk, and squirrel.
>
> In 1896, William F. Fox, superintendent of the state forests, estimated the number of deer in the great northern forest as 30,000.

In another day or so ACD will emerge from the northlands to grumble that he didn't manage to shoot one of them. "The nearest we came to seeing any deer was hearing the baying of the hounds that started out somewhere in the woods, a good ways from us," he will tell an interviewer next week.

And what does he think of these forests and lakes?

> I had studied up the scenery and characteristics of the region as well as I could, and I wanted to see how accurate a conception I had gained of it. I was gratified to find that it was very much as I had pictured it. The trees were not as large as I thought they were. I had failed to take into consideration that the altitude is 1,800 feet and that this naturally would dwarf the trees to some extent. But otherwise, I flatter myself, I had got a pretty good idea of the region.

ACD must return to the status of a hotel-guest tomorrow at the latest. On Wednesday he is to start lecturing.

Tuesday, October 9: The Stars and Stripes

After his visit to America last year, traveller James F. Muirhead had this to say about Yankee hospitality:

> There is probably no country in the world where, at times, letters of introduction are more fully honoured than in the United States. The recipient does not content himself with inviting you to call or even to dinner. He invites you to make his house your home; he invites all his friends to meet you; he leaves his business to show you the lions of the town or to drive you about the country; he puts you up at his club; he sends you off provided with letters to ten other men like himself, only more so.

(Other times he does the very opposite, Muirhead goes on to say.) ACD has had some of those experiences already – back in New York for a few more days, he will be staying again at Appleton's club, the Aldine – but he is not ready yet, for all the reporters' urgings, to begin generalizing about America. One can't tell much by looking out of train windows, he keeps saying.

ACD knows that it is a large country, already larger than Great Britain; patronizing commentators who used to describe America as a child among nations are now using the image of a gangly youth instead. If ACD consulted an almanac at home in Norwood he learned that at the last census the population of the United States was 62,622,250. In economic and military matters America is not yet the titan it will one day become, but there are ominous notes in that almanac:

> The salt-springs are numerous and copious, and appear almost inexhaustible. The financial condition of the United States of America exerts a great influence on that of other nations. . . . It is much to be regretted that the high protectionist duties imposed upon goods from the U. K. limits their import. . . . The number of miles [of railways] open upon which mails are carried and in actual use on the 31st October, 1891, was 160,436, of which 9,422 miles were constructed during the year.

The President of the United States, Grover Cleveland, is in his second term, having left office from 1888 to 1892. He is rapidly losing control of his Democratic Party, but the almanac does not go into such subjective matters. It does enumerate the cabinet, and the officials of the American legation in London (down to the second secretary, Larz Anderson, and still more lowly officials) and the many consuls of Her Majesty across America.

ACD is less interested in purely political affairs than in literature, though he has some strong convictions: a belligerent confidence in the Empire, a faith in the working classes which borders on socialism, and a utopian dream that the English-speaking peoples will one day find a way to undo what he described in a story two years ago as "the folly of a monarch and the blundering of a minister in far-gone years." Remarkably, for a man who was taught heraldry at his mother's knee, he proposed a hideous flag for this hypothetical world-wide country: "a quartering of the Union Jack with the Stars and Stripes." Though his interpretation of the American Revolution puts the blame on the British rather than the American leaders, ACD will be wise enough to avoid raising his proposal of Anglo-American union very often during his present tour. He will content himself with saying mild things about the culture and ideals which British and Americans share – and with writing a stiff note to Rudyard Kipling, expatriate Briton who has been ruffling the feathers of the American eagle.

As ACD travels the United States, he will face the difficulty which always faces foreign travellers trying to understand a country: how to separate the enduring and universal characteristics of this land from the temporary and local ones. Aware that neither cosmopolitan New York nor the Adirondack forest is typical of the country as a whole, he will also see the difference between elegant Philadelphia and brash Chicago and know that neither is like that remote territory which is not yet a state, Oklahoma; but how can he tell whether the attitudes he sees among, say, the lounging unemployed are typically and unchangingly American, or simply the result of the terrible winter of 1893-94, during which there were more than two and a half million men without work? Can he avoid judging the position of American women by what he sees at Smith College, or American journalism by a glance at the *Glens Falls Daily Times*?

He is not here, of course, to study social history or to collect information to retail at home. He must be aware that, as a traveller in first-class coaches and Pullman cars, as a resident of excellent hotels when his schedule allows him to sleep in a bed rather than a berth, and as a constant guest of publishers and followers of the literary scene, he is not seeing the daily life of ordinary Americans. One of his few chances to enjoy social intercourse free of affectations will come in Toledo, when a club of young athletes invite him to a party in their rooming-house. During the trip he will stand in a good many reception lines and sign a good many autographs, submitting himself to what Sherlock Holmes will later call "those unwelcome social summonses which call upon a man either to be bored or to lie."

Wednesday, October 10: Lecture at Calvary
Before giving his "Readings and Reminiscences" for the first time today, ACD must do a little business: he must deal with the American publishers who are eager to bring out *The White Company* in a new edition. (The one published by John W. Lovell is some four years old.) He has already had an offer from Harper & Brothers, publishers of Sherlock Holmes and of *Micah Clarke*, and now he has received a competing offer from D. Appleton and Co. He writes on Aldine Club notepaper, perhaps reflecting that the recipient of this unpleasing letter is in a sense his host here, telling Appletons that he can no more give his permission to them than he can to Harpers; it is all up to Lovells, to whom he has sold all his rights for that book.

By now ACD has had a chance to meet William Dean Howells, who at 57 is already the patriarch of American letters, although he has neither a New England Transcendentalist background (his home is Ohio) nor experience of the Civil War. He was American consul in Venice throughout the war years – one of many nineteenth-century figures who, like Douglas Maberley in a story ACD will one day write called "The Three Gables," combine literature and diplomatic work. Formerly of Boston's *Atlantic* and now of New York's *Harper's*, he is also the author of various romances and novels, most importantly *The Rise of Silas Lapham* nine years ago. He is also in a small way a socialist, and may remind ACD of the much older George Meredith at home in England: now that he has arrived, accepted by even the stuffiest parts of the establishment, Howells does his best to encourage the younger generations of writers. His works are similar to ACD's domestic novels, though ACD might not be completely happy with the comparison, as he will indicate in answer to an Indianapolis reporter's question next week:

> Dr. Doyle spoke of meeting Howells in New York and expressed himself concerning that author's strictures upon art in romance writing. He said that so much was talked about art that there was a tendency to forget what this art was really invented for. He said it was to amuse and comfort the sick and lighten the burdens of the weary. Scott and Dickens had done this and they had been a blessing to the race. If the sole object is to draw life as it really exists, even Goethe and Dante would not be entitled to a place in the world of letters.

The lecture this evening is at the Calvary Baptist Church, a magnificent Early English Gothic building noted for its 229-foot spire and its "Catherine-wheel" window facing onto 57th Street. Under the energetic leadership of Rev. Robert Stuart MacArthur, the church operates uptown missions, conducts chapel services and Sunday school classes in such tongues as Persian and Hungarian, and – as befits a congregation whose members include John D. Rockefeller – is renowned for lavish contributions to home and foreign missions. This building is eleven years old, and cost $525,000, and when it was dedicated it was paid for. In this still largely Christian city (today's observation of Yom Kippur has made a smaller impression on the city than it will do in later year when New York is largely Jewish), it is not unusual for Calvary's 1,500-seat auditorium to be used for lectures not strictly of a religious kind, particularly as it is MacArthur's conviction that

> Ethnology may push her inquiries all over the earth and her scientific conclusions will honor the record of creation by Moses and the speech of Paul at Athens. All the treasures of science and art belong to Jesus Christ . . . all true sciences will cast their crowns at His feet.

The Young People's Association of the church is sponsoring ACD tonight – its lecture series this year will also present General Lew Wallace, the author of *Ben-Hur*, as well as Dean Hole of Rochester, England, and W. Hamilton Gibson. At 8:15 p.m. ACD, a trifle nervous, enters the auditorium to face a crowd who has purchased its tickets at W. A. Pond & Co.'s, 25 Union Square, in the theatrical district.

In his autobiography ACD will recall an awkward moment:

> We had walked from the retiring room and were just coming in sight of the audience when I felt something tickle my ear. I put up my hand and found that my collar was undone, my tie had fallen off, and my stud, the first cause of all this trouble, had disappeared. Standing there, on the edge of the platform, Pond dragged out his own stud. I replaced everything, and sailed on quite as I should be, while Pond retired to refit.

The newspapermen in the audience know nothing of this, of course, though ACD's haberdashery does not go unnoticed: the *World* next day will observe with interest that he

> wore, of course, evening dress, for the church was full of polite women and men. . . . The only bits of color about this broad-shouldered man were his red cheeks, his red ears and a blood-red silk handkerchief stuck in his vest . . . of jewelry he showed only a tiny stud and the bar that held in place his watch chain.

He sits behind a reading-desk just in front of the pulpit, and is introduced by Hamilton Wright Mabie, a scion of Cold Spring, New York, who at the age of 49 has outgrown his legal career to become an author, with two books to his credit already and many more to come. Last year he became associate editor of the *Outlook*, a post he will hold for the rest of his life. (Some thirty years hence, Mabie will contribute in a tiny way to the immortality of ACD's writings, choosing one of the Sherlock Holmes tales to appear in the many-volumed *Pocket University*.)

ACD's talk lasts about an hour and a quarter, half of it taken up with readings of Sherlock Holmes and of an almost new story of the Franco-Prussian war of 1870, "The Lord of Chateau Noir." Members of the audience enjoy those excerpts, laughing "gleefully" over Watson's puzzlement at Holmes's deductions (so the *World*'s reporter will say in print tomorrow) and feeling "the least little creeping of the flesh" at the perspicacity of some of those deductions. "The doctor, feeling entirely at home, stuck his left hand in his trousers pocket," the reporter will further say, and proceeded to tell of still more marvellous deductions in the case of "The Greek Interpreter."

But of more interest to the listeners than the readings are the reminiscences in which ACD recalls Thackeray, his own boyhood reading and first efforts at writing, his literary apprenticeship and eventual success, his creation of Holmes, and the pensive nights and laborious days out of which came his historical novels. He speaks, finally, of the satisfactions of becoming known as a novelist, satisfactions less likely to be expressed in money than in friendship and modest fame. The lecture is received as a success, and afterwards Major Pond tips off a reporter that the author "is contemplating holding a series of literary matinees in some New York theatre." (Those matinees are doubtless already firmly planned; they will take place in the second week of November.) Pond records in his register of speakers, "Audience very large. Introduced by Hamilton Mabie. The lecture was a great success." And on Friday he will write there, "Paid by check 10/12/94."

Thursday, October 11: The Limited Train

There are at least nine ways for ACD to travel from New York to Chicago by rail; further possibilities involve steamers from New York to Albany and, for those with several days to spend on the journey, onward to Buffalo and Chicago. But ACD is in more of a hurry. In thirty-two to thirty-four hours, says Baedeker, he could make the journey via Baltimore and Washington. In twenty-six to thirty-five hours, he could travel by one of several railroads to Buffalo, and from there briefly re-enter the British Empire, travelling through southern Ontario on the Grand Trunk Railway to Detroit and Chicago. A third group of routes would also take him via Buffalo and Detroit, but within the United States. Then there is the Pennsylvania Limited Vestibule Train (not yet the Broadway Limited) through Philadelphia and Pittsburgh. Baedeker notes that this train,

> (fare $28, incl. sleeper), starting from New York at 10 a.m. and reaching Chicago at 9.45 a.m. (central time) next day, consists entirely of Pullman vestibuled cars and offers every imaginable comfort to the traveller. It is provided with a dining-car, a library, a smoking and outlook car, a barber's shop, a bath, a ladies' maid, and a stenographer.

Yet another route would take him on the Erie Railway past such communities as Paterson, Hornellsville, and Jamestown, where he could if he liked get a connecting train to the pretty little village of Chautauqua. It is out of season for the Chautauqua Assembly, and ACD would find the five-hundred-bed Hotel Athenaeum closed until next summer, when thousands of studious vacationers – at Chautauqua that is no oxymoron – will gather there again. It is sixteen years since Lewis Miller and Bishop John Vincent established the Assembly; from their original campground a small settlement has grown (the Pittsburgh House, later to be called the Maple Inn, was added to the inventory of handsome wooden buildings this year), but in bleak October, Chautauquans are concentrating on the home-study course of the Literary and Scientific Circle, administered not from the lakeside village but from an office building in Buffalo. The Erie train continues from Jamestown through a corner of Pennsylvania and then across Ohio, stopping at Marion en route to Chicago.

The route ACD chooses is the fastest of the lot, the New York Central's Limited Train – predecessor of the Twentieth Century Limited – which leaves the Grand Central Depot at 10 a.m. and takes just about twenty-four hours to reach Chicago. Baedeker advises travellers to sit on the left side of the train, for the sake of the view as they race up the east bank of the Hudson River. "I do not think," ACD will write much later, "that finer river-scenery can be found anywhere in the world." The train passes Yonkers, where ACD will be back to lecture in a few weeks; Tarrytown; the prison village of Sing Sing; and Cold Spring, with its great foundry, which has cast much of the cannon for America's wars since it was set up to replace British sources of guns. Across the river stands the military academy at West Point; ACD must have heard stories of the Great Chain which stretched under the Hudson hereabouts to block the progress of British warships, and stories of Benedict Arnold, a black villain to American patriots and a tragic figure to more neutral historians. He will be thinking about lunch in the restaurant car (this train is as elegantly equipped as its Pennsylvania rival) as

October 1894

the fortress recedes in the window to his left, and there looms beside him the steep slope of Storm King. This is Revolutionary War country – on the west bank now is Newburgh, where General George Washington made his headquarters at one time, and on the hill opposite, colonial sympathizers lit signal fires. ACD doubtless thinks, as he is so often prompted to do, about that blundering minister and that foolish king in the 1770's.

The train rattles past Poughkeepsie, and 143 miles from New York reaches Albany, capital city of the state of New York. As Baedeker describes it, Albany is

> well built on the whole, with many really handsome buildings, and retains much of the clean, comfortable, and easy-going character of its original Dutch founders. Brewing and stove-making are its chief industries, and it has a large timber market. . . . The **Erie Canal**, which connects Lake Erie at Buffalo with the Hudson at Albany, was constructed in 1817-25 at an original cost of $7,500,000 (1,500,000*l*.), since increased to $45,000,000 (9,000,000*l*.), including enlargements, feeders, and connections. . . . The canal is 360 M. long, 7 ft. deep, 56 ft. wide at the bottom, and 70 ft. wide at the surface. It descends 570 ft. by means of 72 locks. . . . [T]he little knot of Albany politicians has practically determined the nomination and election of several Presidents of the United States.

ACD has no time to see the state capitol ("only now approaching completion, though it has been partly occupied for some time") or the new Cathedral of All Saints ("the first regularly organised Protestant cathedral erected in the United States"). His train is quickly in motion again, turning west through Schenectady (another city he will revisit next month) and ascending the Mohawk valley, from which sharp eyes can see the Catskills to the south and the Adirondacks to the north. There are stops at Little Falls; Utica, a cheese-making town with a connecting line to Binghamton; Rome; and industrial Syracuse. As a through train, the Limited bypasses the "old route" through Auburn, Geneva, and handsome Canandaigua, instead taking a straighter, more northern route through Palmyra, a town which interests ACD as the place where Joseph Smith discovered the Book of Mormon.

At an average of some fifty miles an hour the Limited races westward through Rochester, reaching Buffalo at dinner-time. At the Union Depot on Exchange Street it leaves the tracks of the New York Central and takes those of the Lake Shore and Michigan Southern Railroad. The stations rush past through the night: Dunkirk, Erie, Cleveland (the seat of the Standard Oil Company), Toledo, Archibald (this through train is following the "Air Line," not the "Old Line" through Adrian), Elkhart, and at 540 miles from Buffalo – 980 miles altogether from his starting-point of yesterday – ACD arrives at the Van Buren Street Station in Chicago.

"It was very beautiful between here and New York, nearly all the way," he says on his arrival. "It has such a homely kind of look. Then the long stretches and the low, waving hills! It is all delicious. The only things that struck me as distinctly American, in an unfavorable sense, were the little wooden houses and the snake-like fences."

Friday, October 12: Chicago's Elite

ACD and his brother are joined by a reporter for the short walk from the railway station. They pass the Monadnock Building, and ACD points it out to Innes as an example of (the reporter has to supply the word) a sky-scraper. "They stimulate and interest and please me," he says earnestly. "In fact, I hope to say they have elevated me!" He intends to get to the top of one, just as he did in New York.

Their destination is the Grand Pacific Hotel, across Clark Street from the post office, a hotel as closely identified with Chicago's Republicans as the Palmer House is with its Democrats. Perhaps more important to a visiting Britisher, it is "richly solid and subdued," in the phrase of one local guidebook. (Other observers might call the structure, occupying a full city block, ornate to the point of surfeit.) As soon as the travellers arrive at their suite, ACD disappears into the bathroom, joking that he needs to escape from the small cloud of bellhops and reporters who accompany them, and leaving Innes to field questions about how they like America and what they thought of theatre in New York.

"The theatres seemed to have more room in them, but it is the same line of plays, you know. We didn't get many impressions out of it," the young man tells the *Post*. ACD sticks his head round the bathroom door. "That 'Shenandoah', though, was a distinctively American play," he declares, "very characteristic of the country, I thought."

Other reporters have questions, about the usual range of matters, especially ACD's opinions of literature and the way he writes his own books. He chats for a while, then pulls out a leather cigarette-case and invites his listeners to join him in a smoke as the conversation continues: Kipling is England's best novelist since Dickens, Dr. Joe Bell is one of the sources of Sherlock Holmes. Chicago is more like London than is New York, he says; Clark Street with its high buildings greatly resembles London's Fenchurch Street. When later reporters arrive, ACD is lounging on the bed, ready to talk once again about his Irish ancestry, his favourite among his own books, his views on home rule: "I believe the Irish and the British can pull very well together. I think their interests are identical."

This evening ACD is the guest of the Twentieth Century Club, which meets in the "bijou theatre" of 2838 Michigan Avenue, the home of Harlow L. and Rachel Higinbotham, located in the Groveland Park area between the Illinois Central Railroad and the South Side Elevated. This is not Chicago's most elegant neighbourhood, but the Higinbotham mansion is noted for its sophisticated furnishings, its Turkish Room, and the second-floor theatre in which ACD is speaking tonight to some three hundred members and guests of the Twentieth Century Club.

October 1894

He finds himself among not merely a moneyed class but a cultured one, the elite which stands behind a great cluster of Chicago's artistic institutions as well as its commercial bastions. This evening's host, a department store magnate, is also a trustee of the Field Museum and the president of the directory of last year's World Columbian Exposition. That exposition, the six-month fair which put Chicago on the map of the world, was both commercial and cultural, and it was dynamic figures such as Higinbotham (considered a member of the younger generation, though he marked his 56th birthday on Wednesday) who made it a success.

Present tonight are Charles L. Hutchinson – president of the Art Institute of Chicago, treasurer of the five-year-old University of Chicago, a guarantor of last year's Exposition – and Martin Ryerson, first president of the new university's board and a trustee of the Art Institute and the Field Museum; he too was a guarantor of the exhibition. "Those three men can raise more money than any other three men in Chicago," said an observer four years ago about Ryerson, Hutchinson and another of tonight's society guests, Clarence L. Peck. No one would try to deny it.

It is the first gathering of the Twentieth Century Club for this season. (Scheduled for the coming months are lectures by Thomas Wentworth Higginson and Very Rev. Reynolds Hole, the dean of Rochester whose path keeps crossing ACD's in these weeks.) The president of the club is George E. Adams, 54, a Republican lawyer who will later be a Harvard College overseer as well as taking his turn on the boards of the Art Institute, the Field Museum, the Chicago Symphony, and the Newberry Library – and, oh yes, has spent eight years in Congress.

"During the five years of its existence," said the *Tribune* this morning, surely repeating the assurances of the club's officials, "the Twentieth Century Club has pursued the policy of having men of reputation and ability whom it would be difficult to hear otherwise. It does not care for professionals, but seeks rather men who would consent only to talk to clubs of this kind." (The club may not have realized when it invited ACD that he will also be speaking at the Central Music Hall in a few days to anyone who can put down a dollar.)

ACD steps onto the little stage of the Higinbotham house theatre with club president Adams, who, in introducing him, makes a slip that will follow ACD for the rest of his trip. He speaks for an instant of "Canon Doyle," and there is a little ripple of laughter. *Chicago Record* columnist Eugene Field, who is in the audience with his mothering wife, Julia, puts his brain to work immediately; in Monday's column he will allege that ACD has been being asked to say grace at luncheons, and in Tuesday's column he will make a punning crack about ACD being "a big gun from England." Some people now have the idea in their heads that ACD is a clergyman, and nothing will get it out.

A little after nine o'clock, ACD begins to speak. Tonight, for the only time during his tour, he gives his lecture "Facts About Fiction," based on a talk which he first gave before the Upper Norwood Scientific and Literary Society a year ago. The hour which it lasts is punctuated with applause and laughter from Chicago's elite. The speaker restricts himself to British fiction, talking about the prominent novelists of this generation: inevitably Meredith, but also Hardy, Stevenson, Kipling, Robert Barr, and Olive Schreiner, whose *Story of an African Farm* is – as he has been saying in interviews as well – "a tragedy and one of the greatest books ever written by a woman. She used her heart for an ink-pot when she wrote it."

Other women writers are mentioned ("only a passing phase of thought, and can have no prolonged influence"). But ACD is kinder to Jerome K. Jerome, Israel Zangwill, Clark Russell (whose sea-stories are a favourite of Sherlock Holmes's companion Dr. Watson), and Canadian-born Gilbert Parker, author of melodramatic tales about the French settlers and the North-West. He speaks of realism and *Gulliver's Travels*, he comments on the growing worth of literature from the farthest reaches of the British Empire, and he earnestly warns against too much attention in books to love and marriage:

> In all Stevenson's novels woman plays a subordinate part. His work and that of his school marks the reaction against the abuse of love in fiction – a reaction which certainly goes too far when it shuts out the most picturesque half of humanity. But the fact is that this one phase of life, ending in the orthodox marriage, has been so hackneyed and worn to shreds in our fiction that it is not to be wondered at that there should be a tendency to swing to the other extreme and to give love less than its fair share in the affairs of men. In British fiction nine books out of ten have held up love and marriage as the be-all and end-all of life. Yet we know in actual practice this is not so.

The listeners laugh, as ACD may have intended; but he may be all too bitterly aware that love and marriage have not brought him all the satisfaction he might have expected. It will be fifteen years before they do.

> In the career of the average man his marriage is the most momentous incident, but only one out of several. He is swayed by many strong emotions, his business, his ambitions, his friendships, his struggles with recurrent difficulties and dangers which tax a man's wisdom and his courage.
> Love will often play a subordinate part in his life. Many luckless ones may go through the world and never love at all. It jars upon truth then to have it continuously held up as the predominating, all-important fact in life, and there is a not unnatural tendency to avoid a source of interest which has been so misused and overdone.

There is applause, and the speaker goes on to talk of how authors choose their words, and of the "pride of national possession" which his native Scotland feels in the works of J. M. Barrie.

October 1894

Among the reporters covering the talk is young Ray Stannard Baker of the *Record*, now 24 and many years away from his Pulitzer Prize. He makes a note of the "aldermanic diamond flashing" on ACD's shirt-front, and of the "wholesome ring of hope in the future and faith in mankind" which his voice carries. Baker began as a stringer for the paper, making enough money from occasional articles to support his addiction to second-hand books, and he will later record his disappointment when, on being hired for the regular staff, he found his weekly income drop from forty dollars to twelve. He covers a little of everything, with special attention to Chicago's tumultuous politics, but takes the keenest interest in literary and cultural events, including a lecture by Thomas Nelson Page and a chance to interview Nordica, the great Wagnerian soprano.

After the lecture, there is a reception at which ACD is introduced to most of the three hundred guests. Mrs. Higinbotham is assisted in serving by Adele (Mrs. George) Adams, Elizabeth (Mrs. William Penn) Nixon, and Mary Elizabeth Matz, whose architect husband, Otto, was one of the chief rebuilders of Chicago after the great fire of 1871. Refreshments are served in a dining room decorated with pink ribbons and pink chrysanthemums.

Saturday, October 13: A Literary Luncheon

Today ACD has some free time for sightseeing in the astonishing city of Chicago. After the famous fire, twenty-three years ago this week, destroyed homes and businesses (as well as civic records and the original Emancipation Proclamation), few people believed that anything more would be heard of Chicago; but today it has more than a million people, and while ACD doubtless is shown the Water Tower which survived the flames, he can also see modern elevated railroads (under which muddy unpaved streets still sometimes run), splendid cultural institutions of the kind built by Higinbotham, Adams and Hutchinson, and the biggest tourist attraction in town: Marshall Field's department store on State Street. It sells gingham and calico, but also Worth gowns and Oriental rugs for the most demanding of customers. This vibrant and rapidly-growing city gives much cause for excitement; much cause, too, for sorrow and righteous anger. Jane Addams opened her Hull House project five years ago to help Chicago's wretched poor, and this year saw the publication of William T. Stead's angry book about the city's slums, *If Christ Came to Chicago!*

The one formal event today is another of those gentlemen's literary luncheons, this one dominated by figures from the newspaper world (which no doubt is why ACD will receive such extensive press coverage throughout his Chicago stay). The host is Melville E. Stone, one of the dwindling number of Chicagoans who can, if pressed, personally recall the great fire: he was a foundry proprietor (his firm had great success making folding chairs for theatres) before the fire destroyed his business. In 1875 he and a partner established the Chicago *Daily News* on such novel principles as honest, comprehensive news and a price of one cent when most papers were charging five. He had to take steps to get more coppers into circulation in Chicago so that people could easily buy the *News*: first he imported barrels of them from the east, and then he talked local storekeepers into pricing their goods at figures ending in nine, so that shoppers would receive pennies in change. Some years ago he sold his newspaper interests, and since has travelled widely and explored business opportunities, becoming among other things president of the Globe National Bank.

He is also general manager of the Associated Press of Illinois, soon to reorganize and become The AP. He will lead the AP through its current fight with a rival, commercial group, the United Press, and through thirty years of growth and success. He will remain generally beloved, though the association's board will try to discourage his friendships with the famous and well-connected for fear that the AP be seen as somehow biased; and his name will give the AP its nickname among journalists – Rocks.

In the course of the day, ACD signs two copies of *The White Company* for Stone: one inscribed to him, "with happiest recollections," and one inscribed more formally to "Melville E. Stone Junr," his younger son, who is away at Harvard.

The luncheon is held at one o'clock at the Union League Club, at the corner of Fourth and Jackson. Such clubs are now found in many American cities, established by Republicans seeking to be patrotic and forward-looking (but not to forget the Civil War absolutely), and at the same time to dine and talk in comfort. This one was organized in 1879, and its building is said by the guidebooks to be "princely" and of particular note for its gallery and its library.

Besides ACD and his brother, Stone has invited to the club eleven men, mostly of literary tastes. One of them is W. Irving Way, now 41, a railroad man from Trenton, Ontario. Led by his enthusiasm for book-collecting, he became a founding member of the Grolier Club, and for the past few years he has been writing and publishing from an office in the Monadnock Building in Chicago. (He is about to join Chauncey L. Williams in forming a respected but short-lived publishing company, Way & Williams.)

Another guest is William Penn Nixon, general manager of the *Inter Ocean* newspaper, a former president of the Associated Press of Illinois and a future Collector of the Port of Chicago. A third is James W. W. Scott: a drummer boy in the Civil War, Scott went into the newspaper business in the 1870's, founded the *Evening Post* four years ago, is former president of the United Press and the American Newspaper Publishers Association – and is fated to die six months from tomorrow.

Also present is Franklin H. Head, 62, an insurance and railroad executive noted for conviviality and for the diplomatic skills of a committee chairman. Trained as a lawyer, he practised in Wisconsin, but after an illness "sought a less confining life and went to Utah," where

October 1894

he was superintendent of Indian affairs and also did some ranching, "incidentally making some valuable research in regard to Mormonism." He came to Chicago just before the 1871 fire and went into business – the Elk Rapids Iron Company, the Chicago Malleable Iron Company, the Chicago and Iowa Railway Company, and so on. He was a director of last year's exposition, and remains interested in fairs: in 1900 he will find himself in Paris as a member of the jury of awards for the Exposition Universelle, and the following year will be named a chevalier of the Legion d'Honneur. He is also a trustee of the Newberry Library and a governor of the Art Institute; his paper "Shakespeare's Insomnia and the Causes Thereof" lives in the lore of the Chicago Literary Club.

Among the other guests at today's luncheon are J. W. Ellsworth; book dealer George M. Millard; F. F. Browne, lawyer, poet, and founder of the little magazine *The Dial*, as well as chairman of the authors' committee for last year's exposition; and W. C. Larned, 43, a Harvard-trained lawyer whose real fame is as a lecturer and author about art, and art editor of the *Daily News* and its sister paper, the *Record*. The list is completed with two noted literary names, Hamlin Garland and Eugene Field, who are well known for the half-serious feud they conducted as representatives of the realists and romantics during the cultural activities of last year's exposition. Field, now 44, is the newspaper columnist who will spread the "Canon Doyle" joke around the country. He is also the author of popular poems for children – most notably the sentimental "Little Boy Blue" – and he is making an astonishing income from a book of his stories, money which he is spending towards the advancement of literary culture (and fine printing) in Chicago. This sociable, yet tormented, balding man will die of heart failure a year and a few days from today, with a package addressed to Millard lying unmailed beside his bed.

Garland, now 34, is also a poet – the proponent, in the words of a later commentator, of something new: "While city dwellers counted the blessings of the pastoral way, men from the farms like Hamlin Garland were simultaneously introducing a different rural literature – of loneliness and poverty and pain." ACD already knows his work, and is pleased to meet him today; he autographs a copy of the just-published *Memoirs of Sherlock Holmes* for him, "with A Conan Doyle's kindest remembrances & best wishes to Hamlin Garland." Oddly, Garland will have little recollection of today's lunch, for in his diary for May 7, 1899, he will note that he called at ACD's home in England during a tour there: "Doyle very fine and hearty . . . I liked him immensely." His reminiscences will mention a later visit with ACD as well, one in 1906 which was enlivened by the host's wild driving around the Sussex countryside. "I resumed acquaintance almost as if six weeks instead of seven years had intervened," he will write, " – of such quality are the friendships established in youth."

The final guest is Stone's younger son, Herbert S. Stone, Chicago's most promising young publisher. He and a friend, Ingalls Kimball, were bitten by the publishing bug during the exposition, and when they returned to their Harvard University studies they devoted more attention to poetry, bibliography, and printing than to their classes. (Some of the faculty were sympathetic, young Stone wrote in a letter home: "You know the faculty is trying to do away with the prevalent idea that Harvard is not practical and so they are mighty glad to have us here."

Herbert Stone left Harvard last spring, without quite finishing his degree, to give full attention to the publishing firm he and his friend have started under the name of Stone & Kimball, to publish elegant and simple books, chiefly in *belles-lettres*. They have already published Garland's *Main-Travelled Roads* and *Prairie Songs*, as well as some two dozen other books (including works by Joaquin Miller, Robert Louis Stevenson and George Santayana), and for five months they have been publishing the semi-monthly *Chap-Book* to promote their books and their authors, from Bliss Carman to William Vaughn Moody. *The Chap-Book* is the first in a tidal wave of small, personal or even precious, iconoclastic literary journals: the "dinkey magazines."

Sunday, October 14: Aladdin, Jr.

If ACD were a churchgoing man, which he is not, he could choose this morning among services at any number of places of worship, though he is too late to hear the magnificent preaching of Professor David Swing, whose voice was stilled forever a few days ago. Chicago has churches of all faiths, from St. Patrick's Roman Catholic, which predates the great fire, to St. James Reformed Episcopal, noted for its boys' choir. But ACD abandoned the faith of his fathers as a young man, turning his back on the church partly out of conviction (or lack of conviction) and partly out of pride, for Catholic connections could have given him a solid medical practice in Southsea. *The Stark Munro Letters*, which he wrote last winter and which is about to be published, will set out some of his religious opinions and uncertainties (the latter will be more extensive than the former for another twenty-five years, until ACD himself becomes a religious leader with his complete conversion to Spiritualism).

ACD today does go to the Opera House, the 2,100-seat theatre at the corner of Washington and Clark Streets which replaced an earlier opera house after the 1871 fire. This house is known as the home of comedy, and on summer nights an Arabian Nights show has been particularly popular. Seats can be had for as little as fifty cents to $1.50, but ACD is one of a party which has taken a box ($10, $12 or $15) for this evening's play: *Aladdin, Jr.* The hit of the season, it opened in June and is now in its final week before leaving on tour.

Subtitled "A Tale of the Wonderful Lamp," *Aladdin, Jr.* is a musical comedy based on the familiar Arabian Nights tale – or perhaps ACD thinks of it rather as a pantomime, considering the presence of Anna Boyd as Aladdin and of "Miss Frankie M. Raymond and Miss Ellene Crater, both incredibly blonde," in the words of a later review, as Chee Kee and Radrombadour. David Henderson's American Extravaganza

October 1894

Company is presenting the show, which is directed by Filberto Machetti and has book and lyrics by J. Cheever Goodwin, music by W. H. Batchelor. Nor is it merely a provincial hit; when it reaches New York and opens on a stormy April night, *The New York Times* will give high praise to its stage design, ballet and music, though admitting to some reservations about the acting.

Also occupying a box at the Opera House is Charles Frohman, the New York theatrical agent whose *Shenandoah* ACD recently saw in New York. He does not know it, but he will be the producer of a yet unwritten drama called *Sherlock Holmes*, starring William Gillette, when it is first performed in Buffalo in November 1899, and for a quarter of a century thereafter. With Frohman is Al Hayman, another of the New York theatre fraternity.

Monday, October 15: With Riley in Indianapolis

> Indianapolis (700 ft.), the capital and largest city of Indiana, with (1890) 105,436 inhab., lies on the W. branch of the *White River*, in the midst of a wide plain. It is a great railway-centre, carries on an extensive trade in grain and live-stock, and produces manufactures to the value of 33 million dollars (6,600,000*l.*) annually.
>
> The *State Capitol* is a large building with a central tower and dome, erected at a cost of $2,000,000. The *Court House* is also an imposing edifice. In *Circle Park*, to the E. of the Capitol, is the *Soldiers' Monument*, 265 ft. high. Other large and important buildings are the *Blind Asylum*, a little to the N. of the Capitol; the *United States Arsenal*, on a hill ot the E. of the city; the *Deaf & Dumb Asylum*, also to the E.; the **Propylaeum*, a unique building, owned and controlled by a stock-company of women for literary purposes; the *Union Depot*; the *Classical School for Girls*; the new *City Library*; and several *Churches*.

So says Baedeker, and to this largest city of Indiana, 197 miles from Chicago on the Cleveland, Cincinnati, Chicago & St. Louis Railway, comes ACD to deliver his "Readings and Reminiscences."

Tickets for tonight's lecture have been on sale for days at D. H. Baldwin & Co., 64-66 North Pennsylvania Street. Chiefly in the piano and organ business, Baldwin's some years ago set up an Indianapolis branch to serve areas too far from its base in Cincinnati. However, their showroom in Indianapolis also houses a ticket agency, from which the literary or curious have been able to acquire fifty-cent tickets to ACD's talk tonight; for a dollar they can hear not just ACD but all the speakers in this season's series of the Montefiore Lecture Course.

When the Doyle brothers arrive at the Union Station they are met by a delegation from the Montefiore Society and are whisked, with their tan valises, to the Denison House. ACD is standing at the front desk – "A. Conan Doyle, London, Eng.," he writes in the register – when a man comes up and greets him enthusiastically. "Well, Mr. Riley, how do you do," responds ACD. "I am most delighted to see you." It is James

Whitcomb Riley, the bibulous poet of rural Indiana, who makes the Denison his home at this time of year and who is eager to talk literature with ACD. Lively conversation ensues – although ACD finds (according to the next day's press reports) that the man who has rescued him from newspaper reporters is asking much the same questions those reporters would have asked. How has the trip been going?

> Dr. Doyle replied that, although he had never been in the country before, he was more than pleased with the American people and with his reception since he had landed at New York a few weeks ago. He spoke with a pronounced English accent and is of commanding presence. . . .

And so on. Eventually Riley gives the reporters a turn, and they ask ACD about contemporary writers, which gives him a chance to praise the familiar names: Meredith, Barrie, Stevenson, Schreiner. "Where did you get your idea of Sherlock Holmes?" he is asked, and he speaks of Joseph Bell and Edgar Allan Poe.

ACD and Riley dine together, and then it is time for his Montefiore lecture in Plymouth Congregational Church, where ACD is introduced by Isidore Feibleman, the president of the society. This church building at the corner of New York and Meridian Streets is eleven years old, though the congregation dates back to 1857. It is popularly known as the Open Door Church, because of the lecture series and other outreach programmes organized by Rev. Oscar Carleton McCulloch, its minister until his death three years ago.

ACD gives his "Readings and Reminiscences" for the second time, and it is well received. "There were very few unoccupied seats," the *Journal* will say tomorrow, "and these were the undesirable ones in the rear of the church." ACD adds some remarks which are not part of his standard lecture text:

> Dr. Doyle referred to the express robbery at New Orleans some time ago and proclaimed the work of Expert Carvalho, of Brooklyn, who found the alleged robber by the imprint of his thumb on one of the seals of the package broken open, as one of the cleverest detective bits in real life, or even in fiction. Dr. Doyle, however, has failed to ascertain that the young man arrested on the discovery of the expert was afterwards acquitted, and compromised a heavy damage suit against the corporation that caused his arrest. Sherlock Holmes would never have lost a case in any such way.

After the lecture there is an "informal reception" back at the Denison – more chance to meet local bigwigs and to talk about literature – and at 10:30 p.m. ACD, Innes, and Riley are among the guests for dinner at 19 West Ohio Street, the home of Dr. Franklin W. Hays and his wife, Luella. Hays, whose handlebar moustache gives him a facial resemblance to ACD, is 36 years old and holds the chair of Materia Medica, Therapeutics and Dermatology in the Medical College of Indiana, as well as being on the staff of the City Dispensary, the City Hospital and St. Vincent Hospital, and being a member of the city board of health. He is a life-long friend of Riley, and will be the model for Doc Sifers when Riley writes "The Rubaiyat" of that country medico:

> Doc's allus sociable, polite, and 'greeable, you'll find –
> Pervidin' ef you strike him right and nothin' on his mind, –
> Like in some *hurry* when they've sent for Sifers, *quick*, you see,
> To 'tend some sawmill-accident, er picnic jamboree; . . .
> Doc's *public* sperit – when the sick's not takin' *all* his time
> And he's got *some* fer politics – is simple yet sublime: –
> He'll *talk* his *principles* – and they air *honest*; – but the sly
> Friend strikes him first, election-day, he'd 'commodate, er die!

Before the evening is over, Riley is taken aside by reporters and made to say what he thinks of ACD: conscientious, honest, true and still readable.

> Those who heard Dr. Doyle's lecture must understand something of the untiring labor to which the writers of such books as he has produced must devote themselves. I admire his stories because I can read them easily. There is nothing heavy about them. Not only are they entertaining, but they are refreshing. People don't want to read the heavy stories produced by some of the old writers. It is nothing short of hard labor – too much like coming from work and then going to work again. The stories that Dr. Doyle has given us will last.

Tuesday, October 16: Ticket to Cincinnati

> It is easy enough to buy a ticket to Cincinnati, but it is somewhat harder to arrive there. Say that all goes well, is it exactly *you* who arrive? [William Dean Howells]

Having a free evening tonight, ACD does not have to hurry to begin his trip to Cincinnati. He can see something of Indianapolis first, in company with his brother, last night's host, and the omnipresent Hoosier poet:

> One of the first things he did was to go to the top of the monument with James Whitcomb Riley. There it was discovered that Dr. Doyle is a kodak fiend. He brought forth his snapshot camera, and turned it upon the beautiful city beneath him. He took almost a boy's interest in all that he saw, and he was enthusiastic in his praise of much.

The vantage point is the Indiana State Soldiers and Sailors Monument, a Civil War memorial in the form of a needle surmounted by a figure with a torch. It will stand for decades as the highest point in Indianapolis. The party also visit the Indiana State House before having lunch at 268 Park Avenue, the home of John M. Shaw, who is the manager of Kingan and Co., a major firm in the city's sizeable pork industry. As usual, reporters are hot on their heels. "You certainly have a delightful atmosphere," he tells them. "It is clearer than that which I have found in any other city, and I have visited most of the cities of Europe." Adds a *News* reporter, "The clear autumn air and the streets lined with trees, whose foliage is just turning to red and gold, made the English visitor enthusiastic."

At three o'clock ACD leaves on that hopeful journey for Cincinnati, and at six he arrives. He finds himself in "the chief city of Ohio, the ninth in the United States," as Baedeker puts it. (A local guidebook ranks the city fifth; it has 296,308 people within the city limits and half a million in the metropolitan area.) Here ACD finds himself as far south as this tour will take him, on a line of latitude with Washington and across the Ohio River from what just half a lifetime ago was a slave state. Cincinnati is, too, the most European of the cities ACD will visit – "the Paris of America," some enthusiasts call it, though with its beer, sauerbraten, and brass bands, it is more like America's Berlin.

> Fragrant memories come to Old-Timers [a guidebook author will write fifty years hence] when they think of the beer gardens and concert halls with sawdust and tanbark floors, singing waiters, dancing girls in tights, and 21 beers for a dollar. Many never closed their doors, and all were *gemuetlich* and respectable, if noisy. . . . Spirits lifted, talk grew wings, and song and laughter enjoyed a perpetual holiday on Vine Street in the 1890's. . . . Entertainment added to the fun at the concert halls and beer gardens, such sterling performers as Helena Mora, Johnny Carrol, Emma Carus, May Howard, Rose Sydell, and Weber and Fields being old favorites. . . . These years brought the theater to its gilded heyday, and variety burlesque, melodrama, and serious make-believe flourished in many a Cincinnati playhouse.

Boxing is popular, the Reds are back in the National League (this year Cincinnati finished tenth out of twelve teams in the baseball standings, with a 55-75 record), and bicycling is the craze, as young "scorchers" terrify decent citizens with their breakneck pace. One of the bookstores on Seventh Street has a window display picturing a man on his deathbed surrounded by snakes, dragons and similar horrors. Says a placard: "You who spend your money on booze instead of books, beware of a like end." ACD can perhaps agree with the sentiment, even if he should find time to visit one or two of Cincinnati's 2,091 saloons.

He is staying at the Burnet House at the corner of Third and Vine Streets, a 340-room palace which was labelled "the best hotel . . . of any in the world" when it opened in 1850. Civil War veterans still venerate its Parlor A, where in March 1864 the great Union generals, Grant and Sherman, spread out their maps to plan the campaign against Georgia and South Carolina. His arrival creates what tomorrow's *Times-Star* will describe as "somewhat of a flurry about the well-lighted corridors of the Third Street hostelry . . . Dr. Doyle was a feast for the reporters, who nabbed the celebrated author before he could escape to his apartments."

He puts most of their entreaties off until eight o'clock, when he has agreed to see all the reporters at once. They have some of the usual questions, and a few new ones. The *Tribune* will report some of his answers thus:

> Another writer whom Dr. Doyle admires is Lafcadio Hearn. He was surprised to find that Hearn was not more widely read in America. He was still more surprised when he was told that Hearn was a Cincinnati man, to all intents.
> But Dr. Doyle's favorite reading is not fiction. He prefers to all else military history. . . .
> Some one asked him what he thought of American vegetables. Corn he could not say that he liked. He thought it really too much trouble for the result. Sweet potatoes were different.
> "And there is a third, egg plant. At first I did not know what it was; and indeed," he continued, with his good humored smile, "I am not sure that I know yet."

He calls Indianapolis the cleanest city he has ever visited, but declines to say anything about Cincinnati until he has a chance to see something of it.

Meanwhile, he has taken a moment to write a note, on a sheet of Burnet House notepaper, to James Whitcomb Riley back in Indianapolis, thanking him for those effusive comments in the Indianapolis papers. (He has not had the boldness to scan the papers himself, but Innes has given him the news.) "You'll send me home," he writes, "all head like a tadpole."

Wednesday, October 17: The Culture of the Queen City

ACD can read reports of his arrival in today's Cincinnati newspapers – the *Commercial Gazette* calling him "charming," the *Enquirer* "delightful." And in the *Tribune*, under the heading "Told in Brief Talks, Some of the Varied Gossip of the Town," is this self-important impression:

> The present visit of Dr. A. Conan Doyle to Cincinnati suggested a very interesting remark to a local literateur yesterday. Said he:
> "I like Conan Doyle. He is one modern writer who has not been ruined by the critics. He has managed to keep the track of genius and persists in writing those things which his natural talents most suggest. How different from many of our American writers. Take Hamlin Garland, for instance. He won his literary fame by cleverly portraying the homely, simple life of what he calls the 'prairie folk.' He never dreamed of being a political economist or the champion of a down-trodden class, but the critics pretended to discover in him a great pleader for the cause of populism, and that ruined him. Now we have lost the best of Garland's work, for he has become a philosopher, a statistician, an essayist and the sorriest failure in the world.
> "Then there is Edward Bellamy. He used to be just a dear, delightful fellow, full of entertaining stories. One day he told one that was a little better than all the others, when, lo, and behold! the smart people said a new light had risen in the field of social

economics. Cranks began forming Edward Bellamy Clubs, and a bright writer became a stupid reformer.

"I like Conan Doyle because he has stuck to his pen and remained loyal to his fancy."

If he chooses the *Times-Star* instead, he will be spared that patronizing endorsement, in favour of this anecdote, which must give him grounds to ponder again the stolidity and uprightness of policemen:

> Rev. Charles Pelton, the reputed detective of the Law and Order league, was in Chief Deitsch's office this morning to make good the charges he preferred against Officer McNulty of going into Kemp's pool room in uniform. The officer showed that what he had done was by order of Lieut. Thornton and Pelton failed signally to make a case.

This newspaper obviously likes such gems. Yesterday it reported the presence at ACD's hotel, the Burnet House, of an Albany bill-collector named C. M. Van Heese – and the presence at the rival St. Nicholas Hotel of an Albany bill-collector named C. T. Van Heese. They are receiving each other's mail and callers, to general embarrassment.

ACD can spend today sightseeing, an activity which in this valley city generally includes a five-cent ride up one of the four Inclined Planes to a hilltop vantage-point. He is taken around the city by A. W. Whelpley, the city librarian, and J. L. Shearer of the Shearer Lecture and Musical Bureau, his local host. "Your air is very bad downtown, but the suburbs are fine," ACD tells a reporter, doubtless comparing this industrial centre with smaller, purer Indianapolis. "I had always heard of Cincinnati as a great manufacturing city, and I am much pleased with it. Your public library is really splendid." So it should be, having cost $296,684.53 when it was built twenty years ago. Patrons walk, a local guidebook explains, through an entrance hall and delivery room to a reading room which is tiered floor to ceiling with alcoves for books. At last count there were 197,484 items; the library (open daily 8 a.m. to 10 p.m.) has room for 300,000. Other public buildings in Cincinnati include a courthouse – in which a 37-year-old circuit court judge named William Howard Taft may be sitting today – and St. Peter's Roman Catholic Cathedral, graced by Murillo's painting "St. Peter Delivered," liberated from its earlier home during the Peninsular War.

Tonight ACD gives his "Readings and Reminiscences" at the new nine-storey Odd Fellows Hall, just opened at the northwest corner of Seventh and Elm Streets. (Tickets, priced at seventy-five cents and one dollar, have been on sale at George B. Jennings Music Co., 76 West Fourth Street.) He is introduced by Hon. Charles Baker, who is back in private legal practice (with a reputation as an authority on cases involving wills) but has not permanently abandoned public life – he will be the unsuccessful Democratic candidate for the United States Senate a few years hence. Tonight he stands "with arms akimbo for several minutes," tomorrow's newspaper will say, telling the audience "that it would be an affectation for him to say anything about the distinguished

October 1894

author, whose fame has preceded him, A. Conan Doyle." Finally allowed to speak for himself, ACD repeats his anecdotes of childhood, apprentice authorship and maturity, and gives the by now familiar readings from *The Sign of the Four* and his other works.

The audience is a good one – "to say that it was representative of the culture of the Queen City is at the same time to say that the box-office has no complaint coming," the *Times-Star* will say tomorrow. To be precise, the box office takes in $313.25.

Thursday, October 18: Harvest Home
Big news in Ohio this morning crowds ACD off the front pages of the Cincinnati papers: there was an attempted lynching during the night at Washington Court House, halfway between here and Columbus. The newspapers spill vast amounts of ink over the matter, but ACD does get some mention, and the *Tribune* also finds room to mention that a gentleman choosing to call himself "Paul Jones" is staying at the Gibson House as he passes through Cincinnati, part of a round-the-world trip which is to win him a five-thousand-dollar bet.

ACD must get back to Chicago, for this evening he and Innes are due at a gala social event which must leave him speechless with amazement. (He has no hesitation in saying that it will stand out conspicuously in his American memories.) It is the regular monthly banquet of the Fellowship Club, a gathering which he would have missed save that it was postponed from its original date because of the death of H. M. Kinsley, a prominent member of the group. He was the proprietor of a popular Adams Street restaurant, famous alike for its Moorish facade and its German cuisine, and the Fellowship Club is accustomed to meeting in the banquet hall at Kinsley's. It does so tonight for almost the last time. Tomorrow's *Tribune* will attempt to describe the occasion:

> The apartment, which the club had on previous occasions converted into the deck of the Fuerst Bismarck, an Oriental bower, and a German beer garden, underwent last night still another magical transformation, and became a barnyard, in which an innocent rural population was celebrating harvest home. The metamorphosis was absolutely stunning.
>
> Just inside the main entrance of the room was a square inclosure of palings and a gate. Inside the fence was a veritable barnyard under the open sky. The electric lights were extinguished, and the full harvest moon beamed upon and lighted up the scene. The floor was covered with wheat straw and barn dust. The walls were tapestried with sheaves of wheat, shocks of corn, and autumn leaves interlaced with grapevines loaded with purple clusters. Lying around on the floor were immense piles of cabbages, squashes, and turnips, and huge baskets of carrots. In one corner of the yard was a dove-cote, to and from which real doves cheerfully flew. Nearby was a henhouse containing fifty or more nice chickens. Elsewhere was a sheep pen containing two old sheep and the cutest of lambs. In another place was a stall containing the

demurest little donkey in the world. Now and then a deep-mouthed watchdog interfered with conversation by barking at imaginary tramps. Down upon the scene looked 100 or more jack pumpkins with red and yellow features. Against the wall hung an immense sign making the following announcement: "The Annual Harvest Home Festival of the Fellowship Club, at Kinsley's Farm, Thursday, Oct. 18, 1894. Music by the Quadrille Band and Singing by the Church Choir. A Hot Supper Will Be Served at 7 O'Clock."

The waiters are dressed in farm shirts and straw hats; in short, the scene is rural and simple to the point of satiation. (The *Inter Ocean*'s reporter notices that Innes is among several revellers who come near "measuring their respective lengths" on the straw, it is so slippery.)

Eighty gentlemen – this is definitely a stag party, save that two women are brought in to sing – sit down to dine on oysters, whitefish, roast suckling pig, roast turkey, chicken, squash, succotash, boiled potatoes, beets, dandelion salad, and "two immense pies three feet long, one a pumpkin and the other a mince." There are doughnuts, popcorn and fruit to snack on, and the official beverage of the meal is applejack.

Among the guests tonight is H. H. Kohlsaat, who started his business career in the bakery business (and was so successful that resentful rivals, in later years when he is a successful publisher and friend of presidents, will still call him "that damned pastry-cook"). Until last May he was part-owner of the *Inter-Ocean*, and he has spent the last few months travelling and dabbling in politics and other interests; he will take over the *Times-Herald* next spring. Tonight Kohlsaat has some good news for ACD: "I am delighted to tell you that your play at Bristol was an enormous success."

"So I am told," says ACD. "The cables are excellent."

Certainly the play, *A Story of Waterloo*, was well received at its production in Bristol a few weeks ago, though reviewers were more effusive about Henry Irving in the title role than about the one-act "sketch" itself. After the first night, *The Times* reported that "The piece was received with enthusiasm, and Mr. Irving, in response to a call for the author, announced that Dr. Conan Doyle was not at present in England." (Actually he was still in England, but could not attend the opening and comfortably make it aboard the *Elbe*.)

Kohlsaat tells ACD that the reports reaching North America "are not half enough" favourable.

"Indeed? I am rejoiced to hear it," says ACD, puzzled. "May I ask if you have had any special report?"

"I didn't need any report. I saw it!"

"Oh, come! That is impossible!"

But Kohlsaat assures him it is true: he attended a performance in Bristol, rushed to the railway station, reached Southampton in time to catch a steamer, and arrived in New York yesterday and in Chicago just minutes ago. "I am," he says, "in all human probability the only man on the American continent who was there!"

October 1894

After coffee, the speeches begin. James W. Scott, the newspaper proprietor, is the club's president, and takes the chair, with ACD, as the most distinguished guest of the evening, seated on his right. Scott and the club's secretary, F. Willis Rice, are followed on the programme by Franklin W. Head, the banker who lunched with ACD at the Union League Club last Saturday. Head introduces ACD, inviting him to tell the assembled farmers how they can go about wringing the tail of the British lion until wheat shall bring them a dollar a bushel. (He does not need to tell his audience that this year's price, in spite of the midwestern drought, was 49.1 cents a bushel.)

> Mr. Doyle said he was reminded of what Daniel said when he saw the lions approaching him, "There will be no after-dinner speaking for me." When he was at sea he found his watch differed from the ship's clock, and he had to push it forward all the time. So with his mental dial in coming West. He thought he had pushed it to its utmost in Chicago. Generally it was thought a man who came to America to lecture came to reap a harvest, but he had reaped only a harvest supper.
>
> Here the club sang, "For He Is a Jolly Good Fellow," after which Mr. Head announced: "The choir will sing the familiar old hymn, 'Old Black Joe'." A quartet then appeared in the balcony, and with the aid of a melodeon rendered the air with admirable effect. Ex-Gov. Oglesby was affected to tears. Mr. Head then introduced Dr. Von Holst, whom he requested to inform them of the bearings of the constitution on amateur farming.

This is a great joke, for Professor Hermann von Holst, who came from Freiburg a few years ago to be head professor of history at the University of Chicago, is an awe-inspiring authority on the springs of the American republic. "His immense forehead and his eyes . . . seem always to be gazing at the departed spirits of the founders of the constitution," an interviewer will write a few weeks hence.

The ex-governor, Richard James Oglesby, also speaks, after being brought to tears again, the newspaper alleges, by "The Old Oaken Bucket." Now 70 and at the end of an eventful career, Oglesby is known as "Uncle Dick" to the voters of Illinois, who have rewarded his talents on the hustings with three elections to the governor's chair. He does not disappoint his listeners tonight, taking the opportunity to refer to corn as the most beautiful vegetable that ever sprang out of the earth.

Hamlin Garland also speaks, and so does Paul du Chaillu, the 59-year-old African explorer, who by now has retired from active adventuring in favour of writing, studying and telling tall tales:

> Paul du Chaillu was asked what effect the discovery of the gorilla migration might have on the market for American cereals. He did not, of course, answer the question, and when the intrepid explorer arose from his chair his head was so near the ground that one of the farmers asked him to stand in a chair. He did not, of course, do it, and began to explain how he happened to remain

a bachelor. His African records showed that he had been proffered by various chiefs no less than a grand total of 22,000 wives. This suggested the topic of love, and while he was telling about the moon kissing the night, the courtship of the flowers, and the like, a farmer to the right wanted to know what it all had to do with corn and May wheat. He said he did not know and finished with a thrilling recital of his first meeting with gorillas.

It is a merry assembly, and getting rowdier as the evening goes on. There are more speakers – Luther Laflin Mills and Rev. E. M. Stires of the Grace Episcopal Church – and even a few words from Innes Doyle, who is so little suited to public speaking that at his own wedding in 1911 his speech will consist of no more than "Well – I say, don't you know! By Jove, what?"

The climax of the evening is the late arrival of actors Joseph Jefferson and Sol Smith Russell after their evening performances. Both are asked to speak and both tell a couple of funny stories.

Friday, October 19: The Toledo Cycling Club

"I expected to find much to like here and much to learn, but it is far finer than I expected," ACD writes in today's letter to his mother in Yorkshire. He is perhaps not thinking just of last night's revels, even though they brought him into the midst of Chicago's rich and influential, but of the whole variety of people he has met and places he has seen in barely three weeks. A less affluent side of American society will be opened to him tonight.

Before leaving Chicago, he writes to *The Toronto World*, which has been ahead of its rivals in asking the creator of Sherlock Holmes for his advice about Toronto's greatest current mystery. Late at night on October 6, someone came to the door of the Westwood home in the quiet residential district of Parkdale, and when young Frank Westwood came to the door, that someone shot him through the chest. He died last Thursday and there is (as far as the press knows) no suspect. Naturally the newspapers are desperate for clues or, at the very least, for some new angle. Hence the request for ACD's opinion. He writes briefly:

> Dear Sir: I shall read the case, but you can realise how impossible it is for an outsider who is ignorant of local conditions to offer an opinion.
> Thanking you, I am, faithfully yours,
>
> A. Conan Doyle

He is travelling today to Toledo, a journey across the full width of Indiana, some five hours, which he makes on the Lake Shore Road's Wagner Vestibule Train. He writes a note on train stationery to Melville E. Stone, referring jocularly to last night's cider and turning down an invitation to spend some time with him before his Milwaukee lecture next Thursday: "as I have to keep myself pretty quiet before a lecture I should have the aggravation of knowing that there was good company there without being able fully to share it."

October 1894

Today he arrives in Toledo to find the *Evening Bee* already carrying what looks like a first-hand interview with him, but is in fact based on a Chicago conversation last week:

> Being interviewed he has modestly confessed to a very ancient ancestry. The Irish sept of the Doyles descend from the puissant Dubhghaill (pronounced do-all), king of Ulster, in the tenth century, from whom they derive their surname. . . . Brigadier Doyle, of the Jacobite army, was successful in raiding the Williamites, but the latter at length caught him, and his head was placed on the walls of Kilkenny. . . .
> "I have always been a very omnivorous reader, and it would be difficult to say what authors I don't like; but I think Dickens influenced me more than any other. . . .
> "Are you conducting material for a novel on American life?"
> "Not on the present occasion. My knowledge of the country is too superficial, being chiefly gleaned through the windows of a railway carriage. But I propose returning next year."

And so on. The rival newspaper, the *Blade*, uses none of this material, being preoccupied with local issues, such as the red tape which is currently preventing women from registering to vote, although legally they are entitled to vote on questions touching on schools.

Tonight's lecture is to be given in the auditorium of the National Union League, whose national headquarters is a seven-storey building in downtown Toledo. The Union is described in reliable sources as "a popular American order, combining patriotic, social and benevolent features. . . . Mr. J. W. Meyers, the courteous secretary, is the resident officer here." However, on this occasion the Union is nothing more than the landlord. The lecture is being sponsored by the Toledo Cycling Club, and reserved seats have been on sale for some days at C. J. Woolley & Co.'s, the popular music store at 311 Superior Street, which for $250 "will furnish you with the best seat in the hall and an upright piano, mahogany case, 3 unisons, 3 pedals, warranted for 5 years."

Everyone is comfortably seated in the gold-and-silver-toned auditorium, and ACD steps onto the stage beside the man who is to introduce him, Robert H. Cochran. "Judge Cochran" did serve for a few years in the 1870's as a judge of the county court, but he has many other distinctions: a judge advocate during the Civil War, a prosecuting attorney, president of the Wheeling and Lake Erie railroad in the early 1880's, a prominent figure in the Grand Army of the Republic, a lawyer in private practice, and at present secretary of the Toledo Chamber of Commerce. (His son, Negley G. Cochran, is managing editor of the *Bee*.

After "Readings and Reminiscences," ACD and Innes are entertained at the home of the Woolleys, 1107 Monroe Street, which is no ordinary home but a merry boarding-house of young artists, writers and gay blades. Living here are George W. Stevens, a reporter for the *Bee*, and Theodore F. MacManus of the *Daily Commercial*, and George P. Brayley, who managed ACD's lecture on behalf of the cyclists' club (though during working hours he is only a clerk for the Woolson Spice Co.), and Harry L. Steiner, another clerk. They flourish on Mrs. Burbank's cooking and black Lizzie's housekeeping, and tonight they and the Woolleys have invited a few kindred spirits (such as Charles O'Brien, a staff artist for the *Bee*) to join them in offering hospitality to the British visitors. Judge Cochran joins the younger men for dinner, which is followed by, as tomorrow's paper will put it, "story telling . . . until a late hour."

The cycling club is secondary tonight: ACD is attending, though no one knows it, an early meeting of the Micawber Club, whose formal creation will come next year when the Woolleys decide to move to New York and the boarding-house must close. MacManus and Stevens and some of the other fast young fellows will hire that same cook and maid, rent themselves premises on Twelfth Street, and set up a bachelors' roost that will become known for beer, poker, music (including the odd Gilbert and Sullivan recital), and endless talk. "Night after night," an old-timer will recall fifty years from now, "the distressed neighbors called the police, who were overjoyed to hear 'riot at the Micawber Club,' and they would rush out to Twelfth St., where they would soon be singing louder than the members." (Wedding bells will eventually break up the old gang, though as MacManus becomes proprietor of Toledo's first advertising agency, and George Stevens the director of the art museum, there will be a tamer successor called the Minor Prophets.) There is no call for the police at 1107 Monroe tonight, although the merriment extends long into what is probably the most relaxed evening of ACD's whole tour.

Saturday, October 20: Dinner in Detroit
ACD takes the train to Detroit, which traveller William Archer will describe with some astonishment as

> a city of considerably more than a quarter of a million inhabitants, beautifully laid out, magnificently paved and lighted, its broad and noble avenues lined with handsome commercial houses and roomy if not always beautiful villas, trees shading its sidewalks, electric cars swimming in an endless stream along its bustling thoroughfares, its imposing public library swarming with readers, its theatres crowded, its parks alive with bicyclists, an eager activity, whether in business, culture, or recreation, manifesting itself on every hand.

ACD observes also that he is close to British soil again: across a narrow river from Detroit lies Windsor, Ontario. He and Innes check in at the Russell House, Detroit's leading hotel, at 2:10 p.m., and he impresses one reporter as "the perfect picture of health and strength . . . a splendid acquisition to any football team." While he is dressing for dinner, he is interviewed by John Hubert Greusel, who fancies himself a local literary lion; a long interview will appear in the Sunday *Tribune*.

> Dr. A. Conan Doyle's manners are hard and brisk [Greusel writes]. . . . He deliberately caused Sherlock Holmes to die.

October 1894

> "I had to do it in self-defense," said Dr. Doyle yesterday. "I was bored to death, you know; I was tired of that sort of thing anyway." . . .
>
> In order to appreciate Dr. Doyle's personality it is quite necessary for one to understand that the trend of Dr. Doyle's intellect is not in the direction of sentiment. He has that sort of mentality which sets the greatest worth on those circumstances which betray the largest element of common sense. You need but to come into the presence of this brisk, bustling man to conclude that he resolves every fact into its antecedent causes and deduces therefrom some rule for the conduct of life. . . .
>
> While he was talking yesterday he ran around the room at times; at others he looked nervously at his watch; he was not guilty of discourtesy; it was his method, for which he has nothing to blame except that splendid physique, with its overflowing spirits. . . .
>
> Dr. Doyle engaged his big, strong hands in the somewhat difficult masculine task of folding a soft white necktie under the bands of a turn-down collar. The tie had been marked in black ink at one end, "A. Conan Doyle." Dr. Doyle put on that cravat so indifferently that the laundry mark showed over his vest.

He is asked about Holmes's death, about the genesis of his literary career, about other authors, and about portraits of women in literature:

> "How about the heroines of your story?" . . .
>
> "I have never seen a woman's character treated successfully," said the doctor quickly. "I am not satisfied with anything in that line within the entire reaches of literature."
>
> "Isn't that a remarkable statement to come from you?"
>
> "I shouldn't wonder."

The *Free Press* also interviews him, getting comments about copyright, his own writings (including a book which the reporter renders as *The White Camp*), and America:

> Unlike most English writers that visit the United States, Mr. Doyle confesses that he has not been in the country long enough to be able to discuss the government and the people. But he has visited New York, Indianapolis, Chicago and Detroit, and has been a close observer of all that has been going on. He thinks he can distinguish a difference in character between the people of New York and Indianapolis, and between the people of that city and Detroit.

ACD will recall tonight's dinner in his autobiography:

> I remember that a banquet was given to us at a club in Detroit at which the wine flowed freely, and which ended by a speech by one of our hosts in which he bitterly attacked the British Empire. My brother and I, with one or two Canadians who were present, were naturally much affronted, but we made every allowance for the lateness of the evening. I asked leave, however, to reply to the speech, and some of those who were present have assured me that

they have never forgotten what I said. In the course of my remarks I said: "You Americans have lived up to now within your own palings, and know nothing of the real world outside. But now your land is filled up, and you will be compelled to mix more with the other nations. When you do so you will find that there is only one which can at all understand your ways and your aspirations, or will have the least sympathy. That is the mother country which you are now so fond of insulting. She is an Empire, and you will soon be an Empire also, and only then will you understand each other, and you will realize that you have only one real friend in the world."

ACD does not tire of this favourite topic. In his autobiography he will add a justification:

It was only two or three years later that there came the Cuban war, the episode of Manila Bay where the British Commander joined up with the Americans against the Germans, and several other incidents which proved the truth of my remarks.

Sunday, October 21: Spiritualism Past and Present

Six years ago today, an overflow crowd in New York's Academy of Music heard a once-famous woman make a remarkable confession. Her name was Margaret Fox (now, she preferred to say, Margaret Fox Kane), and she and her sister Kate had been famous across America in the months and years which followed the astonishing events of March 31, 1848, when Margaret was 13 and Kate was 12. Strange noises had been heard in the family home in Hydesville, near Rochester, New York, and the noises began to respond to commands and questions from the girls. The restless soul of a murdered man, it seemed, had returned to the house to communicate his torment to those still living. Within days the affair was a *cause celebre*; within months, Spiritualism had been born and was on its way to national prominence. Based equally on an interpretation of the mystical teachings of Emanuel Swedenborg and on the yearnings of bereaved relatives everywhere, it is at once a philosophy and a religion, whose most important tenet is "the survival of personality" beyond physical death.

On that day six years ago Margaret Fox – having earned her living as a Spiritualist medium and lecturer for much of her life – confessed that she and her sister had invented the whole original business, making the strange noises, to confound their credulous mother, by cracking their toe-joints against the bedstead. She took off her shoes to demonstrate that she could still do it.

That revelation put paid to Spiritualism, or so the press concluded. By 1888 there was not much left of Spiritualism anyway. It had a flowering in the 1850's, in response to the Fox manifestations, and another in the 1870's – prompted, said the uncharitable, more by the wishful thinking of those who lost loved ones in the Civil War than by any objective evidence or real religious conviction. Consensus had it that the

October 1894

spirit of "Katie King," manifested both in London and in Philadelphia, was a fraud, as was "Violet" when she appeared to Robert Dale Owen in Boston.

Spiritualism has been in decline, but it is by no means extinct. Cora L. V. Hatch, a famous "child medium" in the 1850's, is still pastor of a Spiritualist church in Chicago, and in the summer there is still a camp-meeting in southwestern New York state, at what will soon be renamed Lily Dale, sponsored by the Cassadaga Lake Free Association. But believers will not exist in large numbers again until another great war, that of 1914 to 1918, creates another generation of the bereaved and bewildered – and by that time ACD himself will be their tireless prophet, preaching Christian ethics, scientific progress, and communication with those who have passed over.

What exists now, in 1894, is the Society for Psychical Research, a scientific rather than religious body. ACD has been interested in psychic matters, religious philosophy and "magnetism" since about 1880, and wrote to the journal *Light* in 1887 describing results which he had obtained through a medium. A year ago he joined the SPR, and soon afterwards served it as investigator of mysterious manifestations at Charmouth – which, however, he was unable to explain, though his colleague suspected fraud. The SPR's academic caution is satirized in his novelette *The Parasite*, which is about to be published. Many years hence, when ACD is an ardent Spiritualist himself, he will criticize the Society more violently for its sceptical attitude:

> Psychical research should show some respect for the feelings and opinions of Spiritualists, for it is very certain that without the latter the former would not have existed. . . . In an exaggerated striving after what was considered to be an impartial, scientific attitude, a certain little group within the society has continued for many years to maintain a position, if not of hostility to, yet of persistent denial of, the reality of physical manifestations observed with particular mediums.

He will eventually resign from the SPR in disgust, and become president of the London Spiritualist Alliance and the London College of Psychic Science.

The current president of the SPR is William James, the pioneering psychologist at Harvard, whose special subject of investigation for almost a decade has been a Boston medium, Mrs. Leonora Piper. He is learning much from her, though not necessarily learning what she wants to teach:

> Indeed, during the last two decades of the century the spiritualistic medium played a significant role in the field of psychology by providing such pioneer investigators as Pierre Janet, Theodore Flournoy, William James, and F. W. H. Myers with data for their theories of multiple personality, hysteria, and the unconscious.

It is open to question whether the "science" that is trickling into public attention from the laboratories of such researchers is any more respectable than the simple credulity of twenty or thirty years ago. Thomas Jay Hudson's book *The Law of Psychic Phenomena*, published last year, is on its way to selling copies to a hundred thousand Americans eager to read about the difference between "objective" and "subjective" mind – and to learn that the latter is the proof of human immortality.

ACD does not have any such serious matters on his mind today. He is much sought after by admirers and literary colleagues, and a group of the latter take him for a drive through the city's boulevards and out to Belle Isle. Robert Barr, of the *Idler*, is among them – Detroit is his home, after all, though ACD last saw him in London. Also along are William Savage, Dr. Mann, and Thomas Jerome.

Monday, October 22: Lecture in Detroit

Detroit hospitality continues, as ACD takes a stroll with Cameron Currie this morning, and is invited aboard the yacht of James McMillan this afternoon. (McMillan is nothing less than a United States senator; Ontario-born, he has been in Detroit since his teenage years, and after making a name in business here got himself elected to the Senate as a Republican in 1889.) ACD and "a few friends," the *Evening News* says, "were given a panoramic view of Detroit from the water front."

Tonight he gives his "Readings and Reminiscences" at Detroit's Church of Our Father, a Universalist establishment. ("There has been a large advance sale of seats for Monday night's lecture," the *Free Press* said yesterday, adding, "The plat will be at Schwankovsky's music store until 6 p.m. Monday.") The audience, which nearly fills both floor and gallery, is "composed of the best element of the city," the *Free Press* will say tomorrow, and the *Tribune* will assess the speaker thus:

> On the lecture platform Conan Doyle is a stationary figure, his chief gesture being that of pulling a red handkerchief from between his broad expanse of shirt front and his vest. His voice is loud in volume, but mixed in tone. His words sound a mixture of Scotch, English, Irish and cold, but for all this Dr. Doyle was listened to last night with deep interest. He was talking of himself and his works, which are himself.

Pond's register will record, next to the name of W. E. Brownlee as ACD's local sponsor, that the speaker's fee is $50 and the box office grosses $253.60.

The liquor flows freely in Detroit. At one cordial gathering, a barmaid asks ACD whether he intends to "blow himself," and he is puzzled by the slang phrase. A cynical reporter describes that reaction as "a good illustration of the inevitable slowness of British mental processes":

> Englishmen pretend to make a great mystery out of American slang and they are often foolishly abetted in it by Americans. The fact is that genuine American slang, the slang that really "goes," is instantly and lucidly self-explanatory to everyone with even a casual knowledge of conditions and affairs in this country. Slang that needs a definition dies before the explanation gets around.

October 1894

> An American who had lived in a cloister, confronted by a bar and invited to "blow himself," would know what was meant. Even an Englishman should understand that blowing one's self involves the spending of money, since the term is probably derived from the English slang, "raising the wind."

Tuesday, October 23: George Meredith
A volume of ACD's short stories, titled *Round the Red Lamp*, is published today by the London firm of Methuen & Co., and in a few days there will be an American publisher as well: D. Appleton & Co., which failed to secure *The White Company* but which will get the rights to five more of ACD's books before the 1890's are over. Its author has a day off from lecturing today, before the nightly grind really begins.

In later years Frederick Villiers, the war correspondent and artist who was the model for the hero of Kipling's "The Light That Failed," will take some of the credit for the beginning of ACD's lecturing career:

> I was once lecturing on my war experiences at Norwood when Sir Arthur kindly took the chair. He made a charming, complimentary speech when I had finished, and he had such an excellent, full-toned voice and fine presence that I suggested that he should lecture. The idea had evidently never before struck him, but I pointed out how interested the public was sure to be to hear anything from him on the platform. The suggestion seemed to take ground, for a short time afterward I found him advertised to lecture on the works of George Meredith.
>
> This was hardly what I had expected. I thought the discourse would be on how he evolved Sherlock Holmes – a subject that would have taken the lecture platform by storm.

In that last conviction, Villiers is absolutely right. Not so in his belief that he put the idea of lecturing into ACD's head, for ACD was speaking publicly about Meredith (and other subjects) before he ever lived in Norwood. In his autobiography he will describe the works of Meredith as "one of my youthful cults," and it is certain that he spoke about Meredith on November 23, 1888, at a Friday evening session of the Portsmouth Literary and Scientific Society. In that talk, reported next day in the Portsmouth newspapers, one can clearly see the origin of the lecture which he had hoped to be giving on this American tour, if only someone had asked to hear it.

Seriously crippled, Meredith is still writing in 1894; he has almost completed the metamorphosis from radical crank to grand old man, though general readers are no closer than they ever were to understanding his gnarled and florid writings. An anecdote which ACD will put in his autobiography says it as well as anything:

> I remember that once in the presence of [James] Barrie, [Arthur] Quiller-Couch and myself, he read out a poem which he had inscribed "To the British Working-Man" in the "Westminster Gazette." I don't know what the British working-man made of it,

but I am sure that we three were greatly puzzled as to what it was about.

In that 1888 lecture, according to the *Hampshire Telegraph*, ACD read frequent selections from Meredith's work to illustrate his talk, and

> commenced by pointing out that the greater the originality of a writer the more difficult did it become to measure his genius and assign to him his true place in the world of letters. The reading public was conservative, and looked askance at sweeping innovations in matter and style, and when both were decidedly original an author must be content to bide his time. In England we had had during the present century three men of this class in various ranks of literature. Two had risen to the front rank, and he thought the third would take his true position as one of the greatest writers of English fiction. He referred to Carlyle and Browning, and to George Meredith. The latter had been writing since 1853, but yet his name was less familiar to the public than that of the author of the latest "shilling shocker."

The *Telegraph* does not mention laughter at this point, but members of the audience must by November 1888 have been aware of ACD's own shilling shockers, not least *A Study in Scarlet*, that first Sherlock Holmes tale, published the previous Christmas between lurid covers.

Meredith, by contrast, had been writing serious novels, his latest at this point being *Diana of the Crossways* (1885). Best known perhaps is his earliest real novel, *The Ordeal of Richard Feverel* (1859); still to come were *One of Our Conquerors*, *The Amazing Marriage*, and others. Readers and critics do not generally appreciate just how radical Meredith is, not just in aesthetic terms but in social and political ones as well. The less socialist tone of *Diana* is probably what has made it the most successful of his books. At any rate, there is something in him which by 1888 impressed ACD, and in his 1888 lecture he stoutly championed Meredith as a child of Portsmouth (he was born in 1828 in a tailor's shop in the High Street).

> In a great town like Portsmouth there was not a single private library which contained more than two of his works. The writers of this class had some consolation in the great enthusiasm they had raised in a few, which might be taken as a protest against the lukewarmness of the general reading public; and the essayist cited the Browning Societies in evidence. Having quoted favourable opinions of Meredith's writings to which Walter Besant, Robert Louis Stevenson, and Carlyle had given expression, Dr. Doyle said there were now signs that his reward was at hand. On every side one saw allusions which indicated that the belief was growing that a profound and deep author had been writing among us, unhonoured and unknown. Dealing seriatim with Meredith's works he described "The Ordeal of Richard Feverel" as teeming with witty dialogue, displaying a power of drawing the feelings and doings of boys which was second only to that of Thackeray, tracing a succession of events rather than a plot, ending with tragedy as hard and

October 1894

inexorable as the work of the old character dramatist, and manifesting a scorn of conventionality either in construction or development. "Evan Harrington" might be described as a text book of snobbishness, carried out with such completeness as to make one regret that Thackeray did not live to read it.

Allusions to Thackeray do keep creeping into ACD's remarks. He mentions the great old man in the "Readings and Reminiscences" which he is giving on this 1894 tour, claiming that when he was four years old he sat on Thackeray's knee – and thus a little desperately associating himself, the poor Edinburgh lad, with the great tradition of English letters. One feels sure that he told the same story to Thackeray's former son-in-law, Sir Leslie Stephen, the first time he met him.

The *Telegraph* goes on:

"Emilia in England" and "Vittoria" were dull; and when Meredith was dull he was intolerably so. "Rhoda Fleming" was a novel of great power; more original, perhaps, than "Richard Feverel," but hardly so forcible. Balzac himself never showed such power of analysis of the female mind as did Meredith, who had the Shakesperian trick of treating a character from within as well as from without. "Diana of the Crossways" contained all Meredith's faults and none of his virtues; it was full of wit, and sparkled, but there was an inherent improbability about the incident and a want of sympathy about the various persons introduced, which marred it as a work of art. Regarding "The Egoist," Dr. Doyle said that as a piece of character drawing he knew nothing in the whole range of English fiction to which it could be compared. "Harry Richmond" resembled "Richard Feverel" in its subject, and though inferior in sustained interest it abounded in passages and incidents equal to any which Meredith ever wrote: and there was hardly a character in the book which did not deserve to live. Dealing with Meredith's faults the essayist said he compelled people to read his works for the more intellectual pleasure of his brilliant thoughts, while his characters had an artificial air about them. As a rule the construction of the stories was faulty. Meredith was a phrase-maker, and was so determined not to be commonplace, and never to say anything, as any other man had said it, that the result was now and then so out of place as to be grotesque. Some of his aphorisms should be retained in the English language, but others were ridiculous. Still Meredith's counterbalancing virtues were to the essayist's mind sufficient to place him head and shoulders above any other living writer of fiction.

ACD had probably not yet met Meredith in person when he gave that Portsmouth talk. He will recall later that "articles" from his pen led Meredith to invite him to his cottage at Box Hill, near Dorking in Sussex. Those articles can only have been a piece about Robert Louis Stevenson, with some passing remarks on Meredith, published in January 1890, and a piece "On the Geographical Distribution of British Intellect," with two letters ("Hampshire Worthies" and "Hampshire Celebrities") responding to criticisms, in August 1888.

He will tell of his first visit to Box Hill:
> There had been a good deal in the papers about his health, so that I was surprised when, as I opened the garden gate, a slight but robust gentleman in a grey suit and a red tie [ACD does not comment on this traditional, almost stereotypical, wardrobe accessory of the British socialist] swung out of the hall door and came singing loudly down the path. I suppose he was getting on to seventy at the time but he looked younger, and his artistic face was good to the eye. Greeting me he pointed to a long steep hill behind the house and said: "I have just been up to the top for a walk." I looked at the sharp slope and said: "You must be in good trim to do it." He looked angry and said: "That would be a proper compliment to pay to an octogenarian." I was a little nettled by his touchiness, so I answered: "I understood that I was talking to an invalid." It really seemed as if my visit would terminate at the garden gate, but presently he relented, and we soon became quite friendly.

So friendly were they that Meredith brought out a bottle of Burgundy from his fine cellar and (since the old man was himself forbidden alcohol) encouraged ACD to drink it all. The talk "got upon Napoleon's Marshals," a topic surely congenial to the guest, and after lunch they walked up the steep slope to the little summer-house where Meredith liked to write. He wanted to read to ACD passages from what would eventually become *The Amazing Marriage*.

> The nervous complaint from which he suffered caused him to fall down occasionally. As we walked up the narrow path to the chalet I heard him fall behind me, but judged from the sound that it was a mere slither and could not have hurt him. Therefore I walked on as if I had heard nothing. He was a fiercely proud old man, and my instincts told me that his humiliation in being helped up would be far greater than any relief I could give him.

ACD was back at Box Hill on February 27, 1892, with J. M. Barrie and Arthur Quiller-Couch ("Q") – probably that was the time Meredith read the puzzling poem "To the British Working-Man."

In the autobiography, ACD will speak briefly of Meredith's religious beliefs, which withered away just as his own have done. Indeed, though he never says so, it becomes clear that ACD looks on Meredith as something of a model, if not a father. (By 1894 Charles Doyle is dead, and for years before his death, as a household alcoholic and then an institutionalized madman, he was no father at all to his children.) Meredith himself was deserted by his father in childhood; like ACD he took some schooling in Germany; as ACD will soon be, Meredith found himself caught between two women, and wrote his celebrated sonnet cycle *Modern Love* to describe the experience. Both authors are enthusiasts of cricket and other sports, and of Anglo-American unity, and each has a keen interest in the social position of women; Meredith first used the image of "the old cab-horse" with which ACD will later describe himself.

October 1894

ACD has not yet become a rebel against society and conventional wisdom, a role he will assume only in the 1920's with his full conversion to Spiritualism, but when he does he may feel that he is following in Meredith's steps. And there is an eerie coincidence: that Meredith named his own son (who was born six years before ACD, and who died in middle age in 1890) Arthur.

Wednesday, October 24: Hotels on Wheels
ACD left Detroit for Chicago last night – by rail, of course. America has nearly as many miles of railways as all the rest of the world put together. A web of iron touches every state, almost every town; the trains which speed along these thousands of miles of tracks are chiefly part of city culture, and in small towns adults and children alike stand by the depot and gape as they flash past. It is estimated that not more than three per cent of the population of the United States travels as far as fifty miles from home in any given year. Those who do are obliged to take the trains – there are only a few hundred automobiles in the country, and no highways to run them on. Roads are for getting from the farm or village to the railway station; it will attract some attention when Alexander Winton manages to drive an automobile from Cleveland to New York in ten days in the late summer of 1897.

For all his daily and nightly journeys, the visiting author is experiencing only a very small sampling of the lines. He will have no chance to experience the transcontinental rail journey which has now been possible for some twenty-five years. He is enjoying his travels aboard these luxurious hotels on wheels, or so he told a reporter in Chicago the other day:

> I find it a great treat to use the transportation facilities in this country. One gets to his destination feeling so fresh. It is not that way in Europe.

Indeed, the trains are very different from European ones, not least because of the works of George Pullman. Coaches are different from the European model too (they are one long room, not a series of compartments), but what first-class travellers enjoy on long trips are the sleeping-cars from which Pullman made his millions:

> The parlor and sleeping-cars are generally the property of special corporations, of which the Pullman Palace Car Co. . . . is the chief. . . . The vexed question of whether the American or the European railway-carriage is the more comfortable is hard to decide. It may be said generally, however, that the small compartment system would never have done for the long journeys of America, while the parlor cars certainly offer greater comfort in proportion to their expense than the European first-class carriages do. A *Limited Vestibuled Train* . . . comes measurably near the ideal of comfortable railway travelling, and reduces to a minimum the bodily discomfort and tedium of long railway journeys. . . .

As for the coaches, Baedeker observes, it can be annoying to quarrel with other passengers about whether the windows should be open or shut, and

> the incessant visitation of the train-boy, with his books, candy, and other articles for sale, renders a quiet nap almost impossible; . . . On the other hand the liberty of moving about the car, or, in fact, from end to end of the train, the toilette accommodation, and the amusement of watching one's fellow-passengers greatly mitigate the tedium of a long journey.

Baedeker goes on to explain the desirability of a lower berth, the possibility of a drawing-room for parties of two to four persons, the availability of dining cars, and the necessity to tip no one on board the train except the porter (twenty-five cents a day, since he brushes clothes and boots overnight).

The Doyle brothers are actually lucky to be able to ride these trains and take these Pullman cars. If they had come in July, they would have found the railway system – especially in this part of the country, where all roads lead to Chicago – in terrible disorder as the result of what has already gone into history as "the Pullman boycott." It started at Pullman, Illinois, a model company town outside Chicago, where more than three thousand employees of the Palace Car Co. went on strike in despair when their millionaire employer, George Pullman, announced that because of hard times he was cutting their wages. Their union quickly enlisted support from the American Railway Union, and by late June most members of that union were supporting the strikers by refusing to handle trains which contained Pullman cars – the property of Pullman's company, and a more immediate source of its income than the cars which strikers were refusing to build or repair. Economic pressure did not work fast enough for Pullman and the railroads, who persuaded President Cleveland to intervene, over the strong protests of Illinois governor John Altgeld. On July 2 the President sent federal troops into Chicago, chiefly under the pretext that the strike was interfering with the movement of the mails; there were a few violent incidents; by the middle of July the strikers were virtually all back at work, and Eugene V. Debs, president of their union, was facing conspiracy charges, which are, in October, still before the courts.

Thursday, October 25: Evening in Milwaukee
ACD makes the short journey up to Milwaukee today; the rail fare is $2.55 (thirty-five cents extra for the sybaritic traveller who desires a chair in the parlour car). He is to lecture tonight in Milwaukee, a city which mixes Catholics and Protestants, speakers of English and speakers of German. The most bitter political issue here is whether the state of Wisconsin should pay for the erection at Washington of a proposed statue of the explorer Father Jacques Marquette. ACD the lapsed Catholic is to lead off this year's Popular Lectures series at Plymouth Congregational Church, which later in the season will present such figures

October 1894

as Dean Hole, F. Hopkinson Smith, and the indefatigable George Kennan in his new lecture, "Personal Adventures in Siberia."

ACD's subject has been announced here as "Fads about Fiction," except in *Yenowine's News*, which said two weeks ago that it would be "George Meredith and his Work" and "The Younger Influences in English Literature." Readers of the church's newsletter have been told – in terms which probably owe much to Major Pond – that they should expect only the best:

> It is not often that the privilege is afforded of listening to a man of such rare genius on a subject which he is so well qualified to speak about. In New York and Chicago he has been received by large and delighted audiences, and the press, without exception, speak of him in terms of highest praise. A man who has so captivated the reading and thinking world by his writings and lectures, whom critics speak of only to praise, can scarcely fail to receive a hearty and generous reception upon his first appearance in our city.

He has, indeed, been meaning to give "Facts about Fiction," but has thought better of it and decided to give the popular "Readings and Reminiscences" instead.

Whether he wanted it or not, some of the Chicago literary folk have determined to come up to Milwaukee for the evening. ACD's own train arrives in the city of grain, beer and German culture at 1:45 p.m., so that he has time, if he wishes, to follow Baedeker's advice and visit one of the Milwaukee breweries, such as Pabst's, which produces more than a million gallons of beer annually, or to view the statue of Leif Ericson in Juneau Park. First, of course, at the Pfister Hotel, he must talk with reporters briefly – one is introduced to him as a Republican and one as a Democrat, and he assures them that he knows the difference. He tells the representative of the *Journal* that he will "never write another detective story." At 5 p.m. a later train brings in Melville Stone, Eugene Field, and Paul du Chaillu, who will take whatever opportunity they can to keep ACD company.

It is no coincidence that Plymouth Church is the site of ACD's Milwaukee appearance. Like the Indianapolis church of the same name which he has already visited, this Plymouth, at the corner of Van Buren and Oneida Streets, is an active and outward-looking congregation, led by the able and imaginative Rev. Judson Titsworth. With extensive sewing and cooking schools, a gymnasium, a boys' club and other activities, Plymouth is providing a new kind of ministry in America, serving an urban community of a quarter of a million, half of them identifiably German and many of them newly-arrived immigrants.

The lecture series is less severely practical (extending to the frivolous with "Prof. Carnes, elocutionist" and the Imperial and Arion quartettes of Chicago, due on November 15), but it too tries to make the church a source of support and interest at times other than Sunday mornings. The series is a new venture of the Sunday Evening Club, which "is composed of men only, and any man not connected with other churches will be cordially welcomed to membership upon signing the constitution and paying the entrance fee of one dollar." The club's president, Wesley A. Severson, and its other officers are trying to double the current membership of one hundred.

They are selling tickets for their lecture series at T. A. Gray & Co.'s bookstore, at one dollar for the six scheduled events. "The number to be sold," warned the October issue of the church newsletter, "is limited to one thousand and the limit has been nearly reached." With single tickets sold at the door, the total audience comes to some twelve hundred.

Friday, October 26: Return to Chicago
Eighteen people sit down to luncheon at 1 p.m. at 2 Bank Street, Chicago, the home of the eloquent, cultured, ultra-conservative banker, Franklin H. Head. His wife, Catherine, died two years ago, and his hostess is his eldest daughter, Elizabeth, who among other social distinctions is president of the Wildwood Lunch Club. (A week from today, though neither of them knows it yet, ACD will meet Miss Head's future husband.)

There are more gentlemen than ladies at this luncheon, but it is more evenly balanced than many luncheons in ACD's honour. Besides the hostess, and her younger sister Katharine, the company includes Elizabeth Wallace, Lydia Avery Cowley, Josephine Bates, and Caroline G. Scott, accompanying her husband, the newspaper publisher James W. Scott.

With her husband also is Alice M. Russell, married since 1876 to the literary actor Sol Smith Russell, whom ACD met at last week's rustic dinner. Tall, homely and kindly, Russell at 46 is famous as a comic and character actor, and noted offstage for what an observer calls "quiet dignity . . . he is oftener taken for a clergyman than for an actor. . . . One less delicately organized as a Christian gentleman would be incapable of bringing comedy and pathos into intimate association as Mr. Russell does in his latest and most successful plays." His personal library is said to contain six thousand books, as well as many autographs.

His companion the other night, Joseph Jefferson, is here, and so are several other guests already familiar to ACD and Innes, apart from the host himself: Eugene Field, and the inevitable Melville E. and Herbert S. Stone (whose firm has published Edmund Gosse's book of poetry *In Russet and Silver* since ACD first met him two weeks ago).

There are some new faces as well – George Genowine, and Dr. Frank W. Gunsaulus, a prominent book collector and the minister of Plymouth Congregational Church. Gunsaulus, who preached the memorial sermon for Professor David Swing a couple of weeks ago, is the author of several books himself, not only theological but literary and historical. His life of Gladstone has not yet reached the general public,

October 1894

but his *Monk and Knight: An Historical Study in Fiction* was published three years ago. Gunsaulus will one day soon preach so eloquently on the theme "If I Had a Million Dollars" that meat-packing millionaire Philip Armour will call his bluff and offer to provide that million in exchange for "five years of your life." Gunsaulus will accept and spend the five years creating the Armour Institute of Technology and promoting technical education as its first president.

And there is Alice French, now 44, better known to the public as Octave Thanet. One of the Stone & Kimball stable of authors, she is a successful author of short stories, which began with "The Communist's Wife" in *Lippincott's* fifteen years ago and have been collected in several books. She also has one novel, *Expiation*. An enthusiast about labour reform, she is more old-fashioned in other respects, and in particular has no use for the fad of women's suffrage. Alice French will never marry, devoting her remaining forty years to writing, patriotic organizing, charity, and the Iowa Society of Colonial Dames.

Mrs. Russell composes twenty-six lines of doggerel incorporating all their names:

> Why this joyous turmoil?
> 'Tis to greet Dr. Doyle.
> Oh, who would not hustle
> To see Mr. Russell . . .

Two cards on which she has inscribed the verse are passed around the table for everyone to sign. ACD also signs a large photograph of himself (by Walery, Photographer to the Queen, 164 Regent Street, London) and gives it to Herbert S. Stone.

And he signs a couple of his books for Eugene Field. Field has been using his newspaper column to inveigh against bad printing and bookbinding, and ACD has come in for some of his wrath. Correspondents have pointed out to him that the author can hardly be blamed for poor quality in editions which were pirated (such as those published by the United States Book Company and the firm of Lovell, Coryell), and just last week he responded to a letter from one Walker Thelen, arguing that at least the Harper editions are well made. Not so, said Field:

> The edition of "Sherlock Holmes" published by the Harpers is not a better-made book than the Doyle books made by the United States Book Company and by Lovell; all are so bad as to be a disgrace to the publishing industry in this country. The Harpers are not making uniformly good books. No book is well made that creaks piteously when you open it; that gets out of shape even when reverently handled; and that spills out a leaf here and there after a day's use. That is just the kind of a book the Harpers' edition of "Sherlock Holmes" is. Another Harpers' book, Mr. Du Maurier's "Trilby," is a cheap book, for which, however, an extortionate price is demanded. The Harpers adhere conscientiously and intrepidly to first-class prices without providing therewith first-class work.

> We do not know that we are prepared to ally ourselves with Mr. Thelen in his crusade of extermination against cheap publishers exclusively. A cheap robber is certainly no less desirable than an expensive robber; we are against all robbers, big as well as small. We do not approve of piracy at all; yet we think we should hesitate to kill off the little, measly pirates simply to benefit reformed pirates. We think it would be wise of Mr. Thelen to acquaint himself with the early career of the Harper publishing house before making so truculent a flourish against the pirates and the piracies of the present time.

Now this is not entirely fair. Although in its early years Harpers was guilty of some piracy, it has long prided itself on paying royalties even when the weak copyright laws would not require them. And it is not a Harper volume which Field holds out to ACD to sign, nor yet the authorized Lippincott edition of *The Sign of the Four*, but the despised product of the United States Book Company. ACD sees the impish gleam in Field's eye and responds by drawing a Jolly Roger beside the publisher's name and writing a suitably tongue-in-cheek verse opposite the title page:

> This bloody pirate stole my sloop
> And holds her in his wicked ward.
> Lord send that walking on my poop
> I see him kick at my main yard.

Field also has him sign a copy of Rand, McNally's brand-new *A Study in Scarlet*, an edition so cheap that ACD's ink runs on the rough paper.

Field, Garland and Stone are among a group who often attend Chicago Orchestra concerts on Friday afternoons, and get together afterwards for camaraderie in what is known as "the Little Room." (By 1907 it will evolve into The Cliff-Dwellers, a club of lively literary and artistic folk with premises atop Orchestra Hall.) They will hardly be able to make today's concert, for it begins at two-thirty (presenting soprano Lillian Blauvelt in, among other songs, Mozart's "The Violet," as well as such orchestral works as Tchaikowsky's suite in D Major and excerpts from *Lohengrin*). In any case, the same programme is to be presented tomorrow evening, and today all eyes and ears are on ACD.

In the evening he lectures at the Central Music Hall – for all the social events that have so far taken place, he has still not spoken to the general public of Chicago. This is their chance to hear "Readings and Reminiscences," and to do so they crowd into the 2,000-seat hall, at Randolph and State Streets, which is noted for its roomy stage.

> The audience, which comfortably filled the house, would hardly be called fashionable [the *Herald* will say tomorrow]. It was essentially a gathering of those who had lived with Sherlock Holmes or gone with the little novitiate out of the old priory and down the dusty road to join the white company. There were as many young faces as old ones looking up into the ruddy one of the Englishman, and the sympathy with the speaker was not that of salvos of

applause at every telling point. But when there was a tribute to something pleasing – a quotation or a happy sally – Dr. Doyle appeared to feel that it came from a people who had known him for years before last night.

Major Pond will record in his account-book that ACD's fee for this evening is fifty dollars (he received $200 for last week's private address to the Twentieth Century Club), and that the box office grosses $866.

Introducing ACD is Harlow N. Higinbotham, the man at whose house he spoke last week. Higinbotham refers to "the prospect of a feast of the rich literary viands prepared by one of the most eminent writers of our own time," and ACD bows acknowledgement of what applause greets him. Someone will note in a letter to the editor of the *Bookman*, at home in London, that there is "a large audience. But either they did not appreciate his talk or they are cold and undemonstrative; he certainly was cheered at the end of the performance, but he made several good points which I thought would elicit hearty approval."

Saturday, October 27: Heading Back East

The midwestern part of the tour is over, and ACD is heading back east, leaving behind some new friends. At the end of 1896 he will write to Herbert S. Stone, sending good wishes to all his friends in Chicago, and mentioning Franklin Head and the older Stone, as well as "poor Scott and Field," who had both lately died. Twenty years hence, when he is back in North America, he will write to Stone again, regretting that they cannot get together, and lamenting "how few are left of all the good fellows of '94!" And in 1922 he will still be writing notes to Garland on the letterhead of American hotels, arranging a meeting during his exhausting tour to preach Spiritualism. (Garland will end up taking the chair at one of his New York meetings.)

One piece of literary business, more immediate, connects him with Herbert S. Stone and *The Chap-Book*. He has let himself be talked into having a poem, "The Three Harlots," appear in the little magazine. It should be in good company: "Dr. Arthur Conan Doyle, M. Stéphane Mallarmé, and Mr. Kenneth Grahame are among the contributors to the new volume of *The Chap-Book*," the journal's November 15 issue will announce. (Eugene Field will say in his column that the verse is expected for "the Christmas number.")

In fact, it will never appear, for ACD will write to Stone in March withdrawing it: "Perhaps it would do neither it you me or the public any good. It's moral enough, but the name might alarm." (This is the same man, after all, who has just suppressed "The Cardboard Box" as improper.) When the verse finally does appear in print in 1911, in the collection *Songs of the Road*, it will certainly prove to be moral enough:

> Three women stood by the river's flood
> In the gas-lamp's murky light,
> A devil watched them on the left,
> And an angel on the right. . . .

Welcome to America, Mr. Sherlock Holmes

> Said one: "I am an outcast's child,
> And such I came on earth.
> If me ye blame, for this my shame,
> Whom blame ye for my birth?

With Chicago and Milwaukee, he reached as far west as he will get on this tour, and that is a striking difference between ACD's journey and the spectacle in 1882 which is in many ways his model. That was the year-long tour, managed by Richard D'Oyly Carte, which brought the young Oscar Wilde to lecture in America and Canada on "The Decorative Arts" and "The House Beautiful." In the eastern cities Wilde drew both admiring and mocking crowds, including a turnout of some 200 young men at Yale, who parodied the "aesthetic style" with sunflowers in their buttonholes. As ACD has now also done, Wilde admired Cincinnati, he lectured in Chicago's Central Music Hall, and he made himself conspicuous in Toronto as ACD will in a month's time. But he also went west, not only to Oakland and San Francisco but to Salt Lake City, Denver (on the train between Denver and Ogden he managed to drink $6.75 worth of wine), and even the mining boom town of Leadville, Colorado, where he could not fill the 800-seat Tabor Grand Opera House for his lecture on interior decoration.

ACD is serious about his tour, and less flamboyant than Wilde (though Wilde could be serious and respectable enough, when interviewers took him seriously or when he met with serious folk in the world of art). Accordingly, he has made less of a splash – and Pond, for all that he has been able to do with his hundreds or thousands of circulars in each city, has had nothing like the advertising that D'Oyly Carte could get for Wilde from editorial cartoonists enjoying this real-life comic aesthete straight out of Gilbert and Sullivan's comic opera "Patience." ACD has not even attracted as much attention – the shrieking, the swooning – as Charles Dickens did when he set the fashion for British literary tours of America forty years ago. But he is not doing too badly, judging from the familiar comments and jokes in the newspaper columns. Indeed, one uninformed reporter says it is Doyle who is setting the precedent:

> Oscar Wilde, it is announced, will follow the example of Dr. Conan Doyle and turn lecturer. Jerome K. Jerome also has aspirations in this direction, and both of them are said to be looking forward to the United States lecture platforms.

Sunday, October 28: Literary Tidings

Sherlock Holmes is such a household word that his name came immediately to the mind of a writer on *The New York Times* who wanted to make a few commonplace points about human nature. The result appears in today's edition, sandwiched between an article about the economy of Connecticut and an interview with William Dean Howells. It is titled "Impressions of Sherlock Holmes."

October 1894

>Sherlock Holmes could have communicated wisdom to the reporter if the latter had been young enough to receive it, for he admitted him into the intimacy of his home life, which, in accordance with the dictates of a very moral, though gently cynical, philosopher, one should ardently love. . . .
>
>Facts . . . are trifles in Sherlock's experience. His ideas in their abstract liberty, disengaged from all anecdotic dross, are much more striking, but to express them, a translator is inevitably a traitor. The reporter found at Sherlock's home one day a young stranger, whose rapid thoughts summarize, in concise phrases, universal history. . . .
>
>"Don't affect to ignore the most elementary things," Sherlock said, in a tone which was affable, yet severe. . . .

The article is not a real parody of a Holmes tale, for there is no effort at plot or detection; its author has simply used the name of Holmes as Plato used the name of Socrates, and with as much attention to the master's own opinions.

With the name of Holmes so recognizable, it is no wonder that ACD's own opinions, as well as his movements, are attracting such attention in the press. In Chicago, for example, which he has now left behind him, the *Inter Ocean* has some final thoughts about him today:

>The flattering reception of Dr. Conan Doyle in this country demonstrates that the newspaper novelist has a greater hold upon the public than those who make their reputations in magazines and books alone. Dr. Doyle's best-known character, "Sherlock Holmes," made the acquaintance of the reading public in the newspapers and he had the same experience in dealing with that character that Charles Dickens had in dealing with Little Nell. As one chapter succeeded another, and as the stories in which Sherlock Holmes figured continued to appear, the author says that he received many letters regarding the man, and when at last he decided to dispose of the character the indignant protests from thousands of readers were as violent as though he had been guilty of murder. Charles Dickens had this same experience with his readers over the death of Little Nell.
>
>The novel-reading public today is the same as it was when Dickens made his great success. There is a class who insists that a novel is not to be read piece-meal, but this is a small class when compared with the whole reading public.
>
>Dr. Doyle has made his literary fame rapidly, and while his own genius deserves the larger share of the credit, he has not suffered by using the newspapers as the medium to reach those whom he wished to interest in his stories. The story pages of the Sunday newspapers of today are as huge in literary character as are the magazines, and Dr. Doyle was one of the men to see that here was his opportunity to reach a larger circle than by books or magazines.

There is some truth in it. None of today's newspapers around America contain any of ACD's stories, but there will be an altogether new tale in several of the Sunday papers two weeks from today; earlier this year newspapers have carried such stories as "Sweethearts" and "The Doctors of Hoyland," not to mention the one which he has been reading to audiences along this tour, "The Lord of Chateau Noir."

Magazines are doing their share as well to maintain ACD's literary prominence. The November issue of *McClure's* contains not merely Robert Barr's "A Chat with Conan Doyle," reprinted from *The Idler*, augmented with some 1,500 words of new material, and embellished with several illustrations which had not appeared in the British journal, but also a remarkable short story, "De Profundis." This tale is more than two years old – its first appearance, and its only American one so far, was in a New York newspaper, the *Independent*, on February 18, 1892. It reveals ACD's keen interest, even at that early date, in supernatural matters and the possibility of receiving messages from the dead – a possibility which he will eventually preach as a certainty. This story is grotesque and comic, dealing as it does with a vision at sea which may be a hallucination, a spiritual visitation, or the plain apparition of a drowned man's body thrown up by natural processes from the depths of the ocean.

The story contains, too, some passages which seem to foretell the experiences ACD himself will have more than twenty years in the future, when his brother Innes, his son Kingsley, and his brother-in-law Malcolm are dead:

> . . . when so many have their loved ones over the seas, walking amid hillmen's bullets, or swamp malaria, where death is sudden and distance great, then mind communes with mind, and strange stories arise of dream, presentiment or vision, where the mother sees her dying son, and is past the first bitterness of her grief ere the message comes which should have broke the news. The learned have of late looked into the matter, and have even labelled it with a name, but what can we know more of it save that a poor stricken soul, when hard-pressed and driven, can shoot across the earth some ten-thousand-mile-long picture of its trouble to the mind which is most akin to it.

Those "learned" must be the Society for Psychical Research, which ACD has joined since he wrote these sentences.

The November issue of *McClure's* contains a couple of other items which will catch ACD's eye. One is an article by Rudyard Kipling, in the magazine's continuing series "My First Book." ACD is an admirer of Kipling, though an admirer sometimes impatient with Kipling's bravado, and he of course remembers his own article in the same series, a few months ago. (In that "First Book" article, subtitled "Juvenilia," he omitted to say anything specific about his first book, but he did tell some of the stories about his early literary career which have found their way into his "Readings and Reminiscences" lecture, including the remarkable narrative of the tiger and the man who became one being.) Also in the November issue of *McClure's*, and ACD is sure to devour this piece with interest, is the first episode of Ida Tarbell's life of Napoleon Bonaparte.

October 1894

ACD is not, of course, the only figure in the literary news these days. Much ink, for example, is being spilt over the death last week of James Anthony Froude, the British biographer and historian who – like ACD – abandoned the Christian faith and fell under the influence of Carlyle. To be sure, he was never an uncritical admirer of the essayist, and his candid life of Carlyle, together with his edition of the letters of Carlyle's wife, Jane Welsh, produced a storm of protest. By the time of his death at 76, Froude was a regius professor of history at Oxford, and the author of books on subjects ranging from Tudor England to "English in the West Indies."

Monday, October 29: Lecture in Brooklyn

Back on the east coast, ACD comes today to Brooklyn, the fourth largest city in America. (It was third until the last census, but Philadelphia has gone ahead.) Some civic leaders are now proposing union with the larger city across the harbour, New York, for which it has always been something of a laughing-stock – and something of a dormitory. For a decade the magnificent silver Brooklyn Bridge has linked the twin cities, and ferries by the dozen still carry commuters over the waters of the harbour between them.

> Two hundred and fifty years ago [wrote Murat Halstead, the editor of the *Brooklyn Standard-Union*, in a magazine article published last year] there was established a ferry between the straggling town of New York and the village of Brooklyn, across the strait, and New York's first hotel and Brooklyn's first boarding house were in that year opened to the public. Perhaps one may trace to the distinction between the hotel and the boarding house the beginning of the peculiar regard in which the dwellers on Manhattan island have, if we may believe a line of gossip of which they are fond, held the inhabitants of the other islands in the vicinity, and of the greatest of them above all. . . .
>
> Brooklyn has not sought to dispute with New York her preëminence among the cities on this continent, but she has her large share of the marvellous natural advantages of the locality. The land of west Long Island is admirably adapted for the wholesome foundations of a city of vast proportions. . . . it is wiser to build houses on sand than on rocks, and the view of the magnificent harbor lies under the windows of Brooklyn, while New York has only a glimpse of this perpetual splendor. . . . the imposing front of Brooklyn, her massive store-houses, . . . tell of commerce and offer the characteristics of "no mean city," but of one that is solid and superb. . . .
>
> The fame of Brooklyn as a city of churches may justly be supplemented by a reputation for club houses, in which she is not surpassed in New York. . . .
>
> Brooklyn has a multitude of the natives of other lands, but her percentage of inhabitants whose Americanism dates back two or three or more generations, is far greater than in New York or Chicago.

Welcome to America, Mr. Sherlock Holmes

Convinced that his beloved Brooklyn is a great city, or on its way to becoming one, Halstead is less than enthusiastic about the proposal to unite it with New York and some minor suburbs to the northeast in Queens County – not to mention such villages, nearer at hand, as Flatbush, Gravesend and New Utrecht. After all, Brooklyn's municipal government is already better than that of New York (whose isn't?) and the beloved name "Brooklyn" is unlikely to disappear from daily use in any case.

When ACD crosses the East River to this proud, solid city tonight, he comes to its chief cultural jewel, the Academy of Music, where the Long Island Historical Society is presenting him as the first of its guest lecturers for the season. The Academy, a plain red-brick building with stone trimmings on Montague Street, was built in 1861 for "Musical, Literary, Scientific and other occasional purposes," and its greatest fame probably dates from 1864, when it was the site of the great Sanitary Fair, which raised $400,000 for the relief of the Civil War wounded. Since then it has seen entertainers, educators and civic improvers of every sort; Ellen Terry and Henry Irving have acted here, and in April 1891 Edwin Booth gave his farewell performance as Hamlet in this hall. Next Monday it will be the site of a large meeting in connection with the educational work of the Chautauqua Literary and Scientific Circle, and will be more than three-quarters full in spite of a cold, heavy rain. The Academy has been busier than ever since the Brooklyn Institute, made homeless by a fire, moved in to share its quarters in 1890. (This building will suffer its own fire in 1903, and be replaced by an ugly building not far away.)

Tonight an audience of nearly two thousand people is on hand to hear "Readings and Reminiscences." They are, the *Eagle* will say tomorrow, "thoroughly representative of the intellectual life of the city":

> As is also usual at these lectures, the great audience sat in almost stony silence, broken by a little timid applause here and there, while Dr. Doyle talked about his books and himself for an hour and a quarter. Dr. Doyle knows, however, if his eyes are half as sharp as Sherlock Holmes', that the silence did not mean disapproval or lack of interest. Faces all over the house became most keenly alive after the first fifteen minutes and remained so to the close of the lecture. Dr. Doyle must have seen that, but perhaps he does not know that after he had retired the common voice of the dispersing audience was that he was the most modest and most charming great man who had been introduced to Brooklyn in a long, long time.

ACD is introduced to this demanding audience by Dr. Samuel A. Eliot, the young minister of the fashionable Church of Our Saviour over at the corner of Monroe and Pierrepont Streets. Doubtless marked for greatness by his ancestry – his father is Charles Eliot, the great president of Harvard University – the young man will go on to be secretary of the American Unitarian Association, living his later years in the

October 1894

Unitarian city of Boston where he can keep an eye on his father's university. Today he does his best to fill the shoes of an older and better-known clergyman in the chair at such events as this, and the *Eagle* will label him "a most acceptable substitute, with a touch of humor." Perhaps ACD feels grateful that he has a presiding officer at all – in some cities he has had to introduce himself – and there is also a "fringe of distinguished citizens" on the platform. Eliot comments jovially about ACD's merits, tells the Canon Doyle story, and mentions a rumour that the mayor of Chicago invited him to "name his price" and take over the Second City's detective bureau.

Eventually ACD gets to speak, and the reporters make notes:

> Dr. Doyle looks less like a literary man than does Mr. Howells or Mark Twain, but even less like a detective than he does like a literary man. . . . The voice, when he spoke, was soft and English, without the clearness in consonants and difficult words which comes from elocutionary training, and he read extracts from his stories without the slightest change in the quality of tone to indicate the different speakers.

At the end of the lecture something a little embarrassing happens – these Historical Society lectures are certainly more formal than anything ACD has been used to since, say, the Authors' Society back in London. Again, the *Eagle* (whose thoroughness in local reporting probably explains its status as the largest evening paper in the United States) tells the story:

> At the conclusion of the lecture Frederick A. Ward rose to move the customary vote of thanks. But Dr. Doyle was not used to the Historical society's routine and was too modest to expect any expression of the pleasure of the audience other than its conventional applause. He was moving toward the back door with Dr. Eliot and Mr. Ward had nothing to do but sit down again. So no vote of thanks was passed.

After the lecture there is a dinner in ACD's honour at one of those clubs with which Brooklyn is so rich – the Hamilton Club, a three-storey building at 146 Remsen Street, in front of which stands a fine statue of Alexander Hamilton. Distinguished members of this club include Clarence L. Birdseye, the processed food magnate, former mayor Seth Low, and Dr. Charles E. West, the educator whom ACD met a month ago aboard the *Elbe*.

The host for this dinner is Herbert L. Bridgman – listed prosaically in the directory as a company manager who lives at 604 Carlton Avenue, he is also a journalist, and served this year as historian of Peary's "Auxiliary" Arctic expedition. Among the guests are the club's president, James McKeen, a lawyer who lives in Brooklyn but has his office on Nassau Street in New York; William Berri, president of another Brooklyn club, the Oxford, and himself proprietor of both a carpet firm and the *Standard-Union* newspaper; Murat Halstead, his editor on that paper, who wrote the magazine article about Brooklyn's delights last year; Herbert F. Gunnison, secretary of yet another club, the Hanover; Frederick Mitchell Monroe, another editor; dry-goods merchant Henry Batterman, whose prosperity (he has just opened a new store with five acres of floor space) allows him to take part in many civic activities; Frederick W. Hinrichs, who commutes to an office in New York's Municipal Building, where he is register of arrears; Captain Henry Dishler, Jr.; Horace C. Duval, who lists his occupation in the city directory as "treasurer"; another city lawyer, John A. Taylor; John S. Coleman, who keeps his law practice in Brooklyn, on Joralemon Street; and the chairman of the Historical Society's lecture committee, Joseph E. Brown, a broker.

Certainly the cream of Brooklyn society have come out tonight to do ACD honour. Less discerning people were over at the Columbia Theatre this evening, seeing the premiere of a new farce entitled *Too Much Johnson*. Tomorrow's *New York Times* will say that the show "bubbled and sparkled delightfully" but that there just was not enough substance to this play written by, and starring, a man who will soon loom large in ACD's own life: William Gillette.

Tuesday, October 30: A Tree Grows in Northampton

For the first time ACD is in New England. Today a train brings him to the elm-shaded Massachusetts town of Northampton, where George Washington Cable meets him at the station and takes him home to Tarryawhile. Cable is a novelist, well known for such stories of old Louisiana as *Old Creole Days*, but his heart's passion is gardens, and his three acres are a landscaping paradise. (In 1914 he will publish a book about his labours and reflections here, calling it simply *The Amateur Garden*). Tarryawhile stands south of Elm Street, between a shaded little street called Dryads' Green – named by Cable, who himself planted the post-oaks which shade it – and the Mill River, where

> In the greener seasons of college terms the girls constantly pass upstream and down in their pretty rowboats and canoes, making a charming effect as seen from my lawn's rear edge at the head of the pine and oak shaded ravine whose fish-pools are gay by turns with elder, wild sunflower, sumach, iris, water-lilies, and forget-me-not.

For Northampton – which ACD knows from Parkman's pages as the site of an Indian attack in February 1704 – is above all the home of Smith College, that pioneering institution of higher learning for women in America. Prominent and fascinating men and women are constantly coming to Smith; last year's visitors included Robert Peary, Ignace Paderewski, and Jane Addams; this year Smith has seen Otis Skinner, and Julia Marlowe, who acted "Twelfth Night." William Webster Ellsworth will one day write about Joseph Jefferson, the actor, to point out Smith's confidence in the educational value of visiting celebrities:

October 1894

> He was asked frequently to speak in colleges, and he loved to do it. My eldest daughter was at Smith College when Jefferson was playing for a night at Springfield, Massachusetts, near by. He telegraphed her saying that he would be glad to speak to the girls of Smith at twelve o'clock the next noon. The telegram was taken to President Seelye in some trepidation – to suggest a college speaker seemed a serious matter to the student. But the President said, "Why, surely, telegraph him at once to come." And he came. The chapel was packed to the window-sills, and Mr. Jefferson had his usual good time, talking and giving unbounded pleasure to a thousand girls.

Many of the passing celebrities stop off to see Cable, who five years ago invented a custom: he has each of them plant a tree in his gardens – he keeps a few saplings on hand in case someone should come by unexpectedly. The tradition began when Henry Ward Beecher planted the first tree at Cable's previous house. It was transplanted when Cable moved to Tarryawhile, and in 1914 Cable will be able to write that the tree "is nearly two feet through and has a spread of fifty." By then many famous names will have handled the spade:

> Henry van Dyke's white-ash, Sol Smith Russell's linden, and Hamilton Wright Mabie's horse-chestnut are all about thirty-five feet high and cast a goodly shade. Sir James M. Barrie's elm – his and Sir William Robertson Nicoll's, who planted it with him later than the plantings aforementioned – has, by some virtue in the soil or in its own energies, reached a height of nearly sixty-five feet.

ACD plants a maple at his host's entreaties; alas, the gardener will later write, "it was killed in its second winter by an undetected mouse at its roots. . . . Besides Sir Arthur's maple the only souvenir tree we have lost was a tulip-tree planted by my friend of half a lifetime, the late Franklin H. Head."

Today they dine early – before the lecture, rather than after – at the Greek Revival mansion on Round Hill, off Elm Street, where Elizabeth Maltby keeps house for her elderly father. Lafayette Maltby first prospered as a merchant and slave-owner in New Orleans, but – perhaps seeing what the future held – he sold out just before the Civil War, came to Northampton, and made a fortune (and a reputation) as a banker.

From him and from his wife, Frances, a great-niece of chief justice John Marshall, Elizabeth Maltby has inherited business sense, skill at telling stories, good humour, literary taste, an inclination for lavish hospitality, and an ability to make a friend of virtually anyone. Now 44, she puts these talents to use on behalf of Edwards Church, the Daughters of the American Revolution, and the literary "Monday Afternoon Club." (After her father dies in 1898, she will buy a larger house around the corner and open a boarding-house for Smith students, which will flourish in the young ladies' affections, and then in their reminiscences. She will build more houses on her property until there are more than fifty

Smith girls under her wing. After her retirement in 1921, the houses will be taken over officially by the college.)

With this jovial lady presiding, the company for dinner consists of "a few friends," a newspaper will say the next day, "and every one present was delighted with his charming personality." Among the company is William E. Bryant, one of the editors of the Boston *Transcript*, who is adding ACD to the long list of authors he has interviewed for his paper. Born in Sherbrooke, Québec, in 1842, Bryant is a second cousin of the great poet William Cullen Bryant (whose hundredth birthday would have been this coming Saturday) and is a personal friend of such figures of the drama as Henry Irving and Joseph Jefferson. He is thus well placed to get the visitor talking about his literary career, the excitements of whaling, American writers, Poe's Monsieur Dupin, the death of Sherlock Holmes, and the American press:

> I asked Dr. Doyle what he thought of American newspapers. He said that he was duty bound to like them, in view of the kindness of the American press to him. He had been courteously treated, not only by the reporters sent to interview him, but also by the editors. He rather liked the style of headlines used on the best papers in America, for they were so cleverly put that one could get a pretty good idea of a bit of news without reading more than the headings, and to a busy man that was a consideration of importance. Dr. Doyle added, with a quiet smile:
>
> "American papers do use a good many superlatives in describing events. I wonder, sometimes, what they would do if they had a really big thing to describe. It would seem as if there was nothing more to say."

The busy author must hurry on to give his lecture, in Northampton's City Hall, a Gothic Revival structure (with four towering chimneys atop the facade) built about 1850 by the architect who did most of Northampton's important buildings, William Fenno Pratt. Although the lecture is not actually at Smith, there are many Smith students in attendance – it was listed in the calendar of events in the *Smith College Monthly*. (On Saturday the Alpha Society, a literary group organized by students, has scheduled "An Evening With Holmes," but they have Oliver Wendell, not Sherlock, in mind.)

Among the young ladies who attend is Lydia W. Kendall, a senior, who records it at length afterwards in her journal:

> Tuesday evening mamma, Mrs. B. and I went to hear Dr. Conan Doyle read from his writings; he is English [she first wrote "he is an English writer" but then, recollecting what some strict judge of composition has been telling her, she struck out the unnecessary words] and the author of Sherlock Holmes, The Refugees, The White Company etc. He is a fine looking man of thirty-five, very tall and well proportioned. He read us a paper about his own life and experiences and wove in readings from his own books. . . .

In short, he is giving "Readings and Reminiscences" once again, and

October 1894

Lydia Kendall, of Bristol, Rhode Island, is enjoying it. So, presumably, is her mother, up for a visit in company with Mrs. Brunsen, a family friend.

> He spoke very finely on the subject of good literature for young children, how infinitely valuable it is, and above all that they may have standard books near at hand; at first they will read them because they have nothing else to read, then they will come gradually to see the beauties in them and finally to love them as a part of their very lives.

Although she cannot spell "omnivorous" or "believe," she summarizes the lecture more fully and accurately than some newspaper reporters have been doing, concluding her narrative thus:

> The Refugees is a story of our early Colonial days, written very accurately after reading Hawthorne, Irving and Parkman; the latter he considered our finest historian.
> Wednesday was Hallow E'en and Carrie invited me to the Lawrence House. They had a children's party: fifty girls dressed as children, a number as nurse maids to take care of them. . . .

A reporter from Springfield attends the lecture – Springfield, after all, is the metropolis, and there is a notion that ACD "is to appear nowhere else in this part of the state." (Cable is given the credit for that, but it is not true; he will be in Worcester on Thursday and in Amherst, which is even closer, on Friday.) Not attending are the young ladies from the Mount Holyoke Seminary, over the "mountain" in South Hadley a few miles away. They are kept at home by a rival attraction, the second of two special lectures by a visiting professor, Charles H. Hitchcock of Dartmouth College, who is explaining volcanoes and earthquakes with the aid of stereopticon slides.

Wednesday, October 31: A Cabman in the Athens of America

Today finds ACD in Boston, the Athens of America. One of the many newspapers here, the *Journal*, which sent Bryant to Northampton yesterday, spreads the report of his interview over almost half a page, accompanying it with an engraving of ACD sitting before his door – an engraving based on a photograph which accompanies the recent *Idler* and *McClure's* interview, but with interviewer Barr carefully excised.

William Archer will later compare the city of Parkman the historian and Holmes the physician-poet with the city of his alma mater:

> Not physically, of course, but intellectually, Boston has been likened to Edinburgh. The parallel is fair enough, with this important reservation, that the theological element in the atmosphere is not Presbyterian but Unitarian. The Boston of to-day, it must be added, especially resembles Edinburgh in the fact that its pre-eminence as an intellectual centre has virtually departed. The *Atlantic Monthly* survives, as *Blackwood* survives, a relic of the great days of old; but Boston has no Scott Monument to bear visual testimony

Welcome to America, Mr. Sherlock Holmes

to her spiritual achivement. She ought certainly to treat herself to a worthy Emerson Monument on the Common.

The literary association that is most important to ACD has nothing to do with Emerson. As soon as he can, he crosses the Charles River to Cambridge (there is horse-car service now, forerunner of what will be America's first subway line) and goes to Mount Auburn Cemetery to place a wreath on the still new grave of Oliver Wendell Holmes. The floral tribute consists of "Sago or Cyprus palms" tied with purple ribbon and ornamented with English violets, Bride roses and asparagus vines. There is an inscription: "From the Society of Authors (London). A token of reverence and of love. A. Conan Doyle." He thought to have shaken the great man by the hand, not to have strewn his grave.

It will be said later that ACD's arrival in Boston today is the occasion for a peculiar incident. The story will be told in various ways – here is how William Webster Ellsworth will recall hearing it from ACD himself:

> On his arrival in Boston Doyle told us that he had noticed a dog-eared but familiar volume peeping out of his cabman's pocket. "You may drive me to Young's or the Parker House," he said.
>
> "Pardon me," returned cabbie, "you will find Major Pond waiting for you at the Parker House."
>
> As they parted, the cabman asked for a pass to the lecture instead of a fee, and Doyle said: "Now, see here, I am not usually beaten at my own game. How did you know who I am?"
>
> "Well, sir, of course all members of the Cabmen's Literary Guild knew you were coming on this train, and, I noticed sir, if you will excuse me, that your hair has the cut of a Quakerish, Philadelphia barber; your hat shows on the brim in front where you tightly grasped it at a Chicago literary luncheon; your right overshoe has on it what is plainly a big block of Buffalo mud; and there are crumbs of a doughnut, which must have been bought at the Springfield station, on the top of your bag. And then, sir, to make assurance doubly sure, I happened to see stenciled in plain lettering on the end of the bag the name Conan Doyle."

Ellsworth will hear ACD tell this tale at a luncheon in New York just before he leaves for home at the end of the tour. But the newspapers will be circulating it sooner than that – on November 26 the *Daily Cataract Journal* at Niagara Falls will have the story, and on December 1 the Chicago *Record* will give a fuller version, credited to the Boston *Record*:

> "If it is not too great an intrusion, sir, I should greatly prefer a ticket to your lecture. If you have none of the printed ones with you your agent would doubtless honor one of your visting cards if penciled by yourself. . . .
>
> "If you will excuse other personal remarks, your coat lapels are badly twisted downward where they have been grasped by the pertinacious New York reporters. Your hair has the quakerish cut of a Philadelphia barber, and your hat, battered at the brim in front, shows where you have tightly grasped it in the struggle to stand

your ground at a literary luncheon. Your right overshoe has a large block of Buffalo mud just under the instep, the odor of a Utica cigar hangs about your clothing and the overcoat itself shows the slovenly brushing of the porters on the through sleepers from Albany. The crumbs of doughnuts on the top of your bag – pardon me, your luggage – could only have come there in Springfield, and stenciled upon the very end of the 'Wellington', in fairly plain lettering is the name of 'Conan Doyle'."

"Now I know where Sherlock Holmes went when he died," said this great writer of detective stories, after the cabman had finished his third glass of brandy neat. "That leaves me free to write any more adventures of his that I wish, except that I must locate them in Boston."

It is a fine story – and an apocryphal one.

What ACD does do is give "Readings and Reminiscences" this evening in Association Hall, the auditorium of the YMCA.

It was [the *Post* will say tomorrow] this eminent author's first visit here, despite the fact that one of his best characters at least was to Massachusetts' manor born, and, as is always the case with a man of renown, there was much manifest curiosity on the part of the large audience that was there as to Dr. Doyle's personality.

The hall is full of the more or less intellectual folk for whom Boston is famous. The elite are perhaps unusually interested in what their visitor may have to say about *Micah Clarke*, for the latest issue of the *Bulletin of the Public Library of the City of Boston* has devoted a large section to "Tracts of the Period of English History . . . 1625-1660" which are held in the beautiful new library on Copley Square, and has included a reproduction of a 1637 broadside. ACD's visit is not so important, however, as to attract every prominent Bostonian, not even every one for whom theatre-going is a way of life. William H. Lee, president of the A. J. Houghton brewing company and recently retired member of the city's police commission, will record in his copperplate handwriting at the end of this year that "I drove a good deal and went to places of amusement 108 times" – and this is not one of them.

But representatives of the city's many newspapers are there, including Bryant of the *Journal*, hearing the same lecture he heard last night in Northampton. "This admirer sat on the left-hand side of the balcony in Association Hall last evening," Bryant will write in tomorrow's paper, "and the hearty way in which he manifested his appreciation of both the lecturer and the lecture would warm the heart of a man much less known than Dr. Doyle."

November 1894

Thursday, November 1: Smoke Talk in Worcester
The morning edition of the Boston *Globe* trumpets the news of a great fire at Newburyport, north almost to the New Hampshire line; by the evening editon, international news has taken over: "GLOBE LATEST. CZAR IS DEAD. Sufferings of Alexander III, Ruler of Russia, Ended at 1:30 P.M."

Today's papers also include reports of ACD's lecture, but his Boston visit was very brief, and today he finds himself in Worcester, the second city of Massachusetts, with some 85,000 people. Worcester is a manufacturing city and boasts a large lunatic asylum and the 90,000-volume library of the American Antiquarian Society. It is also in part a college town – the oldest of its three colleges, Worcester Polytechnic Institute, is proud of its brand-new Hydraulic Testing Laboratory, conveniently located next to a 150-acre pond – but, as in Northampton, ACD is a guest of the town, not of the campus. The Woman's Club has invited him to deliver one in its series of lectures.

All 827 seats in the Association Hall are filled when he appears at eight o'clock, on a stage ornamented with large palms, ferns, and white chrysanthemums. It is the first time on the tour that a woman has introduced ACD to his audience. She is the club's president, Annie Wyman Comins, the second wife of Edward Comins, local manufacturer and state legislator, and she introduces ACD as "the author of those famous detective stories which have entertained, delighted and mystified two continents."

The lecture is, as usual, "Readings and Reminiscences," concluding as always with "The Lord of Chateau Noir." The audience is generally pleased, but the critic of the *Evening Gazette* has mixed reactions, seizing as few other critics have done on ACD's taste for blood and torture:

> It was not a lecture. It was a smoke talk, with the smoke left out. Dr. Doyle gave his autobiography, and read a little out of his own books. That was all there was to it.
>
> Viewed calmly, it is a remarkable exhibition when a man stands up before an intelligent audience and talks about himself

for an hour and a half, and he not a very famous man either. . . .

The wonder of it is, however, not the egotism of Dr. Doyle, but the fact that he talks about himself so quietly and simply that the listener is interested and takes it as a matter of course and not as a monumental advertisement of the man, worked out by himself. . . .

Dr. Doyle's mistake was in reading at the end his story "The Lord of the Chateau Noir." . . . This vicarious suffering is painful and there is no excuse for its story. So far as it is real, it is brutal.

There is more of this unpleasant stuff in Dr. Doyle's last collection of short stories, called "Round the Red Lamp." He had better leave the monopoly of this sort of writing to Robert Louis Stephenson [sic].

At about ten o'clock the literary ladies of Worcester carry ACD off to an hour-long "reception" at 1017 Main Street in New Worcester, where ACD will spend tonight at the home of Mr. and Mrs. Frederick L. Coes, whose money comes from the Coes Wrench Company. More than 175 people pass through the receiving line, shaking hands with the hostess and host, the literary lion, his brother Innes, and the hostess's sister, Amie F. Dean, one of the few young ladies whom the young author and his bachelor brother have had a chance to meet in recent weeks. Everyone of any importance in Worcester is present, the list of distinguished guests being headed by the name of Colonel William Swinton Bennett Hopkins, a member of an old Republican family, who between periods in legal practice led troops against New Orleans during the Civil War. Since 1873 he has been a lawyer in this city, and he is so sociable a man that he has been repeatedly elected president of the Worcester Club.

Friday, November 2: Lecture at Amherst College

No one knows yet that Amherst, Massachusetts, is destined to fame as the home of Emily Dickinson, who died in 1886. A few of her poems were published three or four years ago, but her talent is largely unrecognized.

Amherst is known instead for its college, where intellectual life is dominated by such figures as Charles Edward Garman, the liberal professor of philosophy; Merrill E. Gates, the college's president and a much more conservative philosopher, who will in 1913 marry Elizabeth Head, daughter of Chicago's Franklin Head; and astronomer David Todd, whose wife Mabel Loomis Todd is conducting a passionate affair with the treasurer of the college, Austin Dickinson, brother of the late poet.

Intellectual matters are not entirely dominant at the college. In recent years it has gone football-mad, under the influence of the alumni, and the team is almost professional. Interest in sports shares time, among the students, with interest in the girls of Smith College, so that there is natural enthusiasm for the new trolley to Northampton.

Welcome to America, Mr. Sherlock Holmes

ACD travels from Worcester to Amherst today, and gives his lecture tonight in College Hall, a simple old-fashioned building on a high spot on the campus. This hall was built in 1830 for the First Congregational Church in Amherst, and served chiefly for its meetings until the college bought it in 1867. Over the past thirty years, it has been used "for secular purposes entirely," as *The Amherst Student* observed a couple of years ago:

> In that hall have hundreds of alumni received their sheepskins; from that platform have incipient orators thundered their attempts at eloquence – future ministers and lawyers; lecturers of more or less note; musicians of greater or less ability and fame; variety shows; all forms of dramatic entertainment from high tragedy to low comedy – have all charmed large audiences in this hall; mock political conventions, for whose decisions the nation has waited with bated breath, and which have made or marred the chances of candidates; trials with vast issues at stake have been held in this building; old associations for all generations of alumni and undergraduates cluster within its walls thicker than the cobwebs. Nor is the outside without associations. Those mystic numbers above the door have their meaning; they attest the fact that the Ninety-two Freshman team defeated the Yale Freshman 10-3 – ah, what a degenerate age is the present!

There ACD delivers his "Readings and Reminiscences" to what the *Hampshire and Franklin Express* will tomorrow describe as "a rather small but thoroughly appreciative audience." The *Amherst Student* will be more enthusiastic than that, if somewhat vague:

> The college lecture course opened auspiciously Friday evening, November 2, with a lecture by Dr. Doyle. He proved to be a very interesting speaker and reader. After a brief review of his school life, the latter part of which was spent in the study of medicine, he told in a very interesting manner his early experiences as an author, and he related the difficulties he encountered, from the English custom of keeping a young writer's works anonymous.
> The Sherlock Holmes papers were next taken up, the idea that gave rise to them being explained and very well illustrated by the reading of two selections from the stories. The lecture closed with the reading of an intensely interesting story from a magazine article as yet unpublished in book form. Dr. Doyle may be sure of a warm welcome whenever he revisits Amherst.

The lecture course is to continue with Mr. George Riddle and the Boston Philharmonics next Wednesday; William H. McElroy on December 10; the New York Ladies' Quartette on January 7; the inevitable Rev. S. Reynolds Hole on January 14 – the *Student* describes him as dean of "Rochester University," rather than of Rochester or Rochester Cathedral; General Lew Wallace on January 25; and finally, on February 8, "Alexander Black and his picture play, 'Miss Jerry'." All this has been arranged by a committee whose chairman is third-year student Roberts Walker, who will go on to be a railroad lawyer and, during

November 1894

World War I, a member of the draft exemption board for the New York City area.

ACD spends the night in the Amherst House, a four-storey L-shaped brick building on a site which has been continuously occupied by inns since 1757. D. H. Kendrick is its manager, the fifth since this building opened in 1880 in place of an earlier one which had burned.

Saturday, November 3: Lecture at Norwich

The eyes of the artistic world are on New York, where the steamer *Paris* docks today and disgorges both Andrew Carnegie the steel millionaire and Lillie Langtry the sex symbol and supposed actress.

In humbler circles, ACD continues to visit the middle-sized cities of New England. Before leaving Amherst he writes a letter to Sir John R. Robinson, at home in London, sending regards to fellow members of the Reform Club and saying – in terms which show some sympathy for socialist principles – what he thinks of his trip so far:

> Naturally I have only seen the pleasanter side of life, but still I have already travelled many thousands of miles and seen many towns, so I have some experience from which to talk. The people are far more lovable than I expected, so good-humoured and affable, infinitely more so than our own folk. There never was a country so maligned by the travelling Briton as this one. He has picked out all the little things to talk about and missed all the big ones. Every globe-trotter has paragraphs about the number of spittoons in a hotel bar (as if it matters!), but they pass over such trifles as that there are no hereditary chamber and no landlords. There is an absence of affectation and a kindly frankness, too, on all hands which is not to be computed in spittoons. They are naturally hurt at being so maligned, and we have estranged them considerably, though not, I think, irredeemably.
>
> By Jove, when I see all these folk with their British names and British tongues, and when I consider how far they have been allowed to drift from us, I feel as if we ought to have a statesman from every lamp-post in Pall Mall. We've got to go into partnership with them, or else to be overshadowed by them. The centre of gravity of the race is over here, and we have got to readjust ourselves. I've done what I could by tongue and pen over here to plant some seeds. Some of them may sprout. Who knows? We think we are influencing things and we are really floating in a current which is outside ourselves.
>
> I have lectured at New York, Chicago, Milwaukee, Cincinnati, Indianapolis, Detroit, Toledo, Boston, Worcester, etc. etc. etc., so, you see, I have not been stagnant. I came over here with three lectures, one on Meredith, one on the younger school of fiction (both with illustrative readings), and one which is mainly personal, with readings from my own work. This last I included under protest, owing to strong representations from Pond, my agent. His view proved to be correct, for audiences always want that one, so that I have hardly had a chance of delivering the other two. I have had very good audiences – halls full mostly – but I don't

think there is much money in the business. What with the long distances, the hotel prices, the agent's commission, etc., I am sure one could earn much more at one's desk at home. But you have the education and travel gratis, and you wouldn't get that at your desk. Anyhow, I am very glad I came. I have met Howells, Cable, Eugene Field, Riley, Hamlin Garland, and most of the rising men of letters.

That letter written, ACD travels south to Norwich, Connecticut, a mercantile city at a river junction whose sixteen thousand people include at least some lovers of literature: Daniel T. Shea has just opened a bookstore here. There are historic points of interest too, including a shabby settlement of half-breeds, the genuine last of the Mohicans. ACD lectures this evening in Slater Memorial Hall, an impressive old pile in the centre of town. Robert P. Keek is the agent here, and ensures that the speaker receives his reward in financial terms, as well as the "extraordinary salvo of applause" which, tomorrow's newspaper will report, the large audience accords him.

Sunday, November 4: "My Own Theory of Reading"

"I have my own theory of reading," ACD will later write when he recalls the lectures he has given for six nights in the past week and will give more than half the nights of the coming month. He will explain it thus:

> . . . that it should be entirely dissociated from acting and should be made as natural and also as audible as possible. Such a presentment is, I am sure, the less tiring for an audience. Indeed I read to them exactly as in my boyhood I used to read to my mother. . . . Some papers maintained that I could not read at all, but I think that what they really meant was that I did not act at all.

Certainly the opinions have varied, for while today's *Norwich Morning Bulletin* declares that the visitor read "easily and pleasantly" last night, some observers find him boring. A Toronto journalist, Hector Charlesworth, will record for posterity that "for sheer dulness it would be difficult to equal Conan Doyle's readings. Even the most dramatic passages from some of his fine romantic tales seemed incredibly tedious as he read them." And some listeners cannot even understand him easily; in Newark next week, a newspaper will allege that "The first dozen words that he spoke were almost unintelligible, owing to his somewhat peculiar accent. His voice is very deep."

Thirty years later, ACD will still be receiving warnings that he must speak slowly if Americans are to understand him. The difficulty works both ways, of course: all his life he will demonstrate a tin ear when it comes to American accents, putting impossible and comic speech into the mouths of characters who are supposed to be from the United States.

November 1894

One interviewer after another has found it necessary to remark that ACD is hearty, bluff, wholesome, athletic, everything that a man of letters – and an Englishman! – is not expected to be. Those comments have usually been made about the way he appears in an interview, but they apply also to his bearing on the lecture platform:

> At first his attention was pretty closely confined to his manuscript, but after he became warmed up he forgot all about it and talked right out in a frank, pleasant way, frequently peppering his remarks with little sallies of humor of the kind in which Sherlock Holmes often indulged. In fact, the whole bearing of the novelist indicated that he found pleasure and satisfaction in living, and there was often a wholesome ring of hope in the future and faith in mankind in his words.

Reporters may have agreed that ACD is hearty, straightforward and serious (despite that observation about his humour), but they have been unable to agree on what he sounds like. Is his voice that of an Englishman or a Scot?

> . . . He has a slight English accent, and his favorite word for expressing pleasure is "charming." . . . When he laughs you think he is a jolly fellow; when he is talking in a sober strain you are impressed with his great learning.
>
> . . . "My father was born in London of Irish parents," said Dr. Doyle, "my mother is English, and I was born in Edinburgh in 1859." The latter statement was emphasized by the doctor's accent, through which runs pleasantly the Scotch burr, suggestive of heathery hills and shining lochs.
>
> . . . He met them with a cordial grasp of the hand, a hearty American manner, and an accent that is English. And that accent is about the only thing at a casual meeting that impresses one as English.
>
> . . . In his speech he uses an underlying and subdominant pitch of the Northern Doric, which becomes reasonable to the listener as soon as he mentions the fact that he was born and bred in the Athens of the North. . . . With just the least trace of the Scottish twang of voice that gives his vowels a generous breadth, he speaks plainly.
>
> . . . The only peculiarities noticed were a Scotch accent that crept out every now and then and the affectionate manner in which every "r" was rolled out.

That ambivalence will continue for the rest of his tour. The *Rochester Union Chronicle* later this month will say that "A clear enunciation, enriched by a decided Scotch accent acquired during a long residence in Edinburgh, assisted the speaker greatly." But two days later the *Glens Falls Daily Times* will say that "He looked a typical Englishman . . . with a voice as big as himself and a marked accent."

A couple of weeks ago the *Detroit Tribune* had it both ways and more: "His words sound a mixture of Scotch, English, Irish and cold."

Welcome to America, Mr. Sherlock Holmes

Monday, November 5: Lecture in Washington

Guy Fawkes Day finds ACD in America's capital city, where the *Washington Evening Star* mentions his arrival briefly under the heading "Amusements," but gives front-page treatment to a more prominent Britisher who is also in town: "GEN. BOOTH HERE. The Leader of the Salvation Army Arrives in Washington. Reception by the Local Committee. The Other Courtesies to Be Extended to Him While Here. Convention Hall Meeting." The story's lead paragraph gives a lively description of the Sixth Street Station, home of the Baltimore & Potomac Railroad, on whose tracks run Pennsylvania Railroad trains:

> The race track crowd got out of the 6th street station this afternoon just in time to escape being converted by the Salvation Army. The passenger house held a curious mixture of humanity after 1 o'clock, flash costumes of the bookies and the touts mingling with picturesque effect with the blue uniforms and red trimmings of the soldiers and lassies of the army, who had gathered at the depot to give welcome to Gen. Booth, the commander in chief of the army of the world.

ACD checks in at The Arlington (T. E. Roessle, Proprietor) in this now elegant city – like his own London, a capital on an estuary. No longer an unfinished, muddy butt of jokes, and not yet a conglomeration of slums, Washington is a place of elegant society, glittering art and music, imposing architecture. To Britisher William Archer, the rationality of Washington's wheel-and-grid layout, and the breadth of its streets, are a little intimidating:

> The result is dire bewilderment to the traveller; my bump of locality, usually not ill-developed, seems to shrink into a positive indentation before the problems presented in such formulas as "K Street, corner of 13th Street, N.E." But from the Capitol, whence most of the avenues spread fanwise, the views they offer are superb; and Pennsylvania Avenue, leading to the government offices and the White House, will one day, undoubtedly, be one of the great streets of the world. For the present its beauty is not heightened by the new Postal Department, a massive but somewhat forbidding structure in grey granite, which dominates and frowns upon the whole street. From certain points of view, it seems almost to dwarf the Washington Obelisk[.]

Washington is above all a political city, never more than now – tomorrow is election day. The President of the United States, Grover Cleveland, is preoccupied these days with the precarious fortunes of his Democratic Party, and with such other issues as American annexation of Hawaii, immigration rules, extension of civil service protection to more classes of federal employees, the perennial question of tariffs (the central issue in American politics throughout the nineteenth century), and a stubborn bureaucratic dispute over a seventy-dollar expense voucher in the Weather Bureau, which several levels of supervisors have passed to him for final adjudication. Apart from such serious matters, he has

November 1894

the ceremonial duties of his office to undertake; George S. Sicard in Buffalo is writing to him today asking for his autograph on a sheaf of coupons which will then be sold to raise funds for the Buffalo Catholic Institute's public library.

Others besides politicians live in Washington, though historian Henry Adams, observer of political and cultural life from his parlour window – and, like ACD, strong proponent of an Atlantic alliance – is away in Mexico. Frederick Douglass, the great black abolitionist, is here in his old age, his hair snow-white but his voice unweakened. This week he will give an address at a congress in Lowell, Massachusetts, introduced by the same Merrill E. Gates whom ACD met at Amherst.

Living here and working as president of Georgetown University is the Rev. J. Havens Richards, who has been awaiting ACD's visit with some interest. (Born the son of an Episcopalian minister, Richards turned to Roman Catholicism early in life, was ordained as a Jesuit in 1872, and has been president of Georgetown for six years.) He had a letter in August from a fellow Jesuit, Rev. Francis F. McCarthy of the College of the Holy Cross in Worcester, Massachusetts. Richards saw in the author's visit a possible chance to do God's work:

> I've been trying – thus far vainly – to procure for you Dr. Conan Doyle's address. I am told that he is become ashamed of his race & creed. This, I think ought not to be a reason for not engaging him – au contraire. A little timely kindness from the Society from whose members he rec^d a large portion of his Education might awaken thoughts that long have slept, & smooth the way for his return to God and His Church.

McCarthy did not know then that ACD would visit Worcester as well as Washington; in any case, neither Jesuit will have any opportunity to bring the lost sheep back to the church of his fathers.

The lapsed Catholic lectures tonight at the Metzerott Music Hall, a two-year-old building on F Street which as the Columbia Theater will become one of Washington's first cinemas. Tickets (ranging from fifty cents to a dollar) have been on sale since Tuesday morning at Metzerott's Music Store. "His accent is strongly English," a reporter for the *Evening Star* will write afterwards, "but easily understood, and few words escaped the ears of the attentive audience. . . . Many auditors admitted that from reading his books they had conceived a sort of author totally different from their hearty entertainer and the multiplicity of short stories published within the last year was accounted for through the doctor's splendid physique."

Tuesday, November 6: Baltimore on Election Day

Before leaving Washington, ACD writes a note on the Arlington's letterhead. Next Monday he will be lecturing in Yonkers, and he has been invited to have dinner and spend the night at the home of John Kendrick Bangs and his wife. He writes to Bangs at his office ("Harper & Co., Franklin Square, New York") to accept this "very kind invitation."

Welcome to America, Mr. Sherlock Holmes

He pays $1.20 (parlour car twenty-five cents extra) to ride one of the many trains to Baltimore, where he is scheduled to speak tonight. Visitors' first impressions of this city are determined by the railway they choose; those who come in by the Baltimore and Ohio go past "scores of dirty streets with shabby little one and two story dwellings, largely inhabited by Negroes, with plentiful supplies of pigs, chicken coops, and swarming children," but those who come by the Pennsylvania Railroad instead come through tunnels and see the elegant Union Station and "a fine street, full of character, and giving evidence of a luxurious population."

One of the country's major cities, Baltimore has a considerable public library named for the late Enoch Pratt, a much-admired conservatory of music (the country's first), the famed Lexington Market, genteel southern houses with black servants in livery, a Washington monument in a pleasant park, and a multitude of historic sites. Here, eighty years ago, during one of those fratricidal wars that ACD regrets so much, Francis Scott Key wrote a song called "The Star-Spangled Banner" which in 1931 will become America's national anthem.

Baltimore is the home also of the Basilica of the Assumption, a magnificent domed neoclassical building by Benjamin Henry Latrobe, who also designed the United States Capitol. It was the only Roman Catholic cathedral in the United States when it was completed in 1821. Presiding in the Basilica is James Cardinal Gibbons – the only American cardinal at present – whose astonishing career has brought him from a childhood among Irish immigrants to a position as chaplain to Fort McHenry, then the youngest bishop in the country, then archbishop of Baltimore (his see includes the national capital city as well), and now the red hat and intimacy with men as different as President Cleveland and Pope Leo XIII. A friend of democracy – indeed, of the controversial Knights of Labor – he loves to stroll unheralded through the streets, and he regularly argues, to sceptics both among Protestant Americans and among ultramontane Catholics, that the Church can and must be something different, more open and more progressive, in America than it has been in older lands. Gibbons is a witty man and well aware of the scepticism he faces. Just the other day serving coffee to a non-Catholic visitor at his archiepiscopal palace, he poised the sugar over the cup and said ironically, "On my honour, there's not a drop of poison in the house!"

Baltimore means something more to ACD, however, than the Catholic atmosphere and heritage of Maryland. It is the city of Edgar Allan Poe, and the author whose detective disparaged Poe's Dupin is nevertheless here to pay homage to the master. All his life ACD will praise Poe and freely admit a debt to him – as he does in the lecture he is giving on this tour – though persistent questioners will coax him to say that Sherlock Holmes was his own great creation, owing nothing to the detective who had come before. Scholars after his death will carry on the argument, pointing out the similarities (how much "The Dancing

November 1894

Men" owes to "The Gold Bug") and the differences (Poe's delight in the bizarre solution, as of the murders in the Rue Morgue, set against ACD's insistence on the plausible, the everyday).

When Poe died in 1849, he was buried inconspicuously in the family churchyard plot, but in 1875 schoolchildren began collecting "pennies for Poe" and now there is a sizeable marble monument to him at a more prominent spot at the corner of Fayette and Greene Streets in West Baltimore. (Lying beneath it are Poe and his wife, Virginia, as well as her mother Mrs. Clemm; the family which had lived together in the house on Amity Street is reunited in death.)

ACD seeks out that grave as he last week sought out the grave of Oliver Wendell Holmes; as he will, thirty years from now, seek out Poe's cottage in Fordham, by then a part of New York City:

> His face looks at you from every wall, austere, coldly intellectual, cruel in its precise accuracy. He had every quality save humour, and of that there was not a trace. But he was surely the greatest originator of various story-types that ever lived. He was so sure of himself that he never troubled to work out a reef, but he just picked a nugget or two, and then turned away to prospect elsewhere. He was the real father of the detective story, of the buried-treasure story, of the Jules Verne semi-scientific story, of the purely morbid story, and of nearly every other sort that we now use. If every man who owed his inspiration to Poe was to contribute a tithe of his profits therefrom he would have a monument greater than the pyramids, and I for one would be among the builders.

Fifteen years from now, when Poe's centenary is marked with black-tie elegance in a social milieu Poe himself never achieved, ACD will take the chair at an Authors' Society dinner at London's Hotel Metropole. "Never, I should think," he will say, "did any man under such pressure hold so high a standard. . . . This one man's brain was like a seed capsule, which scatters its seeds carelessly to every wind. The capsule withers, but the seed spreads and flourishes without end."

Today, across America, has been election day. Results begin to arrive this evening – they will be trickling in for days – and the news is that men across the United States (and in Colorado, for the first time, women as well) have cast a tidal wave of Republican votes, changing the face of American politics for good. The House of Representatives is expected to have something like 240 Republicans compared with 102 Democrats and perhaps 14 Populists; in the Congress which just came to an end the balance was the other way around, 219 Democrats to 125 Republicans. Democrats have also lost control of the Senate (Populists are expected to hold the balance there), and the Republicans have taken several new state-houses.

In New York, the defeat of the Democrats has meant the defeat of Tammany Hall, the Democratic machine, which was so corrupt that various neutral groups were as eager as the Republicans to destroy it. The new mayor will be Colonel William L. Strong, and among his tasks will be negotiating with the state legislature to arrange the merger of New

York, Brooklyn, and the surrounding areas, which the voters have approved by a slim margin. They were more enthusiastic about rapid transit, voting by almost a 3-to-1 margin to approve the municipal construction of an underground railway. A young reporter named Lincoln Steffens spent today at police headquarters helping to report on Tammany's downfall; when he gets a chance to write to his father on Thursday, he will call the outcome "eminently satisfactory" but add that "There is little crowing, however, for the Republicans are warned and know that they will be watched and turned out as easily and quickly as were their opponents."

At the end of the day ACD is back in Washington, being entertained at the National Capital Press Club, upstairs in the Loughran Building on E Street near Fourteenth. This elegantly equipped club, bought by a crew of newsmen from its previous inhabitants in 1891, is already running into financial trouble because of too-generous credit at the bar; within weeks it is going to become clear that the organization is insolvent, and the furnishings will be sold off in the spring. But for now it is a merry drinking and dining spot, and a suitable place for the entertainment of a visiting literary man who may be prevailed on to say something quotable.

"I feel hardly able to judge what this country needs," he sensibly tells his listeners, "for I have been here so short a time. But from what I have seen I should say that a mausoleum would fill what will some day be, without it, a long-felt want. I have visited the cemeteries of your large cities" – he is thinking of Holmes's grave in Cambridge and Poe's in Baltimore – "and I have seen the illustrious dead of the nation, some in one city and some in another. Now, it seems to me as if it would be much better were you to have some large building for the repose of such people of the republic as we have in Westminster Abbey. I should say, build it for all time and make it as large as your Capitol, even though you wouldn't be able to fill much of it now."

News reports will tell how this dictum was received:

> "No," quoth the listener; "but tomorrow there will be enough of the illustrious lying stiff on the field of battle to fill a good bit of space."
>
> The novelist looked at the speaker quizzically for a moment. Just then a derisive yell from a crowd of gloating Republicans who stood outside the club drinking in the story of the tidal wave came through the window. Doyle heard it and remarked with a smile:
>
> "Ah, yes. I see. Just so. Ha! ha! Very good that, I think, eh?"

Wednesday, November 7: *Round the Red Lamp*

The American edition of *Round the Red Lamp* is finally available. ACD promptly dispatches a copy to Melville Stone in Chicago, with an inscription conveying his "kindest remembrances." This new volume contains fifteen stories, of which half a dozen have never been published before, while others date from as long ago as 1890. All have

November 1894

something to do with the medical life – as ACD will find necessary to explain in the preface to the American edition: "You ask about the Red Lamp. It is the usual sign of the general practitioner in England."

Among the stories in this collection is "A Straggler of '15," ACD's first tale of the Battle of Waterloo, which was turned into that play which is being performed this autumn by Henry Irving. (Originally given the same title as the story, the play was renamed *The Battle of Waterloo* and finally just *Waterloo*.) Another is "The Doctors of Hoyland," in which the author makes a male doctor meet and fall in love with a female doctor, and proves himself something of a feminist by making the woman superior to the man in everything save, perhaps, humanity. The story is reminiscent of William Dean Howells's novel *Dr. Breen's Practice*, published thirteen years ago.

Then there is "The Curse of Eve," one of the most powerful stories ACD will ever write, for it deals in direct bloody terms not just with childbirth but with the vengeance of one sex against the other. Not a mere medical anecdote like, say, "His First Operation," nor yet a sordid story like "The Third Generation," this one is close to being a myth.

Not all readers will be completely comfortable with *Round the Red Lamp*, even after some of the stories have been softened from their original versions. (Jerome K. Jerome refused to publish several of them in *The Idler*.) A reviewer in *Catholic World* will be strongly disapproving:

> The question of moral responsibility for crime is one that thus comes into the purview of the medical expert, in certain classes of disease, and in pursuit of this obscure and delicate subject Dr. Doyle has employed his literary art in a way which, while it fascinates, may be productive of very startling conclusions. Once it is admitted that an apparently rational and level headed person is by nature and heredity powerless to resist the promptings of evil, the foundations of our existing jurisprudence and social safeguards are placed in deadly peril. The group of short stories ranged under the name *Round the Red Lamp* give a vivid idea of Dr. Doyle's method of work. They also induct us into the ethics of pathology which men of his school have been broaching of late, much to the dismay of plainer people.
>
> If we are not easily nauseated, we may wade through professional horrors as ghastly in their way as anything that the feverish imagination of Edgar Allan Poe conjured up in a less sickening school. . . .
>
> It is impossible to question the literary skill with which these tales of medical life are woven. A concise and direct form of narrative, a careful use of detail, and a judicious introduction of medical phraseology are the methods on which the author relies. It is only in a restricted sense that they may be regarded as stories. They are rather brief imaginary episodes, not more startling in their character, it may be assumed, than the everyday experience of many medical men might furnish. . . .
>
> There are doubtless some orders of mind which find pastime in literature of this sort. *Chacun à son gout.* The lovers of a health-

ier page will put them by with the reflection that it is a pity the talent which was expended on them found no better aim than they did.

The Critic will be less censorious:

> It is difficult to pass judgment upon this book: it is in part a human document of undoubted value to all who give to the medical man his true and enviable place in mundane affairs; and in part it is the product of a brilliant storyteller, and as such, of course, of interest to all that read. We are not prepared to say that we like the book in its entirety, but we acknowledge that we have read every line of it with appreciative interest.

Thursday, November 8: Dinner in Philadelphia

ACD is the subject of national publicity today, in the much-read pages of *Leslie's Weekly* – still best known by its former name, *Frank Leslie's Illustrated Weekly*, though not at present operated by its founder's widow, who herself goes by the name of "Frank Leslie." A prominent article in today's issue, titled "Conan Doyle in America," is part discussion of his antecedents as a writer and part summary of his American experiences so far:

> When he went, directly after his landing, to the Adirondack hills to shoot deer and found none, though he waited patiently for four days, his temper as a sportsman was seriously tried, but he nevertheless returned to New York in amiable mood and began his lecture forthwith. Though the deer fought shy of him the people did not, and there was a great crowd to hear his first address. . . .
>
> Dr. Doyle has been interviewed by the reporters wherever he has been since he landed in this country, and an effort has been made to induce him to speak critically of his American contemporaries in the making of the [book]. This Dr. Doyle has declined to do.

There are brief remarks about *Round the Red Lamp*, and there is the proud announcement that beginning next month *Leslie's* will present to America an "absorbingly interesting piece of fiction" from ACD's pen, *The Stark Munro Letters*. The author of this enthusiastic piece, Philip Poindexter, promises that the new book includes "much that is unconsciously autobiographical, though it was in no sense Dr. Doyle's purpose to write his own experiences as a young medical practitioner when he fashioned the story which will in a little while be given to the public through these pages."

ACD was originally supposed to be in Pittsburgh today – Pittsburg, as it is still often spelt, the Iron City, centre of smelting, natural gas extraction, coal mining and glass manufacture, making it a smoky city reminiscent of the English Midlands. He was supposed to be in Pittsburgh, but arrangements for the lecture fell through, and instead he has gone straight to Philadelphia. Here, in a city where a statue of William Penn has just been installed atop City Hall, where the *Times* is

November 1894

headlining "A Window Smasher Caught" and "A Tugboatman's Heroism," and where Wanamaker's is offering gentlemen's overcoats at prices from ten dollars to an astronomical fifty, the visiting author is entertained this evening at the elegant home of Craige Lippincott, 218 South Nineteenth Street.

His host has been president since 1886 of the publishing firm which bears his father's name, J. B. Lippincott & Co. It was their *Magazine* in which was first published *The Sign of the Four*, the novel which made Sherlock Holmes an American success and ensured his fame. Lippincott bought the American rights to *The Sign* (along with three months' British rights) for a lump payment of a hundred pounds, and the firm has earned much more than that from the story, in spite of the many pirate editions which compete against its official ones. After *Lippincott's Magazine* published it first, it was made available in the "Magazine Series" and as part of *Six Complete Novels* and *Five Complete Novels*, and finally last year an edition of *The Sign of the Four* itself saw print. Lippincott's has also published *A Study in Scarlet*, and doubtless hopes to get the rights to other books, in competition with Appletons and other brash New York firms.

"He was a man of great personal charm and youthful spirit," a biographer will write of Lippincott, "and had many friends. His favorite recreations were shooting and diving." This is a man whose company ACD can enjoy, as he can that of the literary colleagues whom Lippincott has invited for dinner. Besides ACD, Innes, and the host, there are the host's brother, J. Dundas Lippincott; Dr. J. William White, a medical man; Edward W. Bok, the immigrant editor whose *Ladies' Home Journal* has become America's largest magazine; Charles Emory Smith, an editor, former minister to Russia, and future postmaster-general of the United States; and Clayton McMichael, editor of *The North American*.

Then there is a rising author of western tales, Owen Wister, whose one book so far is *The Dragon of Wantley* but whose story "La Tinaja," distilling history, love, and the grim heat of the Arizona desert, drew high praise from Frederic Remington in a letter the other day and will soon see print. (In 1902 Wister will do what ACD has already done: create a genre of fiction, without realizing it. His novel *The Virginian* will be the prototype of uncounted Westerns, in print and later on film.) And there is another Lippincott author, Dr. Silas Weir Mitchell, whose book *Hepzibah Guiness* was published in 1887. (He will autograph a copy of it to ACD "With thanks for many pleasant hours.")

A reporter for the *Philadelphia Times* reaches him and asks about his impressions of America:

> "I did not come here to lecture. That was secondary. I only came to see the country, though lecturing is a good way to see things and offers a splendid way of familiarizing one's self with everybody and everything, and now that I am here I propose to give some few lectures. . . .
>
> "To me," he said, "it seems a duty to learn all we can about

America, just as I think it the duty of every American to learn all he can about England. The future of the world depends upon our being able to work together. The Anglo-Saxon race will own the globe. England may be the smallest of the confederacy, but she will be the mother of them all. The English race will neutralize them all. After all, the world is young yet and queer things may happen."

When he was asked to speak of the feeling of Englishmen towards this country he quickly said:

"I think it is much more kindly than the feeling of America towards England. During the five weeks I have been here I have heard some unkind things said about England, but it is rare in England to hear anything harsh said about America. This is the one thing I cannot understand, for there is no question open between the two countries. But this is bound to right itself. As your gallant Erben said, 'Blood is thicker than water.'"

The interview closed by Dr. Doyle saying that much harm was done and wrong sentiment created by globe-trotters, who were taken as representative men, but who, when too late, were found to be the contrary.

Friday, November 9: Next Stop Newark

The weary tour drags on. The lectures nearly every night are bad enough, but in addition there are so many encounters with local celebrities, so many literary enthusiasts who want to shake ACD's hand or hear a few words from him. "I'm sure you wouldn't mind addressing our little society, would you? Just for fifteen minutes?" And then there are the clubs and all the other hospitality, so much of it depending on liquor. "We don't feel we've done the right thing," one expansive host is said to have assured him, "unless we get a guest so drunk he can't tell a silver dollar from a buzz-saw." The offer holds little attraction for ACD, to whom silver dollars and buzz-saws are equally foreign objects, and whose memory of an alcoholic father, dead only a year, is still sharp.

Today the tour brings him to Newark, New Jersey, described by Baedeker as "a prosperous but uninteresting city on the *Passaic*, with 181,830 inhab., large breweries, and extensive manufactures of jewelry, iron goods, celluloid, paper, and leather. . . . *Thomas A. Edison*, the inventor, has his home and workshop here."

Under the management of George Y. Sonn, representing the Agassiz Society of the High School, ACD lectures tonight in the Essex Lyceum. "Readings and Reminiscences" – he must know it by heart by now – fills nearly every seat in the auditorium. As usual, reporters note his solid physique and deep voice; the *Evening News* will say tomorrow that he "greatly resembles J. Lawrence Sullivan, the fallen monarch of the prize ring."

The pugilist to whom the *News* refers, better known as John L. Sullivan, is an Irishman sometimes called "the Boston Strong Boy" who won the championship by knocking out Paddy Ryan in 1882, but lost it through drink and fast living by 1889. He came back briefly and made

November 1894

himself America's last bare-knuckle champion with a 75-round victory, but has now retired from the ring to try acting and keep a saloon. At five feet ten and a half inches and 180 pounds, he is shorter, though no lighter, than ACD, who once saw Sullivan fight and should be delighted by the comparison: he was working earlier this fall on a "boxing play," based on his own experience in the ring and his considerable knowledge of the history of prize-fighting, and will use all that information in a novel called *Rodney Stone* in a couple of years.

After the lecture the visitor has a brief chat with a reporter for the *Daily Advertiser*, and takes the opportunity to promote a new story which is soon to be published in that family journal as well as many other papers: "The Medal of Brigadier Gerard." Tomorrow's paper will note that he "said very emphatically that he considered it his best work."

Saturday, November 10: Siss, Boom, Ah!
Two stories by ACD are in print today for the first time. One is "A Foreign Office Romance," appearing, through a distribution syndicate, in the *Indianapolis News*. The *Chicago Inter-Ocean* and several other papers will carry it tomorrow, and the magazine *Young Man and Young Woman* will use it as the lead item in its Christmas number. The other is "The Parasite," with the first episode appearing today in *Harper's Weekly*. (In England, *Lloyd's Weekly Newspaper* will start carrying it tomorrow.)

ACD himself travels up from Philadelphia today to see a rare sporting treat: an American football game, and not just any game but the annual encounter between those old rivals, the Tigers of Princeton and the Quakers of the University of Pennsylvania. It is played on neutral ground, at the State Fair Grounds in Trenton, where stands have been erected to seat at least fifteen thousand spectators. Decorations in the schools' colours – yellow and black for Princeton, red and blue for Penn – are seen everywhere, with Trentonians favouring their home-state Tigers while merchants are equally ready to make money selling souvenirs to the Pennsylvania rooters who have come up in vast numbers. "The trains bring in fresh contingents every hour," says a telegraph report in today's *New York Herald*. "Speculators have control of the tickets." (The nominal price reaches an astonishing two dollars for grandstand seats.)

In his youth ACD was something of a footballer himself.

> In spite of my wretched training [he will recall] I played for a short time as a forward in the Edinburgh University team, but my want of knowledge of the game was too heavy a handicap. Afterwards I took to Association, and played first goal and then back for Portsmouth, when that famous club was an amateur organization. Even then we could put a very fair team in the field, and were runners-up for the County Cup in the last season that I played. In the same season I was invited to play for the county. I was always too slow, however, to be a really good back, though I was a long and safe kick. After a long hiatus I took up football

again in South Africa and organized a series of inter-hospital matches in Bloemfontein which helped to take our minds away from enteric. My old love treated me very scurvily, however, for I received a foul from a man's knee which buckled two of my ribs and brought my game to a close.

Years later, he will criticize local variations in football rules as an injury to Britain's success in the sport:

> All these local freak games, wall games, Winchester games, and so on are national misfortunes, for while our youth are wasting their energies upon them – those precious early energies which make the instinctive players – the young South African or New Zealander is brought up on the real universal Rugby, and so comes over to pluck a few more laurel leaves out of our depleted wreath.

ACD does not record what he thinks of American football, which is still more different from "the real universal Rugby," but today he has an opportunity to see the game at its best. Pennsylvania relies on its backfield, captained by Knipe at left half, and on its kicking, while Princeton's strength is the rush line, including the Tiger captain, Trenchard. The crowd is helped in following the game by a "novel score board," tomorrow's paper will say, "which showed every play, including the possession of the ball, the number of downs, the yards to gain, and the score." The game begins at 2:10 p.m. American football is less ritualized than it will later become, and has more in common with the scrums of the game ACD knows. A newspaper report tomorrow morning will reflect its style:

> Now Capt. Knipe, with the strength of a giant, wriggled and writhed through the centre of the champions' line for an additional five yards. Osgood made two, Gelbert one, and Wharton two, all through the centre, and the leather rested ten yards from the Princeton goal line. . . .
>
> Cochran punted and Osgood caught the oval in the centre of the gridiron, and when he was tackled he passed the ball to Brooke, who was also seized by Trenchard and rubbed in the wet sod. It was on Pennsylvania's 45-yard line that this happened, and, after two tries by Osgood and Knipe to break the line, Brooke boomed a towering punt that Poe, for the third successive time, muffed, but again Morse, who was near at hand, fell on the ball and was downed on Princeton's 25-yard line.

There is no score in the first half. Pennsylvania gets the ball within six inches of the goal-line once, but is rebuffed. In the second half, though, the Quakers manage two touchdowns – one scored by Williams the quarter-back and one by Osgood the right-half – and both times fullback Brooke kicks the requisite goal. The final score: 12-0 for Pennsylvania. "The ball was rarely in the victors' territory," the *New York Times* will say tomorrow morning in reporting today's chief sporting event, "and the Princeton team was clearly outplayed at every point." Silenced are the voices which were crying before the game,

November 1894

Hooray, hooray! Tiger!
Siss, boom, ah!
Princeton!

ACD returns to Philadelphia after the game, and has dinner at the home of Dr. James William White, one of the men who dined with him at the Lippincotts' the other night, and his wife, Letitia. White, now 44, is a professor at the University of Pennsylvania medical school, a specialist in genito-urinary surgery, and the joint translator and editor of a book ACD may have consulted while he was writing his medical school thesis: *Cornil on Syphilis*. The two men have something to talk about besides medicine, for both have travelled distant seas – at the age at which ACD was whaling in the Arctic and seeing the coast of Africa, White was on the staff of Louis Agassiz for his 1871-72 expedition to the Galapagos Islands.

As if the day has not been long enough, ACD lectures this evening, in the famous (and acoustically admired) Musical Fund Hall on Locust Street. The Musical Fund Society has revived its "lyceum" or lecture series, and ACD is the first speaker for this season; inevitably, he will be followed by Dean Hole and General Lew Wallace. Introducing the speaker – and taking the opportunity to say more than a few words about the Musical Fund Society itself – is Dr. A.   ACD gives, as usual, "Readings and Reminiscences."

Sunday, November 11: Impressions of America

As usual on Sundays, ACD has the day off from lecturing – a chance to relax, to travel from Philadelphia back to New York, to have a conversation with Innes:

> [W]e talked very earnestly of the senseless dissension which at that time was very apparent between the two countries.
> I remember that I said with some earnestness, "Well, Innes, I only hope that in your military career you wil some day find yourself leading British soldiers shoulder to shoulder with American soldiers in a just cause – and may I be there to see!"
> Could any wish have been more grotesquely impossible, and yet I must have spoken with some strange conviction, since the words remain so clear to me after all the years. But see how it turned out.

Perhaps, too, there is time to reflect on what he has seen in America so far and store away ideas for his future writing. He has repeatedly promised not to write one of those odious volumes explaining America to the British on the basis of a few weeks' travel; but there will be nothing to prevent him from using American place names and American references as background material in novels and short stories.

He has no thought of writing more Sherlock Holmes adventures, but some of the places he has visited will eventually find their way into print when he does produce more of those tales ten, twenty, thirty years from now. An example is New York itself: he has seen the city's polyglot colour, and he knows of the Bowery, once a respectable thoroughfare but now a neighbourhood of thugs and cheap bars balanced between Jewish and Italian ghettoes. He will use the Bowery, and respectable Brooklyn across the water, as background as Emilia Lucca tell her life story in "The Red Circle":

> Gennaro was able to do a service to an Italian gentleman – he saved him from some ruffians in the place called the Bowery, and so made a powerful friend. His name was Tito Castalotte, and he was the senior partner of the great firm of Castalotte and Zamba, who are the chief fruit importers of New York. Signor Zamba is an invalid, and our new friend Castalotte has all power within the firm, which employs more than three hundred men. He took my husband into his employment, made him head of a department, and showed his good-will towards him in every way. . . . We had taken and furnished a little house in Brooklyn, and our whole future seemed assured when that black cloud appeared which was soon to overspread our sky.

Chicago must have impressed him for its crime; he will use it twice in Sherlock Holmes tales as the city from which vicious Americans came to England. This is the picture he will draw in "The Three Garridebs" of James Winter, *alias* Killer Evans:

> Native of Chicago. Known to have shot three men in the States. Escaped from penitentiary through political influence. Came to London in 1893. Shot a man. . . . Dead man was identified as Rodger Prescott, famous as forger and coiner in Chicago.

And then there is Abe Slaney, described as "The most dangerous crook in Chicago" in "The Dancing Men." (Oddly, Holmes will get that information from "Wilson Hargreave, of the New York Police Bureau," who presumably will have had it from colleagues in Chicago; perhaps ACD has not noticed that policing is by no means a national affair in the United States.)

Buffalo, which he will visit next week, will figure in "His Last Bow," in which he has Sherlock Holmes mention that he joined "an Irish secret society" there. In other cases, he comes too late to make the best use of an American reference; now that he has seen something of New Jersey, for instance, he may regret that he made it the birthplace of Irene Adler.

One place he will not see on this trip is the Shenandoah Valley of Pennsylvania, a grim district in the east central part of the state, where Irishmen dig coal and drink whiskey. Dense with railways and ugly with collieries, this part of the state is not frequented much by tourists (although a gravity-driven railway at Mauch Chunk is a novelty to sightseers). But ACD might have tried for a detour through it, or a side trip from Philadelphia, had he known that in twenty years he will be writing a novel based on labour unrest, economic misery, and murder which took place here in the 1870's, until the Coal and Iron Police and the Pinkerton men broke the secret society of the Mollie Maguires. He will have to rely on Allan Pinkerton's reminiscences when he writes *The Valley of Fear*, and he will not do badly at describing the desolation, the mud, the paintless houses and the hopeless lives of the miners. Still, for a few dollars' fare and a few hours' exertion he might have seen some of it himself – and they do say that the family of Jack Kehoe, the Mollie boss who was hanged, still keep the Hibernian House at Girardville.

November 1894

Monday, November 12: A Visit with John Kendrick Bangs

Returning to New York, ACD finds that as an attraction he places a distant second, behind the Horse Show at Madison Square Garden. (Indeed, he may also be outdone by an exhibition of "Portraits of Women" which can be seen at the National Academy of Design, for the benefit of the St. John's Guild and Orthopaedic Hospital.) Everyone who is anyone in the city is spending much of this week looking over the twelve hundred entries whose stampings and smells fill the Garden – a four-year-old building, Stanford White's work, at the corner of Madison Avenue and 26th Street. Atop it, above the roof garden where a jealous husband will shoot White in 1906, is a statue of Diana by Augustus Saint-Gaudens, its beauty concealing the gigantic rivets which hold it together.

Tomorrow's *Herald* will sum up the tone of the Horse Show:

> During the dinner hour the Horse Show adjourns to the Brunswick, Delmonico's and the Waldorf, where the tailor made young women are transformed into the most exquisitely costumed women. Amid forests of golden chrysanthemums and bowers of smilax, regaled by sweet strains of music from a hidden orchestra, this world of beautiful women, with handsome men, sits down to dine.

On display at the Garden are coaching stallions, harness horses, roadsters, pairs of carriage horses, saddle horses, thoroughbred stallions, arabs, four-in-hands, ladies' saddle horses, high steppers, and hunters. Fashionable New York knows horseflesh, as, on a lowlier plane, does unfashionable New York – horses no longer pull streetcars, but there are hundreds of thousands of them pulling cabs, milk-wagons and delivery drays.

Although society's attention is elsewhere, ACD is to lecture three times this week in the city. These are matinees, talks and readings at eleven o'clock in the morning, for which the speaker is to receive an unusually generous payment: fifty per cent of the receipts. They are given at Daly's Theatre, at the corner of Broadway and 30th Street, where something livelier is appearing each evening and on Wednesday afternoon: George Edwardes's company in the saucy British review *A Gaiety Girl*.

Daly's Theatre is famous because of the lavish hand of its proprietor and impresario, Augustin Daly. Almost thirty years ago he presented his first original play, *Under the Gaslight*, in which he offered the novel effect of a hero tied to the railroad tracks by the villainous blackmailer, while the beautiful heroine struggled to escape from her own imprisonment to rescue him in time. The following year he repeated that triumph with a heroine narrowly escaping a hideous death in a realistic sawmill. Since those days he has gone from height to height, putting ever more elaborate scenic effects on his stage; nor has he spared effort to bring the finest actors to New York and present them in the finest plays, often commissioned or translated especially for Daly's.

This year he has gone so far as to introduce a new voucher system in an attempt to foil the ticket speculators who cluster on the sidewalks in front of his doors.

Welcome to America, Mr. Sherlock Holmes

For this first of ACD's three New York matinees (tickets $1.50, one dollar, and fifty cents) the audience consists almost entirely of women – gentlemen are at the Horse Show, presumably, and other men are at their offices or shops or factories. The lecture is "interrupted throughout by gentle outbursts of gloved applause," as a newspaper will say tomorrow. He gives the ladies "Readings and Reminiscences" once more, assuming that few of them were at Calvary Church to hear it a month ago, and there is no murmur of dissatisfaction.

He has a moment to write a note on Aldine Club stationery before taking the train to his evening engagement – for the first time, he is to give two formal lectures in a single day. The note is to Ellen Dana Conway of 22 East 10th Street, who has extended a social invitation on behalf of herself and her husband, Rev. Moncure Daniel Conway. ACD is delighted to accept, and sends along a billet "in case you or any of your friends should care to come to my little reading." ACD met Conway in May at that Authors' Society dinner where he spoke, and is doubtless eager to see him again at more leisure. Now 62, Conway is a Unitarian minister who first made a name for himself as an abolitionist, but in the years since the Civil War has gone on to preach (in London for twenty years, and lately back in America) and write a number of books, including *Demonology and Devil Lore*, and countless magazine articles on uplifting subjects. More than a decade ago ACD met Henry Highland Garnet, the great black orator, at the American mission in Liberia, and since then he has maintained a sharp interest in the struggle to end slavery, about which Conway will be able to tell him so much.

ACD's engagement this evening, however, is away from the city, in the Westchester County town of Yonkers. Here he is the guest of John Kendrick Bangs, whose literary talents have earned him the title of Editor of the Departments of Humor for the firm of Harper & Brothers – a position, clearly, of great influence on light journalism and *belles-lettres* in America. "The Editor's Drawer" in *Harper's Weekly* is one province of his empire, but he is also beginning to be known for more sustained work, of the kind collected last year in *Coffee and Repartee*. He is still young, but feels settled now that he and his wife (and first cousin), Agnes, have three fine children and a solid house on North Broadway, packed with nursemaids and in-laws and dogs. Such a solid citizen should take part in civic affairs; so Bangs ran for mayor of Yonkers last year, and lost. But he put his experience to good advantage by writing a book about it, *Three Weeks in Politics*, which has sold fourteen thousand copies.

This merry man is an admirer of ACD and has invited him to dine. Indeed, he is the person behind ACD's invitation to Yonkers in the first place, for this evening's lecture is sponsored by the Yonkers Lawn Tennis Club, of which Bangs happens to be president. He loves bringing celebrities to the club (Richard Harding Davis, Charles Dana Gibson and Anthony Hope Hawkins among them), perhaps to compensate its members for his failure to make their president mayor of the city.

At the North Broadway house, ACD and his host and hostess change for dinner, and the visitor is downstairs first, to be entertained by John Ken-

November 1894

drick Bangs, Jr., six years old. A still younger member of the family will later record the story as the family chooses to remember it:

> As Bangs crossed the hall to the wide doorway of the library, he saw the back of Doyle's head above the plush comfort of a chair which had been drawn up before a blazing fire on the library hearth. At the same moment he was shocked to see his son move swiftly upon Doyle from the rear, and, with a Gollywog Doll poised on high, bring it down upon the crown of the distinguished creator of Sherlock Holmes. Doyle like a flash seized the boy and went to the floor in a wrestling match, easily bringing the attacking party to complete subjection. Looking up and smiling, Doyle eternally subjected Bangs also. "Oh, never mind, Mr. Bangs," he said. "This is only another example of the irrepressible conflict between Old England and Young America!"

ACD must be remembering his own Mary, who is not quite six, and baby Kingsley, who will turn two on Thursday. Such rambunctiousness is nothing new to Bangs; tomorrow, after ACD's departure, he will be sending someone a manuscript with a covering note warning that it may not be up to standard because "I did it Saturday with my small son dancing a fandango upon the back of my chair."

The club where this evening's lecture is given is in Glenwood, an elegant neighbourhood in the northern part of Yonkers. Agnes and John Kendrick Bangs (he had been on the building committee) were conspicuous at the glittering party last New Year's Eve which officially opened this rambling, shingled structure; it has two tennis courts and a ballroom featuring a stage decorated with palms, dressing rooms, thirty-five-foot ceiling and terra-cotta walls.

At 8:30 p.m., Bangs steps out to introduce the celebrity:

> Among the many esteemed privileges I have had as a resident of Yonkers, I know of none that has given me greater pleasure than is afforded by this privilege of introducing to you Dr. A. Conan Doyle. A long and wordy introduction in behalf of one so well known to many through his stories, would be greatly out of place. It would remind me of a certain friend, who, some time ago, invited me to dinner, saying he had two very fine canvasback ducks. I sat down, and went through four or five different courses, and at last exclaimed: "Please bring on the ducks!" I fear, should I continue, that you will say: "Please bring on the ducks!"

The ducks tonight consist of – what else? – "Readings and Reminiscences."

After the lecture, the two literary men return to the Bangs residence and sit together before the fireplace with its tiled inscription: "Hic Habitat Felicitas," here abideth happiness. Late into the night they talk about Sherlock Holmes, literature and life, and breathe a little of the smoke of burning wood. Familiar enough in suburban America, a domestic wood fire is a rarity in England. (Years later, when Bangs returns the visit, ACD will go to great trouble to get the right kind of wood and build the right kind of fire to make his guest feel at home.)

Bangs will remember this visit when in 1897 he writes a sequel to his popular comic novel, *A House-Boat on the Styx*, which he will call *The Pursuit of the House-Boat*. Its chief character will be Sherlock Holmes – or rather the ghost of Sherlock Holmes – and it will be dedicated "To A. Conan Doyle, Esq. with the author's sincerest regards and thanks for the untimely demise of his great detective which made these things possible." Two years after that, Bangs will use Holmes again in "The Mystery of Pinkham's Diamond Stud," a parody set in New York's opulent Walledup-Hysteria Hotel, and after that there will be "Sherlock Holmes Again" in *The Enchanted Typewriter* and "A Pragmatic Enigma: Being a Chapter from 'The Failures of Sherlock Holmes' by A. Conan Watson, M.D.," in *Potted Fiction*. And he will draw on both Holmes and that rival creation of ACD's brother-in-law, Raffles the burglar, for *R. Holmes & Co.: Being the Remarkable Adventures of Raffles Holmes, Esq., Detective and Amateur Cracksman by Birth*.

Tuesday, November 13: Audience in Orange
Before he returns to the city, ACD plays a round of golf with Bangs. There are not many golf clubs in America yet – this one, St. Andrew's, claims to have been the first of its kind, established in 1888. (Members who joined in the spring of 1889 include, besides Bangs, Andrew Carnegie.) Three years from now ACD will write to Bangs that "I still live in hope of playing round the Yonkers links once more."

As soon as he gets back to the city, ACD realizes that he has forgotten something, and sends a telegram to Bangs, which he will follow with a note tomorrow: "I hope you got my telegram about my 'Waterghost' . . . I shall come out to fetch it if you will keep it there, though I don't need a bait to tempt me back to Yonkers." He is referring to a copy of Bangs's book *The Water Ghost and Others*, just published by Harper's, a collection of stories in what is becoming the author's particular province: comic ghosts. ACD may detect in some of the tales echoes of a story he wrote himself eleven years ago, "Selecting a Ghost"; and one of Bangs's sketches, "The Ghost Club," contains the seed of his future *House-Boat* material.

From the Aldine Club today, ACD writes a note to Ripley Hitchcock, who on behalf of the Authors' Club has invited him to dine on Thursday of next week. He sends his regrets – "I shall be many hundreds of miles away," he says, with some exaggeration – but adds that he would be delighted to have lunch with Hitchcock after one of his matinees this week, if Hitchcock should be free. Hitchcock is currently a literary advisor for Appletons; he has tried medicine, been an art critic, organized a mediaeval tournament in New Jersey, prepared a book on art and statuary for last year's Chicago exposition, and confirmed his reputation as a judge of talent by introducing Rudyard Kipling to American publishers.

The lecture tonight is in the Music Hall at Orange, a town which, like all places in New Jersey, is reached by a two-stage journey, first a ferry across the Hudson to Jersey City and then a train. The towns of northern New Jersey are not yet mere bedrooms for New York, in the way they will be after the Pennsylvania Railroad tunnel is opened a decade hence, but there are some well-to-do commuters, such as George Richards, a lawyer who travels from Orange each day to his offices at 62 Wall Street. His wife frequently goes into the city as well, to shop, to make social calls, and to take bicycle lessons in Central Park. Today she has made several calls here in Orange, and undertaken the sad duty, as she will note in her diary, of seeing "Our little George's body moved from Rosedale Cemetery to Litchfield"; but this evening she is in ACD's audience at the Music Hall.

Wednesday, November 14: New Readings at Daly's
It is a wet and unpleasant day in New York, where the morning newspapers are full of last summer's Pullman strike (the commission investigating it has issued its report) and of the autumn flower show of the Farmers' Club, held at the American Institute on West 38th Street. No less a person than Very Rev. S. Reynolds Hole, the Dean of Rochester whose path has been crossing ACD's regularly these weeks, gave an unscheduled talk there yesterday; and in his honour there has been named the Dean Hole carnation.

At eleven this morning, ACD lectures again at Daly's Theatre. The word has gotten around, and he draws a considerably larger crowd than he did on Monday. ACD will later write that he was "weary" during his American tour, and by this stage of the trip he has every right to be so. He will record this "amusing incident" from this morning's lecture:

> [As] I bustled on to the stage at Daly's Theatre I tripped over the wooden sill of the stage door, with the result that I came cantering down the sloping stage towards the audience, shedding books and papers on my way. There was much laughter and a general desire for an encore.

On the assumption that anyone who enjoyed Monday's talk enough to come again today does not want to hear exactly the same material a second time, ACD varies his programme today. He makes no remarks save a few words of explanation now and then, restricting himself to readings from his works: part of "A Scandal in Bohemia," the sketch of Judge Jeffreys from *Micah Clarke*, a passage from *The Refugees* which he titles "An Eclipse at Versailles," and some of "The Green Flag."

Today's crowd is considerably larger than Monday's was, and so is the box office revenue: $335.50, compared to $235.50.

Thursday, November 15: Philadelphia and Princeton
The days are beginning to blur together in ACD's mind. When he writes his autobiography thirty years hence, he will get his recollections slightly wrong:

> Once, for example, I lectured at Daly's Theatre in New York at a matinée, at Princeton College the same evening, some 50 miles away, and at Philadelphia next afternoon. It was no wonder that I got very tired – the more so as the exuberant hospitality in those pre-prohibition days was enough in itself to take the energies out of the visitor.

In fact, today – little Kingsley's birthday, as ACD doubtless remembers – the matinee is in Philadelphia, and the final lecture at Daly's is tomorrow morning.

Welcome to America, Mr. Sherlock Holmes

Between the two he does, indeed, go to Princeton, to lecture for the Casino building fund, the Casino being a proposed hall for student dances, entertainments, and indoor sports. He gets to the pleasant college town (site, as he is doubtless immediately told, of a significant battle in the war between the King and the American colonists) in time for dinner in its chief hostelry, the Nassau Inn, which is already 137 years old.

Dining with him are a group of students and half a dozen professors, headed by Francis Landey Patton, now 51, the Bermuda-born, Toronto-educated Presbyterian minister who has been president of the College of New Jersey since 1888. (It will not officially be "Princeton College" for another two years, nor a university for some decades.) Patton is known as a progressive, capable in business matters and venturesome enough to appoint laymen as well as clergy to Princeton's faculty. Apart from his general interest in what ACD has to say about literature, he can exchange at least superficial recollections of Edinburgh; he visited the Scots city for a theological conference in 1878, while ACD was an undergraduate there.

The dean of the college, James Ormsbee Murray, will mark his 67th birthday in a few days. Also a clergyman, but of the Congregational persuasion, Murray held the Holmes Professorship of Belles Lettres and English Language and Literature before he was promoted to the deanship eleven years ago; he is the author of a hymnbook and several biographical tomes.

Then there is William Milligan Sloane, who has taught Latin, history, and political science since coming to Princeton in 1877. (An ambitious man and still young at 44, he will be leaving for New York's Columbia University in a couple of years.) Sloane is the author of the "Life of Napoleon," a series of articles appearing in the *Century* Magazine this fall. Powerful in build, hearty, genial, known as the proprietor of a wealth of anecdotes, Sloane has a reputation as a good chairman, in a time when a dinner or an evening soiree needs such a figure. ACD is sure to be pumping him about Napoleon tonight, for the French emperor is much on his mind: he has written one or two tales of a Napoleonic warrior named Brigadier Gerard, and is on the lookout for more material.

Henry Burchard Fine, professor of mathematics, is also at the dinner – he has written textbooks and monographs on logic and the singularities of curves. There is Bliss Perry, a professor of English whose novel *Salem Kittredge* was published this year, and who will leave Princeton in 1899 (he came here only last year) to take on the editorship of the *Atlantic Monthly*. There is William Francis Magie, the physicist; there is Leroy W. McCay, the chemist, who has a special interest in arsenic; and there is the youngest of the group, James Mark Baldwin, already something of an authority on "mental development," part of the curious new field of psychology. He came to Princeton last year from the University of Toronto, having acted as vice-president of the international congress of psychology in London in 1892, and six years from now he will be the first man ever to receive an honorary degree in science from Oxford.

The intellectual depth and breadth of the College of New Jersey, thus well represented at dinner, are a credit to the college's former president,

November 1894

Dr. James McCosh, who lies on his deathbed tonight in a house nearby. The students who dine with the group are, in their way, equally impressive. Ernest Haas of Philadelphia, already a graduate and back at the college on a special course, has a unique claim to be among them: when the Class of '94 listed their preferences in life, art and trivia for the *Nassau Herald* last spring, Haas is the only one who wrote "Doyle" in the blank labelled "Author."

The other students are all in their senior year: Richard D. Hatch, who will be going on to the General Seminary next fall; John C. Harding, whose future is in insurance; Lewis F. Pease, who will come back to Princeton at one stage of his career to lecture on music; Howard Colby, the one scientist in the group; and John Work Garrett, a leader of the American Whig Society, one of Princeton's two all-important student debating clubs. Garrett will go on (after a few years in his family's banking business) to a career in the American diplomatic service, ending up as Ambassador to the Netherlands during World War I and a place in the American delegation to the Versailles peace talks.

Tickets have been on sale at Briner's drugstore, 44 Nassau Street, for ACD's lecture, which begins at eight o'clock in Alexander Hall. This gorgeous red romanesque structure was opened only a few months ago; not all the elaborate carving which is eventually to adorn it is finished yet. The hall seats fifteen hundred – a good deal more than the First Presbyterian Church, where the college has held its convocations up to now – and though ACD draws a good crowd, he cannot fill it. The empty sections interfere with the acoustics, the *Princeton Press* will complain. Patton, the college president, introduces ACD, who gives the usual "Readings and Reminiscences."

Sixteen students act as ushers. As the *Daily Princetonian* listed them today, they include several members of Clio, rival of the American Whig Society: Stanley R. McCormick, Edwin A. McAlpin, Jr., and Willis H. Butler. There are also Robert E. Ross of Whig; Algernon B. Roberts, later to be a lawyer and a member of the Pennsylvania state senate; William A. Fisher Jr., on his way to being a Johns Hopkins doctor; Ralph Dusenbury Smith, a future civil service commissioner; William R. Wilson; Fitzhugh Coyle Speer; Robert Forsyth Little, Jr.; Macy Brooks; James Windsor Decker; and Gerardus Post Herrick. The names themselves reflect the genteel, upper-class confidence of half-southern Princeton.

Friday, November 16: North to New Rochelle
Receipts for ACD's third matinee at Daly's are lower than they were on Wednesday, though still better than Monday's level. For the second time this week he has to perform twice in a single day; tonight he is scheduled to be in New Rochelle, a town almost on Long Island Sound and so close to the city it is already becoming a suburb. A decade from now George M. Cohan will discover New Rochelle and immortalize its proximity to the bright lights, as well as its rustic charm, in the greatest musical comedy of forty years, *Forty-five Minutes from Broadway*.

Welcome to America, Mr. Sherlock Holmes

The quick eighteen-mile trip northward starts from the Grand Central Depot on 42nd Street. The trains run through long tunnels beneath Park Avenue, emerge into daylight to cross the Harlem River, pass Fordham and skirt the Sound to deposit ACD at New Rochelle. He gives his "Readings and Reminiscences" in the assembly room of the Trinity Place Public School – the civic pride of New Rochelle, with thirteen classrooms (steam heated, at that), not to mention this hall, a concrete basement, a teachers' room and a library. It has housed primary and "grammar" grades since it was opened a decade ago – the previous school burned, though the library books were saved – and this year the city has established a high school as well.

Miss Ida Babcock is principal of both schools in this single brick building, and supervises the teaching of English composition, physical geography, physiology and hygiene, bookkeeping, Latin, algebra, drawing and spelling to this fall's freshman class.

Saturday, November 17: Dinner at the Lotos Club

A couple of ACD's short stories have been resurrected by American newspapers for publication today. "The 'Slapping Sal'" appears in the *Princeton Press* – it has not been seen anywhere for more than a year – and "The Los Amigos Fiasco," first published in 1892, has for some reason been presented by the *Minneapolis Journal*. It all means more attention for ACD (public interest is high already in Princeton, of course) and perhaps a small fee.

Back in New York, the literary lion has most of the day free, but this evening comes the event which is really the social high point of the trip: a dinner in his honour at the Lotos Club, where that luncheon was held during his first week in the city in October. That was a small affair, but this is a large-scale one, in keeping with the tradition of important Saturday night entertainments at the club. This has been going on for more than twenty years:

> Naturally [the club historian will write next year], the abounding good fellowship and conviviality found its best expression in dinners, which were a feature of club life as soon as the resources of the kitchen and dining room were perfected. The purchase of the first complete dinner set, white china, decorated with red bands and the monogram of the club, was an event which no member of that day has forgotten. It required very little distinction in those days to provoke the honor of a dinner at the Lotos Club. Guests were a necessity, and it was the duty of the directory to provide them, and it did so, whether there was special occasion or timeliness in the demonstration or not. Amusing stories are told of the way in which the committees of the Lotos Club watched the wharves for the arrival of distinguished strangers from Europe. The committee which surprised Charles Kingsley on the deck of the steamer was met with the response, "But, gentlemen, I am trying to view the approaches to New York. I cannot make any engagements now."

The club entertained Wilkie Collins in 1873, Gilbert and Sullivan in 1879, Commander Gorringe (who brought the obelisk to Central Park and whose name supplies the long-sought rhyme for 'orange') in 1881, Oliver Wendell

November 1894

Holmes in 1883, Ignace Paderewski and Mark Twain last year, and Dean Hole just three weeks ago.

Under the leadership of Frank R. Lawrence, who is still its president, the Lotos Club moved eighteen months ago from premises down at 21st Street to this handsome new house at 556-558 Fifth Avenue. A skylight makes the new building's art gallery – so important in a club whose members can present works of art in lieu of initiation fees – so much more satisfactory than its predecessor. (Frederic Remington is among the club's members, and its vice-president is Edward Moran, well known for his paintings of Columbus reaching America.)

Major Pond, though a member of this cultural hive, will not be on the programme this evening: more distinguished men than he will be speaking, including Seth Low himself, former mayor of Brooklyn and since 1889 president of Columbia College. (Two years ago he led the college to its new Morningside campus, and the central library there will be a memorial to his father.) At 44, he still has a political career ahead of him, for in 1897 he will run as a Republican for mayor of the new, united New York City, and in 1901 he will finally be elected to that office. Low must arrive somewhat late for this evening's event – an afternoon reception at his own house requires his presence, he explained when he accepted the club's invitation a couple of weeks ago.

A former mayor of New York, Abram S. Hewitt, is another of the speakers. Hewitt, who is 72, made his money in the iron business with the firm of Cooper & Hewitt, and was the first chairman of the board for the Cooper Union. A Democrat but an opponent of Tammany, he has served in Congress as well as in City Hall; he chaired the 1876 campaign which took Rutherford B. Hayes to the White House, and he is now a trustee at Columbia and chairman of the board of the nearby women's institution, Barnard College.

Tonight ACD gets to hear the magnificent brogue of a young congressman, William Bourke Cochran, which is so often used to oppose the economic heresy of free silver, and which in 1920 will thrill a Democratic national convention with a nominating speech for president: "Victory is his habit! I give you – the Happy Warrior, Alfred E. Smith!" He gets to hear the gentler voice of David Christie Murray, retired mathematics professor and former secretary to the board of regents of the State University, whose book on Japan (he spent six years there) has just been published. Journalist William H. McElroy is here from Albany; also speaking tonight are Charles A. Dana, B. S. Weeks, John W. Goff, Edward Patterson, and Chester S. Lord. The *Daily Tribune* lists "others who will occupy seats at the tables":

> E. B. Harper, George H. Wooster, F. A. Burnham, Colonel E. M. L. Ehlers, J. W. Vrooman, Jerome E. Morse, William H. Hume, James F. Pierce, A. T. Goodwin, W. W. Walker, Dr. A. L. Northrop, F. T. Murray, Chandos Fulton, Colonel E. C. James, General Horace Porter, General J. A. Haldeman, of Washington D.C.; Colonel Richard Lathes, H. C. Du Val, George H. Daniels, H. W. Cannon, Edward H. Low, Judge M. J. O'Brien, Randolph Guggenheimer, Edward Moran, Major J. B. Pond, W. T. Evans and Julius Chambers.

Welcome to America, Mr. Sherlock Holmes

Altogether some two hundred members and guests of the club gather to dine on *consommé princesse*, timbale of chicken, tenderloin of beef, and such other delicacies as "bisque Sherlock Holmes" (as it is identified on a menu card decorated with scenes from ACD's writings, a bust of Sherlock Holmes and a portrait of ACD himself). They hear so flattering a speech from president Lawrence, in the chair, that when the visitor stands up to respond he is blushing.

He speaks to the club about his longstanding desire to see America, and his impressions now that he has seen it:

> I contented myself with reading a good deal about them and building up an ideal United States in my own imagination. This is notoriously a dangerous thing to do. I have come to the United States; I have traveled from five to six thousand miles through them, and I find that my ideal picture is not to be whittled down, but to be on every side.
>
> I have heard even Americans say that life is too prosaic over here; that romance is wanting. I do not know what they mean. Romance is the very air they breathe. You are hedged in with romance on every side. I can take a morning train in this city of New York, I can pass up the historic and beautiful Hudson, I can dine at Schenectady, where the Huron and the Canadian did such bloody work; and before evening I have found myself in the Adirondack forests, where the bear and the panther are still to be shot, and where within four generations the Indian and the frontiersman still fought for the mastery. With a rifle and a canoe you can glide into one of the black eddies which have been left by the stream of civilization.
>
> I feel keenly the romance of Europe. I love the memories of the shattered castle and the crumbling abbey; of the steel-clad knight and the archer; but to me the romance of the redskin and the trapper is more vivid, as being more recent. It is so piquant also to stay in a comfortable inn, where you can have your hair dressed by a barber, at the same place where a century ago you might have been left with no hair to dress.
>
> Then there is the romance of this very city. On the first day of my arrival I inquired for the highest building, and I ascended it in an elevator – at least they assured me it was an elevator. I thought at first that I had wandered into the dynamite gun. If a man can look down from that point upon the noble bridge, upon the two rivers crowded with shipping, and upon the magnificent city with its thousand evidences of energy and prosperity, and can afterward find nothing better than a sneer to carry back with him across the ocean, he ought to consult a doctor. His heart must be too hard or his head too soft.
>
> And no less wonderful to me are those Western cities which, without any period of development, seem to spring straight into a full growth of every modern convenience, but where, even among the rush of cable cars and the ringing of telephone bells, one seems still to catch the echoes of the woodsman's axe and of the scout's rifle.
>
> These things are the romance of America, the romance of change, of contrast, of difficulty met and danger overcome, and let me say that we, your kinsmen, upon the other side, exult in your success and in your prosperity, and it is those who know British feeling – true British feeling – best, who will best understand how true are my words.

November 1894

Sunday, November 18: A Cheque for S. S. McClure
ACD continues to grumble about how little money he is taking home from his tour, but his complaints are not altogether true: one of these days in New York he will off-handedly write a cheque for five thousand dollars – more than the price of a respectable house. It will be payable to S. S. McClure, the struggling publisher, providing desperately needed capital for the *Magazine* he is trying to keep afloat. McClure has known of ACD for several years now, having paid sixty dollars apiece for the right to distribute the original dozen Sherlock Holmes stories to American newspapers through his syndicate. They were well received, but he was less fortunate with *The White Company*, for which he had paid $375, and which he had to resell to the *New York Sun*.

Meanwhile, McClure has been operating a fifteen-cent monthly magazine, started in 1892 in the hope of succeeding in America as George Newnes's *Strand* has done (largely because of ACD's Holmes tales) in Britain. The old-fashioned magazines – *Harper's*, the *Century*, *Scribner's*, the *Atlantic* – cost twenty-five cents or even more, and there is a growing readership which they do not serve. McClure has kept expenses down by filling the magazine with stories to which he, because of the syndicate, already has the rights, and using the new cheap photo-engraving process rather than traditional hand-engraving to illustrate them. *McClure's* has been a literary success, but money has always been a problem – it was launched into the panic of 1893, newspapers have been cutting back on their syndicate material, and the magazine has only made it to the fall of 1894 because of suppliers' credit and a few generous investments. On top of everything else, it now has competition, in the form of *Munsey's Magazine* and John Brisben Walker's *Cosmopolitan*, which have undercut the cover price by charging twelve and a half or even ten cents a copy.

At last report McClure is losing a thousand dollars a month, until an event which he will describe in his autobiography:

> One cloudy afternoon, when I was on the train going home from the city, I looked up from the manuscript I was reading, and noticed that the weather had lifted and that the sun was shining. Instantly I felt an unaccountable rise of spirits. The next morning, before hurrying away to catch my train, I told my wife that there was no possible chance for our success unless God helped us. Every human source of help was exhausted, and without help we could not go on. I asked her to pray God to help us. She said that I must pray also; but I told her that she could pray better than I could.
>
> Conan Doyle was at this time lecturing in America. On that day he was staying at the Aldine Club. I had been so weighed down by business cares that I had not seen him since his arrival in the United States, and I had a feeling of having neglected him. Prompted by this feeling, I went that morning directly from the station to the Aldine Club. In apologizing to him for my seeming indifference to his presence in America, I told him that I had been upset by business anxieties, remarking incidentally that I had had to finance the magazine as well as edit it. Conan Doyle then said that he would like to put some money

> into the business himself, if I needed it; that he believed in the magazine and in me. I lunched with him at the club, and after lunch he walked over to the office with me, and wrote out his check for $5000, exactly the sum we were owing to English authors. When that check was written, it put new life into the office staff. Every one in the office felt a new vigor and a new hope.

But ACD is getting something in return, as is clear from his own more modest account:

> I found after our joint expenses were paid that there was about £1,000 over. The disposal of this money furnished a curious example of the power of prayer, which, as Mr. S. S. McClure has already narrated it, I have no delicacy in telling. He tells how he was endeavouring to run his magazine, how he was down to his last farthing, how he dropped on his knees on the office floor to pray for help, and how on the same day an Englishman who was a mere acquaintance walked into the office, and said: "McClure, I believe in you and in the future of your magazine," and put down £1,000 on the table. A critic might perhaps observe that under such circumstances to sell 1,000 shares at face value was rather hard upon the ignorant and trusting buyer. For a long time I could clearly see the workings of Providence as directed towards Sam McClure, but could not quite get their perspective as regards myself, but I am bound to admit that in the long run, after many vicissitudes, the deal was justified both ways, and I was finally able to sell my holding twenty years later at a reasonable advance. The immediate result, however, was that I returned to Davos with all my American earnings locked up, and with no actual visible result of my venture.

When "The Green Flag" appears in the January 1895 issue of *McClure's Magazine*, its author will be a part-owner of the establishment, and he will indirectly be gaining over the next twenty years when readers buy *McClure's* to read "Life on a Greenland Whaler," "The Début of Bimbashi Joyce," and other stories. But that connection will not stop him from selling tales to other magazines as well, including the *Cosmopolitan*.

The financial side of lecturing will continue to preoccupy Doyle when the tour is over. Early in 1895 a remark in *The Author* about the money to be made from lecturing will prompt him to take pen in hand:

> Any one who goes to America with the intention of seeing the place and the people, and counts on no more from his lectures than the payment of his expenses, will have a most enjoyable experience. He will come back with enlarged ideas, with a pleasant remembrance of hospitality received and with new friendships, which he will hope to retain until they are old ones.
> But if he goes with the primary idea of making money he will be disappointed. Thackeray and Dickens made money, and when we have another Thackeray and Dickens they may do the same; but the British lecturer whose credentials are more modest will find that the margin left over, after his expenses are paid, is probably a less sum than he could have easily earned in his own study.
> In the extract to which I refer from your American correspondence, the sum of $500 a lecture is mentioned. This is nonsense. Tak-

ing an average, a fifth part of it would be nearer the mark, which is no more than could be obtained from the better class provincial societies in Great Britain. For argument's sake, however, let us put the American average at $125. When the agent's commisision of 15 per cent. and the high travelling and hotel expenses have been paid, the lecturer will probably have from $80 to $85 clear. Allow him four lectures a week, and we have from $320 to $350 as his gain. Two months of this will leave him something under $3,000. From this he has to subtract his double passage money and about a month extra spent in the journey and preparations. If the balance will exceed what he would earn in the same period by his pen, it is then worth his while to go to America for money.

If any brother author should go, however, I strongly recommend him to put his affairs in the hands of my friend, Major J. B. Pond, in whom they will find a very sympathetic comrade, as well as a keen business manager.

While he will go on to speak of his own trip as "one of the most pleasant experiences of my life," the letter paints a dismal picture of its financing, with ACD no doubt mentally setting the five thousand dollars which he was able to "invest" with McClure against book royalties he was receiving in America, rather than lecture fees.

The American journal *The Critic* will comment on ACD's observations, to the effect that indeed this lecturer was no Dickens or Thackeray: "The characters of Dickens and Thackeray are intimately associated with the greater part of our lives, but with Sherlock Holmes we have little more than a bowing acquaintance." ACD's reply, citing box-office success as evidence of literary value, will come postmarked Maloja, Switzerland, on September 2, 1895:

I notice that you allude to my recent lecturing tour in America as though it had been unsuccessful. In justice to my most able manager, Major J. B. Pond, will you allow me to say that it was successful beyond all possible expectation, that I had crowded houses nearly everywhere, and that I could have easily doubled the list of my engagements. My remarks about American lecturing were impersonal, and I repeat that an English author should go there with the primary idea of seeing the country and the people, and that the making of money should be a secondary one.

Monday, November 19: Return to Boston

How could any literary man dislike Boston? It is not just the "dear old crooked streets of faded brick," as ACD will later call them; it is also the association with the ghosts of Longfellow, Parkman, Emerson, and of course Holmes. There were giants in those days, and a few giants are left even now that Lowell and Whittier are dead. Thomas Bailey Aldrich lives in Boston still, though no longer editor of the *Atlantic Monthly*, and across the Charles River in Cambridge is the home of what remains of the literary Jameses. Alice is dead, Henry is in England, but William is a professor of psychology at Harvard (and busy this year with a promising graduate student named Gertrude Stein). Younger literary folk are coming along as well: a young Harvard man named George Santayana recently published his first poems.

ACD returns to this enchanted and very English city for two lectures under Pond's direct sponsorship – no local agents here to dilute the profits. Pond's own name is on the advertisements urging the purchase of tickets (reserved seats one dollar) at Connelly's Ticket Office in the Adams House. There is plenty of competition – Ada Gray in *East Lynne* at the Grand Opera House, Boston's first look at *Arms and the Man* by the young Bernard Shaw, and "Prince, the Wrestling Lion" in company with "A Host of Handsome Women," all for just twenty-five cents at the Howard – but a good many cultured folk have responded, and tonight the Association Hall, at the corner of Berkeley and Boylston Streets, is nearly filled for ACD's eight o'clock reading.

As he did last week in New York, he provides a new programme for the benefit of people who heard him on his previous visit. Naturally he includes some of Sherlock Holmes's deductions (including the famous scene from "A Scandal in Bohemia" in which he makes the King of Bohemia look a fool) – but he also reads his sketch of Judge Jeffreys from *Micah Clarke*, a passage from *The Refugees* in which the King of France reads his mail and courtiers offer their opinions, and some of his Waterloo story, "A Straggler of '15."

In today's newspapers, advertisements for ACD's lectures share space with the appointment of O. V. Sage as warden of Sing Sing Prison (an institution which ACD will inspect in 1914), a review of Brander Matthews's new book *Vignettes of Manhattan*, and the news that Boston police raided two seances last night; such fraudulent activities are illegal, and three people have been charged.

"A Boston audience," ACD will write years later, "is very like an Edinburgh one, reserved, dignified, silent, and yet splendidly responsive in a very subtle way, if only by the total absence of movement or sound."

Tuesday, November 20: Reading from "The Cardboard Box"

The great pianist Anton Rubinstein is dying; that will be in tomorrow's newspapers. Today's are full of a matter more in ACD's line, the latest sensational developments in a scandal which has kept Bostonians fascinated for days. "Romance and Crime" is the headline; the news is that the swindler who is charged with defrauding the Fidelity Mutual Life Insurance Company, and who has been giving his name as Holmes – H. H. Holmes – is in reality Herman Mudgett, of Tilton, New Hampshire. (Today also in Boston, a copy of the *Souldier's Pocket Bible*, produced in 1643 for Oliver Cromwell's pious troops, is selling at auction for one thousand dollars. Further afield, in Washington, D.C., President Grover Cleveland is spraining his ankle.)

At 2 p.m. ACD gives his last Boston reading, again in Association Hall. He does not read precisely what the *Boston Evening Transcript* and the *Globe* said he would read (but then, he departed from the announced programme last night as well). Today he reads just three pieces, and two are from the character he claims to be trying to leave behind him, Sherlock Holmes. He reads an excerpt from "The Blue Carbuncle," the famous hat episode in which Holmes amazes Watson by deducing so much from an elderly felt hat. And he reads an excerpt from "The Cardboard Box."

November 1894

That latter is a surprising choice, for "The Cardboard Box" is the story that was suppressed earlier this year. It appeared in the first Harper edition of *The Memoirs of Sherlock Holmes*, but if you go into a bookstore this week and buy *The Memoirs* you will get only eleven stories; that grisly tale of love and amputation has itself been amputated. What is its embarrassed author doing reading from it, here in this very proper city of Boston? The explanation is that the passage he has chosen – later to be known as the "thought-reading episode," for in it Holmes does seem to follow Watson's thoughts from the expressions of his face – is, on the face of it, innocent enough, and certainly it is unconnected with the story which it precedes. So independent is it that some years hence ACD will borrow it for re-use in a new Sherlock Holmes tale, "The Resident Patient," creating a challenge for future bibliographers. Certainly the Boston audience shows no criticism of the passage which is read. The mention of Henry Ward Beecher, the great (if flawed) Brooklyn clergyman, may even draw appreciative nods.

The third reading is the long-promised tale of "The Medal of the Brigadier." ACD reads it from proof-sheets, since it is not yet in print, and the Association Hall audience become the first people in America, except perhaps for a few editors, to learn just how that medal came to be worn on the proud Gerard's breast. A reporter from the *Boston Post* is present and gets down the essentials of the plot, though his three-paragraph summary of it in tomorrow's paper will hardly reflect the story's irony.

Wednesday, November 21: Interview in Rochester
On Voltaire's two-hundredth birthday, the sun shines on ACD as he steps out of the Rochester depot into a noontime street – "but never a ray was brighter or more genial than [the] smile that hovers continually upon his face," notes a *Union and Advertiser* reporter who calls on him in his room at the Powers Hotel, at Main and Fitzhugh Streets.

"Well, I suppose you have come to find out whether I am going to bring Sherlock Holmes back to life," says ACD as he opens the door of his room. He has learned from tedious experience what it is that reporters most want to ask. He gives the usual answer: no.

> I have been reported as saying in nearly every city I have visited that I would write more of the Sherlock Holmes stories. This statement I wish to absolutely deny. I had to kill the omnipresent Sherlock in sheer self-defence. The strain was something I could not endure any longer. Of course had I continued I could have coined money, for the stories were the most remunerative I have written; but as regards literature, they would have been mere trash.

The *Union and Advertiser* man asks the next most popular question: "What do you consider your best work, Doctor?" And then this new one, with its thoughtful answer:

> "In one of your stories in 'Round the Red Lamp,' Doctor," said the reporter, "you say through the medium of Surgeon Walker that a doctor generally dies with the disease that he is especially interested in and has investigated thoroughly. Were you quite in earnest when you made that statement?"

> "I am glad you asked that question," rejoined Mr. Doyle. "The story you mention, though it has been called horrible and other startling names by the critics, is the result of a large number of years of medical practice. I am thoroughly of the opinion that imagination as regards the existence of a disease can affect a doctor as well as the most susceptible of his patients. The story in question relates the life of Surgeon Walker, one of the greatest specialists in nervous diseases in the United Kingdom. He addresses the students in the clinic on a horrible form of nervous disease and concludes his lecture by saying that the only method to determine the evidence of the disease is to close the eyes and endeavor to bring the heels together. Surgeon Walker suits the action to the word, but finds it impossible, and the terrible truth is flashed to his mind that he is afflicted with the very disease he is explaining and which is a lingering one and in the way of exquisite torture could discount seven times any form of torture germinating in the agile brain of the Apache or Sioux Indians. The story is dramatic in the way of climax, for such a position could not be otherwise than horrible. The critics have said that I was stretching my imagination too far and all that, but the story is founded on something more substantial than mere fancy. It has been the result of my observation that a great per cent. of physicians and surgeons die of the very disease which they have so sedulously studied and investigated. I am glad that you asked that question, as I wanted the statement emphasized."

The term "conversion neurosis" has not yet been coined for the phenomenon which ACD is describing, but physicians are well aware of its existence. When he does contradict his promise and bring Sherlock Holmes back to life – "trash" or not – he will use conversion neurosis as the device on which the plot of one of his stories ("The Blanched Soldier") turns. In other writings – such as *The Parasite*, just now being published – ACD also shows a keen interest in "nervous," which is to say psychological, illness.

Rochester, on Lake Ontario, is a thriving commercial city, with garment factories, a lead works, and other businesses of every sort. The Powers Hotel is on a scale to correspond, as a book prepared by local boosters this year makes clear:

> There is an entrance from each street, leading into the rotunda, 60 x 80 feet in size, where the large main stairway is shown, constructed of marble and iron, and eight feet in width. All stairways are built of the same materials, while the ground floor is laid with solid marble, and in the center of the building is a court, 50 x 60 feet, extending to the roof. There are elegant and cosy reading and writing rooms opening out of the office, together with a barber shop and Turkish bathrooms, a finely-stocked bar, a billiard room with six tables, and a solid marble lavatory in the basement. On the second floor are five public parlors, luxuriously furnished; three dining-rooms, one seating 300 and another 100 guests; together with the kitchen, bakery, pastry and carving rooms, pantry, etc.; while the five upper floors contain 231 rooms for guests, each floor having six suites of parlor, bedroom and bath, all furnished regardless of cost, and second to none in the country. The house is thoroughly attractive throughout, richly furnished, artistically decorated, and fitted with all modern improvements, including two ele-

November 1894

vators, an electric light plant, electric bells, steam-heat, and everything in any way conducive to the welfare and comfort of guests. The house is conducted on the American plan, with rates at $4.00 and upward per day.

Rochester is also the city where the Genesee River tumbles over a spectacular waterfall in its rush towards the lake, and the story is still often told of Sam Patch's leap to death over these falls in 1829. Patch, who had performed the feat before and lived to boast about it, was obviously drunk when he tried this last jump, and he was made an object lesson in an 1830 temperance campaign and evangelical revival. But by now Sam Patch is something of a legend, and the best view of the spot where he died is obtained from a comfortable table at a German bierhaus. If ACD has time, he can have a look at the water and perhaps imagine Professor Moriarty and Sherlock Holmes grappling on its brink. What he surely cannot imagine is that he will one day label Rochester "most honoured of all towns" on the grounds that here Spiritualism had its beginning.

His lecture this evening is in the YMCA Music Hall at the corner of Court Street and South St. Paul Street, overlooking that same river. The auditorium in this five-year-old landmark is a large one, and the crowd is far from filling it; the *Herald* tomorrow will dismiss it as "meagre," though giving ample space to ACD's remarks.

After the lecture there is a reception in his honour at the Genesee Valley Club, a solid three-story building at Gibbs Street and East Avenue, where men may dine in style (but may not smoke in the dining room before 7:30 p.m.) and where history is being made with the plan to build a "women's café": few gentlemen's clubs allow the presence of ladies anywhere in the building.

Thursday, November 22: The Female College at Elmira

From Rochester a direct railway line runs south to Elmira, which Baedeker summarizes thus:

> **Elmira** (855 ft.; *Rathbun*, 2 1/2 – 3; *Frasier, Delevan*, $2 1/2; *Elmira Water-Cure*), an industrial town with 30,893 inhab., contains large rolling mills, the car-shops of the Erie Railroad, a Female College, and an Academy of Science. The *Elmira Reformatory* has played an important part in the reformatory treatment of criminals.

The reformatory, a pioneer "social prison," would doubtless be of interest to Sherlock Holmes, or even to an Arthur Conan Doyle of later years, when he has become a public figure and an advocate of penal reform. And Elmira is the home – one of the homes – of an important American author, Mark Twain, who is in Europe throughout ACD's weeks in America.

Instead, it is the "Female College" which brings the traveller to Elmira today. This unusual institution, founded in 1855, is notable as the first women's college to have requirements as rigorous as those of the men's colleges – Colgate, Cornell, Amherst – to which it compares itself. The women who graduate from Elmira College typically become teachers, missionaries, doctors and social workers, and as if that were not startling enough, the college has since the 1860's encouraged its students to travel, and offered them credit for spending a junior year abroad.

ACD lectures this evening in the chapel on the first floor of the college's spectacular building, a five-storey octagon with east and west wings. The pipe-organ rises behind him as he speaks; his audience sits on wooden pews, and when those are filled a large number of chairs are brought in. The audience is not just predominantly female – he had that experience at his New York matinees – but made up largely of young ladies who, however intellectual, are still inclined to rustle at the appearance of a man.

ACD's sponsor here is Kappa Sigma, one of the two student literary societies ("*Per Asperas ad Astras*" is its noble, if not entirely grammatical, motto), and the young ladies are determined to make it an elegant and cultural evening. Before the speaker is introduced, therefore, there is to be music, provided by Josephine Millham, who was a freshman two years ago but did not come back from Rochester for her sophomore year. She is here on a visit, though, and has been prevailed on to use her contralto voice in Meyer-Helmund's "Gondola Love Song" and then, the applause being considerable, in Neidlinger's "Serenade." She is accompanied on the piano by Lena Broughton, professor of piano and harmony at the college.

It falls to Mary Wilson McNair to introduce the guest speaker, for she is president of Kappa Sigma and a very important person at this college. Like so many Elmira graduates, McNair will go on to a professional career. She will spend most of her life working at the Library of Congress, becoming a noted authority on subject headings and the cataloguing of periodicals, and, never married, she will live until 1972.

ACD is "warmly received" by the Elmira College students, as the *Daily Advertiser* will say in its report, for at 35 he is "comparatively a young man of fine physique and a very entertaining speaker." When he reads from "Chateau Noir" the audience is, as the same paper puts it, "thrilled with the rendering of his masterly climaxes."

ACD chooses the first hotel Baedeker mentioned, the Rathbun House, and on its letterhead (H. C. Hayt, Proprietor) he writes a note to Goldwin Smith, a professor and author on economic matters, in Toronto. Smith has offered his hospitality when ACD gets to Toronto next week, but he must decline: he has already accepted the offer of an old acquaintance there, Dr. Latimer Pickering.

Friday, November 23: Pilgrimage to Glens Falls

ACD's itinerary, based on the speaking engagements Pond could arrange, is far from efficient. Tuesday he took the overnight train the full width of Massachusetts and most of the breadth of New York, to get from Boston to Rochester; Thursday he travelled south to Elmira; today he finds himself in the far northeast of the state, at Glens Falls; tomorrow he will head south to Schenectady, and then west (past Rochester once more) to Toronto; by this time next week he will be in the east again, in Vermont. Crack trains travel at high speeds and offer more luxuries than the middle-class traveller's own home, but still this sort of thing becomes a grind after weeks of it.

November 1894

Today's stop, however, is something of a pleasure, for ACD is back on the fringes of Parkman Land, in the little industrial city of Glens Falls, where the infant Hudson River tumbles down a picturesque waterfall fifty feet high. The power from the fall has helped turn Glens Falls into a thriving industrial town, but of much greater interest to ACD is the island at the base of the falls where time and water have carved out a lacing of caves. Cooper's Cave, it is called, for in this very cave, peering out fearfully at the rushing river and the suspiciously rustling trees around it, huddled a party of besieged pioneers, fearful of Indian knives, in the most dramatic scene of James Fenimore Cooper's *The Last of the Mohicans*. ACD knows the book well (in fact he alludes to it in the lecture he has been giving over and over) and here first-hand he can see the landscape which put that scene into Cooper's mind seventy years ago.

Before there is time for sightseeing, however, ACD must do his duty and give his lecture this evening in the Glens Falls Opera House, on the south side of Warren Street, near Glen Street, an 1884 replacement for an earlier 1,600-seat house which burned. "Opera House Block," say the square solid letters above the centre third-floor windows. There is a restaurant at street level, and Loyal L. Davis has his law office on the second floor, as letters painted on his window attest; but in the upper levels, behind that elaborate façade and beneath those three cupolas, is the auditorium itself.

Every available seat is filled for this first of the Union School Course of entertainments, a series which has been brought to Glens Falls – against some scepticism – by the city's superintendent of schools, Sherman L. Williams, who introduces ACD's talk this evening. Perhaps it is because he wisely described the series as "entertainment," rather than "education," that he can be gratified both at the size of the crowd (astonishing, for so small a city) and at its reaction:

> The close attention with which the audience listened and the unflagging interest displayed throughout the entire lecture testified most plainly to the excellence of the entertainment, and probably many of the audience left last night with a resolve to enter immediately into more intimate acquaintance with the delightful company of heroes and heroines to whom their creator had introduced them.

The next speaker in the series is to be William H. McElroy, "second only to Chauncey M. Depew in his happy style of delivery as an after-dinner speaker," whose topic on December 3 will be "Public Men at Public Dinners." Although it is not impossible that his address will include a mention of the Lotos Club dinner for ACD at which he spoke just a few days ago, he does already have a text: he delivered it July 30 at the Chautauqua Institution, with anecdotes about figures from Oliver Wendell Holmes to John Greenleaf Whittier.

Saturday, November 24: Lecture in Schenectady

ACD's companion as he visits the falls and the hallowed cave this morning is Sherman Williams, who brought him to Glens Falls and introduced him on the platform last night. Williams, at 48, wears a modest beard and moustache, in contrast to the receding hairline and walrus moustache which he and ACD will share in another twenty years. Earlier this year he earned the right to put the rare abbreviation "Pd.D." after his name – Doctor of Pedagogy, from the normal college down at Albany. He has been a teacher since the age of eighteen and an education administrator since 1872, first in the New York suburb of Flushing and since 1882 here in Glens Falls. The first of several anthologies and textbooks which he will edit and write was published in 1890. In 1899 Williams will become conductor of the State Teachers Institutes, emphasizing "reading and the creating of a taste for good reading, arithmetic and the development of the habit of accuracy; English and the ability to speak briefly, logically and forcibly; history and how it should be taught and for what purpose; and school management." He will cap his career with appointment as head of the state division of school libraries.

Having climbed down the staircase to that island in the Hudson and seen the place where those childhood tales were set, ACD hurries off to catch the 11:52 train to Schenectady. That city too figures in the stories of frontier settlement and Indian massacre on which ACD and most other English-speaking boys grew up, as William Dean Howells recalls in *Their Wedding Journey*, in which his honeymooning character's bride

> had never even heard of the massacres by the French and Indians at Schenectady, which he in his boyhood had known so vividly that he was scalped every night in his dreams, and woke up in the morning expecting to see marks of the tomahawk on the head-board.

This city on the Mohawk River has more important distinctions nowadays, such as Union College and the new (but rapidly growing) General Electric works – although the conservative Baedeker, not quite aware of the rate at which America and the world are becoming electrified, mentions only "various manufactories." ACD has been in the local newspaper, the *Daily Union*, several times in the past week, what with a report of his Lotos Club dinner on Monday and then on Wednesday a front-page piece, borrowed from Eugene Field's comic note in the *Chicago Record*, about "Canon Doyle." Oddly enough, that piece did not make any mention of ACD's forthcoming appearance here, but yesterday's "Local Notes" announced it, and today there is a two-paragraph announcement, on the same page as a much longer report of Lillie Langtry's arrival in nearby Troy. (She will be here on Tuesday.)

Sponsoring the lecture here are the managers of the free library association (A. L. Roherer is the local manager, Pond notes in his register). The lecture is given in the First Reformed Church, and is preceded by an organ recital given by "Mr. D. Maznenet, a new comer here with the Edison plant," as Monday's newspaper will say.

November 1894

ACD is introduced by Andrew Van Vranken Raymond, the 40-year-old Presbyterian clergyman who became president of Union College earlier this year. Union is approaching its centenary, and has fallen on hard times in recent years, what with scandals, the unhealed wounds inflicted by the Civil War, and the unsteady leadership of a president who took its helm in 1804 and did not relinquish it until 1866. Raymond has been hired to revive it, and is about to take such bold steps as appointing Charles Steinmetz, the genius of General Electric, to head the electrical engineering department. There have even been proposals to move the college to a nearby rival city, Albany, but they will come to nothing. If Raymond has time to chat with ACD, he may mention his plans for improvements to the all-male college – or perhaps ACD will prefer to hear about the maiden, burned at the stake in 1672, who haunts the garden north of the famous sixteen-sided Nott Memorial building.

Sunday, November 25: Tourist at Niagara Falls
Sunday is not exactly a day of rest, although there is no lecture; ACD has to travel the full width of New York state, from Schenectady to the Canadian border, coming most of the way on the same New York Central track on which he travelled to Chicago last month. In Buffalo he gets a connection for Niagara Falls, and late at night he arrives at the Prospect House. The proprietor is Colonel David Isaacs, who originally operated a Prospect House in the village on the Canadian side of the river, when it was still called Clifton; he moved his business to the United States when he lost his Canadian site to park construction in 1887. The building on this side of the river, at Jefferson and Second Streets, is three storeys high, made of brick painted white, and handsomely finished with marble and mahogany (it is said that the mantelpieces in the office and the reception room cost six hundred dollars apiece). A cupola atop the building gives a fine view of the falls – even, on a clear day, of Brock's Monument over at Queenston.

Isaacs loves celebrities; first thing tomorrow he will get ACD to sign his maroon-and-gold autograph book, on the same page signed by Dean Hole just last week. (The book also contains the signatures of Ellen Terry in 1884 and "George" – the young prince who will one day be King George V – in 1883, and Lew Wallace will put his name there in January 1895.)

It is the off-season in Niagara Falls, a tourist town where diversification will begin in a couple of years when the new-fangled hydro-electric power becomes practical. Some of the hotels are closed for the winter, but Isaacs finds it worthwhile to keep his house open year-round. (It is the most expensive hotel in town: some rooms cost as much as $5.50 a night.) Still, there are always some tourists in Niagara Falls, and they find the place less of a trap than it used to be:

> The former extortionate charges and impertinent demeanour of the Niagara hackmen have been greatly abated. The rates are $1 $1/2$ for the first and $1 for each addit. hr., with two horses $2 and $1 $1/2$; but it is always advisable to make a distinct bargain with the driver, and lower terms than the legal rates may often be obtained, especially by a

party. It should be expressly stipulated who is to pay the tolls in crossing the bridges, etc.; and the driver should be strictly enjoined not to stop at any of the bazaars or other pay-places unless ordered to do so. . . .

Since the establishment of the American and Canadian National Parks and Reservations, most of the former extortionate fees have been abolished; and any visitor who is able to walk a few miles can see all the chief points at very little cost. Goat Island and all the best views of the Falls are free; and the only extra expenses which the visitor is advised to incur are the trip in the *Maid of the Mist*, including the visit to the Canadian side (50c.), the *Cave of the Winds* ($1), and the view of the *Grand Rapids* from the Canadian side (50c.). . . .

While the hackman nuisance has been abated, the bazaar nuisance continues in full force; and it is so serious an annoyance that many travellers hurry through their visit and leave Niagara much sooner than they intended. It is impossible to walk through the streets or look into the shop-windows without being annoyed by the most impudent and persistent solicitations. A stony disregard of all such importunity is imperatively necessary, especially in the bazaars through which one approaches the inclined railways. . . .

The American side is seen to greatest advantage in the morning, the Canadian side in the afternoon, the sun being then at our backs as we face the Falls.

If there is one thing more common in Niagara Falls than Indian trinkets, it is guidebooks, ranging from good to awful. Much better than the average is one published in Buffalo last year and titled *The Niagara Book: A Complete Souvenir of Niagara Falls*, and containing "sketches, satires and essays – descriptive, humorous, historical and scientific," including one by Mark Twain and another by William Dean Howells, speaking of the "terrific beauty" and "pristine awe" of the falls themselves.

The tourist here must see the Canadian and American falls, but there are other sights as well: various rapids, the Cave of the Winds, Terrapin Rock, Table Rock, the Whirlpool, and the new tunnel, being driven through solid rock below the village in connection with the planned use of the water's force to generate electric power. ACD will be less articulate than Howells after he sees the falls tomorrow morning; asked what impressed him most about the natural wonder, he will reply, "Its immensity."

Years later, he will visit Niagara Falls again, accompanied by his second wife, and he will remark to Lady Doyle that here, not at Switzerland's Reichenbach, he should have made Sherlock Holmes plunge to his death. One witness will even claim that he carves Holmes's initials on the rock of Goat Island.

Monday, November 26: An Old Friend in Toronto

"Much as I love America, it always gives one a thrill to be under the Union Jack once more with one's feet on British soil," ACD will write one day about an arrival in Canada – and that will be in 1923, when the curious being called Canada is thirty years older than it is now and has gone through the nation-building experience of the World War. So much more

November 1894

he must thrill today as he leaves the United States for a few hours on his way to Toronto.

He and Innes have spent much of the day "driving," the *Niagara Falls Gazette* reports – that is, they have been dashing from one scenic spot to another. Representatives of both the *Gazette* and the *Daily Cataract Journal* call on ACD at the Prospect House; the former interrupts ACD's reading of the morning paper and gets him to observe that he "thought America was a big place," and the latter gets his autograph at the end of a half-hour conversation.

Three bridges at Niagara Falls connect the United States of America with the British Empire: the New Suspension Bridge, so called to distinguish it from the one blown down in a dreadful storm in the winter of 1889, on which pedestrians and carriages cross; the Cantilever Bridge of the Michigan Central Railroad, one of the first cantilever steel bridges, having been built in 1883; and the older Railway Suspension Bridge. Over this third bridge travels ACD's Grand Trunk train, giving him a fine view of the Whirlpool, though the view of the falls themselves is obstructed by the newer Cantilever Bridge a hundred yards above it.

It is not a long journey from Niagara Falls to Toronto, through the rich farmland of the Niagara peninsula and around the shore of Lake Ontario, but it gives ACD a little time to enjoy that thrill of being in the Empire once again. The comment which he will write after a future visit to Toronto, thirty years hence, might be equally true in 1894:

> The insensate hostility which many American newspapers have shown to the British Empire has deeply alienated them from their neighbours, and they are almost fierce in their loyalty. Nowhere else in all my travels have I had "God save the King!" sung as the termination of my lecture.

He will never really understand Canada as anything but a greater Britain spread out on a limitless continent. And most of the people of Canada probably share that idea of their country, if it really is a country. It issues its own postage stamps and it uses dollars, not pounds, but its interests are represented (or more often neglected and abandoned) around the world by British diplomats, its lawsuits are appealed to a high court in London, and the nominal head of its government is a Britisher, Lord Aberdeen, who with Lady Aberdeen is today arriving home in Montréal from a trip across Canada. The internal affairs of Canada are in the hands of a Parliament and a prime minister, the latter position having been held for nineteen years (out of the twenty-seven since Canada's "Confederation") by Sir John A. Macdonald, who bullied a few diverse colonies into a confederation in the first place. He won the most recent election, in March 1891, on the tenacious slogan "The Old Man, the Old Flag, the Old Policy." The old man died a few months later (Sir John Thompson is prime minister now), the Old Flag was the Union Jack with which public buildings in Canada are decorated, and the Old Policy was Macdonald's three-plank platform of heavy immigration to build up home markets, construction of railways to bind the country together, and protective tariffs to keep out Yankee goods.

Welcome to America, Mr. Sherlock Holmes

Toronto is the second-largest city in Canada, and a very sober city it is, known as "Toronto the Good" for its innumerable churches, its strict Sunday-closing laws (it is not even considered decent for streetcars to run on the Sabbath) and its general primness. The murder of Frank Westwood last month came as a naughty delight to the readers of Toronto's many newspapers, ranging from the conservative *Empire* to the racy *World*, which even uses illustrations on its front page. It was the *World* which wrote to ACD shortly after the murder, imploring his opinion of it; naturally, then, it is a *World* reporter who corners him as soon as he reaches the city, and asks his views on the case now that Clara Ford, the mulatto tailoress with the scarlet past, has confessed – and recanted her confession.

> It is a strangely absorbing mystery [ACD tells the reporter], and I discussed it at length with my brother after reading it. However, without a knowledge of local conditions I couldn't attempt to set up an opinion against those of your police officers. I can quite understand how, in the first instance, the public may have thought that the family knew something more of the affair than they stated, but I concluded that the father's story was so unusual that it must be true. As to the present prisoner, Clara Ford, I cannot offer an opinion; I never met with such a case as hers. The system of closeting a prisoner with an officer and cross-questioning her for hours, savors more of French than English methods of justice.

It could be Sherlock Holmes speaking.

The reporter turns to other subjects, and ACD speaks, just as he has done in every American city, about his own writings, and especially the one thing everyone wants to know: "I can say positively that Sherlock Holmes, whose end is shrouded in mystery, will never be revived."

Getting to Toronto at about 5:30 p.m., ACD has gone to 281 Sherbourne Street, the residence of Dr. Latimer Pickering and his wife, also a physician, Dr. Annie L. Pickering. The wife is a Canadian, a medical graduate of Toronto's Trinity College; but the husband is a Birmingham-born Englishman, and an old acquaintance of ACD's. The two of them studied medicine in Edinburgh at the same time, though ACD was at the university, receiving his M.B. degree in 1882, whereas Pickering studied in the hospitals, was examined by the Royal College of Surgeons of Edinburgh, and in January 1880 received its licentiate – LRCS(E) – followed by its licentiate in midwifery. In 1883 Pickering came to Toronto, and in 1889 he was appointed an associate coroner for the city of Toronto, one of several doctors with that additional distinction and source of occasional fees.

Although they studied under different authorities, Pickering and ACD can recall some of the same great Edinburgh medical figures of fifteen years ago: the hawk-eyed and kindly Joe Bell, the bombastic William Rutherford, and even Florence Nightingale, who was often at the Royal Infirmary. Both should have memories of the *cause célèbre* in 1879 when Sophia Jex-Blake, refused the chance to get a medical degree at Edinburgh, arrived back in the city with an M.D. from Berne and a licence from the King's and Queen's College of Physicians in Ireland. Annie Pickering, as one of the early women

November 1894

to study medicine in Canada, must have a special interest in hearing about that affair; and ACD probably based his story "The Doctors of Hoyland" on what he knew of the Pickerings, as well as on his impressions of Dr. Jex-Blake and the few other women who had tried to take the same path.

ACD's lecture in Toronto is at the new Massey Music Hall, on Shuter Street, one of a series of talks which are to be given there under the management of J. E. Suckling. Tickets at fifty or seventy-five cents have been bought by some fifteen hundred listeners; the *Mail* tomorrow will call that "a very large audience," though it is less than half the immense hall's capacity. He is introduced by Goldwin Smith, the professor and writer whose hospitality he was obliged to turn down in that letter from Elmira the other day. Had he accepted it, he would be staying tonight in the most magnificent house in Toronto, for twenty years ago Smith married a rich widow and since then he has made "The Grange, Toronto" his address.

Smith, now 71, has gone a great intellectual distance in his lifetime. Eton-educated, he became a don at Oxford in 1846; after twenty years beside the Isis he came to America and spent a couple of years at Cornell, a land-grant college with pretensions; and then he came to the University of Toronto. In his first years in Toronto he was an enthusiast of the Canada First movement, but he has gradually changed his opinions and is now an advocate of political and economic union between Canada and the United States.

This "continentalist" position is unpopular in Canada, though ACD would doubtless approve, for he will write this in 1923:

> I am assured with that assurance which has never yet deceived me that the time will come, and that soon, when there will be no frontier there. This will come about not through an annexation of Canada, but through a closing-up by common consent of the English-speaking States and their dependencies under some such general title as the United States of Africa, America, Australia, Canada, England, Ireland, New Zealand, Scotland and Wales.

Even now, in 1894, he is constantly saying that the United States has become "the centre of gravity of the race," and he put into Sherlock Holmes's mouth that astonishing proposal for "the quartering of the Union Jack with the Stars and Stripes."

Neither Smith nor ACD will live to see the formal alliances among Britain, the United States, and Canada during and after the Second World War. In 1894 even a reduction in the protective tariffs which Canada and America have thrown up against each other would seem a great step forward. But the ideal ACD is advocating is not unique to him; "Imperial Federation" is a lively issue, and in July George B. Adams of Yale University spoke on it at the Chautauqua Assembly, prophesying that "The idea of leadership of the United States among nations will come to be universal."

Making his introduction, Smith tells the audience that the characters which ACD has created have been the delightful companions of most of those present as they sat by their firesides during the long winter evenings – in Toronto there are, to be sure, a good many long winter evenings. He says it must therefore give them a decided satisfaction to welcome in person someone who has given them so much enjoyment through his books. To these gratifying words he adds a comment which ACD may wish he had omitted: his hope, on behalf of thousands of readers, that Sherlock Holmes may enjoy a speedy resurrection, for they all deplore his death. ACD gives his usual "Readings and Reminiscences," and receives a standing ovation for it.

After the lecture ACD returns to Sherbourne Street, where a *Globe* reporter gets a few minutes with him before dinner. ACD is, not surprisingly, "very fatigued with his long journey," for Niagara Falls has not given him much of a rest – but, as always, he answers questions about his life, his work and his impressions of America "good-naturedly . . . he expressed himself as delighted with the October weather and the autumn tints of the country." He is asked about the Canon Doyle story, and inevitably about the Westwood murder, and he mentions one reason for his special affection for Toronto:

> "The first friendly notice I had was from a Toronto paper," he said, as the interview concluded; "it was in either The Globe or The Mail. 'Micah Clarke' had recently come out, and it had several kind notices in England, but there was a warmth and friendliness in the article in the Toronto paper that pleased me very much. I have it at home, but the top has now been cut off so that I do not know which paper it was. Yes, I was much pleased. . . ."

(Someone at *The Week* will read that paragraph and hurry into print with the claim that it was that journal's review which ACD must be remembering. Another paper will credit J. S. Willson of the *Globe*.)

Smith is a guest at the Pickering home for dinner, and so are two Toronto doctors, one of whom will enjoy those Edinburgh recollections. He is Dr. George Sterling Ryerson, who graduated from Toronto's medical school before going off to Edinburgh for licentiates in 1876 and 1877 (while ACD was at the university) and then specializing in ophthalmology and otology in London (ACD took specialist studies in ophthalmology in Vienna). He is a nephew of preacher and educator Egerton Ryerson, served as an army surgeon in the North West Rebellion, helped to found the Toronto Clinical Society – of which he is this year's president – and has been elected to a term as Member of the Legislative Assembly, Ontario's parliament. He will write a couple of books, as ACD will, about the South African War, and he will end his career holding the military rank of Surgeon-General.

The other is Dr. Arthur J. Johnson, a few years older than the rest of the company. Also Toronto-educated and with later training in London, though not in Scotland, he specializes in anatomy, along with the kindred fields of pathology and microscopy; he is an associate coroner, like Pickering, and he is noted for an article on cancer of the stomach in the *Canada Lancet* fifteen years ago. In 1911 he will write a book which might interest Sherlock Holmes: *Inquests and Investigations: A Practical Guide for the Use of Anyone Holding Inquests in Ontario*.

November 1894

Tuesday, November 27: Lecture in Buffalo

Reminiscences no doubt continue at breakfast, and there is time for ACD to have a quick look at Toronto – time, too, when a neighbour of the Pickerings asks for his autograph, for him to write neatly on the letterhead of 307 Sherbourne Street: "For Miss Evelyn Cameron. Yours very truly, A. Conan Doyle. Toronto. Nov 27/94."

In the afternoon he retraces the journey he made yesterday, returning to the United States and arriving in Buffalo at 6:30 p.m. He could, if he had arrived sooner, have renewed his acquaintance with John L. Sullivan, the boxer, who is performing in "A True American" at the Lyceum Theatre here. (There was a matinee today.) At the Star Theatre, where in a little less than five years William Gillette will begin his life-long role of Sherlock Holmes, this week's attraction is Sadie Martinot, "America's favorite comedienne," in *The Passport*.

But as things are, ACD has just time to get to the Women's Union Hall, in Niagara Square, and prepare to give his lecture. This brand-new building, first opened to the public on October 29, is the property of the Women's Educational and Industrial Union of Buffalo, whose founder (in 1884) and still president is Mrs. George W. Townsend. Tickets for the lecture have been on sale for the past week at Peter Paul Book Co., 420 Main Street, who specialize in "School Books for the Night Schools," according to their advertisements.

ACD is introduced by Rowland H. Mahany, who at the age of 30 has just been elected to represent the Thirty-Second District in Congress. Briefly a journalist, he first ran for the House in 1892, but the electors chose a Democrat instead; he has spent the past two years as a diplomat in Latin America and claims some of the credit for the Santos Treaty last year. Now, he uses the title "Hon." with his name, and has learned to speak with a brevity and point rare in a public figure:

> Ladies and Gentlemen – It is my privilege this evening to announce as your lecturer a man who needs no introduction to a cultivated audience anywhere in the world.
>
> A profound student of human nature, a keen analyst of social conditions past and present, he has given us the benefit of his researches, his conceptions and his originality in a series of admirable and splendid books. I take great pleasure in introducing to you the author of "Micah Clark [sic]," Dr. A. Conan Doyle.

"Readings and Reminiscences" is well received, but hardly lucrative: ACD and the sponsors each net eighty-one dollars. When the talk is over, the speaker hurries back to the station to catch the 11 p.m. eastbound train. A holiday is before him at last.

Wednesday, November 28: Mark Twain's New Book

The original plan had been for ACD to head west from Buffalo, not east, and to lecture tonight in Cleveland. "Hold until Thurs.," Pond wrote in his register. But in the end there is no engagement in Cleveland, and ACD is free to make the long trip to Brattleboro, Vermont, where Rudyard and

Caroline Kipling are waiting to be his hosts for Thanksgiving. They invited him a month ago, and at first he was "stuffy," Caroline Kipling wrote in her journal, and declined. A few days later he wrote again to apologize and to accept, and late today ACD and Innes arrive at "Naulakha" for the holiday.

Today is a day of some significance for American literature, for it is the official publication day of Mark Twain's new book, *Pudd'nhead Wilson*. It is no surprise to readers, having been serialized last winter and spring in the *Century* Magazine – and reviewed (as "the work of a novelist, rather than of a 'funny man'") in the October issue of the *Idler*, adjacent to the first installment of ACD's "Stark Munro Letters." But now it is official, and commentators can start arguing about whether it is a heartless picture of a heartless time, or a satirical work in which reason is made superior to prejudice.

Though it is among other things a parody of detective stories, *Pudd'nhead Wilson* is also clearly its author's homage to ACD and his Sherlock Holmes, who will appear even more clearly in some of Twain's later work. Equally clear is this book's influence on ACD, though he may not be reading it today as his train races across New York, Massachusetts and Vermont. He will have read it by the time he writes "The Norwood Builder" in 1903. Wilson's triumph in the climactic trial scene of Twain's book depends on fingerprint evidence (regarded even in 1903 as the work of eccentrics), over which Holmes and Lestrade will clash. And the bloody fingerprints on Wilson's dagger are as unexpectedly decisive as the bloody thumbprint with which Lestrade will confront Holmes.

Thursday, November 29: Thanksgiving with the Kiplings

Thanksgiving Day, not yet permanently fixed on the fourth Thursday of November, is a venerable American custom. The household in which ACD has been invited to observe it, on this fifth Thursday of the month, is far from a typical American establishment, even though it lies near the pleasant Vermont town of Brattleboro, home of the Vermont maple sugar industry and of a sizeable organ factory. Brattleboro's new electric street lights were turned on for the first time two days ago, so that Yankee conservatism is not untempered by progress.

The man of the house is no Yankee, but that unquenchable Anglo-Indian, that critic of so much that is American, that teller of tales of the frontier and bard of military verses, Rudyard Kipling. He is living in rural Vermont out of kindness to his wife, for this is her home territory – the nearest neighbour to the Kiplings is Caroline's brother Beatty Balestier. Bliss Perry, whom ACD met at Princeton two weeks ago, saw Kipling here during a visit last summer:

> I was driving up a long hill to fish a trout-brook, and overtook the alert, eager little figure already so famous. Mr. Kipling was marching along, arrayed in a Vermont farmer's wide-brimmed, flopping straw hat, a black seersucker coat, and linen trousers far too short. On his shoulder, as he peered rapidly and cautiously over the fields from left to right, was the biggest rifle I had ever seen. He was evidently out for a woodchuck, but if it had been a rhinoceros he could not have been more earnest about it.

November 1894

Kipling tries to get some writing done here, and is having some success. Just a month ago he sat down and wrote another of his characteristic lays, "The Mother-Lodge," straight off, and he is now working on a poem in Scots dialect which is to be called "McAndrew's Hymn." He guards his privacy here, or his wife does so on his behalf: a young woman representing the *New York Recorder* showed up at Naulakha earlier this week, but Rudyard Kipling would not see her and Caroline sent her away.

They were probably trying, for once, to avoid controversy. Kipling has found it hard to avoid jumping into issues in the press, and particularly to avoid, as ACD will later put it, pulling "a few feathers out of the Eagle's tail." For he is nothing if not an Imperialist, and feelings between Britain and America are very touchy these days. They have always been so – some now alive can remember how close the two countries were to war in 1844 – and if there were nothing else about which to be prickly, there is always sport. This month Lord Dunraven has been clearing his throat preparatory to issuing a challenge for the world yachting championship, soon to be known as the America's Cup, and the committee of the New York Yacht Club is in no hurry to meet his terms. Over this and much more serious matters, Americans are resentful of the British, as ACD learned at that banquet in Detroit when someone drank a little too much and spoke too freely, and Kipling has been unable to refrain from putting in his oar. ACD will record later that "I, as a passionate believer in Anglo-American union, wrote to Kipling to remonstrate," and it was that letter which led to his invitation for this holiday at Brattleboro. Of course Kipling the wunderkind and ACD the established author have plenty of literary subjects in common too, and Kipling owes ACD a little debt, unless it is just chance that he borrowed the name Teddy from "The Crooked Man" to use in his own tale about a mongoose, "Rikki-Tikki-Tavi."

Thanksgiving services are held at eleven o'clock this morning at the Brattleboro town hall, with "God in America" the theme, but the Kiplings and Doyles do not attend. Instead, they play golf. ACD has found some clubs somewhere and brought them along, and will later record that he gave Kipling "lessons in a field." (In fact golf is not new at Naulakha: Kipling has been playing it with neighbours, the Cabots. Vermont rustics are puzzled enough, though, by this new sport.) There is also time for much talk, of course, and for ACD to hear Kipling's newest work:

> The poet read me "McAndrew's Hymn," which he had just done, and surprised me by his dramatic power which enabled him to sustain the Glasgow accent throughout, so that the angular Scottish greaser simply walked the room.

The poem will be the first item in the December issue of *Scribner's* Magazine.

The Kiplings, the Doyle brothers, and Miss Cabot have their Thanksgiving dinner at Maplewood, brother-in-law Balestier's house – for, Balestier says, "No one would want to keep Thanksgiving in an Englishman's house."

Kipling is not amused.

Welcome to America, Mr. Sherlock Holmes

Friday, November 30: Lecture in Morristown
"It was a wild, tempestuous night, towards the close of November," ACD will write in a Sherlock Holmes story still unimagined, "The Golden Pince-Nez." Setting that story in November 1894, he will perhaps stop to recall where he himself was as November 1894 came to an end.

ACD and Innes can spend most of the day with the Kiplings at Brattleboro; there may even be time for a little more golf. ACD is impressed by Kipling's interest in sport – next year, wishing to make a present to Kipling, he will send him a pair of skis from Norway. As he leaves, he makes a final plea for Kipling to stop aggravating the misunderstandings between Americans and Britons. "For God's sake," he puts it, thinking of the eternal symbol of American coarseness, "let's stop talking about spittoons."

His train this afternoon must take him to New York, and from there he goes across the Hudson into New Jersey again, this time to Morristown. St. Bartholomew's School, a local boarding school for boys, has invited him to lecture here, in the Lyceum Hall. This hall is part of the library building on South Street, occupying its second floor; a school and the library are on the first, and there is a dance floor on the top storey, though it is not much used. The hall is the centre of culture in this very affluent town: Henry Ward Beecher has spoken here, Lillie Langtry has trod these boards, Paderewski and Twain have been here – and now a Morristown audience hears ACD tell of his literary apprenticeship, his albatross Sherlock Holmes, and his hope that such books as *The Refugees* have helped to bring Americans and Britons a little closer together.

A story will appear in an English newspaper, months after this visit to Morristown, about ACD's apparent rudeness to a local resident who invited him to dinner:

> Then a strange thing happened. He would not on any account join the party at the table, but asked for roast beef and potatoes, which he could eat in his own room. And this programme was carried out.

The explanation: somehow his dress coat had gone missing, and he could not possibly insult his hosts by appearing in ordinary grey trousers and blue coat and waistcoat. Better to seem eccentric about one's eating habits than rude about one's attire. But then what about his clothes for the lecture itself?

> He pulled out his pocket knife and cut all the buttons from his sack coat, and pinned back the lapels; and when he did face his audience, later, they were some distance from the platform, and supposed he was wearing a Tuxedo coat.

He might be amused if he knew that fifty years hence a man named Edgar W. Smith, who is now eight months old, will live at 221B Baker Street, Morristown, and devote much of his time to bringing Americans a little closer to Sherlock Holmes through a group called the Baker Street Irregulars.

December 1894

Saturday, December 1: Rain in Paterson
This dark and stormy night finds ACD in another town of northern New Jersey – Paterson, which in another fifty years will be the name of a book-length poem as well as of a mill-town. Why should William Carlos Williams, today an eleven-year-old boy in nearby Rutherford, grow up to choose Paterson as the subject of his historical, biographical, patchwork poem about a city and a life?

> I thought of other places upon the Passaic River, but, in the end, the city, Paterson, with its rich colonial history, upstream, where the water was less heavily polluted, won out. The falls, vocal, seasonally vociferous, associated with many of the ideas upon which our fiscal colonial policy shaped us through Alexander Hamilton, interested me profoundly – and what has resulted therefrom. . . . The Falls let out a roar as it crashed upon the rocks at its base. In the imagination this roar is a speech or a voice, a speech in particular; it is the poem itself that is the answer.

The Falls roar tonight, answering the roar of the wind and rain.
But wind and rain do not keep a sizeable audience from coming to Paterson's Association Hall to hear ACD lecture. Monday's newspaper will record that they "filled nearly all the seats on the lower floor and a considerable number of those in the gallery."
The speaker is introduced by Eugene Stevenson, who met him at the Lotos Club the other day, and whose words are taken down by the *Daily Press* reporter as follows:

> The honor has been conferred upon me by the members of the Tuesday Club of introducing to you this evening Dr. Doyle. This is no arduous task, for wherever the English language is spoken or read, the author of the "White Company" and the originator of that fascinating personality, "Sherlock Holmes," is no stranger but a friend. Since Dr. Doyle has been in this country the question has been raised as to whether Sherlock Holmes was really dead. We may not be able to answer this question definitely, but I feel sure that when Dr. Watson returns to his lodgings in Baker street, he will find Sherlock Holmes waiting to welcome him.

ACD may wince at yet another raising of this sore topic, but he must smile at the thought of being "no stranger but a friend" – that is exactly what he has been saying, in his lectures as well as his interviews, since he reached American shores just two months ago.

After the lecture, he presents to Rosa Murray, the president of the Tuesday Club, a copy of *The Adventures of Sherlock Holmes*; the newspaper will report that it is the very copy from which he has been reading in the course of his tour. He spends the night at the home of Eugene Stevenson, enjoying his hospitality until lunchtime on Sunday.

Sunday, December 2: The Napoleon Fad

The December issue of the *Strand*, back in England, is telling the world of Brigadier Gerard for the first time. The name is known here in America too, since ACD has been telling reporters that a Napoleonic tale with a hero of that name is forthcoming and is not to be missed; he even read it to a Boston audience the other day. But readers everywhere will have to wait another month to find out, in truth, "How the Brigadier Won His Medal." In North America, the tale will appear first in the December 16 issue of the *San Francisco Examiner*, which will boast that it cost twelve and a half cents a word, and then in the January 1895 issue of the American *Strand*.

Brigadier Etienne Gerard, flamboyant champion of the Hussars of Conflans, an Englishman's idea of the ultimate French soldier, makes his début in an auspicious year, for 1894 is the year of Napoleon, and it was ninety years ago today that he was crowned Emperor of the French. It seems that these days every historian, novelist and hack has Bonapartist ink in his pen. Sloane of Princeton, whom ACD met on Thursday, is just one of them; Lippincott is about to publish a *History of the Consulate and Empire of France under Napoleon*, by Louis Adolphe Thiers, in twelve octavo volumes. Then there are two separate works by Frederic Massor, *Napoleon at Home* (which is scandalous enough) and *Napoleon and the Women of his Court* (which is positively indecent, even when every possible consideration is given for its importance as history). A series on the "Military Career of Napoleon the Great" by Montgomery P. Gibbs is running in the *Pittsburg Post*, and a play titled *Napoleon Bonaparte* has been playing at New York's Herald Square Theatre (former president Benjamin Harrison was in the opening night audience last month).

And certainly it was news in mid-September when a large sale of Napoleonic relics took place at the Fifth Avenue Auction Rooms. A lock of the conqueror's hair fetched fifty dollars from a collector; a piece of tapestry from his bedroom at St. Helena sold for $97.50, and a pair of bronze candelabra went for $570. What was certified to be the Emperor's own medal of the Legion of Honour – certified in a letter, which was sold with it, signed by his valet – was knocked down for $245. In short, as *The New York Times* put it three weeks ago, "The Napoleon fad is strong in this country just now."

Of course Napoleon is no new fad with ACD. His first novel of the Napoleonic era, *The Great Shadow*, was published two years ago, but attracted very little attention. Even before that, early in 1891, came the short story "A Straggler of '15," on which is based *Waterloo*, the play in which Henry Irving is making such a success this season. He will have less success in 1897 with *Uncle Bernac*. What has happened with Sherlock Holmes is about to happen with Brigadier Gerard: ACD's lighter tales, written for entertainment or money, will appeal to readers much more than anything he will ever do in the way of serious fiction.

The tales are, it will appear, based more or less on the memoirs of Jean Baptiste de Marbot, a genuine Napoleonic general and baron, which were published in French in 1891 and in English the following year. Some of these other writers owe their inspiration to Marbot just as much as ACD does; publication of those *Mémoires* was, in the words of a later bibliographer, the signal for the "*Début d'une avalanche de mémoirs civils et militaires sur l'Empire.*" But ACD is following Marbot the boaster and hero with a wry fidelity, and somehow making his deeds read better in fiction than they do in sober history.

There will be seventeen of these wonderful stories altogether: eight between now and 1896, another eight in the first years of the new century, and "The Marriage of the Brigadier" in 1910, which will, to some readers' exasperation, contradict many assertions made in the earlier ones. Historical verisimilitude is important to ACD, but consistency within his own works has never been one of his strengths. The strength he will reveal in the stories of Gerard is in his use of irony (shading into comedy), his depiction of a larger-than-life personality, his choice of the perfect detail to illuminate a man, an event, an age. In these stories he is drawing with a broad brush, and yet deftly:

> I am an excellent soldier. I do not say this because I am prejudiced in my own favour, but because I really am so. I can weigh every chance in a moment, and decide with as much certainty as though I had brooded for a week. Now I saw like a flash that, come what might, I should be chased, and on a horse which had already done a long twelve leagues. But it was better to be chased onward than to be chased back. On this moonlit night, with fresh horses behind me, I must take my risk in either case; but, if I were to shake them off, I preferred that it should be near Senlis than near Soissons. . . .
>
> I turned to the door, and my hand was upon the handle, when the Emperor called upon me to stop.
>
> "You will see," said he, turning to the Duke of Taranto, "that Brigadier Gerard has the special Medal of Honour, for I believe that, if he has the thickest head, he has also the stoutest heart in my army."

For all that ACD loves France, it is also England's traditional enemy. But the campaigns of which these stories tell took place a lifetime ago, and the great figure of Napoleon, bestriding Europe, can now be seen with a somewhat less partisan eye. ACD is aware of the resonances which Napoleon's name arouses in England, however, and will make good use of them in 1904 in a Sherlock Holmes tale, "The Six Napoleons." Inevitably, the very appearance of the French Emperor in that story will turn out to be a red herring; but until the denouement in which Holmes demonstrates that fact, journal-

Welcome to America, Mr. Sherlock Holmes

ists, policemen and good old Watson will worry away at the idea of someone with an idée fixe about Napoleon, a madman with a hereditary injury acquired during the Napoleonic wars, whose English constitution could not stand up against the child-frightening bogey of the Emperor who commanded Marbot and, we are all asked to believe, Brigadier Gerard.

Monday, December 3: Evening in Flushing

Today's newspapers, in which Bloomingdale's department store is advertising iron beds for $3.98, boys' bicycles for $4.99, and rolled white oats at four cents a pound, also have a funny story about the English theatrical company with whom ACD was sharing Daly's Theatre last month. The *World* tells it best:

> A real Anglo-American farce in one act was enacted on the stage of Daly's Theatre yesterday morning. It was a very amusing little comedy, too, and made an unqualified hit with a small but appreciative audience of newspaper men. The plot of the piece was all about the vaccination of the sixty-odd members of the "Gaiety Girl" company because Harry Monkhouse, the leading comedian, was taken down with the small-pox last week. . . .
>
> [When] the ominous-looking instrument cases were produced and the gleaming lancets exhibited there was a marked hesitation all around. Nobody wanted to be first. Then Charles Ryley, Fred Kaye and Louis Brafield remembered that they were bold soldier boys in the cast of "A Gaiety Girl," and their reputation for fearlessness must be sustained. They therefore bravely threw off their coats and bared their arms to the glittering steel. . . .
>
> Dr. Doty brought matters to an unexpected climax by asking where [Maud Hobson] wanted to be lanced. Confusion reigned supreme in the feminine ranks for several minutes. No one had thought of that all-important point.
>
> Hurried consultations ensued, mingled with giggles and anxious exclamations. Finally Miss Hobson decided that a scar upon her arm would be more becoming than a loss of dignity under the present circumstances. So the arm was bared, and a lovely one it was, too. A bit of a scrape, a drop of blood and all was over.
>
> Demure little Decima Moore thought she preferred the arm, too, but Cissy Fitzgerald thought otherwise, and – but under the circumstances it would not be fair to tell on her. . . .
>
> About sixty in all were inoculated, besides the stage hands of Daly's Theatre, who looked upon the whole affair as a huge joke.

(The *Sun* has other details, such as the various ways in which bedraggled chorus girls, with and without admirers at their sides, struggled through the rain to report so early – at eleven o'clock – on their day of rest.)

ACD is engaged to speak tonight in Flushing, a town of 8,500 in Queens County, accessible by an eight-mile trip on the Long Island Railway. Before he goes he writes a quick note to John Kendrick Bangs, making a luncheon appointment for 11:30 a.m. tomorrow, "if that is compatible with getting from Flushing. But perhaps I'll get from Flushing tonight." W. J. Ballard, who has acted for Pond in several other towns, is ACD's agent in Flushing – as he will be in another Queens County community, Jamaica, on Wednesday.

December 1894

Another speaker named Doyle is making a much bigger splash than ACD in New York tonight. He is Rev. Alexander P. Doyle, of the Paulist Fathers. Now 35, Father Doyle is said to have been the first man born in California ever to become a priest. His career has been in city missions and in the work of the Catholic Total Abstinence Union, and for the past couple of years he has been manager of the Catholic Book Exchange and editor of the *Catholic World*, whose current issue is so scathing about ACD's *Round the Red Lamp*.

Well known already in Catholic intellectual circles, Father Doyle will wake up tomorrow to find himself an object of much broader public interest, for tonight he is the invited speaker before the Homiletical Society of the Union Theological Seminary. "It is," the *Sun* will explain, "the custom of the society to invite clergymen of various denominations to address it at certain periods. No Catholic priest, however, had ever been invited." The invitation was diplomatically extended, however, in view of Father Doyle's talents and reputation, and he comes tonight and speaks on the undoctrinal subject "Methods of Preaching." The *Sun* will publish part of his text tomorrow morning and have a profile and portrait of him next Sunday.

Tuesday, December 4: Fire, Blood, and Corruption
Today's newspapers – ACD may have a chance to read them, for he has no engagements today – are full of the usual fire, blood and corruption. A mysterious shooting is reported from Wantagh, out in Nassau County; a fire yesterday afternoon drove artists out of their studios at the Manhattan Club at the corner of Fifth Avenue and 15th Street. And the commission investigating the reformatory at Elmira has yet to make its report, but is expected to have plenty to say when it does.

ACD will be interested in one small item of news: suit was filed yesterday on behalf of Oliver Wendell Holmes, Jr., who seeks standing to represent his late father's estate in copyright disputes. ACD is bound to wince whenever he sees the word "copyright," for though a Copyright Act is now on the books in Washington, it is not retroactive, so that several of his books are still available for reprinting by any "pirate" who thinks they might bring in a profit. Passage of such a law came very slowly and uncertainly, though both American and foreign writers wanted it – the latter for obvious reasons, the former so that publishers would not find foreign books cheaper to produce than American ones, and so neglect the native product. Reputable publishers favoured it too: now they can buy a foreigner's work with some confidence of having it all to themselves, rather than seeing a cheaper edition on the shelves a few days after they bring out the authorized one. Less reputable publishers, and trade unions fearing the loss of jobs in the printing industry, were its strong opponents.

There are other matters in today's *New York Times* as well – politics, for example: yesterday the Congress began its lame-duck session, and the paper contains the long dull text of President Cleveland's message. And last night the Sons of Tammany met, for the first time since the disastrous election defeat, to lick its wounds and discuss what might come next. An editorial in the *Times* deals with the longstanding topic of sugar tariffs, and other articles discuss the disgraceful massacre of Armenians by order of the Sublime Porte, which is to say, the government of the Ottoman Empire.

There is also the awkward incident involving Madame Nordica, the Maine-born opera singer, who "has stirred up unpleasantness in Brooklyn by her refusal to fulfill her contract to sing next Monday night at the second concert of the Seidl Society at the Brooklyn Academy of Music." ACD may have a passing interest in that, recalling that Madame Nordica was born Lillian Norton, and that her career at Covent Garden and elsewhere carries at least hints of one of his best-known characters, the late Irene Adler (later Mrs. Godfrey Norton), of dubious and questionable memory.

And no reader of the newspapers can miss the endless articles about the progress of what will come to be known as the Sino-Japanese War. The dispute is ostensibly about whether China or Japan shall hold the real power in the puppet kingdom of Corea, but shrewd observers realize that domination in the whole of East Asia is at issue, and is far from settled even by the recent Japanese capture of the mainland fortress known as Port Arthur. Today it is reported that Japan would be willing to accept an indemnity of four hundred million yen in settlement of the whole matter – at least for now.

Wednesday, December 5: The Town Hall, Jamaica
ACD's lecture in Jamaica, Queens County, was moved back from this Saturday to tonight – the author is eager to start his homeward voyage in time to be with Louise for Christmas. The lecture is given at the Town Hall, at the corner of Fulton Street and Flushing Avenue, a brick building which includes the police headquarters and other offices as well as an opera house. It is sponsored by the Jamaica Library, which presents ACD as the third of seven events in its Lecture Course for 1894-95. (Still to come are Alexander Black, the Ollie Torbett Concert Co., George Kennan, and Madam Lineff's Russian Peasant Choir. Season tickets are priced from fifty cents to three dollars.)

ACD gives his usual lecture, in a manner which earns him the flattering label of "an easy and graceful speaker" from the *Long Island Farmer*. Introducing him is Rev. J. Howard Hobbs, of the Presbyterian Church, Jamaica, who boasts Mayflower descent but birth in humbler circumstances – his father was a missionary to the Choctaw Nation in the Indian Territory which will later be called Oklahoma, and he himself has spent time as both a missionary and a cowboy.

Thursday, December 6: Last Lecture
ACD gives the thirty-fourth and final rendition of his "Readings and Reminiscences" almost within sight of that Statue of Liberty which welcomed him to America more than two months ago. There had been some thought of a final matinee in New York tomorrow, but as things work out, tonight's will be the last lecture, and the weary traveller gives it in a church, as he did his first one early in October. The church is the First Presbyterian in Jersey City, a town which is closer to his roost at the Aldine Club than are some

parts of New York itself; it is reached by a few minutes' ferry ride across the Hudson River.

ACD speaks in the Sunday school room and – perhaps because of his reputation, not entirely deserved, as the author of exciting stories for boys – his audience includes the local members of the Boys' Brigade, in uniform. Founded eleven years ago in Scotland, this organization has rapidly spread in North America. Its purpose is "the advancement of Christ's Kingdom among Boys, and . . . the promotion of habits of Obedience, Reverence, Discipline, Self-respect and all that tends toward a true Christian manliness." Activities include Bible class, physical drill, camping and first aid training.

Finally ACD comes to that familiar last paragraph, and perhaps there is a hint of nostalgia in his voice:

> It is the novelist's happy lot to be known and perhaps loved by thousands in all parts of the world, to know that one has written what occasionally cheers a heart or brightens a dark hour. He can carry, as it were, his profession in his hat and have it for his service at any time and place. His part is to be apart from and a part of all that has been and that is. These are the joys of the author, and they repay him for the griefs which come to him when a good story goes wrong or a bright idea grows dark in the telling. An author has his dark hours, but if he knows he has brought a smile upon sad lips or cheered one hour of pain, his own troubles are all the lighter for that.

There – it is over. After the lecture, a good many of the audience are presented to the visitor. Eventually he can crawl back to the ferry and his bed in New York; save for a social occasion tomorrow, his work in America is done.

Friday, December 7: A Toast to Arthur Conan Doyle

Some literary men are not without honour, save in their own country. Emile Zola has been snubbed yet again in his efforts to become a member of the Académie Française, this morning's newspaper reports. But ACD is not in his own country, and the Aldine Club, which has been his home during much of his nine weeks in America, is to honour him tonight.

He takes luncheon with Hamilton W. Mabie, the man who introduced him at his first American lecture some two months ago, and who is to take the chair at tonight's dinner. After luncheon there is some formal talk – the two of them interview one another on behalf of the *Ladies' Home Journal*. That estimable periodical has been promising an article by ACD on "How Your Women Impressed Me," but someone has thought better of so risky a venture and decided that he is better qualified to speak to the magazine's nearly one million readers about literature than about women. The interview, as the *Journal* will publish it next March, covers familiar subjects: James Fenimore Cooper, Edgar Allan Poe, Nathaniel Hawthorne (*The Scarlet Letter* is "the greatest novel yet written in America").

ACD is asked almost the same question Barr asked him in that interview for the *Idler*, and gives a similar response:

Welcome to America, Mr. Sherlock Holmes

> I think the special tendency at present is toward what may be called local fiction – the presentaton of local types, and I think this is likely to become a great danger. Provincialism is a thing to be avoided in art. The value of the local type depends entirely upon the power of the writer to make it significant of universal traits.

Mary Wilkins has achieved that feat in *Pembroke*, he repeats. The discussion ranges over English and French literature, Uncle Remus, and the relative popularity of reading in America and England:

> I am of opinion that books are more read in England than in this country. The workingmen in England seem to me to be, in a sense, better read than the workingmen in this country, because they read books where the American workingman reads newspapers. I should say that, taking magazines and newspapers into account, the reading habit is more general in America than in England, but that, on the whole, more time is given to the reading of books of the best literature in England than in America.

Inevitably, he gets onto Anglo-American relations, and the role of literature in improving matters: "English writers addressing an American audience will be educated out of insular prejudices and misconceptions, and American writers speaking to English readers will forget the old-time hostilities."

Tonight's event at the Aldine Club is a dinner for some sixty guests. They include familiar names: William W. Appleton, Sam McClure, John Brisben Walker, even President Frost of Berea College, Kentucky. Among the many speakers are Sir Henry Cunningham, retired Anglo-Indian judge and novelist, who takes the opportunity to say something about the late James Russell Lowell (whose letters have just been published) as well as about ACD; the Rev. Henry Van Dyke, minister of the Brick Presbyterian Church in New York and author of a book which must endear him to ACD immediately: *The National Sin of Literary Piracy;* Thomas Nelson Page (whose *The Burial of The Guns*, just published, contains just the sort of story ACD writes himself); F. Hopkinson Smith, Frank R. Lawrence (president of the Lotos Club), Ripley Hitchcock, and half a dozen others. Even Innes Doyle speaks. Letters of regret are read from a few other distinguished men of letters: William Dean Howells, Charles Dudley Warner, George Washington Cable up in Northampton, and Rt. Rev. Henry Codman Potter, the Episcopalian bishop of New York.

In the chair is Hamilton Wright Mabie, the president of the club, the same man who introduced ACD to his first New York lecture audience almost two months ago. Introducing him tonight, he quips that the affair is indeed an international one, for the guest of honour is Irish by ancestry and Scots by birth, but speaks English!

When a toast to ACD is proposed, he of course rises to respond, saying that on such occasions he recalls with envy the remark of Daniel the prophet on his introduction into the den of lions: "There will be no after-dinner speaking for me." Nevertheless, Daniel lived to prophesy, and ACD does find something to say. "It is possible that you may wish to know my impressions of this visit to America," he begins, but claims he can hardly give any,

December 1894

for there have been so many images in so short a time that they are all blurred. He has felt like a hurdler, challenged one after another by obstacles which are the east, the west, the north and the south of this broad land; "but the greensward between them will always appear to me as the Aldine Club."

Then ACD the amateur photographer tries a second metaphor: Time, he says, will serve as a reagent, bringing out the tints in these mental views. He does make a few more specific comments, rather like those to which the Lotos Club was treated a few days ago. He characterizes Chicago as a schoolboy growing too fast for his parents to keep him in clothes; he mentions the delightful old Dutch towns up the Hudson, and his glimpses of midwestern manufacturing and of staid old Philadelphia. When he leaves tomorrow, ACD says, he will leave a part of himself behind.

After that, the chairman calls on the speaker everyone has been waiting for: Edgar, or "Bill," Nye, the funniest man alive. Tall, thin, self-deprecating, and bald, Nye is best-known for his weekly syndicated newspaper column, though he has also been a star of the lecture platform, often coupled with James Whitcomb Riley or Mark Twain. He is not lecturing this year, but is living in Washington making satirical comments about the government; his *History of the United States* has just been published, joining earlier books of comic but pointed essays. Nye congratulates ACD on renouncing medicine and joining the ranks of the literary toilers; and as for himself, he assures tonight's company that he has been leading a blameless life lately, looking after the business of the family farm in North Carolina (as indeed he has, once in a while). Upright? He has been so upright that the whole farm stands up edgewise!

Saturday, December 8: Aboard the *Etruria*

As ACD finishes packing, an important literary event is taking place in New York, the authors' reception for the "Round Table Fair," which is being held to raise money for an industrial school. At today's reception (a second one is scheduled for Monday), everyone from William Dean Howells to Owen Wister is confidently expected to put in an appearance – not to mention John Kendrick Bangs, Agnes Bailey Ormsbee and Edward Eggleston.

ACD and Innes board the Cunard liner *Etruria* at midday. It has been an exhausting few weeks: for a day or two ACD will rest, leaving it to Innes to explore the ship's amenities, from the music saloon (panelled in satinwood) to the central saloons, lighted at night by incandescent electric bulbs. He will not get to see the ladies' boudoir, with four marble bathrooms and a barber shop, but the smoking-room is no less lavishly equipped.

The nine-year-old *Etruria*, captained by Henry Walker, is a big ship and a fast one. The engine-room alone requires a crew of eleven engineers, 109 firemen and an electrician, and their ingenuity and strength, added to those of the builders (Scots, of course: John Elder & Co., of Glasgow), helped the ship set the eastbound speed record of six days, four hours and thirty-six minutes in the spring of 1887. It is carrying, besides its hundreds of passengers, a load of mail and a shipment of $298,000 in specie.

One very important man making this crossing is Sir Donald Smith, who nine years ago at a little place called Craigellachie, British Columbia, drove the last spike to complete Canada's transcontinental railroad. Since that steel ribbon was completed, one can cross the North American continent, from Montréal to the Pacific coast, in five days – faster than this crack steamer can traverse the Atlantic. Smith, soon to be ennobled as Baron Strathcona, entered business as a clerk in the Hudson's Bay Company, but he knows how to handle money, and in 1889 he reached the position he still holds, governor of what is formally the Company of Adventurers of England Trading into Hudson's Bay. His involvement in the railway scheme was inevitable, for as a veteran Hudson's Bay man he knew the Canadian West intimately (he was a prisoner for two months during the 1869 Riel rebellion) and as a Montréal money man he knows politicians. He was a director of the CPR at the time he drove the last spike; his knighthood came the following year. Smith will list his "Profession, Occupation or Calling" on British immigration documents as "Gent.," making no mention of his business interests. His wife, Isabella, will fittingly list herself as a "Lady."

A couple of livelier and younger persons are also on board, Jessie and Georgina Preston, who register themselves as actresses. Jessie starred in London last summer in the title role of *Little Jack Sheppard* – a role played in New York a decade ago by no less a charmer than Loie Fuller. Jessie Preston at 23 (though she will later shave half a dozen years off her age) is every inch a woman, or, as one London commentator put it, she has "an unfortunate figure for 'principal boy' characters." Her sister Georgina, three years younger, had a smaller part in *Little Jack Sheppard* in London. Theatrical immortality for them both will come when they pose together for a photograph to illustrate the popular song "You Shant Come and Play in Our Yard" – one of them holding a stick of candy, the other clutching a doll.

Actress sisters, railway magnate and his lady wife, popular author and his military brother: they are among the eighty-five passengers in cabin class and ninety in the second cabin. The *Etruria* is also carrying 524 steerage passengers.

The ship leaves its New York berth at four o'clock. Their voyage is beginning, and for ACD the American tour is over.

Afterword

The *Etruria* passed Browhead at 10:30 p.m. on Friday, December 14, made its call at Queenstown at 2:20 a.m. to drop off the mails, and arrived at Liverpool on Saturday.

> I noticed on board the boat coming back [ACD will write much later] a dark, silent man with a hevy moustache – a sort of cavalry officer type – as free from apparent emotion as a man could be. When we arrived at Liverpool it was midwinter, pouring rain, and the quay was all slush. I was about to walk down the gangway when someone brushed violently past me, the heavy dragoon man blundered down the gangway, and I saw him throw himself upon his face on the pier and press his lips to the muddy ground. Much inner pain must have been endured before such a man was in such a plight as that.

Not until after Doyle disembarked and reached London did he hear a shocking piece of news: Robert Louis Stevenson had died on December 3 in remote Samoa. Much later, getting the year wrong, he would recall his reaction:

> I cannot forget the shock that it was to me when driving down the Strand in a hansom cab in 1896 I saw upon a yellow evening poster "Death of Stevenson." Something seemed to have passed out of my world.

Doyle never met Stevenson – though he notes that he may have brushed elbows with him in an Edinburgh crowd – but he loved his tales. (During his week on the boat there was other news, of course: the death of Canada's prime minister, Sir John Thompson, during a visit to Queen Victoria at Windsor Castle, and a sentence of six months' imprisonment for Eugene Debs, the man behind that American railway strike.)

Doyle found London as exciting as ever, still the largest city in the world and with such projects under way as the construction of a new Claridge's hotel in Brook Street, based on the European interpretation of American-style luxury.

During and after the 1894 tour, Doyle's own works continued to be printed and read. The first sections of *The Stark Munro Letters*, in print in the British *Idler* since October, appeared in *Leslie's Illustrated* for

Welcome to America, Mr. Sherlock Holmes

December 13. Then on December 16 the *Philadelphia Inquirer* and the *Atlanta Constitution* both published a piece in a new genre, which the Philadelphia paper titled "Mountain Climbing on Norwegian Ski." It described the novel sport of "ski-ing," and in particular Doyle's expedition, later to be famous, from Davos to Arosa over the Furka Pass. On December 22, *Publishers' Weekly* in New York made this comment:

> Harper & Brothers have just ready "The White Company" and "The Parasite," both by Dr. A. Conan Doyle, the former of which is considered by the author to be his best work – the latter story having just been making its own impression during its publication as a serial in *Harper's Weekly*.

The February issue of *The Bookman* noted that Doyle's works were "in steady demand," though he was on the best-seller lists only in Chicago and St. Louis (with *Round the Red Lamp*) and Toledo and Washington (with *The Memoirs of Sherlock Holmes*). In March the same journal quoted a remark by A. P. Watt, the titan of literary agents: "Mr. Kipling, Dr. Doyle, Mr. Crockett, and Mr. Stanley Weyman are among the writers for whom I can get the largest prices, both here and in America."

Doyle was eager to get back to Switzerland, not only for the wholesome outdoor activity – so different from the way he had been spending the past three months – but for his darling Louise and the children. The January issue of *The Bookman* had this brief note:

> Dr. Conan Doyle returned from America in the *Etruria*, but is only making quite a short stay in London. He leaves again almost immediately to join Mrs. Doyle and his family on the Continent. His lecture tour in the States has, we understand, been a great success.

After Switzerland, Doyle went to Egypt, in search of healthy air for Louise. She did not recover from her tuberculosis there, but experienced some remission – she did not die until 1906 – and Doyle arrived just in time to see a little war, which he was able to report in a series of dispatches to the *Westminster Gazette*. He contionued to write fictin as well, including stories about Brigadier Gerard and others which would eventually be collected in *The Green Flag* and *Round the Fire Stories*.

The versatile author was extending his range and exploring new genres. English fiction was to about to turn toward "realism," with the publication of such startling works as Stephen Crane's *The Red Badge of Courage* in 1895 and Theodore Dreiser's *Sister Carrie* in 1900, and Doyle would never be a member of that school, despite the use of some modern themes in the 1920's. But in the 1890's he was a generally respected and ever more popular author. Real fame came at the turn of the century, with two developments: the grudging return of Sherlock Holmes in *The Hound of the Baskervilles*, and the war propaganda efforts which earned Doyle his knighthood. By 1901 he apparently saw himself as a public man, not merely an author; he gave a lecture that November, for example, on "Typhoid and the Army."

Afterword

A couple of weeks after his return, Doyle was in print with strong opinions about Anglo-American relations:

> I saw many points in which I thought that we had much to learn. As to the better feeling between England and America I was convinced that it was on the increase, and I believe one of the chief obstacles which it has to encounter is the irritating criticisms made by travellers, who generalise upon a short experience, and who fail to allow for the fact that conditions which are dissimilar to our own must evolve different types and different methods.

Rapprochement between America and England became more palatable by the late 1890's than it had been at the time of Doyle's American tour. Some of the factors were economic: the 1893 depression in the United States, for which Britain had been popularly blamed, gave way to prosperity, and Britain was seen as the model of a dynamic and prosperous land. In addition, shrewd British handling of the Venezuela boundary dispute in 1895, over which some American leaders had been ready to provoke a war, led instead to mutual respect. In January 1896 Doyle could propose an Anglo-American Society to work for the removal of "bitter feeling" between the two nations. Such feeling was starting to dissipate anyway; one sign of permanent change would be the creation of the English-Speaking Union in 1918.

The twentieth century was beginning, the century of gritty literature, of economic warfare (which Doyle predicted), and of something like a real understanding between America and Britain. When Doyle next landed in New York, in May 1914, he was greeted by officials, taken on tours, followed by even more reporters than had attended the 1894 trip. He had become indisputably a great man.

Appendix I
Readings and Reminiscences

Text of Doyle's lecture as delivered during his 1894 tour of North America, reconstructed by Christopher Redmond.[1]

Ladies and gentlemen: It is naturally repugnant for a man to stand up on a public platform and to talk about himself and his own work, for never until a man attempts to do so before an audience does he realize how very insignificant things both himself and his own works are, and how very difficult it is to make either the one or the other interesting to any third person. It would be more pleasant for me to speak of the work of my friends and contemporaries. Before I came to America, however, it was pointed out to me that if anybody should come to hear me lecture, it would not be because they want my criticism on this or that, but because something I have written has come in their way and they want to make a bond of sympathy between us. So tonight I must make my work the subject of my remarks.

I can very distinctly recollect, away down among the very earliest misty remembrances of a child, the first connection that I ever had with a literary man. My own father was an artist, as were all his people. He had himself gone to live at Edinburgh, and it was there that I was born. Well, I can remember that into the little flat in which we lived there came one day a great man – gigantic he seemed when viewed from the height of two-foot-nothing. His shoulders, I remember, spanned the little door and his head was somewhere up near the gas chandelier. His voice, too, was as big as his body and I have since learned that his heart was in the same proportion. I can still remember the face of the man, clean-shaven, pugilistic, with an old man's hair, a young man's eyes and a child's laugh. Above all I remember his nose, which fascinated me by its strange distortion.[2] Long after I had been tucked into my little crib I could hear him roaring and rumbling in the next room, and his bare personality left as vivid an effect upon my three-year-old mind as his name and fame could do upon the thousands who knew him as William

Makepeace Thackeray.³ Considering that the great man died within four years of my birth I feel myself fortunate in being able to say that I have been danced upon his knee.

Well, that was the first personal knowledge that I had of the world of letters. But before long, I myself began to make little trial trips into that enchanted region. It is, I think, to my mother that I owe the very vivid feeling which I had quite early in life as to the delight which lay in a well-told story. She had, and I am thankful to say still has, a remarkable power in that direction, and the best I could ever wish myself would be that I could make a reader thrill and palpitate and long for a next installment as she could in these long stories carried on for weeks and served out in very small doses between bathtime and bedtime.

It must have been her influence which started me writing a book at the rather immature age of six. I took a sheet of foolscap and wrote in a fine bold hand about four words to the line. It was illustrated with sketches by the author and the characters were a tiger and a man. They were separate at first, but they became blended about the time when the tiger met the man, and I did not know how to get them apart again. I remarked that it was easy to get characters into a scrape, but not so easy to get them out again, and I have often had cause to repeat the precocious aphorism of my childhood.⁴ In this instance the situation was beyond me, and my book like my man was engulfed in my tiger. There is an old family bureau with secret drawers in which lie little locks of hair tied up in circles and black silhouettes and dim daguerrotypes and letters written in the lightest of straw-coloured ink. Somewhere there lies my primitive manuscript, where my tiger, looking in the picture like a many-hooped barrel with a tail to it, still envelops the stranger whom he has taken in.

While I was yet a child I became an omnivorous reader.⁵ The circulating library which I attended was compelled to pass a new by-law for my especial benefit, saying that no reader should be permitted to change his books more than three times in a day. Ever at my elbow there was Fenimore Cooper and Mayne Reid⁶ and although I have shot bear and harpooned whale since I read their tales, the actual experience never touched me as did the dreams I conjured over those pages. We lose that interest as we grow older: in youth it is you who suffer and weep and triumph with the hero of the tale; it is you who, with your Kentucky rifle, ramble through the wild forest. I remember that in my youthful fancy I had fought with pirates on the Pacific Ocean, and although my boyhood was spent in an Edinburgh flat, I knew the Rockies as if they had been my own back garden. The number of Indians which I killed in hand-to-hand conflicts in Edinburgh would fill a large graveyard, and I myself was nursed to recovery after every fight by a faithful young squaw.

Once I had a money-box so full I could hardly slip a knife blade into it. This accumulation of wealth was a source of both pleasure and anxiety to me: I did not know what to do with it. Fortunately, my parents solved the problem for me. I can remember one morning finding on the breakfast table, reaching from one side of it to the other, the thirty volumes of *Waverley*, which had been purchased with that money. I remember thinking as I looked at the books what a pity it was that that money could not have gone into a football and a bow and arrow. I mentally placed Sir Walter Scott beween cod liver oil and English grammar in the list of my antipathies. But I have since learned to appreciate my parents' wisdom. It is a good thing for a lad to have good books at his elbow; he reads them because he has nothing else to read, and eventually he prefers them. In those grand books I found a fascination for the past which not even the dull teaching of history during my school days could dispel. I believe that the whole course of my thoughts was altered by those books, which laid the foundation for my future work.

In the eight years of my public-school life the thing which I can remember most clearly is that innumerable times I was punished for sitting with my Virgil or my Euclid on my desk and Washington Irving or some other congenial author on my knee, and it gives me a squint yet to think how I managed to be lookng at the one thing while I was, in fact, looking at the other. I might have easily passed undetected had it not been that it is not in nature for any schoolboy to be so absorbed in Latin or mathematics, and I endured unnumbered punishments as a result. It was prophesied that I would never come to any good, for neither I nor my master realized that the real education for the work of my life was going on not on the desk but under it.

I have perhaps been rather too long-winded over these childish memories, which must seem trivial enough to you although I can see that they were essential to me. With your permission, now, I shall move on a little faster. When I left school and began the study of medicine, at seventeen or so, my hero-worship of favourite authors was certainly the strongest emotion in my nature. I well remember how when as a lad I visited London, the first thing I did was leave my luggage at the station to go and stand by the tomb of Macaulay, whose writings had stimulated in my mind that interest in the past which had first been awakened by Scott.

I think perhaps the less I say about my first literary flutterings, the better. Some writers seem to spring into maturity at a bound. Any development which I have made has always been a slow and painful matter. It was in 1878, I think, that with many misgivings I sent a small manuscript to the publisher of a provincial journal. I expected its return, and when I look at the story now I think the expectation was fully justified. However, it was accepted, and the small cheque which accompanied the editor's letter was the bounty money that enrolled me in the army of letters.[7] It is very sweet to the young man, especially to the poor young man, to earn money by his pen; it seems like creating something out of nothing. When he has once done it, whatever may come later, he is bound to struggle until he does it again.

For the following ten years I wrote short stories without advancing a step, and I might, I think, have gone on writing them for the rest of my life without making the slightest progress, but for comparative chance. During that time I also sailed for seven months in the Arctic seas, visited the coast of Africa, and took my degree as Doctor of Medicine and settled in practice. Yet during the whole of this time literature was always in my heart and I never ceased to write short stories, yet I never in all that time made more than $250 a year by my pen.[8] There is a bad system in England, which prevails, I believe, to a much lesser extent in this country, of keeping the stories anonymous in many of the leading magazines. I was so far a victim to this system that at the end of ten years of apprenticeship my name was as unknown to the public as at the beginning. I have no doubt that I escaped many a slating through these articles being anonymous, for I do not think that the average of them was at all high, but it is better for the young author to be slated than to be ignored. The adverse criticism may set someone to read your book, but a critic's silence cannot.

Yet I got some slating, too. I had been contributing short stories to provincial papers, and at last secured one in the *Cornhill*, which in England is regarded as the first of our magazines.[9] After it was published a friend came running after me on the street waving an evening paper. "Have you seen what they say about your *Cornhill* story?" he cried. "No," I said, bracing myself up to look modest. He turned the pages over until he had found it for me, and it read: "*Cornhill* has a story this month that would have made Thackeray turn over in his grave." Now as Thackeray was the first literary man of my acquaintance, and I had a great admiration for him, this seemed like a pointed personal insult. It was then I realized that English criticism had fallen into a sad state of decay – although when someone has a pat on the back for you, you understand that after all there are some very smart people in the literary press.

It dawned upon me that I must drop the short story and write a book to which I could put my name.[10] It was a sensational novel, very incoherent and disjointed, written during the little scraps of time a medical man can steal between patients. The publishers wrote to say they could see no merit in it, and I was of the same way of thinking. Finally it found its way into print, and I must say now in looking back at it that my conscience would be lighter if it had never seen the light of day.[11]

At this period a gentleman appeared in my life who certainly has been a very good friend to me, and to whom I think I afterward behaved in a very ungrateful manner – I mean the late Mr. Sherlock Holmes, of Baker Street. Now the detective story is no doubt an exceedingly primitive form of literature. At the same time it is a very good setting for a dramatic idea. I conceived the idea that a detective story could be built on scientific and literary lines, and carried out that plan. Resenting the idea that seemed to prevail in all detective stories that the hero reached his result by chance, and not by any special sharpness of his own, I resolved to make a detective who should succeed by observation and deduction. I modelled my character after an old professor at Edinburgh, whose powers of observation and logic were wonderful.[12] He used to electrify students by the manner in which he would read a total stranger. He was able, at a glance, to tell what disease a man had, and what were his habits, his trade, his circumstances. The patient's scarf pin, his watch charms, the knees of his trousers, the sleeves of his coat would provide him with information. The effect was so striking that I have seen the patient spring out of his chair and stare around in bewilderment.[13]

And then of course there is Edgar Allan Poe's Monsieur Dupin, who must be the father and the hundredfold superior of every detective in literature. His system of reasoning was so exactly analogous to that of my old professor that it is impossible to separate the two influences. But Monsieur Dupin is so masterly that he must affect the reader who comes in contact with him; and certainly it was Poe also who first showed the possibility of making such a story extremely sensational and yet making it literature.

I illustrated Sherlock Holmes's facility of deduction in this way in the story *The Sign of Four*:

> "I have heard you say," [says Watson,] "it is difficult for a man to have any object in daily use without leaving the impress of his individuality upon it in such a way that a trained observer might read it. Would you have the kindness to let me have an opinion upon the character or habits of the late owner?"
>
> I handed him over the watch with some slight feeling of amusement in my heart, for the test was, as I thought, an impossible one, and I intended it as a lesson against the somewhat dogmatic tone which he occasionally assumed. He balanced the watch in his hand, gazed hard at the dial, opened the back, and examined the works, first with his naked eyes and then with a powerful convex lens. I could hardly keep from smiling at his crestfallen face when he finally snapped the case to and handed it back.
>
> "There are hardly any data," he remarked. "The watch has been recently cleaned, which robs me of my most suggestive facts."
>
> "You are right," I answered. "It was cleaned before being sent to me."
>
> In my heart I accused my companion of putting forward a most lame and impotent excuse to cover his failure. What data could he expect from an uncleaned watch?
>
> "Though unsatisfactory, my research has not been entirely barren," he observed, staring up at the ceiling with dreamy, lack-lustre eyes. "Subject to your correction, I should judge that the watch belonged to your elder brother, who inherited it from your father."
>
> "That you gather, no doubt, from the H. W. upon the back?"
>
> "Quite so. The W. suggests your own name. The date of the watch is nearly fifty years back, and the initials are as old as the

watch; so it was made for the last generation. Jewellery usually descends to the eldest son, and he is most likely to have the same name as the father. Your father has, if I remember right, been dead many years. It has, therefore, been in the hands of your eldest brother."

"Right, so far," said I. "Anything else?"

"He was a man of untidy habits – very untidy and careless. He was left with good prospects, but he threw away his chances, lived for some time in poverty with occasional short intervals of prosperity, and finally, taking to drink, he died. That is all I can gather."

I sprang from my chair and limped impatiently about the room with considerable bitterness in my heart.

"This is unworthy of you, Holmes," I said. "I could not have believed that you would have descended to this. You have made inquiries into the history of my unhappy brother, and you now pretend to deduce this knowledge in some fanciful way. You cannot expect me to believe that you have read all this from his old watch! It is unkind and, to speak plainly, has a touch of charlatanism in it."

"My dear doctor," he said kindly, "pray accept my apologies. Viewing the matter as an abstract problem, I had forgotten how personal and painful a thing it might be to you. I assure you, however, that I never even knew that you had a brother until you handed me the watch."

"Then how in the name of all that is wonderful did you get these facts? They are absolutely correct in every particular."

"Ah, that is good luck. I could only say what was the balance of probability. I did not at all expect to be so accurate."

"But it was not mere guesswork?"

"No, no: I never guess. It is a shocking habit – destructive to the logical faculty. What seems strange to you is only so because you do not follow my train of thought or observe the small facts upon which large inferences may depend. For example, I began by stating that your brother was careless. When you observe the lower part of that watch-case you notice that it is not only dinted in two places but it is cut and marked all over from the habit of keeping other hard objects, such as coins or keys, in the same pocket. Surely it is no great feat to assume that a man who treats a fifty-guinea watch so cavalierly must be a careless man. Neither is it a very far-fetched inference that a man who inherits one article of such value is pretty well provided for in other respects."

I nodded to show that I followed his reasoning.

"It is very customary for pawnbrokers in England, when they take a watch, to scratch the number of the ticket with a pin-point upon inside of the case. It is more handy than a label as there is no risk of the number being lost or transposed. There are no less than four such numbers visible to my lens on the inside of this case. Inference – that your brother was often at low water. Secondary inference – that he had occasional bursts of prosperity, or he could not have redeemed the pledge. Finally, I ask you to look at the inner plate, which contains the keyhole. Look at the thousands of scratches all round the hole – marks where the key has slipped. What sober man's key could have scored those grooves? But you will never see a drunkard's watch without them. He winds it at night, and he leaves these traces of his unsteady hand. Where is the mystery in all this?"

"It is as clear as daylight," I answered.

And in the story "The Greek Interpreter" is this dialogue between Sherlock Holmes and his brother Mycroft, who speaks first:

"Look at these two men who are coming towards us, for example."

"The billiard-marker and the other?"

"Precisely. What do you make of the other?"

The two men had stopped opposite the window. Some chalk marks over the waistcoat pocket were the only signs of billiards which I could see in one of them. The other was a very small, dark fellow, with his hat pushed back and several packages under his arm.

"An old soldier, I perceive," said Sherlock.

"And very recently discharged," remarked the brother.

"Served in India, I see."

"And a non-commissioned officer."

"Royal Artillery, I fancy," said Sherlock.

"And a widower."

"But with a child."

"Children, my dear boy, children."

"Come," said I, laughing, "this is a little too much."

"Surely," answered Holmes, "it is not hard to say that a man with that bearing, expression of authority, and sun-baked skin, is a soldier, is more than a private, and is not long from India."

"That he has not left the service long is shown by his still wearing his ammunition boots, as they are called," observed Mycroft.

"He had not the cavalry stride, yet he wore his hat on one side, as is shown by the lighter skin on that side of his brow. His weight is against his being a sapper. He is in the artillery."

"Then, of course, his complete mourning shows that he has lost someone very dear. The fact that he is doing his own shopping looks as though it were his wife. He has been buying things for children, you perceive. There is a rattle, which shows that one of them is very young. The wife probably died in childbed. The fact that he has a picture-book under his arm shows that there is another child to be thought of."

I began to understand what my friend meant when he said that his brother possessed even keener faculties than he did himself.

Of course when it is all explained this way it is very plain and simple, but lest you should think even more lightly of it than it deserves, I will mention one case that occurred between Holmes and his friend Watson that has not found its way into print. It was when they were out on the track of a mysterious murder, and Watson picked up a charred wad of tobacco from the ground. "It has been smoked in a pipe," said Watson. "Yes, in a meerschaum pipe," said Holmes. Now I will leave you to deduce that for yourselves. It is not so easy as it seems.[14] The fact is, everything is easy when you know how to do it. And you should not attempt to carry out this method in real life. I have been among people who expected me to know all about a person from the button on his coat. But so far from having any such occult or mystical power, I am really absent-minded, and never would notice trifles unless my attention was directly called to them.[15] I have received letters from people in many parts of the world, from Moscow to San Francisco,[16] asking me to come and solve some mystery for them. I did not know there were so many mysteries in existence. Though not sharp myself, I believe a man, by attending to details, might be able to do such work.

These detective stories arose, as I explained to you, half in joke and half in experiment at first, and then I was drawn on from one to another, until I brought them to an abrupt end. As a matter of fact, my heart was never in it, and I had very different views about literature. Well, as you know, in 1893 Mr. Holmes came to grief at last and met with his end, as he was opposed to a criminal as determined as himself. I think it was well; he had been imposed long enough upon the good nature of the public. But it was only after Holmes's death I realized what warm friends he had made. I assure you, if I had killed a real man I could not have received more vindictive letters than those which poured in upon me after that event. The fact that he was a very real person to many people is evident by other letters, which ranged from the funny to the pathetic. People went so far as to write asking me for a lock of his hair, and one asked for his photograph at different ages. But it was justifiable homicide, and when a man has been the hero of twenty-six stories it is about time for him to get out before he outstays his welcome.[17]

The historical romance was the field which had always attracted me the most, and when I found myself drifting away into this other work I felt as a young artist might who has had an ambition to exhibit in oils and large classic canvases at the American Academy, but who finds somewhat to his chagrin that his sketches in a comic journal pay better and are more popular with the public. Even if his sketches are better than his oils, he would rather be doing the work in oils.[18]

Now I had a theory that it is almost impossible after a lapse of two hundred years to make a merely individual experience, such as a man's love affair, interesting to the reader, and consequently that a love story should not be introduced into historical novels. Even such a master of narrative as Sir Walter Scott could not make the love scene between a crusader and high-born dame human or interesting, and no one cares whether Ivanhoe marries Rebecca or Rowena or neither of them. What strikes the attention in the book is the tournament, the outlaws, the black knight, Friar Tuck with his great fist, the robber baron torturing the Jew – the romance of the period, in fact, rather than the romance of the individual. One resents almost as an impertinence the intrusion of a conventional love story on a canvas which should contain the typical incidents and characters of a great age. When one has the wit to write such a love story as that between Gerard and Margaret in *The Cloister and the Hearth*, of course, that is another matter, for I think that the greatest novel of this century.[19] These were my perhaps rather ungallant views when I wrote *Micah Clarke*, and the result was that there was hardly a skirt in it.[20]

A historical romancer should, above all, learn not to be a partisan, to be broad-hearted, to understand that in every political cause and in every religious faith there are beautiful characters, and also, alas, that in every one there are characters which are by no means beautiful. There is no use in drawing a Bible-and-Commonwealth man as an angel and a king, and churchmen as the other thing. There were noble souls on both sides, and Falkland[21] was as good a man as Hampden. Loyalty is a virtue as well as liberty. Both the Puritan and the Cavalier were noble fellows at their best, and on both sides they degenerated at their worst into the brawling ruffian and the sour bigot. I tried to draw various types of them in *Micah Clarke* and to give a glimpse of the England of the day, when it was like a bursting pod, all ready for the expansion which was to scatter the seed of the English-speaking races all over the whole wide world.

It was with difficulty that I found a publisher for *Micah Clarke*. One publisher told me it lacked only one thing – interest.[22] Another said experience showed historical novels didn't pay. A third assured me that people did not talk like that in the seventeenth century. I was depressed, and often, when I looked at my dog-eared manuscript when it used to come back for a whiff of country air after its periodic visits to London, I used to wonder what I should do if some sporting kind of a publisher were to stride in and bid ten dollars or so for the lot. I persevered, however, and finally, the critic Andrew Lang introduced me to the house of Longmans, who published it. Its sale in England has been considerably greater than that of any of the Sherlock Holmes books, so I think I can claim to have helped to confute the view that the public cannot be induced to read a historical novel. That was in '88. From that time onward, I have always found the door open to the temple of literature, if only I could find something worthy to bring in.

The White Company followed, an attempt to bring into existence again the days of the fourteenth century, and the great English and French wars. This necessitated the study of heraldry, archery, armoury, monastic institutions, and other subjects,[23] in order to produce a conscientious study of the times. I had recourse to the study of 115 books before I could put a pen to paper. It was very much as Charles Reade had said of *The Cloister and the Hearth*: "I milked three hundred cows into my pail, but the butter was my own for all that."

Then came *The Great Shadow*, dealing with the campaign of Waterloo, in which battle five of my ancestors took part and one was slain;

and *The Refugees*, which was prompted by the great interest I take in and the admiration I have for your own country.[24] Among the deepest convictions of my life is this one: that whatever tends in the smallest degree to excite the interests of one branch of the English-speaking race for another is working to a good end. It is a pity that the language is too often used for the purpose of libel and detraction.

I wished to come to this country to study my characters for that work, but was told not to do so: that the types I wished had disappeared, and that even your forests were but second growths. It was a labour of love to trace your history back to the early settlements, and to endeavour to reconstruct the types of men who inhabited them. I think of the American frontiersman, his customs and his language, as I have pictured them in this book, as a new twig upon the old English-speaking tree. All the different types of character seem to have been intensified by their crossing the water. I took the liberty of transporting two typical Americans and introducing them to court life in France, and I reversed the thing by putting two European characters in southern Canada. Parkman, Hawthorne, Cooper and Irving were my guides, along with the annals of the Jesuit missions in northern North America, as I endeavoured to realize that slow and somewhat lurid daybreak which was to prove the herald of so brilliant a sunrise. I believe that such errors as I have made in that work are few and unimportant. One curious coincidence was that a Mr. Savage, of Boston, wrote to me and sent the documents that proved beyond dispute that he had an ancestor named Captain Ephraim Savage living in Boston at the very time written about. Captain Ephraim Savage was a leading character in *The Refugees*.[25]

I should like to end by reading one of my recent stories, titled "The Lord of Chateau Noir," which has not yet appeared in book form. . . .[26]

In England, and I learn that conditions are the same here, an author may not hope for the same returns that come to a physician in the practice of medicine, nor can he earn as much as one in the profession of law, nor does his profit reach that of the clergy. But it is not to worldly gain that the novelist looks in choosing his profession. It is the novelist's happy lot to be known and perhaps loved by thousands in all parts of the world, to know that one has written what occasionally cheers a heart or brightens a dark hour. He can carry, as it were, his profession in his hat and have it for his service at any time and place. His part is to be apart from and a part of all that has been and that is. These are the joys of the author, and they repay him for the griefs which come to him when a good story goes wrong or a bright idea grows dark in the telling. An author has his dark hours, but if he knows he has brought a smile upon sad lips or cheered one hour of pain, his own troubles are all the lighter for that.

Notes to "Readings and Reminiscences"

[1] This text has been reconstructed from reports in newspapers all along Doyle's tour, chiefly using a technique demonstrated by Kevin O'Brien in his book *Oscar Wilde in Canada* (Toronto: Personal Library, 1982). While I have often had to use personal preference to choose among different plausible readings, and in some cases have had to use imagination and a sense of Doyle's style to provide continuity, I think the text which appears here would not have seemed unfamiliar to him.

Doubtless the lecture varied in small details from one evening to another; certainly the news reports do not always use the same words, even in what are presented as direct quotations. But the variations are usually small – the Yonkers *Statesman* is unique in saying that the gift of the *Waverley* novels delighted the young Doyle, when every other paper agrees that he says they distressed him.

[2] Apart from the good heart, this is the portrait which Doyle later drew (in The Speckled Band) of Dr. Grimesby Roylott. (I am indebted to the perceptive Karen Campbell for this observation.)

[3] Arthur Conan Doyle, *Memories and Adventures* (Boston: Little, Brown, 1924), p. 6.

[4] See *Ibid.*, p. 7. A portion of the manuscript of this rarity is reproduced in *Sir Arthur Conan Doyle: Centenary 1859-1959* (Garden City: Doubleday, 1959), p. 41. It reads as follows, and shows early evidence of Doyle's later tendency to capitalize words beginning with the letter "c" whether they need it or not:

> each man carring a knife gun pistle We ran on till we Came to a Cave on the Side of the rock we rushed in the first thing we saw Was a fine Bengal

[5] Doyle will use this same phrase, thirty years later, to describe Sherlock Holmes (in The Lion's Mane).

[6] Thomas Mayne Reid, 1818-1883, author of *The Scalp-Hunters* (1851), etc.

[7] This story must have been "The Mystery of Sasassa Valley," which appeared in *Chambers's Journal* for 6 September 1879. (Indeed one newspaper report has Doyle specifying *Chambers's* – which is hardly a "provincial" journal.)

[8] *Memories and Adventures*, p. 67, says the figure was £10 to £15, which at the customary rate of about $5 to £1 is even less.

[9] This must be "J. Habakuk Jephson's Statement," which was published in the January 1884 issue of *Cornhill*. Other reviews were more favourable – and then there were the many commentators who took the story as fact, not fiction.

[10] *Memories and Adventures*, p. 68.

[11] *Memories and Adventures*, p. 69. The book to which Doyle refers must be *The Mystery of Cloomber* (Ward and Downey, 1889). There is an earlier novel, *The Firm of Girdlestone*, but the description Doyle gives here hardly suits it.

[12] *Ibid.*, p. 69.

[13] *Ibid.*, pp. 20-21.

[14] As far as I am aware, this incident has never been published, this deduction never explained.

[15] *Memories and Adventures*, p. 95.

[16] *Memories and Adventures*, p. 104.

[17] *Memories and Adventures*, p. 94.

Notes: Readings and Reminiscences

[18] Doyle must be thinking here of the work of his uncle Richard (Dicky) Doyle, whose work in *Punch* was well known – and, perhaps, of his frustrated father, Charles Altamont Doyle, whose life was in the end devoted to alcohol rather than to art.

[19] It is the work (1881) of Charles Reade, 1814-1884, the uncle of Winwood Reade, whose book *The Martyrdom of Man* is mentioned by Sherlock Holmes as "one of the most remarkable ever penned."

[20] This statement is not true, as Karen Campbell has pointed out to me. *Micah Clarke* does contain a significant love story (and one which, as Doyle presumably expected, does little to strengthen the book as a whole). One wonders why the author made so broad a disclaimer.

[21] Lucius Cary, second Viscount Falkland, an ambivalent Royalist.

[22] *Memories and Adventures*, p. 71. The publisher mentioned is apparently Bentley.

[23] Beyond doubt, this episode in Doyle's life is the origin of the often-discussed list quoted by Jabez Wilson, the encyclopaedia copyist in "The Red-Headed League," a story which Doyle wrote not long after completing *The White Company* in 1890. Says Wilson, "I had written about Abbots and Archery and Armour and Architecture and Attica, and hoped with diligence that I might get on to the B's before very long." Attica is the odd one out, but the other subjects were clearly studied by Doyle as he prepared to write a novel of mediaeval times. It would be of interest to know whether he sorted his material alphabetically in quires of foolscap.

[24] *Memories and Adventures*, pp. 92-93.

[25] The programme leaflet for Doyle's reading at Yonkers indicates that his lecture would include a reading from *The Refugees*, presumably at about this point, but the newspaper accounts, from Yonkers and elsewhere, do not indicate that there was any such reading.

[26] One newspaper report complains that Doyle pronounced this title "Chateau Gnaw."

Appendix II
Notes and Comments

Epigraph

J. B. Pond: From a typescript by Major Pond, Doyle's agent during the 1894 tour, now held in microfilm by the State Historical Society library, Madison, Wisconsin.

Introduction

Memoirs of Sherlock Holmes: See also the chapter for November 20.

Micah Clarke: This edition, mentioned by Gibson and Green (*op. cit.*, p. 19), was reported in *Publishers Weekly* for September 29, 1894. Published by Longmans, Green, it sold for fifty cents. The Harper edition described by Gibson and Green (p. 18) as published in September 1894 does not appear in *Publishers' Weekly* at all.

Innes Doyle: ACD's brother was born March 31, 1873 and formally named John Francis (some records say Fraser) Innes Hay Doyle. His posting at Fort Efford (not Aldershot, as Charles Higham assumes in *The Adventures of Conan Doyle*, London: Hamish Hamilton, 1976, pp. 133, 139) is reported in the *Monthly Army List* for October 1894. (The November and December issues show him listed as at Devonport; there is no mention of the leave, which may not have been formally gazetted.) His commanding officer at Fort Efford, again according to the *Monthly Army List*, was Major H. P. Hickman. Details of Innes's later career can be found in *The New Annual Army List* (H. G. Hart), 1894 ff. I am grateful to Maj. (ret.) A. S. J. Bake of the Massey Library, the Royal Military College of Canada, for some assistance with information about the Royal Artillery. Detailed information about Innes's career was assembled for me by D. A. Redmond. That Innes collected souvenirs is demonstrated by the existence of several of them in the collection of Gerald O'Hara of Edmonton, who I understand received them from Innes's son, Brigadier John Hay Doyle. The diary which Innes Doyle apparently kept is not publicly available.

Trolley incident: The locale is Brooklyn, in this tale told in the *New York Sun*, November 13, 1894 ("Sat in Her Escort's Lap").

Brochure: J. Bliss Austin of Pittsburgh kindly provided me with a photocopy of the Pond brochure from his collection.

Notes: Introduction

Letter to Greenhough Smith: This letter, dated July 11, 1894, is in the Arthur Conan Doyle Collection of the Metropolitan Toronto Library.

Doyle's letter to Pond: This letter, dated May 31, 1894, is in the collection of the Buffalo Historical Society, where it was located and copied for me by Allen De Loach.

Society of Authors: There was a modest report of this dinner in *The Times* for June 1, 1894. Through the courtesy of Philippa MacLiesh of The Society of Authors, I have a copy of the evening's proceedings as they were reported in *The Author* for July 2, 1894. It includes a full list of those in attendance; other names of interest include Marie Belloc, Walter Besant, "Maj.-Gen. Sir F. J. Goldsmid, C.B.," and "Rev. Prof. W. W. Skeat, LL.D.." *The Author* includes the text of Doyle's remarks, in which he observed that "Our colleagues of poetry, of science, and of history have made their way as high as the House of Peers and the Privy Council. But fiction has always been the Cinderella of the family. . . . Within the last ten years several noble novels have come from the pens of men and women which would have been, I think, impossible a decade earlier." The "Miss Doyle" who accompanied ACD to the dinner was not Connie, the literary sister, who by this time was Mrs. Willie Hornung; most likely it was Caroline (Lottie), now 26 years old.

Major Pond: J. B. Pond's autobiography is *Eccentricities of Genius: Memories of Famous Men and Women of the Platform and Stage* (London: Chatto & Windus, 1901); it tells a little about his own life, though it is chiefly about his performers. Pond is discussed a good deal by William Webster Ellsworth in *A Golden Age of Authors* (Boston and New York: Houghton Mifflin, 1919), especially pp. 225-228, 251-260. One of Pond's critics was Winston Churchill, who referred to him in a letter as "a vulgar Yankee impresario [who] poured a lot of very mendacious statements into the ears of the reporters" (Randolph Churchill, *Winston Churchill: Youth 1874-1900* (Boston: Houghton Mifflin, 1966), pp. 526-527. George Kennan is referred to on p. 258. John Nieminski points out that Kennan had met Doyle in England in the summer of 1893, according to a brief note in the *Chicago Evening Journal* for July 22, 1893. Major Pond's role in the lyceum and lecture movement is discussed by Carl Bode in *The American Lyceum* (New York: Oxford University Press, 1956), especially pp. 248-252.

Doyle's autobiography: *Memories and Adventures* (Boston: Little, Brown, 1924), with Pond at pp. 116-117. Doyle refers to Pond as "my old friend and manager . . . typically American" in *Our American Adventure* (London: Hodder and Stoughton, Ltd., [1923]), p. 17. That book is chiefly a narrative of Doyle's 1922 American tour.

Mark Twain: Ellsworth, *op. cit.*, pp. 225-227.

Eugene Field: This letter to Pond, dated April 10, 1893, is available in microfilm at the State Historical Library of Wisconsin, Madison.

Nothing after December 1: ACD originally sets this deadline in the May 31 letter referred to above. By the time he reached America, he was telling reporters that he would be leaving by December 10. (In the end, he sailed on the 8th.)

Bill Nye: Ellsworth, *op. cit.*, p. 219.

The *Elbe*: The Norddeutscher-Lloyd line advertised regularly in *The Times*, promising a westward voyage of seven and a half days from Southampton. (Trains from Waterloo Station in London met the ship at the docks.) Some information about the *Elbe* is found in Henry Fry, *The History of North Atlantic Steam Navigation* (London: Sampson Low, Marston and Company, 1896; reprint by Cornmarket Press, London, 1969).

"The Wreck of the Deutschland": This poem, written by young Hopkins probably in 1876 (while Doyle was a schoolboy in Germany), had certainly been shown to Splaine by the middle of 1884 – so Hopkins says in a letter to Robert Bridges (*The Letters of Gerard Manley Hopkins to Robert Bridges*, edited by Claude Colleer Abbott. Oxford University Press, 1955). Splaine's connection with Doyle was first brought to light by Owen Dudley Edwards in *The Quest for Sherlock Holmes* (Edinburgh: Mainstream Publishing, 1983), pp. 104-5, 121.

Low-roofed hotel: William Archer, *America To-Day: Observations and Reflections* (New York: Scribner, 1899; Arno Press, 1974), p. 8.

Sinking of the *Elbe*: Lively accounts of this event appear in *The Chautauquan* xx (March 1895) No. 6, pp. 734-735, under the title "An Appalling Ocean Disaster," and in *The Illustrated London News* cvi (February 9, 1895) no. 2912. Just twenty of the 336 passengers and crew were saved when the British steamer *Crathie* struck the *Elbe*, making another trip from Bremen to Southampton, in an early morning storm.

Dining salon: Doyle reports this incident briefly in *Memories and Adventures* (Boston: Little, Brown, 1924), p. 116. He says the flags were hung to mark "some fête day."

Passengers: A list of passengers disembarking from the *Elbe* (presumably only those from the cabin classes) appeared in *The New York Times* for October 3, 1894. It is much longer than the brief cabin-class list (transcribed for me by D. A. Redmond) in the Passenger Lists Outwards maintained by the Public Records Office, London; those Lists name only the forty-two adults and three children who boarded at Southampton, and omit the dozens of (mostly German) names in the *New York Times* list. Those people presumably boarded at Bremen. A considerable number of steerage passengers came aboard at both ports as well.

Geheimrath Gutsch: A "Geheimrath" is a Privy Councillor, holder of a minor Imperial German distinction. I have not been able to identify Gutsch, though Don Redmond has identified three possibilities: Friedrich Gutsch, 1838-1897, Karlsruhe historian and writer; Julius Gutsch, apparently an engineer; and Ludwig Gutsch, author of *Uber die Ursachen des Schockes nach Operationen in der Bauchhohle*.

John Harington Gubbins: His books were reviewed in *The Times Literary Supplement*, November 2, 1911, and November 2, 1922. His *Who's Who* entry notes that he also compiled a Japanese dictionary and translated the Civil Code of Japan into English. Barton-Wright's "bartitsu" is probably the original of the "baritsu" which Sherlock Holmes mentions in "The Empty House" (published 1903).

Charles Sumner Tainter: The story of the Tainter-Edison, graphophone-phonograph, rivalry is told, rather from an Edisonian point of view, by Oliver Read and Walter L. Welch in *From Tin Foil to Stereo* (Indianapolis: Howard W. Sams & Co., Inc., 1976, second edition). See especially pp. 28, 31, 56. The passage from *Hamlet* is, "There are more things in heaven and earth, Horatio, than are dreamed of in our philosophy." The story in which Holmes uses a gramophone is "The Mazarin Stone" (1921).

Notes: October 1894

Charles E. West: An obituary appeared in *The New York Times* March 10, 1900. Much of the information summarized here is taken from the files of the archives at the Schaffer Library, Union College, Schenectady, from which West graduated in 1832; the material was generously photocopied for my use by Sibylle Schweidt of the Union College alumni office. The catalogues from the sales of West's books, in 1895 and 1901, make no mention of any of Doyle's books, I am kindly informed by Allen Asaf of The Grolier Club, New York, who however points out that this is not proof that he never owned any books by an author whom he must have met.

October 1894

Tuesday, October 2: Arrival in New York
Hudson River piers: The *New York World* for October 3, 1894 ("A. Conan Doyle Is Here") does say that ACD landed at Hoboken (across the Hudson from New York). This is unlikely – liners generally docked in Manhattan – but possible. The *World* reporter is unlikely to have invented such an idea; on the other hand, he weakens his credibility by saying that Doyle claimed to be 34 years old (he was 35).

Cabin passengers: The procedures for landing passengers of various classes are affectingly told by Ann Novotny in *Strangers at the Door* (Riverside, Connecticut: Chatham Press, [1971], pp. 10-13.

Inevitable reporters: In addition to the *Times* and *World*, quoted here, other papers were represented, including the *Tribune*, which had a brief report October 3 ("A. Conan Doyle Comes to Lecture").

Sherlock Holmes: *New York World*, October 3, 1894.

He is tall: *The New York Times* for October 3, 1894 ("Conan Doyle As He Appears Here").

Louise will come: *New York World*, October 3, 1894.

Mr. Appleton: D. Appleton & Co. would publish *Round the Red Lamp* at the beginning of November (*Publishers' Weekly*, November 3, 1894). It is not certain which Appleton was Doyle's sponsor at the club. There were a good half-dozen of the family involved in the firm. William Worthen Appleton, 48 years old at this time and head of the firm, had been one of the publishing leaders who secured passage of the 1891 copyright law; he appeared at a dinner in Doyle's honour later in his visit (see the chapter for December 7). His cousin Daniel Appleton, 42 years old, would become vice-president of the firm (W. W. Appleton became president) when it incorporated in 1896. For a younger brother of Daniel, Edward Dale, see the chapter for October 8. Doyle's host may even have been William Henry Appleton, senior member of the firm from 1848 and a former president of the American Publishers Copyright League; aged 80 in 1894, he lived to be 85.

Aldine Club: The club is described in New York guidebooks of the period; its move to Fifth Avenue is announced in *Publishers' Weekly* for February 10, 1894. In his autobiography Doyle says that he was lodged in "a little hotel beside the Aldine Club, . . . in which we had our meals." *Memories and Adventures*, p. 116. The Kensington is identified in a brief piece, "A Man of Few Words," in *The New York Dramatic Mirror* for November 24, 1894, which observes that "by the courtesy of the members of the Aldine Club, he uses the Club's rooms, which are situated in the adjoining house."

I wrote short stories: *New York Times*, October 3, 1894.

I make no exception: The report in the *Times* gives no basis for Higham's statement, in his biography of Arthur Conan Doyle, that his subject "roared" this famous line (*The Adventures of Conan Doyle*, New York: W. W. Norton, 1976, p. 133). Higham also says that this press-conference took place in the first-class lounge of the *Elbe*, and that the Aldine Club was at 20 Lafayette Place.

Of course I know: *New York World*, October 3, 1894.

Miss Wilkins: Known to history as Mary E. Wilkins Freeman, she was the author of several books of stories, starting with *The Adventures of Ann* (1886) and including *Giles Corey* (1892). *Pembroke*, her most ambitious book to date, was described by one critic as "one of the strongest and least engaging novels of the year. We cannot praise too highly the close and fine texture of Miss Wilkins's art, both in style and composition; but her people and scenes are dreary, and even repellant, almost beyond endurance." (*New York Independent*, as quoted in the *Vermont Phoenix* for November 23, 1894.)

Never saw such an atmosphere: *New York World*.

The World building: Built by Joseph Pulitzer in 1889-90 in newspaper row, near City Hall, it was in 1894 the tallest office building in the world, 309 feet from sidewalk to lantern (twenty-six storeys, surmounted with a golden dome).

Shenandoah: Doyle's attendance at this play is mentioned by *The New York Times*. The review quoted appeared in the *Times* for August 31, 1894.

Wednesday, October 3: The Metropolis of the United States
Leading guidebook: The guide I have used is the 1892 edition of *King's Handbook of New York City*, "Planned, Edited and Published by Moses King, Boston, Mass." This quotation is from page 45; the statistics cited are from pp. 45-66.

University of the City of New York: This institution is the forerunner not of the City University of New York but of the private New York University, although the University Heights campus in the Bronx now belongs to CUNY (NYU abandoned it in 1973).

Proposal to unite New York: *King's Handbook*, p. 48.

In a long tradition: A major study of the subject is Richard L. Rapson, *Britons View America* (Seattle: University of Washington Press, [1971]). a book of sources is Allan Nevins, ed., *American Social History as Recorded by British Travellers* (New York: Henry Holt and Company, 1923, 1931).

Five years hence: William Archer, *America To-Day: Observations and Reflections* (New York: Scribner, 1899; Arno Press, 1974), pp. 11, 26, 45, 56-57.

Tribune: The news items mentioned do all appear in the *Tribune* for October 2, 1894.

Green fields: It is in The Three Students that Holmes babbles of "green peas at seven-thirty."

New York Times: The quotations and other references are from *The New York Times* for October 3, 1894.

Notes: October 1894

Governesses: ACD, whose younger sisters had become governesses and whose grandmother had rented rooms to governesses, was well aware of their ambiguous social status and the ways in which they could be exploited. Several of the Sherlock Holmes stories present governesses as their heroines.

Prince Ruspoli: Emanuele Ruspoli, principe di Poggi Suasa. At 57, he had enjoyed a military career – and a political one since the unification of Italy – and had been a syndic of Rome for twenty years.

David Swing: See also the chapter for October 14.

Thursday, October 4: Luncheon at the Lotos Club
Lotos Club: John Elderkin, *A Brief History of the Lotos Club* (New York: [Press of Macgowan and Slipper, ca. 1895]).

Luncheon: A list of those present is given in a brief paragraph in *The New York Times* for October 5, 1894.

Edgar Saltus: The first biography of this curious man is *Edgar Saltus: The Man*, by his third wife, Marie Saltus (Chicago: Pascal Covici, 1925). It is short on dates and long on anecdotes which make Saltus seem a madman, unrestrained in emotion or behaviour. But his literary output was substantial enough to suggest that he was more. His presence at a respectable luncheon in 1894 must have required some tolerance, both because of his indecent reputation and because of his agnostic (not yet Theosophist) views. Still more tolerance, perhaps, might have been required after his second marriage the following year, or his later involvement with the much younger Marie.

Traveller of 1899: William Archer, *America To-Day: Observations and Reflections* (New York: Scribner, 1899; Arno Press, 1974), p. 82.

Collier's Cyclopedia: The edition of this huge one-volume compendium which I have seen also includes sections on rainfall, bicycle riding, grammar, and Instructions to Ladies Desirous of Entering the Civil Service.

Expansion: Archer travelled in 1898, when the leading political question was the American presence in Cuba and (especially) the Philippines.

John Lawson Stoddard: The *Boston Evening Transcript* for November 21, 1894, reporting one of ACD's lectures in that city, notes that Stoddard will shortly arrive to speak about the places listed.

Friday, October 5: A Chat with Conan Doyle
Thomas Carlyle: I have been unable to locate this paragraph in the works of Carlyle, though I do not doubt that it is there. Doyle was interested in Carlyle as early as January 19, 1886, when he read a paper on him to the Portsmouth Literary and Scientific Society. (The *Hampshire Post* for January 23, under the heading "Our Literary and Scientific Society," observed that on Carlyle's character, principles, and literary importance, "Dr. Doyle holds the most orthodox views," which was to say, there was nothing very original in his remarks.) A useful discussion of Doyle's early interest in the survival of personality, which eventually led him to become a Spiritualist, is found in Pierre Nordon, *Conan Doyle* (London: John Murray, 1966), pp. 144-152.

Favourite quotation: This solemn hopeful page, along with other photographs and holograph quotations apparently also from *New Age*, was republished in *Portraits, Quotations, Autographs*, edited by F. A. Atkins (London: Partridge, 1894).

Welcome to America, Mr. Sherlock Holmes

ACD's page is opposite that of a bemedalled Lord Charles Beresford, who betrays that he is no literary man by offering a two-word favourite quotation and spelling one of the words wrong: "Never dispair."

"A Chat with Conan Doyle": *Idler* vi, pp. 340-349; *McClure's Magazine* iii pp. 503-513 (the November 1894 issue). See also the chapter for October 28 for more about the *McClure's* version.

Robert Barr: Born in Scotland in 1850, Barr was raised in Ontario, taught school, and in the 1870's began to write. In 1876 he crossed the St. Clair River from his home in Windsor, Ontario, to Detroit, where he joined the staff of the *Free Press*. That paper sent him to England in 1881 to work on establishing a weekly European edition, but he turned to more serious writing (a first book was published in 1883) and in 1892 he and Jerome were the central figures in the establishment of *The Idler*. His article "Literature in Canada" (*Canadian Magazine*, 1899) is probably his most lasting work. See also the chapters and notes for October 21 and October 28. One of the few available biographical sources is the Introduction, Chronology and Bibliography to *Selected Stories of Robert Barr*, edited by John Parr (University of Ottawa Press, 1977).

Works written in Norwood: Bibliographical details for the titles cited can easily be found in Gibson and Green's *Bibliography*. Clearly the most important title of the autumn of 1894 is *Round the Red Lamp*, which was first published by Methuen in London (October 23, 1894, say Gibson and Green) and in New York by D. Appleton (*Publishers' Weekly*, November 3, 1894). *The Great Keinplatz Experiment* was originally published in 1885. *The Great Keinplatz Experiment and Other Stories*, published by Rand McNally in its Globe Library paperback series, is reported in *Publishers' Weekly* for October 6, 1894. Gibson and Green class it under "Unauthorized and Cheap American Editions." The story appears in *The Captain of the Polestar and Other Tales*, of which Longmans in New York published editions in 1890 and 1892. *Beyond the City* (first published 1893) and *Micah Clarke* (1889) are reported in *Publishers' Weekly* for November 3, 1894. Gibson and Green indicate that the former was a twenty-five-cent paperback in the Dora Thorne series, and that *Micah Clarke* appeared at twenty-five cents in that series and fifty cents in the Sunnyside series. Some of the serial publications are mentioned in later chapters of this study, and Brigadier Gérard is discussed in more detail in the chapter for November 18.

Saturday, October 6: Parkman Land

Parkman Land: Doyle frequently used this term for the Adirondack region, recognizing that his interest in it arose from the writings of historian Francis Parkman (1823-1893), who spent his life at Harvard University writing the history of New France. The definitive edition of his nine-volume work is *France and England in North America* (New York: Frederick Ungar Publishing Co., 1965), a facsimile of the nine original volumes (1865-1884) with an introduction by Allan Nevins. (ACD speaks of Parkman's twelve volumes, but that includes minor works not part of this opus.) My citations to Parkman are to book title and chapter. A pleasant digest is *The Parkman Reader* (Boston: Little, Brown and Company, 1955), with an introduction and notes by Samuel Eliot Morrison.

Langy and Trepezec: Francis Parkman, *Montcalm and Wolfe*, chapter xx.

State park: I have drawn general information about the Adirondack region from *Adirondack Country* by William Chapman White (New York: Alfred A. Knopf, 1967).

Notes: October 1894

Baedeker: *Baedeker's United States*, 1893 edition, p. 166ff; steamer to Albany, p. 143.

Died a year ago: Parkman died at home November 8, 1893.

Autobiography: *Memories and Adventures pp. 290-291.*

James Fenimore Cooper: One thinks especially of *The Last of the Mohicans*, a book which ACD read and which apparently influenced one of his stories in particular: "The Copper Beeches." He borrows the name of the British commander in Cooper's book, Colonel Munro, and that of his daughter, Alice, and attaches Munro to a fort in the new world (Halifax, which, like Fort William Henry, figures in such histories as Parkman's). It seems likely that what suggested the connection was hair: in *The Last of the Mohicans* the danger that Alice will be scalped amounts to an obsession, and of course scalping of the young lady is exactly what takes place in "The Copper Beeches." See also the chapter and notes for November 23.

Standing at sunset: Francis Parkman, *Pioneers of France in the New World*, Part II, chapter x.

Sunday, October 7: The Sage of Boston

Holmes is dead: *The New York Times*, October 8, 1894, a long front-page article embellished with an engraved portrait of Holmes (illustrations were rare in serious newspapers in this period) and including three brief quotations from his verse.

March 3, 1881: Catherine Drinker Bowen, *Yankee from Olympus* (Boston: Little, Brown and Company, 1944) is a popular biography of the senior and junior Holmeses; the 1881 dedication is mentioned at p. 284. I have argued elsewhere (in a letter in *The Baker Street Journal* XXXIII no. 2, June 1983, pp. 100-101) that ACD may have been aware of this date and echoed it more or less deliberately in his dating of the major scenes of *A Study in Scarlet*.

A book in 1907: *Through the Magic Door* (London: Smith, Elder & Co., 1907, and New York: The McClure Company, 1908). In the edition accessible to me (London: John Murray, 1920) Oliver Wendell Holmes is dealt with on pp. 254-257. It is perhaps of interest that ACD refers to the author by what looks like a compound surname, Wendell Holmes, just as he eventually came to treat "Conan Doyle" as inseparable, and to introduce such ambiguous names in his writings (for example, Arthur Cadogan West in "The Bruce-Partington Plans").

Monday, October 8: Hunting in the Adirondacks

In the Adirondacks: Newspapers from Adirondack towns during the period seem to make no mention of Doyle; I inferred that he was at a more remote camp or hunting-lodge. Thanks for efforts to locate him, however unsuccessful, are due to Richard H. Kimball of the North Country Reference and Research Resources Council; Shirley McFerson of the Caldwell Library, Lake George; Eleanor Rossiter of the Essex County Historical Society; William K. Verner of *Adirondack Life* magazine; Pamela Vogel, historian of Warren County; Mary McKenzie, town historian of Lake Placid. Finally a letter which I wrote to the *Adirondack Daily Enterprise* in Saranac Lake attracted the attention of Rod Swenson of Ridgefield, Connecticut, who generously wrote to give me a photocopy of Doyle's signature in the visitors' book of his grandfather's lodge at Upper Saranac Lake, and subsequently provided much more information about Bungalow Bay (later called Saranac Pines). Gerry O'Hara of Edmonton has two photographs showing Doyle in the Adirondacks, presumed to date from this visit.

General information about the Adirondacks is drawn from William Chapman White, *Adirondack Country* (New York: Alfred A. Knopf, 1967): Paul Smith, pp. 130-134; Adirondack League Club, p. 150; Saranac Lake, pp. 165-174; Bonapartes, pp. 181-194.

In this chapter, for the first of many times in my study, I cite an article from a Chicago newspaper which was available for consultation because of the painstaking research of John Nieminski. In 1983 he assembled the Chicago press coverage of ACD's tour, transcribed the articles and published a few copies under the title *Conan Doyle in Chicago*. Without the existence of this compendium, and its creator's kindness in providing me with a copy, my researches would have been vastly more laborious.

Baedeker: The 1893 *Baedeker's United States*, already quoted, p. 167.

The game animals: *Where to Hunt American Game* (Lowell, Massachusetts: United States Cartridge Company, 1898), passim.

Tell an interviewer: *Chicago Times*, October 13, 1894, part of a long interview headed "Dr. Doyle on Writers . . . He Likes America and Its People."

Tuesday, October 9: The Stars and Stripes
James F. Muirhead: *The Land of Contrasts: A Briton's View of His American Kin* (Boston, etc.: 1898), excerpted in Neil Harris, ed., *The Land of Contrasts, 1880-1901* (New York: George Braziller, 1970), pp. 32-41, at p. 41.

Consulted an almanac: As Sherlock Holmes did in *The Valley of Fear*, I have referred to Whitaker's *Almanack for the Year of Our Lord 1894* (London, 1893), which describes the United States at pp. 572-575. The population of the United Kingdom in 1891, according to Whitaker's, was 37,787,953.

Larz Anderson: Born 1866, later to serve briefly (1912-1913) as ambassador to Japan, Anderson would be remembered by a bridge between Boston and Cambridge, Massachusetts, which bears his name.

Folly of a monarch: This cloying peroration appears in "The Noble Bachelor."

Rudyard Kipling: See the chapters for October 29 and November 29.

Social summonses: This quotation too is from "The Noble Bachelor."

Wednesday, October 10: Lecture at Calvary
American publishers: ACD's October 10 letter to someone at Appletons is in the Appleton-Century Manuscripts collection of the Lilly Library, Indiana University, Bloomington. (I am grateful to Cheryl Baumgart of that library for arranging to make a photocopy available.) ACD's dilemma over a new edition of *The White Company* is noted by Gibson and Green in their *Bibliography*, p. 48. The new edition was in the end published by Harper & Brothers in 1895.

William Dean Howells: I have been unable to find out what the occasion was on which ACD met Howells, but it was certainly during his first stay in New York, for he mentioned it, as the chapter notes, when he was in Indianapolis on October 15. The passage quoted is from "Dr. A. Conan Doyle Here," *Indianapolis Sentinel*, October 16, 1894. He again mentioned Howells in a letter written November 3 – see the chapter for that date.

Notes: October 1894

Calvary Baptist Church: It still exists on that 57th Street site, though in a new building; Rev. Nelson Schoen of its pastoral staff kindly helped me obtain a copy of William R. DePlata's book *Tell It from Calvary* (Calvary Baptist Church, 1972), which on pp. 23-35 tells the story of MacArthur's pastorate and describes the church at that period.

Young People's Association: The *New York Herald* and *Tribune* for October 11, 1894, and *The Critic* for October 13 all mention this sponsorship; both *Tribune* and *Critic* mention the other lecturers in the year's series. Of Hole, more will be said in the chapter for November 30.

Advertisements: For example, in *The New York Times* for October 10.

Autobiography: *Memories and Adventures* p. 117.

Haberdashery: New York *World*, October 11, 1894, has the fullest account of the October 10 lecture I have seen.

Hamilton Wright Mabie: Only the *Herald* mentions that it was Mabie who introduced Doyle. Karen D. Drickamer of the archives of Williams College, where a room is named in Mabie's memory, reports that the college has none of his papers which might mention an encounter with ACD.

The Pocket University: There are several editions of this book, the bibliography of which is somewhat confused. Through the kindness of Patricia Brandt of the William Jasper Kerr Library at Oregon State University, I have first-hand information about the edition of 1924-25, which contains ACD's story "The Dancing Men" in volume 22, part I, pp. 63-100. Volumes 22 to 25, covering Fiction, are said to have been edited by Mabie, who however died in 1916. ("The Dancing Men" was first published in 1903, so Mabie had full opportunity to read it and include it in earlier editions of *The Pocket University*.)

ACD's talk tonight: New York *World*, October 11.

"The Lord of Chateau Noir": This tale had already been published in the New York edition of the *Strand* magazine (August 1894) and in at least five American newspapers, but it was generally hailed as new throughout Doyle's tour. See also the notes for October 28.

Tips off a reporter: Pond "told me after the lecture" that future matinees were contemplated, the October 11 *Herald* reports. No other paper makes this promise.

Received as a success: Following are the October 11 press reports of this lecture which I have seen: "A. Conan Doyle's Lecture," in the *Herald*. "Doyle Tells of Doyle," in the *World*. "Conan Doyle's Lecture," in the *Sun*. "Dr. Doyle Makes His Bow," in the *Herald*. Two days later "Conan Doyle's First Lecture" appeared in the literary weekly *The Critic*.

For some reason Pond did not present ACD in Carnegie Hall, just around the corner from Calvary Baptist Church. Aside from the fact that the Young People's Association was willing to sponsor his lecture, doubtless taking some of the financial risk, it may also be that Carnegie Hall was not available. Susan L. Laufer of the staff of Carnegie Hall kindly drew my attention to the book *The World of Carnegie Hall* by Richard Schickel (New York: Julian Messner, Inc., 1960), pp. 71-72. This book confirms that Carnegie Hall underwent some renovations during 1894; when the Philharmonic Orchestra opened its season on November 16 the gala event was enlivened by falling plaster.

Welcome to America, Mr. Sherlock Holmes

Register of speakers: This manuscript book is now in the Berg Collection of the New York Public Library. It does not indicate the amount of the cheque; under "Fee" for this lecture is the symbol "HTX." Later lectures are variously marked "HTX," "CBT," "CRX," "CRB" and "ATX"; in a few cases, however, a fee is stated in dollars or percentage.

Thursday, October 11: The Limited Train
Baedeker: *Baedeker's United States*, 1893 edition. Routes are described as follows: New York to Chicago, overview, pp. 276-279. Pennsylvania Limited Vestibule Train, p. 276. New York to Albany (with advice to choose the left side of the train), pp. 150-152. Albany to Buffalo, pp. 186-192. Buffalo to Chicago, pp. 267-270.

The route ACD chooses: "Dr. A. Conan Doyle reached Chicago today over the Lake Shore Road from New York," begins a report in the Chicago *Post* for October 12. The *News* and *Journal* speak of his arrival "this morning" without mentioning the railroad.

No finer scenery: *Our American Adventure* (London: Hodder and Stoughton, [1923]), p. 102.

Chautauqua: There is no substitute for personal experience of Chautauqua, including the Maple Inn. At the Smith Memorial Library facing on Bestor Plaza in Chautauqua I did some small part of the research for this book, and I am grateful for the assistance of Alfrieda Irwin and Barbara Haug there. In particular I looked into the 1894 summer Assembly at Chautauqua, when lecturers included Anthony Comstock, Edward Everett Hale, Hermann von Holst (whom ACD met in Chicago), Theodore Roosevelt, the great Anglo-Saxonist A. S. Cook, and Miss K. E. Hogan, a New York lawyer. The assembly ran from June 30 to August 27 and included Political Equality Day, with attention to women's suffrage, on July 14, as well as graduation ceremonies for the 1894 class ("The Philomatheans") of the Chautauqua Literary and Scientific Circle. During 1894-95, CLSC members were studying *The Growth of the English Nation, Europe in the Nineteenth Century, From Chaucer to Tennyson, Renaissance and Modern Art*, and *Walks and Talks in the Geological Field*, as well as the monthly educational magazine *The Chautauquan*.

Cold Spring: Background information for this paragraph was acquired during a personal visit to Cold Spring and nearby places under the hospitable supervision of Edward F. Clark Jr. and Rosemary Clark.

Joseph Smith: Doyle's *A Study in Scarlet* is of course largely about the early days of the Mormons.

It was very beautiful: "Conan Doyle Here," Chicago *Post*, October 12, 1894).

Friday, October 12: Chicago's Elite
This chapter, probably more than any other, relies on newspaper reports transcribed by John Nieminski in *Conan Doyle in Chicago*. Among the important ones: "Conan Doyle Here," *Post*, October 12, which provides the Monadnock Building anecdote; "Dr. Conan Doyle in Town," *News*, October 12, which less convincingly says that "a carriage" brought the travellers to their hotel; "An English Opinion," *Journal*, October 12; "An Author of Note," *Inter Ocean*, October 13; "Fiction as a Theme," *Tribune*, October 13; "Conan Doyle Talks," *Record*, October 13; "Dr. Doyle on Writers," *Times*, October 13; "Doyle as Lecturer," *Herald*, October 13.

Notes: October 1894

Grand Pacific Hotel: Several newspapers mention this hotel. The bathroom incident is reported in the *Post*, the cigarette-case in the *Journal*, Doyle lolling on the bed in the *Inter Ocean*. The hotel is described in *The Artistic Guide to Chicago and the World's Columbian Exposition* by Charles Eugene Banks (R. S. Peale Co., 1893), p. 153. Writes David Lowe in *Lost Chicago* (Boston: Houghton Mifflin, 1975, p. 66): "Turning for inspiration to the extensions of the Louvre just completed for Napoleon III by Louis Visconti and Hector Martin Lefuel, [architect William] Boyington created an edifice which would be a model for Chicago hotels for years to come. In a daring display of prodigality, he brought together Doric, Ionic, and Corinthian columns, balconies, domes, pavilions, a forest of chimneys, and caryatids to compose a building which had in the words of a contemporary guide to the city, not one, but 'four grand entrances.' Here was indeed a palace for the people."

The theatres: As reported in the *Post*, this conversation seems to indicate that ACD and Innes had seen more than one play, perhaps several plays, in New York. If they did, I have found no record of it; the conversation may reflect a glance at playbills rather than actual attendance at performances.

2838 Michigan Avenue: The phrase "bijou theater" was used by the *Inter Ocean*, October 13. (The *Record* called the same room a "dainty little theater" and the *Herald* used the phrase "spacious ballroom.") The Turkish Room, "Miss Higinbotham's Room" and another – unidentified – room of this house are dignified with full-page engravings in *Interior Views of Chicago Residences* (1900), made available to me in photocopy through the kindness of Janice Soczka of the Chicago Historical Society Library.

Moneyed and cultured class: The circle in which Higinbotham, Adams, and the others moved is the subject of *Culture and the City* by Helen Lefkowitz Horowitz (University Press of Kentucky, 1976). The first hundred pages of this book are sprinkled with names which were on the guest list for ACD's lecture; the comment about raising money was made by Thomas W. Goodspeed in a letter (October 5, 1890) quoted by Horowitz, pp. 42-43. A useful appendix lists the major figures and their institutional connections.

Charles L. Hutchinson: A president of the Art Institute, trustee and treasurer of the University of Chicago, guarantor of the 1893 Exposition. I am grateful to Carolyn A. Sheehy of the Newberry Library for consulting those of Hutchinson's papers which that library holds, but they do not include diaries from 1894.

Scheduled for the coming months: *Tribune*, October 12. Higginson, born 1823, was a lifelong resident of Cambridge, Massachusetts, known for his poetry, stories and histories, including *Army Life in a Black Regiment* (1869), based on his Civil War experience leading black troops; *Common Sense about Women* (1884); and *Larger History of the United States* (1885). He also served as president of the Free Religious Association. For Dean Hole, see the chapter for November 30.

Twentieth Century Club: *Tribune*, October 12, under the title "Society Affairs."

Canon Doyle: The narrative given in this chapter is the best explanation I can devise of how the story arose that Doyle was regularly called "Canon" by people who thought he was a clergyman. Eugene Field's column "Sharps and Flats" in the *Chicago Record* told the story October 15 and 16, and, through the "exchanges" in which American papers delighted, it reached many of the cities which ACD would later visit. Field solemnly describes George Adams's slip of the tongue as "an error which is likely to give rise to complications and to involve Dr. Doyle in embarrassment." It is unlikely that Adams really believed ACD to be a cleric, but apparently some people who had heard the name second-hand did.

By November 24, the *Literary Digest* (crediting the *New York Sun*) was telling the story in detail, with Higinbotham ("who became famous during the World's Fair by appearing at a luncheon given to the Spanish Infanta, in a dress suit") the butt of the joke: "He presided at a breakfast, and addressing the guest as Father Doyle, requested him to 'ask a blessing.' The accounts stated that Dr. Doyle has been overwhelmed with requests to preach in half the churches in Chicago." ("Literary Chicago and Conan Doyle," *Literary Digest* volume x number 4, November 24, 1894.) There is much to be said for the caveat of the Chicago *Tribune* in its "Notes and Gossip" column December 1, 1894: "This little tale must be taken with caution . . . for I am informed by one who ought to know that it originated in the fertile brain of Maj. Moses P. Handy of the *Mail and Express*, who told it at a recent dinner in the Waldorf."

Doyle himself gave this explanation to a reporter in Toronto:

> It was quite true, he said with a smile, that in Chicago a mistake was made whereby he was introduced as "Canon" Doyle, but he laughingly protested that the tales of the invitations to preach which flowered in upon him in consequence were a gratuitous addition to the story.

("Dr. A. Conan Doyle," *Toronto Globe*, November 27, 1894.) It was an easy enough mistake to make, however, and Doyle was happy to confirm such incidents in his autobiography:

> There was an amusing episode connected with "The Refugees," when it was read aloud in some strict Irish convent, the innocent Reverend Mother having mistaken my name and imagined that I was a canon, and therefore of course a holy man. I am told that the reading was a tremendous success and that the good sisters rejoiced that the mistake was not found out until the story was completed. My first name has several times led to mistakes, as when, at a big dinner in Chicago, I was asked to say Grace, as being the only ecclesiastic present. I remember that at the same dinner one of the speakers remarked that it was a most sinister fact that though I was a doctor no *living* patient of mine had ever yet been seen.

(*Memories and Adventures*, Boston: Little, Brown, 1924, p. 93.) "It is amusing, I think," wrote the learned John Nieminski in a letter to me, "to note that in a brief, unsigned review of *The Great Shadow* carried in the *Inter Ocean* for December 10, 1892, page 10, either the reviewer or a careless typesetter also gave the author's name as 'Canon Doyle'."

"Facts About Fiction": Doyle gave the lecture "Some Facts About Fiction" on October 4, 1893, according to reports October 7 in the *Norwood News and Crystal Palace Chronicle* and the *Norwood Review*, and October 19 in the *Anerley & Norwood Times*. He repeated it at Bayswater on October 10 (*Norwood Review*, October 14). He had also been giving lectures that season on such topics as "Recent Fiction" and "Fiction as a Part of Literature," according to newspaper reports listed in the Gibson and Green *Bibliography* – some fifty of them across England and Scotland by May, according to the *Norwood News*, May 19, 1894. The summary in this chapter is based on the newspapers already mentioned; the passage about love is quoted from the *Tribune*, October 13. I regret being unable to present this lecture *in extenso*.

Notes: October 1894

Ray Stannard Baker: That it was Baker who covered this lecture for the *Record* is stated by Robert C. Bannister, Jr., in *Ray Stannard Baker: The Mind and Thought of a Progressive* (Yale University Press, 1966), p. 66. Baker mentions the Page lecture and the Nordica interview, as well as telling about a Chicago newspaperman's life in general, in *Native American* (New York: Charles Scribner's Sons, 1941), pp. 268-270, 291-307.

After the lecture: The *Record* indicates that "supper" was served; other papers mention refreshments in the dining room. The names mentioned appear in the *Herald*. The *Record* indicates that Mrs. Higinbotham was "assisted . . . in receiving" by Mary (Mrs. Chauncey) Blair, wife of a bank president, and Mrs. Frederick W. Becker.

Saturday, October 13: A Literary Luncheon
The astonishing city: *The Artistic Guide to Chicago* has already been cited and provides a general impression of Chicago in the 1890's, as do passages in Horowitz's *Culture and the City*, also noted in the October 12 chapter, and Lowe's *Lost Chicago*, from which the description of Marshall Field's is taken.

Literary luncheon: Reported in "For Dr. Conan Doyle," Chicago *Inter Ocean*, October 14, and "very similarly worded items" in other newspapers, notes Nieminski in *Conan Doyle in Chicago*, adding that some of the reports identify the younger Stone, Herbert S., as the host.

Melville E. Stone: Some of this information is from Oliver Gramling, *AP: The Story of News* (New York: Farrar and Rinehart, Inc., 1940).

Autographs *The White Company*: Both copies of the book are now in the collections of the Newberry Library, Chicago; I am grateful for photocopies of their title pages.

Union League Club: *The Artistic Guide*, p. 175.

W. Irving Way: Joe W. Kraus, "The Publishing Activities of Way & Williams, Chicago, 1895-98," *The Papers of the Bibliographical Society of America* 70 (1976) pp. 221-260.

Franklin H. Head: A typewritten biographical sketch of this fascinating man was made available to me from the files of the Chicago Historical Society. Born in Paris, New York, he attended Hamilton College (which gave him an LL.D. degree in 1896) and developed both commercial and literary talents in an enormous number of directions. The Historical Society sketch notes that among his writings were some unpublished humourous papers, including "Dante and the Boodlers of His Time." One treasure of his Bank Street home was a collection of autographed portraits of celebrities. More will be said of Head and his family in the chapter for October 26.

F. F. Browne: Francis Fisher Browne, born 1843, was author of "The Every-day Life of Abraham Lincoln" (1886) and *Volunteer Grain* (poems, 1893) as well as editor of many anthologies. He founded *The Dial* in 1880.

Eugene Field: My chief source on Field is Robert Conrow's book *Field Days* (New York: Charles Scribner's Sons, 1974). Gerry O'Hara of Edmonton reports that he has a copy of a note from Field to Doyle, dated October 10, inviting Doyle to Field's home in Buena Vista, Illinois, on Saturday, presumably in the evening.

Hamlin Garland: This copy of *The Memoirs* (the second edition, lacking "The

Cardboard Box") is now in the Berg Collection of the New York Public Library. The inscription is on the title page. The diary passage quoted here is from *Hamlin Garland's Diaries*, edited by Donald Pizer (San Marino: Huntington Library, 1968), p. 22. The volume of reminiscences in which Garland mentions Doyle is *Companions on the Trail* (New York: Macmillan, 1931), at p. 297. William Jankos of the library at the University of Southern California kindly consulted Garland's papers and informs me that there are more than twenty letters and cards from Doyle to Garland, but most deal with Garland's visit to England and apparently none date from 1894. Nor do Garland's notebooks appear to mention the 1894 encounter. Garland, sceptical but sympathetic, took the chair when Doyle lectured on Spiritualism in New York in 1922 (Doyle, *Our American Adventure*, London: Hodder and Stoughton, 1923, p. 26).

Herbert S. Stone: Sidney Kramer, *A History of Stone & Kimball and Herbert S. Stone & Co. with a Bibliography of Their Publications 1893-1905*. University of Chicago Press, 1940. Stone's letter home about Harvard is quoted, p. 23.

Sunday, October 14: Aladdin, Jr.

Places of worship: *The Artistic Guide*, pp. 141-143. David Swing, who had died October 3, had drawn crowds to his Central Independent Church, conducted in the city's Central Music Hall.

Opera House: *The Artistic Guide*, p. 123.

Aladdin, Jr.: Nieminski in *Conan Doyle in Chicago*, p. 65, gives brief information about this play, which, he says, "opened to rave reviews on June 7, 1894, and was clearly the hit of that theatrical season." The cast list and the reference to the "incredibly blonde" soubrettes appear in the *New York Times* review published April 9, 1895.

Also occupying boxes: "Plays and Players," Chicago *Dispatch*, October 15, is the sole authority for ACD's attendance at this play, and mentions these names in the same sentence. There is no indication that these parties occupied the same box, although it is recorded that Frohman was a friend of J. M. Barrie, as was Doyle, so that they may have already formed an acquaintance. Frohman, at this time 34, was noted for his development of the "Star System"; William Gillette would be perhaps his biggest star. As for Al Hayman, it is not certain which of two theatrical brothers by that name attended the Opera House that evening: the theatrical manager (born 1850) or the producer (born 1865). Neither seems to have had interests in anything on a Chicago stage in the fall of 1894. The younger one, Alfred, would later be associated with Frohman, and is therefore the likelier candidate.

Monday, October 15: With Riley in Indianapolis

Indianapolis: *Baedeker's United States*, pp. 302-303. It is perhaps to be regretted that Doyle did not (apparently) visit the Propylaeum, let alone speak there.

D. H. Baldwin & Co.: Advertisements in Indianapolis *Journal* for October 14, the *Sentinel* for October 15, and probably other papers and dates mention Baldwin's. Diane Peters, music librarian at Wilfrid Laurier University, and Colleen R. Cahill of the Indiana Historical Society Library, Indianapolis, kindly helped me confirm that this ticket agency is the same firm now famous for pianos and organs. Unfortunately George F. Carr, Jr., vice-president of what is now the Baldwin-United Corporation, was unable to provide any further information about the company's Indianapolis establishment in the 1890's.

Notes: October 1894

Montefiore Lecture Course: Frederick P. Fellers of the Indianapolis Marion County Public Library reports that the library was unable to provide any information about the Montefiore Society, which sponsored Doyle's appearance in Indianapolis.

Lobby of the Denison House: This incident is most clearly told in "Conan Doyle in Town," Indianapolis *Journal*, October 16.

James Whitcomb Riley: At this time aged 45, Riley had been recovering from an illness brought on by hard work, lecture touring, and probably drink, a recurring problem for him. His collection of poems *Armazindy* had just been published. And he was becoming interested in Spiritualism, the faith to which Doyle had not yet turned. See Richard Crowder, *Those Innocent Years* (Indianapolis: Bobbs-Merrill, 1957).

Lively conversation: "Dr. A. Conan Doyle Here," Indianapolis *Sentinel*, October 16. A further paragraph of this report is quoted in the chapter for October 10.

ACD and Riley dine: The chronology of this afternoon in Indianapolis is puzzling. According to the *Journal*, October 16, Doyle's train arrived at the Union Station at 5:30 p.m.; he registered at the Denison; he met Riley; "the remainder of the afternoon was devoted to a delightful interchange of literary gossip" until ACD and Riley "dined together at 6 o'clock." The schedule seems impossibly tight. According to the *Sentinel* for October 15 (an untitled squib), Doyle arrived "early this morning"; that day's *Journal* uses the expression "will arrive early this morning," so perhaps that had been the announced plan. Next day the *Sentinel* has Doyle arriving in the "afternoon," meeting Riley – the conversation is quoted at length – and giving interviews. "Mr. Riley returned and the two went to Dr. Doyle's room, where they talked pleasantly for several hours." ACD's autobiography mentions Riley visiting his room and sitting on an "unmade" bed, but that can hardly have been when he had just checked in. It could have been Riley's room – he lived in the hotel, probably in a bohemian style. None of the papers indicate the time of Doyle's lecture, but the *Journal* says dinner, which followed not only the lecture but the reception, was at 10:30 p.m.

Plymouth Congregational Church: I am grateful to Richard M. Doolen of the library at the Christian Theological Seminary, Indianapolis, for providing some information about Plymouth Church (and its successor, the First Congregational Church) and drawing my attention to Genevieve C. Weeks's book *Oscar Carleton McCulloch, 1843-1891* (Indianapolis Historical Society, 1976), the biography of the minister who established Plymouth's cultural and outreach programme.

Isidore Feibleman: This man seems to have escaped all biographical dictionaries. His surname is mentioned in the newspapers, and his full name is given in Pond's register, which wrongly records that Doyle's topic in Indianapolis was "Facts about Fiction."

Robbery at New Orleans: Quoted from the *Journal*, October 16. I have so far failed to find further information about this incident, but I am kindly informed by Peter Costello of Dublin, who is doing research about Doyle's interest in true crime, that the "expert" was Solomon Solis Carvalho, crime reporter for the New York *Sun*. Costello observes that Carvalho "was well ahead of the times" in trying to use thumbprints for evidence in 1894. This incident probably finds an echo in "The Norwood Builder," in which a thumbprint provides ambiguous evidence.

Welcome to America, Mr. Sherlock Holmes

Franklin W. Hays: I am grateful to Colleen R. Cahill of the Indiana Historical Society Library and particularly to Lori L. Klein of the School of Medicine Library, Indiana University, for helping me to locate information about this talented man. Sources are Hays's entry in *Biography of Eminent American Physicians and Surgeons*, edited by R. French Stone (Indianapolis; C. E. Hollenbeck, 1898) and his obituary in the *Indiana Medical Journal* xvi (April 1908) pp. 412-413. Riley's cloying "Rubaiyat" appears in, among other places, *The Hoosier Book: Containing Poems in Dialect* by James Whitcomb Riley, ed. Hewitt Hanson Howland (Indianapolis: Bobbs-Merrill, 1916).

Riley is taken aside: *Journal*, October 16.

Tuesday, October 16: Ticket to Cincinnati

William Dean Howells: *Their Wedding Journey* (Boston and New York: Houghton Mifflin, 1895), p. 19.

One of the first things: "Conan Doyle's Lecture," *News*, October 17. The later quotation about autumn foliage is from the same article.

The monument: Colleen R. Cahill of the Indiana Historical Society Library has kindly provided a picture of the monument as it stood in 1936, with the English Theater and Hotel curving around it and not a building of more than ten storeys visible anywhere.

John M. Shaw: Mentioned in the *News* article already quoted, and identified through the kindness of the Indiana Historical Society.

A kodak fiend: This seems to be the only newspaper reference, at any point on the 1894 tour, to ACD taking pictures. But there is little reason to doubt it; he was a camera enthusiast and had contributed a number of essays to the *British Journal of Photography* in the early 1880's. They have been collected in *The Unknown Conan Doyle: Essays on Photography*, edited by John Michael Gibson and Richard Lancelyn Green (London: Secker & Warburg, 1982). There apparently was a camera with the Doyle brothers during their 1894 tour: see the notes for October 8.

Chief city of Ohio: *Baedeker's United States*, p. 307. The local guidebook cited is *Illustrated Guide to Cincinnati and the World's Columbian Exposition*, by D. J. Kenny (Cincinnati: Robert Clarke & Co., 1893), which notes that (besides the 2,091 saloons) the city had 186 churches, twenty-one kindergartens, and eight intelligence offices.

America's Berlin: The descriptions of Vine Street night life are from *Cincinnati: A Guide to the Queen City and its Neighbors* (American Guide Series; Cincinnati: The Wiesen-Hart Press, 1943; Somerset Publishers, 1973), pp. 105-109.

Bookstore on Seventh Street: *Publishers' Weekly*, November 10, 1894, under the column heading "Pick-Ups."

Burnet House: *Cincinnati: A Guide* (1943), pp. 50, 156-157.

Dr. Doyle was a feast: Newspaper articles reporting Doyle's arrival in Cincinnati include "A. Conan Doyle, Author," *Commercial Gazette*, October 17; "A. Conan Doyle," *Tribune*, October 17; "Conan Doyle," *Enquirer*, October 17; and the report quoted here from the *Times-Star*, October 17. I am grateful to Yeatman Anderson III of the Public Library of Cincinnati and Hamilton County for providing photocopies of some Cincinnati press reports, and to the staff of the

Notes: October 1894

Ohio Historical Society Library and Archives for assistance in locating others, as well as collateral information, during my visit to Columbus.

Lafcadio Hearn: As odd a figure as ever passed through the 19th-century literary scene, Hearn was born in 1850 in Ireland, and suffered seriously damaged vision as the result of a childhood accident. Coming to America, he waited on tables in New York, worked in Cincinnati's public library, and by 1874 was a reporter for the *Enquirer*. He lost his job in a scandal over a mulatto mistress, but eked out a living as a newspaper correspondent (seldom writing the informative copy which editors had commissioned) and writing fantastic essays and stories, as well as an 1890 book which reflected his adoration for the "golden, childlike" women of the West Indies. He went permanently to Japan in 1890, and by 1894 was on the staff of the *Kobe Chronicle* as well as writing books purporting to explain Japan to the western world. The one published in 1894, *Out of the East*, had something to say about jiu-jitsu – Doyle's "baritsu." One wonders whether Doyle, with his continuing interest in psychical matters, was aware that one basis of Hearn's reputation in Cincinnati was his 1875 exposé of fraudulent mediums and "spirit photographers."

Note to Riley: I am grateful to Cheryl Baumgart of the Lilly Library, Indiana University, Bloomington, for providing me with a photocopy of this letter, which is in its collection of Riley's papers.

Wednesday, October 17: The Culture of the Queen City
Reports of his interviews: See the Notes for October 16.

This valley city: *Baedeker's United States*, p. 307.

Taken around the city: Doyle's sight-seeing is briefly reported in the *Times-Star* for October 18, where the comments about the air and the public library are reported. The identification of Shearer and Whelpley, and the description of the public library and the Odd Fellows Hall, are based on *Williams' Cincinnati Directory* (Williams & Co., props., June 1893) and *Illustrated Guide to Cincinnati*, already cited. (The *Illustrated Guide* has an impressive picture of the Odd Fellows Hall at p. 158.) The Shearer Lecture and Musical Bureau, northwest corner of Seventh and Walnut Streets, was operated by J. L. Shearer and Samuel Ellis.

Tickets: Advertised in the *Enquirer*, October 16, and other papers.

Hon. Charles Baker: The "arms akimbo" description is from "Dr. A. Conan Doyle," *Tribune*, October 18. For Baker's life see William W. Morris et al., eds., *The Bench and Bar of Cincinnati* (Cincinnati: New Court House Publishing Co., 1921).

Audience is a good one: Quoted from *Times-Star*, October 18. The *Tribune*, as mentioned, had a substantial account of the lecture; the *Enquirer* just two brief paragraphs. The figure of $313.25 appears in Pond's register.

Thursday, October 18: Harvest Home in Chicago
Big news in Ohio: From the *Tribune* comes the Paul Jones anecdote; the Washington Court House affair was all over the front page of the *Enquirer* and in other papers.

Fellowship Club: This account is taken from newspaper reports collected in Nieminski's *Conan Doyle in Chicago*, especially "Down on the Farm," *Tribune*, October 19; "Down on the Farm," *Inter Ocean*, October 19; "Jolly Farmers Dine,"

Herald, October 19; "Pranks at Kinsley's," *Record*, October 19; "Amid Rural Delights," *Times*, October 19.

Adams Street restaurant: David Lowe, *Lost Chicago* (Boston: Houghton Mifflin, 1975), p. 188, with a fine photograph of the cast-iron Moorish facade of Kinsley's.

The apartment: Quoted from the *Tribune*'s report next day, as indicated.

H. H. Kohlsaat: The premiere of *A Story of Waterloo* took place at the Princes Theatre, Bristol, on September 21, 1894; it was reviewed next day in *The Times* and soon thereafter in other publications. If Kohlsaat had attended the premiere, his appearance in Chicago four weeks later would hardly have been miraculous; presumably then he saw a later performance. (It is my inference that it was this dinner at which this famous conversation took place; Kohlsaat is not listed as a guest at any of Doyle's earlier appearances in Chicago, and he was certainly at this one. The newspapers list his name last among those in attendance, which supports the statement that he arrived late.) I have chosen the version of the Kohlsaat-Doyle conversation which is reported by Bram Stoker, Irving's secretary, in *Personal Reminiscences of Henry Irving* (London: William Heinemann, 1906), pp. 250-251. It seems more plausible than the version given by Charles Higham in *The Adventures of Conan Doyle* (New York: W. W. Norton and Company, 1976), p. 136. Higham identifies Kohlsaat as editor of the *Times-Herald*, which at this time he was not. He reasonably has Kohlsaat identifying his "magic carpet" as the S. S. *City of Rome*, which docked in New York on October 6, 1894. (The *New York Times* for October 7 noted that Kohlsaat was in town and staying at the Holland hotel.) Kohlsaat thus had many leisurely days to reach Chicago.

Two women are brought in: The *Herald*, alone among the newspapers, refers to "the Weber quartet, assisted by Miss Carpenter and Agnes Hill Dodge," as part of the entertainment.

Price of wheat: Harold U. Faulkner, *Politics, Reform and Expansion 1890-1899* (New York: Harper & Brothers, 1959), p. 54. The price had been as high as $1.19 a bushel in 1881. "In 1894, the worst year of all, drought destroyed the crops in sixty-one of Nebraska's ninety-one counties," Faulkner writes. "Decline in production brought with it no compensating rise in price, because, while Kansas, Nebraska, and the Dakotas lay stricken, other states enjoyed fine years and produced large crops."

Hermann von Holst: "Seen at the Campus," *Inter-Ocean* for April 21, 1895, quoted in Richard J. Storr, *Harper's University: The Beginnings* (University of Chicago Press, 1966).

Ex-governor Oglesby: Born in Kentucky in 1824, Richard J. Oglesby would later say that he had been made an abolitionist by the boyhood experience of seeing the family slaves, including beloved "Uncle Tim," sold after his parents' death. (He later managed to find, buy and free the black man.) Oglesby was called to the bar of Illinois in 1845, but left the law to fight in the Mexican War, seek gold in California as a forty-niner, tour Europe and the Holy Land for almost two years, and eventually enter politics, joining the Republican Party on its formation in 1854. He held minor offices, returned to military life during the Civil War (and rose to be a major-general), and in 1864 was elected governor of Illinois. He was elected to the post a second time in 1872 (but quickly resigned in order to accept election to the United States Senate) and a prec-

Notes: October 1894

edent-setting third time in 1884. He was known for his bluff, friendly manner and his talent at stump speaking.

Paul du Chaillu: Born in France in 1835 and educated in West Africa (by Jesuits, as was Doyle), he came to the United States in 1852 but returned to Africa repeatedly between 1856 and 1863, making journeys of exploration into a continent still mostly "dark" a generation after Livingstone's great explorations. By the 1890's he had written several books and was concentrating on scholarly work, though he would soon catch the travel bug again and would die during a Russian journey in 1901.

Innes Doyle: John Dickson Carr, *The Life of Sir Arthur Conan Doyle* (New York: Harper & Brothers, 1949), p. 211.

Joseph Jefferson and Sol Smith Russell: Information about these actors appears in the chapter for October 26.

Friday, October 19: The Toledo Cycling Club
Letter to his mother: Quoted in Pierre Nordon, *Conan Doyle* (London: John Murray, 1966), p. 39. Nordon apparently had access to Doyle's letters to his mother, which are no longer available. At that time she was living at Masongill, Yorkshire, on the estate of a family friend, Dr. Bryan Charles Waller.

Toronto's mystery: I am particularly grateful to Janice McNabb of the Metropolitan Toronto Library for assembling information about the Frank Westwood murder. This case has fascinated historians and dramatists. The consensus is that Clara Ford, who was tried for the murder early in 1895 and acquitted, did shoot the young man, apparently out of sexual jealousy or revenge; but there are other possibilities. The case comes up again in the chapter which sees Doyle in Toronto (November 26). The letter which ACD wrote to *The Toronto World*, apparently the most sensational of the city's newspapers, was reproduced in facsimile on the front page of its October 29 issue. It is dated "Chicago, Oct. 19, 1894," with "Chicago" and "189_" in copperplate (apparently printed on the stationery) and the rest in Doyle's hand.

Writes to Stone: This note on the stationery of the Wagner Vestibule Train is now in the Newberry Library, Chicago, laid into Stone's copy of *The Hound of the Baskervilles*. It is not dated, but must be from October 19, as the only day between October 18 (when Doyle was introduced to Chicago hard cider) and October 25 (when he lectured in Milwaukee) that he travelled on the Lake Shore Road. The handwriting is wobbly, and in the note Doyle attributes it to "a rather skittish train," not the cider. (For a copy of this letter, as of several other items in the Newberry's collections, I am indebted to Carolyn A. Sheehy of the special collections department there, and grateful also to John Nieminski for assistance in mining the Newberry's riches.)

Evening Bee interview: "Conan Doyle in Toledo," *Evening Bee*, October 19. This material is apparently based closely on one of the Chicago interviews a few days previously, published as "An Author of Note," *Inter Ocean*, October 13. It is striking that Doyle (as quoted) makes no mention of any descent from the Breton nobility, in which his mother took such pride.

National Union League: So described in *Souvenir of Toledo* (Toledo: Mercantile Advancement Co., 1897). I briefly entertained the idea that this Mr. Meyers was a source of Meyers the bootmaker in *The Hound of the Baskervilles*. Alas, apart from any other improbability, I discovered in the city directory (R. L. Polk &

Co.'s Toledo City Directory for the year beginning July 1894; Toledo: Polk, 1894) that he really spelt his name Myers.

C. J. Woolley & Co.'s: This clever advertisement appeared in the *Evening Bee* for October 18.

Steps onto the stage: The lecture is described in October 20 issues of the *Daily Commercial*, the *Blade* ("He Looked the Physician"), and the *Bee* (which chose the headline "Killed for Good" since its first sentence reported Doyle's statement that Sherlock Holmes would not rise again).

Robert H. Cochran: This brief biography, like other incidental information about Toledo which I have used in this chapter, was assembled from reference books at the Ohio Historical Society library and archives, Columbus. I am grateful for assistance from the staff during my visit there.

The Woolleys: I regret that research has failed to turn up the given name of Mrs. Charles J. Woolley, partner with her husband in the music store and the boarding-house.

The Micawber Club: Tana Mosier Porter of the Toledo Lucas County Public Library made efforts beyond the call of duty in helping me confirm my impression that the boarders at 1107 Monroe were something more than a casual group of acquaintances, and further helping me document parts of their lives and connections. The most colourful report on the birth, heyday and successors of the Micawber Club is "The Micawber Club and the Minor Prophets," *Blade*, April 29, 1951, which identifies Mrs. Burbank, Lizzie and many of the young men. "They were all under 30," writes Dorothy Stafford in that article, "and few earned more than $100 a month, but they were all making their way in art, literature, music, architecture or business."

Saturday, October 20: Dinner in Detroit

Beautifully laid out: William Archer, *America To-Day: Observations and Reflections* (New York: Scribner, 1899; Arno Press, 1974), p. 98.

Detroit: I am grateful to Anna DiPiazza and Alice C. Dalligan of the Detroit Public Library for information about Detroit and assistance in finding press reports of Doyle's visit.

Windsor: If any trace of Doyle's visit was left among the papers of the literary community of Windsor, or in its newspapers, it has not been located through the efforts (for which I am most grateful) of Gail P. Juris and her staff at the Windsor Public Library, the staff of the Hiram Walker Historical Museum, or the municipal archivist of Windsor, Mark Walsh.

They check in: "Conan Doyle's Here," *Evening News*, October 20, 1894.

Dressing for dinner: It is my inference that the dinner which Doyle mentions in his autobiography (it is not mentioned in any press reports I have seen) is the reason he was putting on his white tie – and looking anxiously at his watch – during his interview with Greusel.

Greusel's interview, titled "Dr. Doyle" in enormous letters, ran on the first column of page one of the *Sunday News-Tribune* for October 21. Greusel, at this time 28, was already the author of *The Ethics of the Law, or, What it Means to Die for a Crime of Which You Are Innocent*, and would go on to write books, mostly brief, about Bismarck, Edison, and assorted other subjects. He worked for McClure's syndicate in New York and became noted for a series of "Hours with Famous Americans."

Notes: October 1894

Showed over his vest: This sartorial observation contradicts the statement made by Charles Higham in *The Adventures of Conan Doyle* (New York: W. W. Norton, 1976), p. 135, that on this tour Doyle "lectured in a frock coat buttoned up to the neck so that he could dispense with a waistcoat." References to his visible vest, i.e. waistcoat, made by newspaper reporters have also been quoted in the chapters for October 10 and October 22. When he lectured in Newark on November 9 he wore (according to the next day's *Newark Evening News*) "a dress suit and in his shirt front a large diamond sparkled." And see the anecdote quoted in the chapter for November 30.

The Free Press: "Differs with His Readers," issue of October 21, helpfully reprinted in *The Commonplace Book* (new series) 1 (summer 1964), p. 4.

Autobiography: *Memories and Adventures* (Boston: Little, Brown, 1924), pp. 118-119. One would certainly like to know more about this late evening of dining, drinking and bombast, including the identity of the "one or two Canadians."

Sunday, October 21: Spiritualism Past and Present

Spiritualism: There are many books on the subject, including Doyle's own *The History of Spiritualism* in two volumes (George H. Doran Company, 1926), republished in one volume (New York: Arno Press, 1975). Two books from which I have extracted general information are R. Laurence Moore, *In Search of White Crows: Spiritualism, Parapsychology, and American Culture* (New York: Oxford University Press, 1977) and Howard Kerr, *Mediums, and Spirit-Rappers, and Roaring Radicals: Spiritualism in American Literature, 1850-1900* (Urbana: University of Illinois Press, 1972).

Six years ago today: Kerr, p. 119; Doyle's *History*, vol. I p. 105.

March 31, 1848: Kerr, pp. 4-9, any source on Spiritualism tells this basic story.

Katie King: A commonplace of Spiritualist history, this affair is for some reason discussed in detail by Charles Higham in *The Adventures of Conan Doyle* (New York: W. W. Norton and Company, 1976), pp. 118-123.

Violet: Kerr, p. 145.

Lily Dale: Moore, p. 67. The camp-meeting continues in modern times, under the name of the Lily Dale Assembly, and is a depressing and squalid enterprise, though dozens of energetic mediums deliver messages from the spirits at services several times a day.

Doyle's interest: See especially Pierre Nordon, *Conan Doyle* (London: John Murray, 1966), pp. 139-157.

Society for Psychical Research: Moore, pp. 139ff; Doyle, vol. ii, pp. 63-95 (the quotations are from pp. 63 and 70). Higham, p. 117, states that ACD joined the SPR in November 1893. A date of December 1893 is given by Jeffrey L. Meikle in what is certainly the best-documented study of Doyle as Spiritualist: "Over There: Arthur Conan Doyle and Spiritualism," *The Library Chronicle of the University of Texas at Austin* new series number 8, fall 1974, pp. 22-37. Texas at Austin holds a mass of material, including some SPR records, which collectively form the Doyle Spiritualism Collection.

William James: Moore, p. 147; the quotation is from Kerr, p. 117.

The Law of Psychic Phenomena: Moore, p. 156.

Today: "He's Not Lonesome," *Evening News*, October 22, 1894. It begins thus: "Time does not hang heavy on the hands of Dr. A. Conan Doyle. Every moment of his leisure is taken advantage of by friendly admirers, who insist that he shall see everything of interest about Detroit, and many call to pay their respects to the literary lion at his rooms in the Russell house."

Robert Barr: It came as a surprise to me to find Barr in Detroit at this time; and there is apparently no coherent biographical source which can be consulted about his movements. Janice McNabb of the Metropolitan Toronto Library, who knows as much about Barr as anyone I have found, reports that "his contributions to *The Idler* dropped to virtually nothing at all in the late 1894-95 period. . . . Jerome took over the sole editorship of *The Idler* in 1895 . . . this would effectively free Barr from a lot of regular duties on the magazine, were he planning a trip to North America in late 1894." For more about Barr, see the notes for October 5 and October 28.

Thomas Jerome: Apparently it is only coincidence that this man has the same surname as Doyle's friend Jerome K. Jerome. He is described in one dictionary of authors as a "consular agent," and was born in Michigan in 1864; he died in Capri in 1914.

Monday, October 22: Lecture in Detroit

Hospitality: "He's Not Lonesome," *Evening News*, October 22, 1894.

The Detroit lecture is reported in the Detroit newspapers for October 23, 1894: the *Evening News* ("Conan Doyle's Lecture"), the *Tribune* ("Dr. Doyle's Lecture") and the *Free Press* ("Very Pleasant Introduction"), which observes that ACD "looks like a man who is fond of the open air . . . might be mistaken for a comfortable country squire." The paragraph quoted from the *Free Press* was from the article "Differs with His Readers," October 21.

To blow himself: "As to Slang," *Chicago Daily News*, October 24, 1894; "Comment of the Day," *Chicago Record*, October 25, as transcribed by the invaluable Nieminski. The paragraph says the incident happened "last night," which may be the 22nd or the 23rd.

Tuesday, October 23: George Meredith

Bibliographical information about *Round the Red Lamp* is taken from *A Bibliography of A. Conan Doyle*, edited by Richard Lancelyn Green and John Michael Gibson (Oxford: Clarendon Press, 1983), pp. 79-83.

Reviews: "Talk about New Books," *Catholic World* 60 (December 1894) pp. 419-420. "Round the Red Lamp," *The Critic* number 665, p. 326.

Frederick Villiers: *Villiers: His Five Decades of Adventure* (New York and London: Harper & Brothers, 1920), pp. 190-191. The date of this incident is open to doubt; immediately after it (pp. 191-192) Villiers tells of another visit to Doyle, when he found the author trying to work out how to kill off Holmes. That must have been some time in 1893.

Doyle's autobiography: Pages 242-245 of *Memories and Adventures* contain the various Meredith anecdotes.

Portsmouth Literary and Scientific Society: Doyle took an active part in this group, and at the time of his 1888 talk was one of its Hon. Secretaries. The

Notes: October 1894

November 23, 1888, meeting is reported in the November 24 *Hampshire County Times* as well as the *Hampshire Telegraph*, here quoted. It is notable that at the end of the evening, the vote of thanks to Doyle was proposed by the chairman (Mr. A. W. Jerrard) and seconded by Dr. James Watson, the Portsmouth physician who may have given his name to Sherlock Holmes's amanuensis.

George Meredith: There are of course many books about Meredith. The one I have chiefly used, and an eccentric one it is, is the Marxist work of Jack Lindsay, *George Meredith: His Life and Work* (London: The Bodley Head, 1956).

Thackeray: The story may not be true (Thackeray's last visit to Edinburgh likely took place before Doyle was old enough to sit on any knee), or may be true of the author's older sister rather than of himself.

Articles by ACD: They are listed in the Gibson and Green *Bibliography*, pp. 417-418 (and commentaries on them, p. 502).

Barrie and Quiller-Couch: This date is fixed by Denis Mackail in *The Story of J.M.B.: A Biography* (London: Peter Davies, 1941), pp. 190-193. Barrie was a regular visitor to Box Hill, ACD and "Q" apparently less so.

Wednesday, October 24: Hotels on Wheels
Left for Chicago: "Town Talk," Detroit *Evening News*, October 24, 1894.

A web of iron: For an interpretation of the railway system as an extension of urban civilization along a thin right-of-way throughout the nation, see John R. Stilgoe, *Metropolitan Corridor: Railroads and the American Scene* (Yale University Press, 1983). The journey of Alexander Winton is mentioned by William H. Marnell in *Vacation Yesterdays of New England* (New York: Seabury Press, 1975), p. 112.

Enjoying his travels: "An English Opinion," *Chicago Journal*, October 12.

The sleeping-cars: *Baedeker's United States*, pp. xix-xxii.

The Pullman boycott: A convenient compact source is Colston E. Warne, ed., *The Pullman Boycott of 1894*, Problems in American Civilization series (Boston: D. C. Heath and Company, 1955).

Thursday, October 25: Evening in Milwaukee
The rail fare: *Baedeker's United States*, p. 287.

"Fads about Fiction": This title is given in the newsletter *Plymouth Rock* (explained in the next paragraph) and in the *Milwaukee Telegraph* for October 20, 1894 ("A. Conan Doyle"). *Yenowine's News* had it in a brief paragraph October 21, and the *Evening Wisconsin* made a point of correcting it in a brief item October 25. The alternative titles are found in *Yenowine's* for October 13, 1894 ("Conan Doyle's Views"). The *Sentinel*, having on October 24 published what amounted to a publicity blurb, on October 25 reprinted a portion of the Robert Barr interview with Doyle, originally in *The Idler*, which by this time had also appeared in *McClure's*.

Plymouth Church: I am grateful to Rev. Mary Ann Neevel of Plymouth Church, Milwaukee (now of the United Church of Christ), for information about Plymouth as it was in 1894, and for a photocopy of the October 1894 issue (volume 12 no. 5) of its newsletter, *Plymouth Rock*.

Welcome to America, Mr. Sherlock Holmes

Doyle in Milwaukee: ACD's arrival is reported in "Dr. Doyle Makes a Change," *Milwaukee Journal*, October 25, 1894. Pfister's and the rival reporters are mentioned in the *Evening Wisconsin* for October 25, 1894 ("Conan Doyle Arrives"). The same paper for October 26 published a brief review of the lecture ("A. Conan Doyle Makes Friends"). The figure of twelve hundred people comes from an untitled paragraph in *Yenowine's News* for October 27, 1894. A review paragraph appeared in *Milwaukee's Abend-Post* for October 26, 1894 ("Vortrag in der Plymouth Kirche") and noted that ACD had spoken about "seinen Hauptwerken" (his masterwork) "Sherman Holmes." Another German-language paper, the *Milwaukee Herold*, had a brief report ("Doyle's Vortrag") on October 26. The *Milwaukee Daily News* for October 26 had one sentence about Doyle; its editors devoted a large share of the front page to a campaign aimed at cleaning up the brothels of the National Avenue Extension: "The Dives Must Go."

Friday, October 26: Return to Chicago
Luncheon at Bank Street: "Some Notes on Society," Chicago *Record*, October 26, 1894. John Nieminski in his invaluable *Conan Doyle in Chicago* notes that "similarly worded items were carried" in the *Post, Journal, Tribune, Inter Ocean*, and *Times*. The item is very brief; the full guest list can only be derived from the signed cards which also bear Mrs. Russell's poem. One of those cards is now held by the Newberry Library, the other by the Humanities Research Center of the University of Texas at Austin.

Herbert S. Stone: Sidney Kramer, *A History of Stone & Kimball and Herbert S. Stone & Co* (University of Chicago Press, 1940), with Edmund Gosse's book noted (pp. 216-217) as published October 23, 1894.

Sol Smith Russell: William T. Adams, "Sol Smith Russell," in *Famous Actors of Today*, edited by Frederic Edward McKay and Charles E. L. Wingage, (New York: Thomas Y. Crowell and Company, 1896), pp. 372-376, quoted in William C. Young, *Famous Actors and Actresses of the American Stage*, volume 2 (New York: R. R. Bowker Co., 1975). Russell's clerical bearing may have been learned from his father, who was a clergyman for a few years.

Frank W. Gunsaulus: The Philip Armour story is told in Ray Stannard Baker, *Native American* (New York: Charles Scribner's Sons, 1941), p. 291.

The photograph of Doyle is also in the Newberry Library, Chicago; again I am grateful for the use of a photocopy.

The Sign of the Four: This story has been variously told – first of all by Field himself in his column "Sharps and Flats" in the *Record* for October 29, 1894. The passage quoted from Field about bad printing is also from "Sharps and Flats," for October 22. That the signing happened at the October 26 luncheon is my inference. That it was Field's own book which was signed has been generally accepted, though there is no primary evidence to that effect. I am indebted to Donald A. Redmond for extensive bibliographical information about editions of *The Sign of the Four* which were in circulation in the United States in 1894, including the dark-blue Lippincott edition (bibliographically listed as DeWaal 26a) published in the fall of 1893, the only legitimate edition then in print. Field writes of "the United States Book Company's edition," presumably DeWaal 754a, which also contained "A Scandal in Bohemia" and which is known in both light-green and red cloth bindings. "They were," Redmond writes in a private communication, "rather undistinguished cheapo jobs, though the paper wasn't as bad as the later reprints from the same plates with American Publishers

Notes: October 1894

Corp. imprints." His definitive study of the legitimate, semi-respectable, and pirated editions of *Sign* in the United States before and just after the passage of the 1891 Copyright Act is forthcoming. I do not know the present location of this copy of *Sign*, once owned by Vincent Starrett, but through the kindness of J. Bliss Austin (who does not own it) I have seen a photocopy of the title page and inscription. Austin does own the copy of *A Study in Scarlet* and has also provided a photocopy of that one, also once owned by Starrett. The autographs of Doyle and Field on the title page were questioned – but defended by Starrett – in 1956, when Lew D. Feldman bought it with others of Starrett's books. The title page of that edition bears the printed date October 29, 1894; but, as Austin points out, the book may well have been available a few days before its official publication date.

Chicago Orchestra concerts: The Little Room soirées are described by Helen Lefkowitz Horowitz in *Culture and the City* (University Press of Kentucky, 1976); she notes that their chief organizer was Garland's brother-in-law, Lorado Taft. Information about the concerts of October 26 and 27, 1894, has kindly been provided by Megan McCaffery of the Chicago Symphony Orchestra office. Information about The Cliff Dwellers was lavished on me by Roy A. Berg, one of its former presidents and a true lover of Doyle; I wish the scope of this book allowed for much fuller use of the names and anecdotes he provided.

Central Music Hall: "Conan Doyle Reads," *Inter Ocean*, October 27; "Listen to Dr. Doyle," *Herald*, October 27; "Speaks of His Pen," *Tribune*, October 27; "Tells the Story of His Life," *Record*, October 27; "Talks About His Books," *Times*, October 27. The quotation from Higinbotham is from the *Inter Ocean*.

ACD's fee: Both figures about the speaker's fees, and the box office figure, are found in Pond's manuscript register, at the Berg Collection of the New York Public Library.

The Bookman: This unidentified correspondent's comment appears in "News Notes," *The Bookman* vii (December 1894) p. 71.

Saturday, October 27: Heading Back East

Letters in later years: All the letters referred to here are held by the Newberry Library, Chicago: to Stone, not dated but offering "happiness in '97"; to Stone, not dated but apparently 1914, on the letterhead of The Plaza, New York, and undated but apparently 1922, on that of The Ambassador, New York; to Garland, not dated but apparently 1922, on the letterhead of The Ambassador, New York, and that of The Blackstone, Chicago.

"The Three Harlots": The forthcoming appearance of a poem by Doyle was announced in *The Chap-Book* itself, as quoted, and by Eugene Field in "Sharps and Flats" for October 29. A letter from Doyle to Stone, dated March 15, 1895, from the Grand Hotel Belvedere, Davos-Platz, Switzerland, refers to "our discussing the possibility of putting my 'Three Harlots' into the book," and makes the comment quoted here. The letter also includes a rhyme thanking Stone for his "journalette," and extends greetings to the senior Stone and to Scott, Head, Field, Garland, "Kimball and all of them." The letter is now held by the Newberry Library, in a copy of *The Memoirs of Sherlock Holmes* (the London first edition) formerly owned by Herbert Stone. The Newberry also holds a copy of the second American edition of *The Stark Munro Letters* in which ink from this letter has been offset opposite the title page. The dates of the letter and that book make it impossible that the two were originally transmitted together, and it seems likely that Stone, who owned the book, later stuffed the letter into it, and over a period of time humidity or pressure caused some ink to migrate. I am grateful to Carolyn Sheehy of the Newberry Library for information about these items, and to Donald Redmond for plausible chemical speculations about how they came to be as they are. It is my conjecture — but it seems a safe one — that the poem is the same as the one published under the more innocuous title in *Songs of the Road* (London: Smith, Elder & Co., and New York: Doubleday, Page & Co., 1911). It might have shocked some readers, but it was safely in the then popular tradition of soiled-dove literature, and it certainly has none of the fleshly specifics of, say, Dante Gabriel Rossetti's "Jenny" (1870). It is a serious, almost political poem.

Oscar Wilde: Two major books treat Wilde's 1882 tour: Lloyd Lewis and Henry Justin Smith, *Oscar Wilde Discovers America* (New York: Harcourt, Brace and Company, 1936, reissued by Benjamin Blom, 1967), and Kevin O'Brien, *Oscar Wilde in Canada* (Toronto: Personal Library, 1982).

One newspaper has decided: "Jerome and Wilde Want to Lecture," *Chicago Journal*, November 3, 1894.

Sunday, October 28: Literary Tidings

The New York Times: "Impressions of Sherlock Holmes," *The New York Times*, October 28, 1894, p. 20.]

The Inter-Ocean: "The Newspaper Novelist," *Inter-Ocean*, October 28, 1894.

Stories in newspapers: "Sweethearts" was in the *Louisville Courier-Journal* on June 2, the *Boston Sunday Globe, Philadelphia Inquirer* and *New York Sun* on June 3. "The Doctors of Hoyland" was in the *Louisville Courier-Journal* on April 8. Both had seen book publication in October in *Round the Red Lamp*. "The Lord of Chateau Noir" was in the *Chicago Tribune, Louisville Courier-Journal, Pittsburgh Dispatch*, and *Detroit Sunday News-Tribune* on July 15, and the *San Francisco Examiner* on July 22. It would not see book publication until 1900.

McClure's: Robert Barr, "A Chat With Conan Doyle," volume iii (November 1894) pp. 503-513. "De Profundis," pp. 513-518. Arthur Conan Doyle, "My First Book," vol. III (August 1894), pp. 225-228. "The additional photographs are of interest," writes Janice McNabb in a still unpublished bibliographical essay, "in that they show Robert Barr and Robert McClure, the magazine editor's younger brother, together with the author Doyle and his wife and sister, as well as another of Robert Barr in the Idler offices with a prominently displayed copy of *McClure's Magazine*." She speculates that S. S. McClure was the author of the additional material and that he met Doyle at the time of the original Barr interview. Robert McClure was his brother's agent in London from 1893 to 1903. When Doyle visited America again in 1914, he asked after the younger McClure, who had been in poor health. A day or two later the newspapers would report that McClure had shot himself dead (*New York Times*, May 31, 1914). The "My First Book" pieces were shortly to be published in book form by Lippincott.

James Anthony Froude: See the obituary in *Publishers' Weekly* No. 1187, October 27, 1894.

Notes: October 1894

Monday, October 29: Lecture in Brooklyn
The basic research for this chapter was generously done (at the Brooklyn Public Library) by my friend Paula Cohen. Her location and transcription of articles from the Brooklyn *Eagle* and *Times* has been particularly valuable. Later research was done by me, some of it at the Long Island Historical Society (with the kind assistance of librarian Lily Hammock) and at the Business Library of the Brooklyn Public Library.

Fourth largest city: For general information about Brooklyn I have relied heavily on the article by Murat Halstead to which I refer: "The City of Brooklyn," in *The Cosmopolitan* xv no. 2 (June 1893) pp. 131-144.

Academy of Music: *Bulletin of the Brooklyn Institute of Arts and Sciences*, March 27, 1920; "The Brooklyn Academy of Music," by Samuel L. Leiter, in Rita Seiden Miller, ed., *Brooklyn USA* (Brooklyn College Press, 1979), pp. 149-156.

Chautauqua Literary and Scientific Circle: Letter from John H. Vincent, chancellor of the CLSC and co-founder of the Chautauqua Institution, to Kate Kimball, life-long secretary of the CLSC, dated New York, November 6, 1894; this letter is in the Smith Memorial Library, Chautauqua, New York.

Tonight's lecture: "Dr. A. Conan Doyle in Brooklyn," New York *Daily Tribune*, October 30, 1894; "Conan Doyle's Lecture," Brooklyn *Eagle*, October 30; "Of Sherlock Holmes," Brooklyn *Times*, October 30. This last-mentioned article is, as Paula Cohen points out in a letter to me, one of the earliest Sherlockian pastiches. It begins thus:

> "That man is Conan Doyle," said Sherlock Holmes to me last night, after giving a single quick but comprehensive glance at the figure who stepped upon the stage of the Academy of Music, and with a bow acknowledged the applause which greeted him.
>
> "Marvelous acumen," I said. "It is a wonder to me how you find out such things."

Reporters make notes: This quotation is also from the *Eagle*.

One of those clubs: *Club List of Brooklyn* (Brooklyn, 1896) lists the membership of many clubs, including the Hamilton, and provides photographs of their houses.

Among the guests: Their names appear in the *Eagle*. Their identities are found in the usual biographical sources.

"Too Much Johnson": Gillette's farce was reviewed as "A New Farce in Brooklyn" in *The New York Times*, October 30, 1894. The *Times* discussed it again December 2, 1894, by which time it was playing at the Standard Theatre.

Tuesday, October 30: A Tree Grows in Northampton
Northampton: Newspaper reports about Doyle's visit to Northampton, and background information about the references in them, were kindly provided to me by Elise Bernier-Feeley of the Forbes Library, Northampton, and Ed Lonergan of the Springfield City Library. The newspaper items include "A. Conan Doyle's Recital," *Daily Hampshire Gazette*, Northampton, October 31, 1894, and "Novelist Doyle at Northampton," Springfield *Daily Republican*, also October 31.

George Washington Cable: Arlin Turner, *George W. Cable: A Biography* (Duke University Press, 1956), p. 332. (And on p. 308, Turner notes a visit which Cable paid to Doyle at "Undershaw" in Sussex in May 1898. "From the time he

Welcome to America, Mr. Sherlock Holmes

took the train on Friday until he returned to the city on Monday, he was on the peaks of enjoyment, and his report of the visit in his diary is punctuated with exclamations.") Also, George Washington Cable, *The Amateur Garden* (New York: Charles Scribner's Sons, 1914), pp. 6-29.

Parkman's pages: The incident, known to history as the Sack of Deerfield, is recorded in chapter IV of *A Half-Century of Conflict*.

Smith College: In my research for this chapter, great help was provided by Mary B. Trott and Sondra Lee Slesinski of the College Archives at Smith College. Additional comments about the general atmosphere of Smith was provided by one of its graduates, my dear friend Lois Gardiner Clark. Smith's tradition of welcoming distinguished guests is told at length in *Through the Gercourt Gates: Distinguished Visitors to Smith College 1875-1975*, by Eleanor Terry Lincoln (Smith College, 1978). The Joseph Jefferson story is told by William Webster Ellsworth in *A Golden Age of Authors* (Boston and New York: Houghton Mifflin, 1919), pp. 82-83.

Elizabeth Maltby: Eleanor Lincoln and John A. Pinto, *This, the House We Live In* (Northampton: Smith College, 1983), pp. 100-101. Obituary of Lafayette Maltby, *Daily Hampshire Gazette*, December 30, 1898. Obituary of Elizabeth Maltby, *Daily Hampshire Gazette*, November 14, 1921.

City hall: Documents of the Massachusetts Historical Commission were kindly photocopied for me by the staff of the Forbes Library.

Alpha Society: The events listing from the *Monthly* for November 1894 was provided for me by the Smith College Archives, as was the explanation of the Alpha Society. Other events between October 10 and November 10 include a lecture on Tolstoi by Rev. W. W. Newton; a concert by the Beethoven Quintette Club; the Dickinson House dance; an informal talk by Charles Dudley Warner; and a performance of *She Stoops to Conquer*.

Lydia W. Kendall: This diary is now held by the Smith College Archives, from which I was generously provided with a photocopy. I am grateful for permission from the diarist's grandson, Dr. Kendall W. Foster of Okemos, Michigan, for permission to quote from it. Lydia Williams Kendall, later Foster, later studied home economics, taught Greek and Latin, acted as housekeeper of Boston's Elizabeth Peabody House, worked as a proofreader for the Athenaeum Press, was business manager of an apartment house for ten years, and was librarian of Trinity Church. (This biographical information is taken from the Smith College *Alumnae Biographical Register*.)

Mount Holyoke College: Information about the rival attraction at Mount Holyoke was kindly provided by Elaine D. Trehub, College History Librarian there.

Wednesday, October 31: A Cabman in the Athens of America

The first research for this chapter was generously done by two of my friends: Ursula Moran (at the Public Library of the City of Boston) and Carol Sandström (at the Widener Library of Harvard University). I am very grateful to them both. I later was able to continue the research myself at the Public Library.

Journal: "Conan Doyle: Some Characteristics of the English Novelist," *Boston Journal*, October 31, 1894.

Notes: October 1894

Boston and Edinburgh: The quoted passage is from William Archer, *America To-Day: Observations and Reflections* (New York: Scribner, 1899; Arno Press, 1974), pp. 92-93.

Mount Auburn Cemetery: Oddly, this incident seems to have escaped mention in Boston's newspapers. It is reported in such other sources as an untitled note in the *Philadelphia Times*, November 9, 1894. John Dickson Carr in *The Life of Sir Arthur Conan Doyle* (New York: Harper & Brothers, 1949), quotes from Doyle's letter home (pp. 87-88), describing his visit to the grave. He would make a similar pilgrimage in 1922, as he reports in *Our American Adventure* (London: Hodder and Stoughton, [1923]), p. 66.

The story of the cabman: Ellsworth tells the story in *A Golden Age of Authors* (Boston and New York: Houghton Mifflin, 1919), pp. 247-248. The longer version appears in "A Puzzled Novelist," Chicago *Record*, December 1, 1894. But where did the story of the Boston cabman come from? Did the incident which has so often been retold, with some embellishment, in fact take place?

Doyle does not tell the story in his autobiography, but gives this comment:
> There are certain Sherlock Holmes stories, apocryphal I need not say, which go round and round the press and turn up at fixed intervals with the regularity of a comet.
>
> One is the story of the cabman who is supposed to have taken me to an hotel in Paris. "Dr. Doyle," he cried, gazing at me fixedly, "I perceive from your appearance that you have been recently at Constantinople. I have reason to think also that you have been at Buda, and I perceive some indication that you were not far from Milan." "Wonderful. Five francs for the secret of how you did it?" "I looked at the labels pasted on your trunk," said the astute cabby. (*Memories and Adventures*, p. 103.)

It is clearly the same joke.

The story does not appear in any of the Boston newspapers – where one would expect to see an early telling of so good a story, if it originated in Boston. On the other hand, it is certain that Doyle did tell the story, with a Boston setting, at the dinner at New York's Aldine Club on December 7, the night before he sailed for home, when William Webster Ellsworth heard the tale. Writing in 1919, Ellsworth calls it "an original Sherlock Holmes story," which suggests that he did not exactly believe it. I am inclined to think that Doyle told it as a joke and some later enthusiasts took it as truth. Richard Lancelyn Green comments on the story's resilience thus:
> The following day [after Doyle told the story at the Aldine Club] there were full reports of the speech in the newspapers, and six years later, in his book *Eccentricities of Genius*, Major Pond gave Doyle's full version. The other people who had been present, such as William Ellsworth and Frederic Villiers, were also to recall the story on many subsequent occasions, but it was the version given by Pond which appeared most often; the American *Bookman* was particularly fond of it and never missed an opportunity of repeating it, and it was soon equally well known in England. It then assumed a life of its own and resurfaced under various different guises. [*The Uncollected Sherlock Holmes*, Penguin Books, 1983, pp. 72-73.]

Still, the story was in circulation before December 7. The earliest version I have seen is "He Got the Tickets," in the *Daily Cataract Journal* for November 26, 1894, which credits it to the *Brooklyn Eagle*. The Chicago *Record* had the longer version in print on December 1 ("A Puzzled Novelist"), and if the attribution to the Boston *Record* can be believed (I have not seen any appearance of it in that paper), there is a good chance that it dates from Doyle's return visit to Boston in late November. Perhaps Doyle mischievously told it to friends on that occasion, it found its way into print, and he then polished it for use at the Aldine Club. It is also possible that someone else, such as Major Pond, invented it in the interests of publicity.

The story is implausible on the surface, and it smacks too much of things Doyle had himself written:

> "My dear Mr. Grant Munro – " began Holmes.
> Our visitor sprang from his chair. "What!" he cried, "you know my name!"
> "If you wish to preserve your incognito," said Holmes, smiling, "I would suggest that you cease to write your name upon the lining of your hat, or else that you turn the crown towards the person whom you are addressing. . . . " ("The Yellow Face.")

It may be worth adding that even if the outline of the story could be believed, the details are wrong. Doyle had not been to Philadelphia at the time of his first visit to Boston (he did get there before his return) or to Buffalo until after both of his Boston sojourns. He did get sufficiently close to Springfield that the newspaper there reported on his visit to Northampton (see the chapter for October 30), but it appears that he never got to Utica, New York, at all. Doyle did write in 1923 that he had done so: "Schenectady, Utica, Syracuse – I had lectured in all of them nearly thirty years before." (*Our American Adventure*, London: Hodder and Stoughton, [1923], p. 103.) But Utica and Syracuse are not listed in the Pond manuscript register, and it is hard to see where in the schedule there was time for them. (For the Schenectady visit, see the chapter for November 24.) Possibly Doyle noticed the cities' names as his trains passed through them, and recalled them later. (A final note: Elizabeth Pattengill, of the Utica Public Library, tells me that a volunteer kindly searched the files of Utica's newspapers for the fall of 1894 and found no mention of Doyle.)

Lecture this evening: "Letters to Conan Doyle," *Globe*, November 1, 1894, morning edition; "'His First Boston Lecture," *Herald*, November 1; "Conan Doyle's Lecture," *Daily Advertiser, November* 1; "Dr. Conan Doyle's Talk," *Evening Transcript*, November 1; "Doyle's Lecture," *Post*, November 1; "With Conan Doyle," *Journal*, November 1. The *Journal* on this day also published a sizeable article, "A. Conan Doyle's Opinion of Women," under "The Women's Corner"; it admits to being based on "every available source," and those sources seem to include Greusel's interview in Detroit and others in which Doyle had spoken of Olive Schreiner, George Meredith, and his own childish handwriting. The article is accompanied by an engraving showing Doyle standing between his mother and one of his sisters.

Period of English history: *Bulletin of the Public Library of the City of Boston* xx no. 3 (whole no. 98), October 1894, containing thirty-eight pages of titles as well as the reproduction mentioned.

William H. Lee: The copperplate "summary" which Lee (1841-1916) made of his diary is now in the rare book collection of the Public Library of the City of Boston. In it he includes an exhaustive list of attractions which came to the city during the year, whether or not he attended them; Doyle's name appears under "Readings" along with those of James Whitcomb Riley, Mrs. Erving Winslow, H. A. Clapp and various others. I am grateful for the assistance of Roberta Zongki

Notes: November 1894

at the Boston Public Library for assistance in finding this and other contemporary manuscripts.

November 1894

Thursday, November 1: Smoke Talk in Worcester
Worcester: "Killed Sherlock Holmes," *Worcester Daily Telegram*, November 2, 1894. "Dr. Conan Doyle," *Worcester Daily Spy*, November 2. "Timely Notes," *Worcester Evening Gazette*, November 2 (with Robert Louis Stevenson's name misspelt as I have quoted it).

I am grateful to Nancy E. Gaudette of the Worcester Public Library for making photocopies of these reports available, and to Jessica S. Goss of the Worcester Historical Museum for assistance with background information. The Historical Museum was the only public institution which volunteered that it has a copy of the original program booklet from ACD's talk. From a photocopy I judge that it was based on the brochure which Pond sent out earlier in 1894 to advertise Doyle's services. It also notes that tickets for the 8 p.m. lecture were on sale "at Gorham's and at the door."

Blood and torture: The Sherlock Holmes tales do not particularly show this tendency, which can be observed in the medical tales (see the reviews of *Round the Red Lamp* quoted in the chapter for November 7) and the historical novels (the classic example is the Iroquois torture of the priest in *The Refugees*). It is a black side of Doyle frequently overlooked.

Reception: The *Telegram* has an extensive list of the guests, mentions the receiving line, and observes that "The affair was prettily arranged and was unusually enjoyable."

Amie Dean: Amie Dean marked her twenty-ninth birthday the following Sunday (November 4). On July 11, 1895, she married Herbert A. Aikins, and they subsequently moved to Cleveland, where she died in 1932, leaving him a widower. One thus sees her as a young society lady, perhaps seeming attractive to Doyle and even more so to Innes. "In no country," wrote James Bryce a few years before this, "are women, and especially young women, so much made of [as in America]. The world is at their feet. Society seems organized for the purpose of providing enjoyment for them." (*The American Commonwealth*, London, 1888, vol. III p. 515, quoted in Richard L. Rapson, *Britons View America* (Seattle: University of Washington Press, 1971), p. 108). I am grateful to Nancy E. Gaudette of the Worcester Public Library and to Tom Stetak of the Lorain County (Ohio) Historical Society for assistance in identifying Miss Dean and finding her vital statistics.

Friday, November 2: Lecture at Amherst College
Amherst College: Thomas LeDuc, *Piety and Intellect at Amherst College 1862-1912* (New York: Arno Press and The New York Times, 1969), pp. 102-111, 132-139.

Merrill E. Gates: Gates's first wife was still living. She would die in 1905, and eight years later he would marry Elizabeth Head (see the chapter for October 26). By that time Gates would be living in Washington and serving as president of the United States Board of Indian Commissioners; he also served for a period as president of the American Missionary Association.

Mabel Loomis Todd: This lady's love life forms an important part of the material for Peter Gay's remarkable book *The Bourgeois Experience, Victoria to Freud: Education of the Senses* (Oxford University Press, 1984). Unfortunately Doyle's visit seems to have made no impression on her; the diary entries for November 1, 2 and 3, 1894, "are mainly concerned with the social activities held in connection with the meeting of the College Presidents in Amherst," I am helpfully informed by Judith Ann Schiff of the manuscripts and archives section at the Yale University Library.

Lecture in College Hall: "The College Lecture Course" *The Amherst Student*, October 27, 1894; "Dr. A. Conan Doyle," *The Amherst Student*, November 10, 1894; one-sentence note in *Hampshire and Franklin Express*, November 7, 1894. I am grateful to Daniel Lombardo of the Jones Library, Amherst, and John Lancaster of the Amherst College Library for finding these reports and making photocopies available, and to John Lancaster for assistance with information about the Amherst House, College Hall and Roberts Walker.

In that hall: Quotation from "College Hall," *Amherst Student*, May 21, 1892.

Amherst House: *The History of the Town of Amherst, Massachusetts* (Amherst: Press of Carpenter & Morehouse, 1896), pp. 380-383.

Saturday, November 3: Lecture at Norwich

The steamer *Paris*: Presumably many newspapers reported this incident; I first encountered it in the *Pittsburg Post* for November 4, 1894.

Letter to Robinson: This letter appears in full in John R. Robinson, *Fifty Years of Fleet Street* (London: Macmilland and Co., 1904), pp. 358-359.

Norwich, Connecticut: I am grateful to my friend Glenn J. Shea, then of Norwich, for doing the basic research for this chapter. The one newspaper report of Doyle's visit to Norwich is "Dr. Doyle's Lecture," *Norwich Morning Bulletin*, November 5, 1894. There was a brief advance notice of his talk ("Dr. Doyle Tonight") in the *Bulletin* of November 3. The reference to Shea's bookstore is found in *Publisher's Weekly* for October 13, 1894, under "Business Notes." The reference to the half-breed colony is from *Baedeker's United States*.

Robert P. Keek: This name is found in Pond's manuscript register, though not in any record from Norwich that I have seen.

Sunday, November 4: "My Own Theory of Reading"

My own theory of reading: *Memories and Adventures* (Boston: Little, Brown, 1924), p. 117.

Norwich Morning Bulletin: "Dr. Doyle's Lecture," November 4, 1894.

Hector Charlesworth: *Candid Chronicles: Leaves from the Note Book of a Canadian Journalist* (Toronto: Macmillan, 1925), p. 299.

Newark next week: "Listened to A. Conan Doyle," *Newark Evening News*, November 10, 1894.

Thirty years later: Doyle mentions this incident in *Our American Adventure* (London: Hodder and Stoughton, [1923]), p. 26.

Tin ear: I am indebted to Edward F. Clark, Jr., for this observation.

At first his attention: "Conan Doyle Talks," *Chicago Record*, October 13, 1894.

Notes: November 1894

He has a slight English accent: "An English Opinion," *Chicago Journal,* October 12, 1894.

My father was born: "An Author of Note," *Chicago Inter-Ocean,* October 13, 1894. The statement that his mother was "English" is startling: her Irish ancestry is indisputable, and she claimed ancestors from Brittany, but this comment, if correctly reported, may mean that she was born in England, something scholars have not known.

He met them: "A. Conan Doyle, Author," *Cincinnati Commercial Gazette,* October 17, 1894.

In his speech: "Of Sherlock Holmes," *Brooklyn Times,* October 30, 1894.

The only peculiarities: "His First Boston Lecture," *Boston Herald,* November 1, 1894.

Rochester Union Chronicle: "A Famous Novelist," November 22, 1894.

Glens Falls Daily Times: "Conan Doyle Delightful," November 24, 1894.

Detroit Tribune: "Dr. Doyle's Lecture," October 23, 1894.

Monday, November 5: Lecture in Washington

The newspaper material for this chapter was in part gathered by my friend Lois Gardiner Clark of Washington. I also acknowledge efforts by Jack D. Brewer of the Columbia Historical Society, Washington, to find other contemporary sources.

Evening Star: November 5, 1894, titles as cited.

The Arlington: Evidence for this is the letter which he wrote on the hotel's stationery next day, as described in the chapter for November 6.

To an Englishman: William Archer, *America To-Day: Observations and Reflections* (New York: Scribner, 1899; Arno Press, 1974), p. 71.

Cleveland is preoccupied: I gleaned these impressions from a cursory look at the appropriate microfilm roll of the Grover Cleveland Papers, representing the President's incoming correspondence. I am happy to acknowledge the help of James H. Hutson and his staff at the manuscript division of the Library of Congress for assistance in beginning that search, and for a separate brief search which, I was sorry to learn, produced no evidence or suggestion that Doyle called on the president during his Washington visit.

Frederick Douglass: It seemed to me that Doyle, on whom a meeting with Henry Highland Garnet had once made such an impression (Owen Dudley Edwards, *The Quest for Sherlock Holmes,* Edinburgh: Mainstream Publishing, 1983, pp. 243-276), might have been eager to meet Douglass. But the great black orator may already have been in Massachusetts; my authority for his presence there is "Frederick Douglass: A Spirited Picture of an Historical Character," *The Vermont Phoenix,* Brattleboro, November 9, 1894. At any rate, several authorities on Douglass say they are aware of no meeting with Doyle. For that information I am indebted to Marilyn W. Nickels of the National Park Service, Benjamin Quarles of Morgan State University, and John W. Blassingame of Yale University.

Letter from a Jesuit: This letter from McCarthy to Richards is in the archives of Georgetown University; a photocopy (with some helpful background) was kindly provided by Anna T. Zakarija of the staff there, and permission for its publication was given on behalf of Georgetown University by its archivist, Jon Reynolds.

ACD lectures tonight: "Conan Doyle Deduces," *The Washington Post*, November 6, 1894. "Amusements," *Evening Star*, November 6. Pond's register indicates that the lecture grossed $118.75 and that the local agent was W. J. Murtagh. For the Metzerott Music Hall, see a brief passage in *A Guide to the Nation's Capital* (New York: Hastings House, 1942, American Guide Series), pp. 90-91.

Tuesday, November 6: Baltimore on Election Day
ACD writes a note: This letter and its envelope are now in the collection of Ted Schulz of San Rafael, California, who generously provided me with a photocopy of it.

Visitors' impressions: Sherry H. Olson, *Baltimore: The Building of an American City* (Johns Hopkins University Press, 1980), pp. 198-99; in part the author is quoting from a piece in the *London Daily Chronicle* which was reprinted in the *Baltimore Sun*, January 6, 1894.

Baltimore has: Eric Garland, "Historic Baltimore," *American Way*, July 1984, pp. 30-40.

James Cardinal Gibbons: The "poison" anecdote is told by Thomas Beer in *The Mauve Decade* (New York: Vintage Books [Random House], 1960, first published 1926), p. 97.

Edgar Allan Poe: For information about the Poe grave I am indebted to my friend Ann Byerly, now of Baltimore. She notes that at the present day there are several Poe sites for tourists to visit, but that the only one known in the 1890's was the grave. It is notable that ACD did not discuss Poe in "Before My Bookcase," the series of articles on his literary idols which he wrote for the journal *Great Thoughts* earlier in 1894. But when he turned those articles into a book (*Through the Magic Door*, London: Smith Elder, 1907, and New York: McClure, 1908), he included several pages on Poe.

Authors' Society: "The Poe Centenary," *The Times*, March 2, 1909. Doyle's son Kingsley was in the audience, the newspaper notes.

Thirty years from now: *Our American Adventure* London: Hodder and Stoughton Ltd., [1923]), pp. 168-169.

Election day: "The watershed in American politics that has traditionally been the 1896 election of the Republican William McKinley to the White House should more accurately be placed at 1894," writes Robert Kelley in *The Transatlantic Persuasion* (New York: Alfred A. Knopf, 1969), p. 340. "The oscillation that for decades had taken place in Congress, first one party and then the other winning majorities, was suddenly terminated. For a generation thereafter the Republicans were to dominate American political life completely." A useful contemporary summary under the title "The General Elections" appeared in *The Chautauquan* xx number 3 (December 1894), pp. 354-359. The Steffens letter appears in *The Letters of Lincoln Steffens*, volume 1, 1889-1919, edited by Ella Winter and Granville Hicks (New York: Harcourt, Brace and Company, 1938), p. 107.

Press Club: "Gossip of the Capital," *Chicago Post*, November 9, 1894. The item is datelined "Washington, November 9," and says the affair took place "last night"; but that is impossible, since he was dining in Philadelphia on the evening of

Notes: November 1894

November 8, and it sounds like an election-night incident. For information about the club, I am grateful to Barbara Vandegrift, archivist of the present National Press Club; she also drew my attention to a book published in 1942 under the title *A Short Story of Newspapers, Newspapermen, and Newspapermen's Clubs in the Life of the National Capital.*

Wednesday, November 7: *Round the Red Lamp*
A copy to Stone: This inscribed and dated volume is now in the Newberry Library, Chicago.

Reviews: "Talk about New Books," *Catholic World* 60 (December 1894) pp. 419-420. *Round the Red Lamp*, *The Critic* number 665, p. 326.

Doyle probably did not see a copy of the British edition of the book until his return home in December. When he did, he gave Innes a copy of it, writing on the title page a modest inscription: "from your affectionate brother ACD." (That copy is now in the Berg Collection of the New York Public Library.)

Thursday, November 8: Dinner in Philadelphia
Frank Leslie's: A lively life of (Mrs.) Leslie, and inevitably the story of her magazine, is Madeleine B. Stern, *Purple Passage* (Norman: University of Oklahoma Press, 1953). The article referred to is "Conan Doyle in America," *Leslie's Weekly*, November 8, 1894. The magazine had of course been publicizing the forthcoming *Stark Munro Letters* in previous issues – on October 25, for example, in an issue which also featured the new Boston Public Library, an advertisement promised that "Dr. Doyle regards this as THE BEST WORK he has yet produced, and this will no doubt be the conclusion of all who read it."

Supposed to be in Pittsburgh: This at least can be inferred from Pond's manuscript register, where Baltimore and Pittsburgh have been written in for November 7, and Pittsburgh for November 8, and both lines have then been erased. There is no evidence of a visit by Doyle in Pittsburgh newspapers of the time (so I am informed by Eileen Finster of the *Pittsburgh Press*). Pittsburgh's distinguished Sherlockian, J. Bliss Austin, has looked into the matter and also found no trace of such a visit.

Craige Lippincott: "A. Conan Doyle in Town," *Philadelphia Times*, November 9, 1894 – a report embellished with the usual engraved portrait of Doyle, presumably supplied by Pond to newspapers all along the tour. (The same article includes the comments which I quote later in the chapter: "I did not come here to lecture." It seems an unlikely thing for Doyle to have said.) A telegram to Lippincott from Charles King, accepting an invitation to dine with Doyle, is in the collection of Gerry O'Hara of Edmonton. The telegram is dated November 5, 1894, and may refer to this November 8 dinner, although the newspaper makes no mention of King's presence.

Owen Wister: Ben Merchant Vorpahl, *My Dear Wister* (Palo Alto: American West Publishing Co., 1972), pp. 106-108.

Silas Weir Mitchell: The copy of *Hepzibah Guiness* which Mitchell signed for Doyle is listed in Catalogue 276 of George S. MacManus Co., a Philadelphia bookseller. Unfortunately the listing does not indicate the date of the inscription (the book was the second, or 1887, edition), and MacManus are unable to provide any more information or to say who bought the book or when. I am indebted to Jack D. Key, librarian of the Mayo Foundation and scholar of

Doyle's medical connections, for bringing this tantalizing paragraph to my attention, but no further information about encounters between Doyle and Mitchell has been forthcoming, in spite of efforts both by him and by G. S. T. Cavanagh of the Duke University Medical Center Library, which holds many of Mitchell's papers.

Friday, November 9: Next Stop Newark
So many encounters: The two invitations quoted here sound almost apocryphal; the authority for them is John Dickson Carr in his *Life of Sir Arthur Conan Doyle* (New York: Harper & Brothers, 1949), p. 87. Carr may be quoting from Doyle's letters, which were available to him, but he gives no source. I am equally puzzled by a quotation which Charles Higham presents in *The Adventures of Conan Doyle* (New York: W. W. Norton & Company, 1976), p. 135: asked to meet yet another unidentified society group, Doyle is said to have blurted, "I cannot, I cannot! What do they want of me? Let me go away! I haven't the courage to look these people in the face." Higham credits it to *The Bookman*, but I do not find it in either the British or the American periodical of that title. As for clubs, I learn that the collection of Gerry O'Hara, of Edmonton, includes copies of complimentary cards extending to Doyle the privileges of the Union League in New York, the Fellowship Club in Chicago, the Detroit Club, the Rittenhouse Club in Philadelphia, and other such houses.

I am grateful for the assistance of my friend Linda Van Zandt Morris, of Middlesex, New Jersey, for her assistance in finding information about Doyle's excursions to New Jersey. For reasons not clear to me, the New Jersey lectures were by far the least accessible in my research.

Baedeker: *Baedeker's United States*, p. 208.

ACD lectures tonight: The name of the local manager is found in Pond's manuscript register. The lecture was reported in the *Newark Evening News* ("Listened to A. Conan Doyle," November 10, 1894, and the *Newark Daily Advertiser* ("A. Conan Doyle's Lecture," November 10). I am grateful to James Stuart Osbourn of the Newark Public Library for assistance in obtaining these reports and for other help.

John L. Sullivan: ACD mentions in *Memories and Adventures* (Boston: Little, Brown and Company, 1924), p. 267, that he had "seen nearly all the great boxers of my time, from J. L. Sullivan down to Tommy Burns." That presumably was during Sullivan's tour of England and Ireland in October 1887.

A boxing play: Carr, p. 83.

Saturday, November 10: Siss, Boom, Ah!
Stories in print: Details are of course taken from the Gibson and Green *Bibliography*.

Up from Philadelphia: Records of Doyle's presence at this football game are frustratingly few. The Newark *Daily Advertiser* for November 10, 1894, says at the end of its report of Doyle's lecture the previous night ("A. Conan Doyle's Lecture") that the visitor "will attend" the game. The *Daily Pennsylvanian* of the University of Pennsylvania says in an untitled note in its November 13 issue that he "was . . . an enthusiastic witness" at the game.

American football game: Reports of the preparations and the game include "The Big Football Game," *New York Herald*, November 10, 1894; "Pennsylvania,

Notes: November 1894

12; Tigers, 0," *The New York Times*, November 11; "Tigers are Vanquished," *New York Sun*, November 11; "Trentonians Who Saw the Game," *Trenton Sunday Advertiser*, November 11; "Tigers Shorn of Their Claws," *Philadelphia Inquirer*, November 11; "How the Game Was Played," *New York World*, November 11. There was a good deal about the game in the *Daily Princetonian* on the days immediately before and after the game. The description of the scoreboard, the long description of play and the Princeton cheer are all taken from the *Sun*. I am grateful to Elizabeth Mosiman of the Van Pelt Library, University of Pennsylvania, and Richard W. Reeves of the Free Public Library, Trenton, for assistance in finding some of the information about the big game.

ACD was a footballer: The passages quoted are from *Memories and Adventures* (Boston: Little, Brown, 1924), pp. 269-270. He would draw on memories of his football days when he wrote the Sherlock Holmes tale "The Missing Three-Quarter" in 1904.

James William White: The same valuable paragraph from the *Daily Pennsylvanian* is the authority for this incident. Doyle's thesis for the M.D. degree from Edinburgh was a study of tabes dorsalis, a form of syphilis. Alivin E. Rodin and Jack D. Key do not mention Cornil in their *Medical Casebook of Doctor Arthur Conan Doyle* (Malabar, Florida: Robert E. Krieger Publishing Company, 1984). White kept extensive diaries, but those now at the University of Pennsylvania library regrettably do not cover the later months of 1894, I am informed by Maryellen C. Kaminsky of the library there.

Lecture in Philadelphia: "Evening With Conan Doyle," *Philadelphia Inquirer*, November 11, 1894; "Dr. A. Conan Doyle," *Public Ledger*, November 12.

Sunday, November 11: Impressions of America

Conversation with Innes: Doyle writes these recollections in *Our American Adventure* (London: Hodder and Stoughton, [1923]), p. 95-96. He states that the conversation took place "in Philadelphia," not giving a date; this day when ACD had no lecture seems to me a likely one for a conversation between the brothers, and is particularly appropriate since November 11 would later become Armistice Day. Innes rose to a high rank during the First World War, but I know of no evidence that he literally commanded American as well as British troops.

Descriptions of New York which I have found particularly useful are – besides those cited in the notes for October 3 – those in *The WPA Guide to New York City* (New York: Random House, c. 1939; Pantheon Books, 1982).

Shenandoah Valley: *Baedeker's United States*, pp. 226-230. Bruce Kennedy and Robert Watson Douty, *In the Footsteps of Birdy Edwards* (Privately printed, 1980) is a study of the coal and iron country from a Sherlockian point of view.

Monday, November 12: A Visit with John Kendrick Bangs

The Horse Show: The New York papers were full of the Horse Show that week; the *Herald* report quoted is "During the Dinner Hour," in the issue of November 13, and the list of attractions is taken from an advertisement in the *Herald* of November 12.

Generous payment: The fifty per cent figure is found in Pond's manuscript register for the November 16 lecture; I assume it applied also to Monday and Wednesday.

Welcome to America, Mr. Sherlock Holmes

"A Gaiety Girl": Advertisements in the New York papers for that week; for more about this show see the chapter for December 2.

Daly's: Howard Taubman, *The Making of the American Theatre* (New York: Coward McCann, Inc., 1965), pp. 197-198; Jack Poggi, *Theatre in America* (Ithaca, New York: Cornell University Press, 1968), p. 94; Richard Moody, *America Takes the Stage* (Indiana University Press, 1955), p.p. 225-226; John Ranken Towse, *Sixty Years of the Theater* (New York: Funk & Wagnalls, 1916), p. 341.

ACD's matinee: Prices are given in an advertisement in the *New York Herald*, November 12. A report is "Conan Doyle's Readings," *New York Sun*, November 13.

Note to Ellen Conway: The original of this note is now in the libraries of Columbia University, New York. I am grateful to Bernard R. Crystal, assistant librarian for manuscripts, for arranging to make a photocopy available.

Henry Highland Garnet: This fascinating influence on Doyle's life is discussed at length by Owen Dudley Edwards in *The Quest for Sherlock Holmes* (Edinburgh: Mainstream Publishing, 1983), pp. 243-276.

John Kendrick Bangs: I am grateful to Jon L. Lellenberg for looking at a draft of this section of the book and providing suggestions and information about Bangs. Valuable in addition to standard references is a biography by Bangs's son Francis Hyde Bangs: *John Kendrick Bangs: Humorist of the Nineties* (New York: Alfred A. Knopf, 1941). Describing Doyle's visit on pp. 152-155 this biography is the source for the gollywog episode. (Some North American readers nowadays may need to be told that a gollywog is a blackface rag doll, the English – and nineteenth century American – equivalent of a teddy bear.) Though still a young man, Bangs was well known in 1894. Early in December, a plastic surgeon giving a public talk at Sherry's, an authors' hangout in New York, used the "strong, pleasant countenance" of Bangs to argue that even a handsome man could be improved with a little work: "If he so desired, the Woodbury Dermatological surgeons could straighten his nose ever so little," and so on. Drawings of Bangs as he was and Bangs as he might be appeared with the article "Famous Authors' Faces" in the *New York Sun*, December 9, 1894.

Dancing a fandango: This letter, directed to "Miss Laughlin," is now in the Beinecke Rare Book and Manuscript Library, Yale University; I am grateful to David Schoonover there for making a copy available.

Yonkers Lawn Tennis Club: I am indebted to Frances C. Roberts of the Yonkers Public Library for assistance in finding information about the club, and about Doyle's Yonkers visit in general. Now occupied by the Amackassin Club, the building "is said to have changed relatively little over the years," she writes. She was able to provide a 1902 photograph of it, as well as reports of the opening festivities: "A Brilliant Opening," *Yonkers Herald*, January 2, 1894. and "Yonkers Lawn Tennis Club," *Yonkers Statesman*, January 2, 1894.

This evening's lecture: "Sherlock Holmes," *Yonkers Herald*, November 13, 1894; "Dr. A. Conan Doyle," *Yonkers Statesman*, November 13, 1894. I am grateful to Ted Schulz of San Rafael, California, for providing me with a photocopy (and also a modern reproduction) of the miniature programme leaflet which was distributed on the occasion.

To the Bangs residence: This incident also is told in the Bangs biography by his son.

Notes: November 1894

Writes a sequel: An extensive study of Bangs's Sherlockian writings is Jon L. Lellenberg's article "Bangsian Sherlockiana," *Baker Street Miscellanea* 39 (autumn 1984), pp. 31-36. The major items: *A House-Boat on the Styx* (New York: Harper & Brothers, 1895). *The Pursuit of the House-Boat* (New York: Harper & Brothers, 1897). "The Mystery of Pinkham's Diamond Stud," *Harper's Bazaar*, April 1, 1899, and *The Dreamers* (New York: Harper & Brothers, 1899). "Sherlock Holmes Again," *Harper's Weekly*, September 2, 1899, and *The Enchanted Typewriter* (New York: Harper & Brothers, 1899). "A Pragmatic Enigma," *New York Herald*, April 19, 1908, and *Potted Fiction* (New York: Doubleday, 1908). "The Remarkable Adventures of Raffles Holmes," *Harper's Weekly*, July 29 and August 5, 12, 19 and 26, 1905, and then as *R. Holmes & Co.* (New York: Harper & Brothers, 1906).

Tuesday, November 13: Audience in Orange
Golf with Bangs: Also reported in the biography by Francis Bangs (cited in the previous chapter). The letter quoted is dated June 27, 1897, and is now held by the New York Public Library in its Berg Collection, tipped into the holograph manuscript of Bangs's *The Pursuit of the House-Boat*.

Forgotten something: This note on Aldine Club stationery is held by the Harry Ransom Humanities Research Center, University of Texas at Austin. I am grateful to Jon Lellenberg for identifying the "waterghost" for me. The book had just been published (New York: Harper & Brothers, 1894).

Note to Ripley Hitchcock: The original of this note is now in the libraries of Columbia University, New York. I am grateful to Bernard R. Crystal, assistant librarian for manuscripts, for a photocopy of it.

Orange, New Jersey: In tracking down this lecture I have been kindly assisted by Arthur Klimowicz of the South Orange Public Library; Paul Chao of the library of Seton Hall University, South Orange; Edith Bolden of the Orange Public Library; and my friend Linda Morris. The entirety of what was found is a brief paragraph which appeared under "Concerts and Entertainment," *East Orange Gazette*, November 15, 1894.

Mrs. George Richards: I very much regret that I was unable to discover the given name of this lady, whose diaries are now held by the New-York Historical Society. I was able to examine them (and many other diaries which proved to have no mention of Doyle) through the kindness of Stephen E. Novak, assistant curator of manuscripts.

Wednesday, November 14: New Readings at Daly's
The papers are full: See especially the *New York Daily Tribune*, November 14 (with the report on Dean Hole) and November 15 ("Dr. Doyle's Second Reading at Daly's").

The box office: These figures are from Pond's manuscript register, now in the Berg Collection of the New York Public Library.

Amusing incident: *Memories and Adventures* (Boston: Little, Brown, 1924), p. 118. It is not certain that it was the Wednesday lecture at which this incident took place; I have arbitrarily assigned it here rather than Monday or Friday.

Varies his programme: As reported in the *Daily Tribune*. See also the chapter for November 20.

Welcome to America, Mr. Sherlock Holmes

Thursday, November 15: Philadelphia and Princeton

His autobiography: *Memories and Adventures* (Boston: Little, Brown, 1924), p. 117.

Matinee in Philadelphia: I have found absolutely no newspaper record of this event, which is attested in Pond's manuscript register; the local sponsor is noted there as Mrs. E. H. Barrows.

To Princeton: For information about the Casino, and for much else in connection with Doyle's visit to Princeton, I am indebted to the knowledge and patience of Earle E. Coleman, the University Archivist at Princeton University. I was able to collect some additional information from Princetoniana held in the Seeley G. Mudd Manuscript Library, during a brief visit to Princeton. A version of this chapter appeared as "A. Conan Doyle's 1894 Visit to Princeton," *The Princeton Recollector* ix no. 9 (Autumn 1986) pp. 1, 11-15.

Dining with him: The surnames of the faculty and students who dined with Doyle appear in "A Dinner to Dr. Doyle," *The Daily Princetonian*, November 15, 1894, and in the *Princeton Press* for November 17. In most cases it was easy to identify them from standard sources, from Princeton's published register of graduates, or from the *Nassau Herald* for 1894, as indicated. (Leroy Wiley McCay suffered the indignity of having his name published as McCoy in the *Princetonian* and as McKay in the *Press*.)

John Work Garrett: I could not resist the hope that Garrett had met Doyle again in later life, when the former was an American diplomat in Europe and the latter a historian of World War I, with connections in the highest military circles. No evidence of such a connection has, however, come to light. I did obtain a transcript of a letter from Garrett dated November 30, 1922, and beginning "Dear Doyle," but finally concluded that it was not directed to Arthur Conan Doyle. I am nevertheless grateful to Jane Katz, John Work Garrett Librarian at the Johns Hopkins University, for finding it for me, and to Ann S. Gwyn of the Milton S. Eisenhower Library there, as well as Harrison Garrett of Brooklandville, Maryland, for permission to refer to it.

ACD's lecture: Ticket information was advertised in the *Daily Princetonian*, and in the issue of November 14 there was a front-page promotional article ("Dr. A. Conan Doyle"). The lecture was reported in the *Daily Princetonian* for November 16 ("Dr. Doyle's Lecture") and in the *Princeton Press* – the newspaper of the city, as opposed to that of the university – for the same date ("Dr. A. Conan Doyle").

Ushers: The names appeared in the same *Daily Princetonian* article which listed the students and faculty who dined with Doyle. It was easy to identify most of them. Not mentioned in my text are Pease '95 (the same one who dined with Doyle) and Morris '95 and Grant '96 (whom I could not identify). A couple of the names are spelt differently but identifications seemed clear.

Friday, November 16: North to New Rochelle

Matinee at Daly's: This final matinee produced a brief paragraph ("Dr. Doyle's Third Reading at Daly's") in the *Daily Tribune* for November 17, 1894. The receipts were $290.50, Pond's register records.

New Rochelle: For information about this city I am indebted to Hillel Ausubel of the New Rochelle Public Library and to Thomas A. Hoctor, City Historian of New Rochelle; the latter also pointed out to me the relevance of George M.

Notes: November 1894

Cohan's musical play and song, about which I found some information in John McCabe, *George M. Cohan: The Man Who Owned Broadway* (Garden City: Doubleday, 1973), pp. 68-71.

He gives his readings: "The Alumni Lecture," *New Rochelle Paragraph*, November 24, 1894. Pond's manuscript register indicates that the local agent or manager for this lecture was W. J. Ballard – the same name which appears for the Glens Falls lecture on November 23, the Flushing lecture on December 3 and the Jamaica lecture on December 5. I have no further information about him.

Trinity Place Public School: Austin D. Devane, *History of the New Rochelle Schools, 1795-1952*, a doctoral dissertation at Columbia University and Teachers College; and newspaper information supplied by the New Rochelle Public Library.

Saturday, November 17: Dinner at the Lotos Club

"The 'Slapping Sal'": This appearance in the *Princeton Press* for November 17, 1894, has not been previously reported by bibliographers.

Dinner at the Lotos Club: There was apparently very little press coverage of this event. A brief item ("The Lotos Club to Entertain Dr. Doyle") appeared beforehand in the *New York Tribune* (November 17, 1894), and it lists the intended speakers and the names, as I have quoted them, of some of those who would be attending. Much more information, including the passages of Doyle's speech from which I have quoted, appears in John Elderkin, *A Brief History of the Lotos Club* (New York: Press of Macgowan and Slipper, ca. 1895), pp. 131-134. That book, *passim*, is the source for my general comments about the Lotos Club and its house.

Low must arrive late: This letter from Seth Low to Chester S. Lord, secretary of the Lotos Club, is dated November 5, 1894, and is remarkable for being typewritten. It is now in the collections of the Columbia University Libraries, to whose staff I am indebted for a photocopy.

The menu: The menu card from this dinner, indicating these delicacies and many others, and decorated as I have described, is reproduced in facsimile in *Sir Arthur Conan Doyle: Centenary 1859-1959* (Garden City: Doubleday, 1959), p. 49.

A paragraph of an after-dinner speech by Doyle, said to have been given at the Lotos Club in 1912, appears in the souvenir book *Sir Arthur Conan Doyle Centenary 1859-1959* (Garden City, New York: Doubleday, 1959), p. 62. Doyle was not in New York between 1894 and 1914. It is possible that he did use those remarks at the 1894 dinner:

> I am aware that the division of opinion among us at the time of your civil troubles has been taken to mean lack of sympathy with you. Far from being so, it was exactly the contrary. Our sympathies are so close and vital that when you are rent in two we are rent in two, and with a bitterness and completeness which was a counterpart of your own. So it would be to-morrow, and when it ceases to be, it will be a proof that we have finally lost touch with you. It is only when a great American or a great Britisher dies, when a mighty voice is hushed for ever, a Tennyson, a Lowell or a Holmes, that a thrill through both countries tells of that deep-lying race feeling in the development of which lies, I believe, the future history of the world. Little waves and eddies may disturb the surface, but there is an unseen current, a thousand fathoms deep, which sweeps us onward to the same goal.

Welcome to America, Mr. Sherlock Holmes

Sunday, November 18: A Cheque for S. S. McClure
Magazines: Frank Luther Mott, *A History of American Magazines 1885-1905* (Cambridge, Massachusetts: Harvard University Press, 1957), especially pp. 43-47.

S. S. McClure: S. S. McClure, *My Autobiography* (New York: Frederick A. Stokes Co., 1914; Frederick Ungar Publishing Co., 1963), *passim*, with the story of Doyle's visit to him on pp. 215-217. McClure had probably met Doyle before: see the chapter and notes for October 28.

ACD tells the story: *Memories and Adventures* (Boston: Little, Brown, 1924), p.119.

The Author: "New York Letter," by "H. R." *The Author*, June 1895, pp. 10-12. Doyle's reply was a letter, "Lecturing in America," in the July issue, p. 35. It was reprinted under the same title in the *New York Tribune*, September 1, 1895, p. 22, and quoted at length under "The Lounger" in the American journal *The Critic*, July 20, 1895. Doyle's reply to *The Critic*, dated from Maloja, then appeared in the issue of September 21, 1895, p. 189.

Earnings from the trip: Doyle presents his figures as a hypothetical case, but they seem, from the fragmentary information available, to be a not unreasonable summary of his own experience. The fees noted in Pond's register (where most entries are missing or in code) range from $250 at Baltimore and $200 for the first Chicago talk to fifty per cent of a $290.50 gross on November 16 in New York and a mere $50 each at Cincinnati, Detroit and Chicago. There were thirty-nine lectures, and if the average net earnings were $85 the total was $3,315. To write a cheque for five thousand dollars before the journey was finished certainly required further resources; royalties, perhaps including advances for *The Stark Munro Letters*, seem the obvious source.

Monday, November 19: Return to Boston
General comments about Boston will be found with the chapter for October 31. Doyle uses the "dear old streets" phrase in *Our American Adventure* (London: Hodder and Stoughton, [1923]), p. 59.

George Santayana: I had hoped to find some indication that Santayana met Doyle or at least heard him speak. None came to light, despite assistance from two people whose help I am happy to acknowledge: Susan Bellingham of the rare books room at the University of Waterloo libraries and Dr. John McCormick of Rutgers, the State University, New Jersey.

The advertisements: "Last Appearances Here of Dr. A. Conan Doyle, The Distinguished English Author," says the heading on an advertisement, signed by Pond, in the *Boston Globe* for November 19, 1894. The same newspaper was the source of the information about competing theatrical events – which also included "In Old Kentucky" at the Boston Theatre, with two hundred people and ten horses on stage.

Association Hall is filled: "Read His Own Tales," *Boston Globe*, November 20, 1894. "Last Readings," *Boston Post*, November 20. "Lectures and Readings," *Boston Evening Transcript*, November 20. "Dr. A. Conan Doyle's Readings," *Boston Journal*, November 20. "Dr. Doyle's Reading," *Boston Advertiser*, November 20. There was also a note in the *Boston Herald*.

Today's newspapers: The review of *Vignettes of Manhattan* was in the *Boston Herald*.

Notes: November 1894

A Boston audience: *Our American Adventure* (London: Hodder and Stoughton, [1923]), p. 63.

Tuesday, November 20: Reading from "The Cardboard Box"
Today's newspapers: The headline quoted appeared in the *Boston Globe* for November 20. A still better headline was in the *Globe* the next day: "Holmes a Hypnotizer."

Last Boston reading: "A New Story by Doyle," *Boston Post*, November 21, 1894.

"The Cardboard Box": As the chapter for October 27 notes, Doyle was somewhat prudish about his work. "The Cardboard Box" had been suppressed for reasons still not absolutely clear; my fullest discussion of that incident appears in *In Bed with Sherlock Holmes* (Toronto: Simon & Pierre, 1984), pp. 33-37. As I note there, the "thought-reading episode" does include some resonances of the story's sex-related plot, although the author may not have been consciously aware of them; in the early 1890's mention of Henry Ward Beecher was bound to bring to many minds a recollection of the Tilton-Beecher scandal and adultery trial of 1874 which almost ended his pastorate. This whole episode fits somewhat uneasily with "The Resident Patient," onto which Doyle grafted it beginning with the first book publication in Britain and the second (revised) book edition in the United States. That second edition had appeared by the time of this lecture in Boston, and it is odd that he referred to the episode as belonging to "The Cardboard Box" when he could have mentioned "The Resident Patient."

"The Medal of the Brigadier": See the chapter for December 2.

Wednesday, November 21: Interview in Rochester
Union and Advertiser: "Conan Doyle," Rochester *Union and Advertiser*, November 21, 1894. The question and answer about doctors and their diseases were picked up by the *Cleveland Plain Dealer* and published under the title "Queer: A. Conan Doyle Answers an Interesting Question" in the issue of December 2, 1894.

Conversion neurosis: For this interesting insight into "The Blanched Soldier" I thank Thelma Beam, who raised it in a paper delivered to The Bootmakers of Toronto in March 1985.

Rochester: General information about the city was kindly provided by Wayne Arnold and Carol Emrich of the Rochester Public Library. The book quoted from is *History and Commerce of Rochester* (New York: A. F. Parsons Publishing Co., 1894), p. 53. For the Sam Patch story, see any guidebook, but also Whitney R. Cross, *The Burned-Over District* (New York: Harper & Row, 1950, 1965), p. 154, and more humourously William Dean Howells, *Their Wedding Journey* (Boston and New York: Houghton Mifflin, 1895), pp. 134-135.

Most honoured: *Our American Adventure* (London: Hodder and Stoughton, [1923]), p. 103.

Lecture this evening: "A Famous Novelist," Pond's manuscript register indicates that the local agent for this lecture was Algernon D. Crapsey, and that there was a payment of "10% to Furlong," whom I am not able to identify.

Rochester was noted as a centre of such causes as Spiritualism and women's rights. ACD would return to it in 1923, observing in his book *Our Second Ameri-*

can Adventure (Boston: Little, Brown, 1924), p. 16-17, that "I was interested in my sally to Rochester, for this city is near the place where the Hydesville rappings occurred in 1848, the first time in modern days that actual systematic intercourse has taken place between the two spheres."

Thursday, November 22: The Female College at Elmira
Baedeker: *Baedeker's United States*, p. 197.

The reformatory: I enquired whether there was any record of Doyle visiting the institution, but I am told both by John B. Wilmost, Superintendent of what is now the Elmira Correction and Reception Center, and by Peter Lu of the library there that no records are available. On his 1914 tour Doyle, by then world-famous for his involvement in criminal justice reform, inspected both New York's "Tombs" prison and the penitentiary at Sing-Sing (*Memories and Adventures*, pp. 288-289).

Elmira College: For extensive and patient help with information about Elmira College I am indebted to its archivist, Herbert A. Wisbey, Jr., who provided photocopies of contemporary publications as well as his own explanations of various matters. See also W. Charles Barber's *Elmira College: The First Hundred Years* (New York: McGraw-Hill, 1955). Page 132 of that book notes the crisis which the college was facing late in 1894: a deficit of $6,500 – and that just after the arrival of a new president, the Rev. Dr. Rufus S. Green, of Orange, New Jersey.

Lectures this evening: "Society Notes," *The Sibyl* xxiv no. 2 (December 1894), p. 91, the college's student publication, with a report on the work of Kappa Sigma. "Dr. A. Conan Doyle," *Elmira Daily Gazette and Free Press*, November 23, 1894. "Dr. A. Conan Doyle," *Elmira Daily Advertiser*, November 23.

Her contralto voice: For what little information about Josephine Millham is available I am again indebted to Herbert A. Wisbey, Jr. I have found no information about the songs, but have tentatively identified their composers as Erik Meyer-Helmund (1861-1932), Russian-born composer of more than two hundred light songs and five operas, and William Harold Neidlinger (1863-1924), of Brooklyn, best known for his music books for kindergartens.

Mary Wilson McNair: She probably outlived everyone else who saw Doyle during his 1894 tour, and seems almost a link with the present. A brief obituary appeared in the *LC Information Bulletin* from the Library of Congress shortly after her death on August 31, 1972.

Writes to Goldwin Smith: The original of this note is with a mass of other papers of Smith held at Cornell University, and available on microfilm at various libraries. I am grateful to Kathleen Jacklin of the John M. Olin Library at Cornell for pointing me in the right direction.

Friday, November 23: Pilgrimage to Glens Falls
Glens Falls: General information, including descriptions of the opera house, has helpfully been provided by Gayle A. Rettew of the Glens Falls-Queensbury Historical Association and by Bruce Cole of the Crandall Library, Glens Falls.

Cooper's cave: The edition of *The Last of the Mohicans* which I have used is the one with an introduction by James Franklin Beard (Albany: State University of New York Press, 1983). The cave is described in the text at p. 55, and Cooper's own interest for it is discussed at p. xx of the introduction.

Notes: November 1894

Lecture this evening: "Conan Doyle Delightful," *Glens Falls Daily Times*, November 24, 1894. See the note about the local agent at New Rochelle with the chapter for November 16.

William H. McElroy: His Chautauqua lecture was titled "Famous Men at Famous Dinners," according to a report in the *Chautauqua Assembly Herald*, July 31, 1894, p. 5.

Saturday, November 24: Lecture in Schenectady

Sherman Williams: An engraving of Williams in profile, which could pass for Doyle in his later years, appears with the entry for him in volume viii of *American Biography: A New Cyclopedia*. An informative obituary appeared in the *New York State Historical Society Proceedings*, 22 (1924) pp. 164-167.

Train to Schenectady: The train time is mentioned in the report of the previous night's lecture in the *Glens Falls Daily Times*.

Indian massacre: William Dean Howells, *Their Wedding Journey* (Boston and New York: Houghton Mifflin, 1895), p. 106.

Schenectady: Most of the research for this chapter was done by my friend Tom Dandrew of Schenectady, who has subsequently reported his findings in "Conan Doyle's Visit to Schenectady, N.Y.," *Naval Signals* 21 (December 18, 1984) pp. 3-6. The items from the *Daily Union* include "Dinner to A. Conan Doyle," November 19; "Dr. A. Conan Doyle: Culture in Chicago," November 21; "Local Notes," November 24.

The lecture: The manuscript register, indicating A.L. Roherer's name, adds the note "Arranged by EPH." I do not know whose initials those are. The lecture was reported in "Dr. A. Conan Doyle," *Schenectady Daily Union*, November 26, 1894.

Andrew Van Vranken Raymond: Much of this information is abstracted from the catalogue of Union College.

Sunday, November 25: Tourist at Niagara Falls

Niagara Falls: For most of the information about Niagara Falls I am indebted to Donald E. Loker, local history specialist at the Niagara Falls (New York) Public Library, where the collection includes David Isaacs's autograph books. The help I was given at that library, coming early in my research, was both productive and encouraging. A useful source about David Isaacs was a typewritten letter written in 1963 by Marjorie F. Williams, then city historian of Niagara Falls (New York), made available to me there. Additional material was found through the assistance of Mary Joselin at the Sir Harry Oakes Room of the Niagara Falls (Ontario) Public Library. I also briefly consulted microfilms at the public library of Niagara-on-the-Lake, Ontario.

Late last night: One newspaper report does say that the Doyle brothers "arrived at the Falls this morning," that is, November 26. It is possible that he took an overnight train, but since he apparently put up at the Prospect House it seems more likely that at least part of a night was involved.

George V: The young prince George was a midshipman aboard HMS Canada, commanded by Capt. Francis Durrant, during 1883, and visited Niagara Falls on September 27, 1883, signing Isaacs's book on that occasion; he was eighteen years old.

Welcome to America, Mr. Sherlock Holmes

A tourist town: These descriptions (together with the assessment of the rates at the Prospect House) come from *Baedeker's United States*, pp. 199-206.

The Niagara Book: "By W. D. Howells, Mark Twain, Prof. Nathaniel S. Shaler, and Others." Buffalo: Underhill and Nichols, 1893.

Years later: ACD apparently did not get to Niagara Falls during his second trip to North America, in 1914, but he and his family did visit there in May 1922. He devotes several paragraphs to the visit in his book *Our American Adventure* (London: Hodder & Stoughton, 1923), pp. 110-112, but they are limited to conventional descriptions and comments on the future of hydroelectric power. The report that he he spoke there about Reichenbach, and that he carved his initials – a vandalistic act most unlike him – depends entirely on the recollections of Borden Clarke, former proprietor of Old Authors Farm booksellers in Morristown, Ontario, who was fond of weaving literary anecdote and fantasy into his catalogues. In 1971 he wrote of "the days when I made pocket money as a Niagara Guide. . . . After two-hour Tour with Conan Doyle (. . . about 1923) he paused to scratch 'SH' on a rock. Gazing out over the Canadian Falls, he said to Lady Doyle, 'A Glorious Trail's End for anyone . . . I should have killed Holmes over there, not the Swiss Alps.'" (Quoted in *Baker Street Journal* 21 (September 1971) p. 191.

Less articulate: "Its Immensity," *Niagara Falls Gazette*, November 26, 1894.

Monday, November 26: An Old Friend in Toronto
Much as I love America: *Our Second American Adventure* (Boston: Little, Brown, 1924), p. 198.

Spent much of the day: "Its Immensity," *Niagara Falls Gazette*, November 26, 1894. "Dr. A. Conan Doyle," *Daily Cataract Journal*, November 26, 1894.

Three bridges: See the sources of information about Niagara Falls cited for the preceding chapter.

The insensate hostility: *Our American Adventure* (London: Hodder and Stoughton, 1923), p. 114.

Lord Aberdeen: John T. Saywell, ed., *The Canadian Journal of Lady Aberdeen 1893-1898* (Toronto: The Champlain Society, 1960), pp. 152-155.

The World: "Sherlock Holmes on the Westwood Case," *The Toronto World*, November 27, 1894. This article also mentions the time of Doyle's arrival in Toronto, and is one of several newspaper reports to indicate that Pickering was his host.

Latimer and Annie Pickering: There were two ways to become a physician or surgeon in Edinburgh in the 1880's: through study at the university, or though a process something like apprenticeship, with instruction at the city's hospitals from the "extra-academical" lecturers who also gave the university students some classes. Doyle chose the university programme, which led to the M.B. (Bachelor of Medicine) degree, and later returned to write a thesis and earn the more advanced M.D. (Doctor of Medicine) degree. Pickering chose the other method, which led after a series of examinations to the distinction of L.R.C.S.(E.) (Licentiate of the Royal College of Surgeons, Edinburgh). He also received the College's licentiate in midwifery. Although in later years he used the distinction M.D., which was the North American convention for medical doctors, there is no indication that he ever earned an M.D.

Notes: Monday, November 26: An Old Friend in Toronto

Having practised medicine in Birmingham, where Doyle briefly also worked, Pickering came to Canada in 1883, and on October 1 he was registered with the College of Physicians and Surgeons of Ontario. Directories show several addresses for him before, in 1892, the Toronto city directory has him at 281 Sherbourne Street, with a "branch" at Queen Street and Carlaw Avenue in the east end. He is listed as "M.D., L.R.C.S., L.M.E.," and "Coroner, city of Toronto" – there is a mention also of Annie Louise Pickering, "M.D., C.M., phys. & surg." The Sherbourne Street address continues for several years, but Dr. Annie Pickering is not mentioned in city directories after 1894.

The records of the City Clerk for Toronto indicate that as of September 10, 1891, Latimer Pickering lived at, and owned, 281 Sherbourne Avenue; he was a physician and surgeon; he gave his age as 36 and his religion as Anglican; there were three people in the family, none of them being of school age. (This information was provided by Victor L. Russell, manager of the City of Toronto Archives.)

Although one directory listed him as coroner of the city, he never held that position, but was an associate coroner for the city of Toronto, from the time of his appointment on February 8, 1889, according to records consulted by Richard W. Ramsey of the Archives of Ontario. "These appointments were 'at pleasure'," I am told, "and it is probable that he functioned in the office until his death." A brief obituary which appeared in the *Canadian Medical Association Journal* and a death notice in the August 5, 1923, issue of the *Toronto Globe* indicate that Dr. Latimer Pickering died at home August 5, 1923. The *Globe* says he was to be buried in the cemetery of St. John's, Norway, near the office he had once maintained at Queen and Carlaw.

Dr. Annie Louise Pickering graduated in 1887 from Trinity University, Toronto, and held the qualifications of "M.D., C.M.," according to Sheila Swanson, of the William Boyd Library of the Academy of Medicine, Toronto, and Marie Cuthbert of the alumni records office at the University of Toronto. "The Archivist of Trinity College, Henri Pilon, informs me that she matriculated on 12 January, 1885 and that she received her MD CM . . . on 12 April, 1887," writes Harold Averill of the University of Toronto Archives in a letter to me. He explains: "Women at that time took courses at the Woman's Medical College (later Ontario Medical College for Women) which was affiliated with the U. of T. and Trinity College. The women, though, chose to take their degrees from Trinity." Probably Annie Pickering was a member of the first class to graduate from that institution. There were a few women doctors in Ontario before that date; the first one, trained in Pennsylvania, was registered in 1875, and Augusta Stowe (later Stowe-Gullen) received her qualifications in Ontario in 1883. (Carlotta Hacker, *The Indomitable Lady Doctors* (Toronto: Clarke Irwin, 1974), pp. 29, 32, 39, 51.)

The Academy of Medicine Library reports as follows: "I have checked with the College of Physicians and Surgeons of Ontario for a death date for Dr. Annie. She last appeared in the Register for 1937 and on her card there is a note that Dr. Stowe-Gullen had made inquiries. Dr. Annie Pickering had gone to live in England 'where her husband came from'. In 1953, the College [listed her] 'presumed dead'."

I speculate that the two doctors were married at about the time Annie Pickering graduated from Trinity; that the third member of the family in 1892 was an infant child – though there is no later indication of a child – and that, once she had become a mother, Dr. Annie Pickering did little in the way of medical practice, maintaining her registration but not being listed in the city directory.

It seems surprising that she would have gone to England, whether or not to her husband's home, at the end of her life if she had grown up in Ontario and if he was buried in Toronto.

I regret that I do not have more information about these doctors, starting with Annie Pickering's maiden name. Clearly she was a pioneer among woman physicians in Canada, and the Pickerings must have been an interesting couple indeed. (Augusta Stowe-Gullen was also married to a physician, a medical school classmate.)

Much of the information assembled here was collected on my behalf by Donald A. Redmond. A general picture of medical education at Edinburgh in the 1880's can be found in Ely M. Liebow, *Dr. Joe Bell: Model for Sherlock Holmes* (Bowling Green, Ohio: Bowling Green University Popular Press, 1983). A chapter on the subject also appears in Owen Dudley Edwards, *The Quest for Sherlock Holmes* (Edinburgh: Mainstream Publishing, 1983), pp. 177-221. A more detailed biography of the Pickerings appears in my article "The Toronto Doctors Who Welcomed Doyle," *Canadian Holmes* 10 no. 2 (winter 1986) pp. 35-38.

ACD's lecture: "Dr. Conan Doyle," *Toronto Mail*, November 27, 1894. "'Sherlock Holmes' in Town," *Toronto World*, November 27. "Dr. A. Conan Doyle," *The Globe*, November 27. "An Author's Life," *Toronto Daily Star*, November 27. "Conan Doyle a Speaker," *The Empire*, November 27. "Lecture Hall and Theatre," *The Evening News*, November 27. "How They Were Written," *The Evening Telegram*, November 27. John B. Withrow, who has had a life-long association with Massey Hall and whose father was a functionary there, writes to me, "I doubt if any programme would have been printed – they rarely were for a speaker – and I cannot recall my father making special mention of Mr. Doyle's appearance." He kindly provided some information about the hall.

I am assured: *Our Second American Adventure*, p. 196. The Chautauqua lecture by George B. Adams was reported in the *Chautauqua Assembly Herald*.

The first friendly notice: "Dr. A. Conan Doyle," *The Globe*, November 27, 1894. One response to this comment came in *The Week*, November 30, 1894, and the other in *The Evening News*, November 28 ("Micah Clarke; How a Toronto Editor Gave Conan Doyle his First Boost." I have found brief items about *Micah Clarke* in *The Week* for March 1, 1889, and (the same item) August 9 and 16, 1889, but nothing which would seem to justify Doyle's fond recollections of a favourable review. Janice McNabb of the Metropolitan Toronto Library reports no success in finding a review of *Micah Clarke* in the *Globe* in 1889 or 1890.

Guest for dinner: "Sherlock Holmes on the Westwood Case," *The Toronto World*, November 27. For biographical information about Ryerson and Johnson I am grateful to Donald Redmond. In addition to the things I mention in the text, Ryerson served in the Austrian Army of Occupation of Bosnia (1878), founded the St. John's Ambulance Association in Canada and the Canadian Red Cross Society, and served as a senator of the University of Toronto. Johnson's book, with the title noted, was published in 1911 by the Canadian Law Book Company.

Tuesday, November 27: Lecture in Buffalo

His autograph: This autograph is now owned by David B. Clark of Willowdale, Ontario, who tells me that it was given to him and he knows nothing of the circumstances under which it was written. A photocopy is on file at the Metropolitan Toronto Library.

Notes: December 1894

Hall is from pages of *Morristown's Forgotten Past, "The Gilded Age"*, by John W. Rae and John W. Rae, Jr., provided to me by that library.

Coat and waistcoat: *Norwood Review*, May 18, 1895.

Edgar W. Smith: Born April 1, 1894, Smith was "commissionaire" of the Baker Street Irregulars from about 1940 until his death in 1960, and editor of the first thirteen volumes of the *Baker Street Journal*. His son, Edgar P. Smith, now of Far Hills, New Jersey, kindly advises me that he has no reason to believe that his father ever investigated Doyle's visit to Morristown.

December 1894

Saturday, December 1: Rain in Paterson

William Carlos Williams: *Paterson* was published in sections between 1946 and 1958. The passage quoted is from the author's note "The Poem Paterson," borrowed from Williams's autobiography for publication in the New Directions Paperbook edition of *Paterson* (New York, 1963), pp. [vii-viii].

Tonight: "Dr. Doyle's Lecture," *Paterson Daily Press*, December 3, 1894. This article includes the passage from Stevenson, as quoted, and also mentions the bad weather. "Dr. A. Conan Doyle," *Paterson Morning Call*, December 3, 1894. I am grateful to Linda Van Zandt Morris, to Jack De Stefano of the Paterson Free Public Library, and to Jessica Peters of the Passaic County Historical Society for help in finding these reports.

Eugene Stevenson: No report which I have found mentions Stevenson's presence at either of the Lotos Club events in Doyle's honour. The luncheon early in the tour was a small event; more likely, then, Stevenson introduced himself to Doyle at the dinner on November 17, and invited him to be his guest in Paterson.

Rosa Murray: The *Press* gives only her surname; but the full name appears in Pond's manuscript register, indicating that she, on the club's behalf, was the sponsor of the Paterson lecture. One wonders whether the book Doyle gave her really was the one he had been using – and, if so, what he used on subsequent days in Flushing, Jamaica, and Jersey City. Perhaps he knew the passages by heart by that time.

Sunday, December 2: The Napoleon Fad

The Brigadier: Bibliographical information is of course taken from the Gibson and Green *Bibliography*.

Every novelist and hack: Various advertisements and references in literary journals. I have no doubt that many other Napoleonic works from the period could have been cited. The "fad" quotation from *The New York Times* is taken from an October 28 review of the play *Napoleon Bonaparte* at the Herald Square Theatre.

Auction sale: "Napoleon's Hair at Auction," *New York World*, September 17, 1894.

Based on Marbot: Jack Tracy, "How the Brigadier Came to Be Written," in ACD, *The Return of Gerard* (New York: Jove Publications, Inc., 1982), pp. 174-182. The quotation in French is from Jean Tulard, *Le Mythe de Napoléon* (Paris: Librairie Armand Colin, 1971), p. 22.

Welcome to America, Mr. Sherlock Holmes

I am an excellent soldier: A quotation taken almost at random from that first story, "How the Brigadier Won His Medal."

Monday, December 3: Evening in Flushing
Today's newspapers: The Bloomingdale's advertisement appeared in the *New York World* for December 3, 1894. That paper's story about the Gaiety Girls is headed "Gaiety Girls Vaccinated"; the same day's *New York Sun* headed its piece "Immune Gaiety Girls."

Note to a friend: This letter is now in the author's collection.

Flushing: The only evidence of this lecture is the entry in Pond's register, which indicates that W. J. Ballard was the agent (see the note with the chapter for November 16) and adds "1000 circulars sent Miss Lyles 10/16/94." Apparently there are no files of the *Flushing Daily Times* and *Flushing Evening Journal* for late 1894, and no mention of Doyle appeared in the *Long Island Democrat*. I am grateful to William Asadorian of the Queens Borough Public Library and Carol Ahrens of the Hempstead Public Library for their attempts, however unsuccessful, to turn up press reports.

Alexander P. Doyle: See particularly the profile of him, "Father Alexander P. Doyle," *New York Sun*, December 9, 1894.

Tuesday, December 4: Fire, Blood, and Corruption
These news items are taken from *The New York Times* for December 4, 1894.

Copyright law: A detailed study of the copyright issues surrounding Doyle's books in the United States in the 1890's is far beyond the scope of this book. The Gibson and Green *Bibliography* touches on the matter; the definitive study, at least of the extreme case, *The Sign of the Four*, is awaited from Donald Redmond. The *New York Times* for December 9, 1894, carried a long article under the title "Advantage to Authors," discussing the workings so far of the Copyright Act of March 3, 1891, and the international agreements which followed it. The consensus of American publishers' views quoted there is as I have summarized them in this chapter. Details of the law's functioning were still being worked out in 1894, and Doyle's friend H. Rider Haggard was in court in New Jersey (Haggard et al. v. Waverly Pub. Co.) to maintain his rights to the book *Mada the Lily*. I am grateful to my friend Paula Perry for helping me to find the case report (144 Federal Reporter p. 490).

Wednesday, December 5: The Town Hall, Jamaica
Jamaica: Through the kindness of William Asadorian, of the Queens Borough Public Library, and Vincent Seyfried of Queens, I have transcripts of brief items about Doyle which appeared in Jamaica's newspaper, the *Long Island Farmer*, on November 23, November 30 and December 7, 1894. In addition, I have an article from the *Brooklyn Times*, December 6, 1894: "Dr. Doyle's Lecture. He Pleases a Large Audience at Jamaica." The November 30 item mentions that the lecture was rescheduled from December 8 to December 5.

J. Howard Hobbs: Information about him from the *Portrait and Biographical Record of Queens County (Long Island), New York* (1896), and about the Jamaica Town Hall, was provided by Robert Friedrich of the Queens Borough Public Library.

Notes: December 1894

Thursday, December 6: Last Lecture
The Jersey City lecture is reported in that city's *Evening Journal* for December 7, 1894 ("Conan Doyle's Lecture"). As with Doyle's other excursions into northern New Jersey, I found this occasion particularly difficult to document. Even the Pond register does not indicate the name of a local sponsor – only the initials or symbol "BB." It does provide the justification for my statement that a December 7 lecture in New York had been considered: the pencil notation "Dalys" opposite that date. Newspapers I have consulted do not contain any advertisements for such a lecture, let alone any report of it; I conclude that Pond throught better of it, or Doyle drew the line.

Friday, December 7: A Toast to Arthur Conan Doyle
Emile Zola: "Zola Didn't Get a Vote," *New York World*, December 7, 1894.

Interview with Mabie: It was published as "Literary Aspects of America," *Ladies' Home Journal*, March 1895, p. 6. The *Journal*, which had previously been advertising Doyle on the subject of American women, mentioned the change of topic in a note introducing the published article. A brief note in volume 1 number 1 of *The Bookman* of New York (February 1895, p. 9) observed that the conversation "took place . . . on the eve of [Doyle's] departure for Europe. . . . Those who are aware of Mr. Mabie's strong aversion and instinctive dislike to interviewing and being interviewed will interpret this announcement as an evidence of Mr. Mabie's strong personal regard for Dr. Doyle."

Aldine Club: Names, quotations and paraphrases are extracted from three brief newspaper reports: "Conan Doyle at the Aldine," *New York World*, December 8, 1894; "Farewell Dinner to Conan Doyle," *New York Times*, December 8; "A Farewell to Dr. Doyle," *New York Daily Tribune*, December 8. The *Times* mentions "Charles W. Warner," but Charles Dudley Warner must surely be meant.

Bill Nye: Biographical information is from David B. Kesterson, *Bill Nye* (Boston: Twayne Publishers, 1891). Nye had been in London the previous winter and made some acquaintance with active members of the Authors' Society, as he reported in comic tones in a syndicated column. (Among its appearances: "The Lights of London," *San Francisco Examiner*, December 31, 1893. It is not certain that he had met Doyle on this occasion, but it seems likely.

Saturday, December 8: Aboard the *Etruria*
Round Table Fair: "An 'Authors' Reception' for Charity," *Publishers' Weekly*, December 8, 1894.

Etruria: Descriptive information about the ship, together with confirmation of its sailing and arrival times, were provided by Michael Cook, of the archives at the University of Liverpool, which hold the records of the Cunard Steam-Ship Co., Ltd. Additional information came through him from the Cunard public relations office.

Will rest: Charles Higham in his *The Adventures of Conan Doyle* (New York: W. W. Norton and Co., 1976), p. 138, states that Doyle spent much of the trip in bed. I have no idea how he knows. John Dickson Carr is even vaguer in his *The Life of Sir Arthur Conan Doyle* (New York: Harper & Brothers, 1949), p. 89: "In the reaction after stimulus he was exhausted and depressed."

$298,000 in specie: This additional shipment is noted in *The Times* for December 10, 1894.

Welcome to America, Mr. Sherlock Holmes

Sir Donald Smith: It is astonishing how many archives do not have the personal papers of this important historical figure. For information I am nevertheless indebted to H. T. Holman of the Public Archives of Canada; Dave Jones of the Canadian Pacific corporate archives; Leslie Hoffman of the Hudson's Bay Company; Anne Morton of the Provincial Archives of Manitoba; and the present Lord Strathcona.

Immigration documents: Records from the Public Record Office, London, indicating the number of passengers and the names of those in the cabin classes, were copied for me by Donald Redmond.

Jessie and Georgina Preston: The London production of *Little Jack Sheppard* was reviewed in *The Times* August 13, 1894. Another description, including the comment I have quoted about Jessie Preston's figure, is found in William Archer, *The Theatrical World of 1894* (London: Walter Scott, Ltd., 1895), pp. 218-221 and 392-393. The statement that she later shaved some years off her age is based on her dates (1877-1928) as listed in J. P. Wearing, *The London Stage 1890-1893* (Metuchen, New Jersey: Scarecrow Press, 1976). The song-sheet illustrated by the sisters posing as little girls is held at Harvard College and listed in its *Catalogue of Dramatic Portraits*, edited by Lillian Arvilla Hall (Harvard University Press, 1932), p. 361.

Afterword

The *Etruria*: The time of sighting at Browhead was mentioned in *The Times* for December 15, 1894. The time of the call at Queenstown was noted by Michael Cook of the University of Liverpool archives, who notes that the total length of passage was officially 6 days 5 hours 45 minutes, which is clearly the time to Queenstown; time of arrival at Liverpool is, oddly, not recorded.

Cavalry officer: *Our American Adventure* (London: Hodder and Stoughton, 1923), p. 179. The available passenger lists of the *Etruria* give no clue to the man's identity.

Robert Louis Stevenson: Two of Doyle's biographers state that he received the news of Stevenson's death before he left New York: John Dickson Carr in *The Life of Sir Arthur Conan Doyle* (New York: Harper & Brothers, 1949), p. 89, and Charles Higham in *The Adventures of Conan Doyle* (New York: W. W. Norton and Co., 1976), p. 138. Higham adds that the news came in a telegram from A. P. Watt. But this seems impossible. Stevenson died December 3 on a remote island, from which the news had first to be carried by naval steamer. *Publishers' Weekly* reported on December 22: "A cable despatch, dated Apia, December 8, confirms the report that had reached San Francisco by way of Auckland, New Zealand, that Robert Louis Stevenson had died suddenly of apoplexy a few days before." Whatever the route, the newspapers in the western world did not report the news until December 18 (both *The Times* and *The New York Times* had it on that date) and they were hardly noted for self-restraint. Surely Watt, Doyle and other literary folks cannot have had the news for ten days before any newspaper got wind of it. In any case, there is the almost conclusive evidence of Doyle's own recollection, as quoted from *Memories and Adventures* (Boston: Little, Brown, 1924), p. 254. He may have erred in the year but he can hardly be mistaken about the sensation. December 18 was Wednesday, and Doyle thus had

Notes: Afterword

ample time to travel from Liverpool to London and be in the Strand when the headlines appeared.

Norwegian Ski: The headline in the Atlanta paper was equally odd to a modern ear: "Conan Doyle's Adventures on Ski." The word was not yet familiar. Bibliographical details are from the Gibson and Green *Bibliography*.

Doyle's works: The paragraph quoted from *Publishers' Weekly* was a note in the December 22 issue. The *Bookman* material is from the American journal of that title: "Eastern Letter," in volume 1 number 1, February 1895, p. 62, and "Sales of Books During the Month," pp. 64-65. The March item is a brief paragraph from volume 1 number 2, p. 75.

Short stay in London: This quotation is from the British, not the American, *Bookman*: volume vii (January 1895), under "News Notes," p. 103.

Anglo-American relations: Doyle's letter – an effort to contradict earlier reports of what he had said about America – was published as "Mr. Conan Doyle and America," *Daily Chronicle*, January 1, 1895. His proposal for an Anglo-American Society was published as "England and America" in *The Times*, January 7, 1896, and reprinted in *The New York Times*, January 19, 1896.

Index

Aberdeen, John Campbell Gordon (Lord) 135
Académie Française 149
Academy of Music, New York 29
Actresses 54, 146, 152, 222
Adams, Adele (Mrs. George) 51
Adams, George B. 137
Adams, George E. 49
Adams, Henry 101
Addams, Jane 51, 88
Addicks, W. H. 40
Adirondacks 37, 40-41, 47, 106, 174-175
Adler, Irene 112, 148
Adventures of Sherlock Holmes 22, 79, 144
Agassiz, Louis 111
Aikins, Herbert A. 199
Aladdin, Jr. 54-55
Albany, New York 37, 47, 60, 93, 121, 132
Alcoholic entertainment 108, 187, 189
Aldine Club 28, 43, 114, 116, 123, 148-150, 171-172
Aldrich, Thomas Bailey 125
Alexander III, Czar 17, 32, 94
Altgeld, John 76
American Publishers Corp. 192-193
American Revolution 46-47
Americas' Cup 141
Amherst, Massachusetts 95-97, 101
Anderson, Larz 42

Anglo-American relations 42, 47, 67-68, 74, 97, 108, 111, 115, 122, 137, 141, 142, 150, 155, 208, 222
Appleton, D., & Co. 28, 43, 71, 107, 116, 171
Appleton, Daniel 171
Appleton, Edward Dale 40, 171
Appleton, William W. 150, 171
Archer, William 30, 33, 66, 91, 100
Armour, Philip 79
Associated Press 52
Atlantic Monthly 43, 91, 118, 123, 125
Author, The 124
Authors, lectures *see* Lecture circuit, Twain, Wilde
Authors' Club (U.S.) 116
Authors' Society 22-23, 87, 92, 103, 114, 169
Automobiles 75

Babcock, Ida 120
Baker Street Irregulars 142
Baker, Charles 60
Baker, Ray Stannard 51
Baldwin, D. H. & Co. 55
Baldwin, James Mark 118
Balestier, Beatty 140-141
Ballard, W. J. 146
Baltimore 101-104
Balzac, Honoré de 73
Bangs, John Kendrick 101, 113-116, 146, 151, 206-207
Barmaid's slang 70
Barr, Robert 35, 50, 70, 84, 91, 149, 174, 190-191, 194

Barrie, James M. (Sir) 50, 56, 71, 74, 89, 182
Barton-Wright 25
Barton, Clara 32
Baseball 58
Batchelor, W. H. 55
Bates, Josephine 78
Batterman, Henry 88
Battle of Waterloo, The, see *Waterloo*
Becker, Frederick W. (Mrs.) 181
Beecher, Henry Ward 19, 89, 127, 142, 211
"Before My Book-Case" 39, 202
Bell, Alexander Graham 25
Bell, Joseph (Dr.) 29, 48, 56, 136, 160, 216
Bellamy, Edward 59
Belloc, Marie 169
Benziger, Louis 34
Beresford, Charles (Lord) 174
Berri, William 87
Besant, Walter 72, 169
Beyond the City 36
Bicycling, see Cycling
Birdseye, Clarence 87
Black, Alexander 96, 148
Blackwood's 91
Blair, Mary 181
"Blanched Soldier, The" 128, 211
Blauvelt, Lillian 80
"Blue Carbuncle, The" 126
Bok, Edward W. 107
Bookman, The 154, 197
Booth, Edwin 86
Booth, William (General) 100
Boston, Massachusetts 91-93, 125-127
Boxing 108-109, 204
Boyd, Anna 54
Boys' Brigade 149
Brafield, Louis 146
Brattleboro, Vermont 139-142
Brayley, George P. 65
Bridgman, Herbert L. 87
British soil 46, 66, 134-135
British visitors 30, 33, 41, 48, 66, 71, 91, 100, 107-108, 172
Broadway, New York 31

Brock, Isaac (Sir) 133
Brooklyn, New York 30, 85-88, 121, 127, 148
——, streetcar anecdote 18
Brooklyn Heights Seminary 26
Brooks, Macy 119
Broughton, Lena 130
Browhead 153
Brown, Joseph E. 88
Browne, F. F. 53
Browning, Robert 72
Brownlee, W. E. 70
"Bruce-Partington Plans, The" 174
Bryant, William Cullen 90
Bryant, William E. 90, 91, 93
Bryce, Lloyd 34
Buffalo Bill 31
Buffalo Female Academy 26
Buffalo, New York 47, 55, 92, 93, 101, 112, 133, 139
Burnham, F. A. 121
Burns, Tommy 204
Butler, Willis H. 119

Cable, George Washington 36, 88-89, 98, 150, 195-196
Cabman story 92-93, 197-198
Cabots, of Brattleboro 141
Cambridge, Massachusetts 92, 125
Cameron, Evelyn 139
Canada – see British soil, Toronto
Cannon, H. W. 121
Canon Doyle 49, 53, 87, 138, 179-180
"Cardboard Box, The" 21, 81, 126-127, 211
Carlyle, Thomas 35, 72, 85, 173
Carman, Bliss 54
Carnegie Hall 177
Carnegie, Andrew 97, 116
Carnes, Prof., elocutionist 77
Carrol, Johnny 58
Carus, Emma 58
Carvalho, police expert 56
Cary, Lucius 167
Central Park, New York 30
Century magazine 118, 123, 140
Chambers, Julius 121

Chambers's Journal 166
Champlain, Samuel de 38
Chap-Book, The 54, 81
Charlesworth, Hector 98
Charters, old English 22
Chautauqua, New York 46, 131, 137, 178
Chautauqua Literary and Scientific Circle 46, 86, 195
Chicago, Illinois 8, 47-55, 61-64, 75, 78-82, 92, 112
Churches, lectures in 44, 56, 70, 76-77, 132, 148
Churchill, Winston (Sir) 169
Cincinnati, Ohio 57-61, 82
Civil War, American 29, 34, 43, 52, 57, 58, 68, 86, 95, 114
Civil War, British 93, 126, 164
Clapp, H. A. 198
Clemens, Samuel, *see* Twain, Mark
Cleveland, Grover 17, 42, 76, 100, 102, 126, 147
Cleveland, Ohio 75, 139, 217
Cliff-Dwellers 80, 193
Clubs 33, 52, 87, 129, 204
Cochran, Robert H. 65
Cochran, William Bourke 121
Coes, Frederick L. 95
Cohan, George M. 119
Colby, Howard 119
Cold Spring, New York 46
Coleman, John S. 88
Collins, Wilkie 120
Columbia College 121
Columbian Exposition 49
Comins, Annie Wyman and Edward 94
Comstock, Anthony 32
Conversion neurosis 128, 211
Conway, Ellen Dana 114
Conway, Moncure Daniel 22, 114
Cooper, James Fenimore 30, 37, 41, 131-132, 149, 157, 165, 174
Cooper Union 121
Copyright 34, 80, 147, 171, 192-193, 220
Corea, *see* Korea
Cornhill magazine 23, 159

Cosmopolitan magazine 34, 123, 124
Cowley, Lydia Avery 78
Crane, Stephen 154
Crapsey, Algernon D. 211
Crater, Ellene 54
Crime 111-112, 183
Crockett, author 154
Cromwell, Oliver 126
"Crooked Man, The" 141
Cunningham, Henry (Sir) 150
"Curse of Eve, The" 105
Cycling 58, 65-66

D'Oyly Carte, Richard 82
Daly, Augustin 113
Daly's Theatre 113, 117, 119, 146
Dana, Charles A. 121
"Dancing Men, The" 102-103, 112
Daniels, George H. 121
Dante Alighieri 44
Davis, Loyal L. 131
Davis, Richard Harding 36, 114
De Maupassant, Guy 33
"De Profundis" 84
Dean, Amie F. 95, 199
Debs, Eugene V. 76, 153
"Debut of Bimbashi Joyce, The" 124
Decker, James Windsor 119
Delmonico's 113
Denmark, Royal Antiquarian Society 26
Denver, Colorado 82
Depew, Chauncey M. 131
Detroit, Michigan 66-71, 75
Deutschland (steamship) 24
Dial, The 53
Dickens, Charles 44, 48, 65, 82, 83, 124-125
Dickinson, Austin 95
Dickinson, Emily 95
Dictionary of National Biography 23
Dishler, Henry, Jr. 88
"Doctors of Hoyland, The" 84, 105, 137
Douglass, Frederick 101, 201
Doyle, Alexander P. (Rev.) 147
Doyle, Arthur Conan, accent 56, 70, 98-99, 101, 167

——, ancestry 21, 65, 99, 150, 187, 201
——, attire 44-45, 67, 70, 142, 188, 189
——, childhood 22, 101, 156-158
——, description 27-28
——, early life 159
——, fees 81, 123-125, 178, 210
——, handwriting 166, 187, 198
——, knighthood 23
——, lecturing 71-72, 180, 190-191
——, letters 7, 97, 187
——, luggage 55
——, photograph 79
——, religion 54, 68-70, 76, 101
——, surname 174
——, trips 13, 155
Doyle, Caroline (Lottie) 169
Doyle, Charles Altamont 74, 108, 167
Doyle, Connie 169
Doyle, Innes Hay 7, 23, 25, 48, 64, 67, 84, 107, 111, 142, 150, 151, 168, 205
Doyle, Jean (Leckie) 23
Doyle, Kingsley 23, 84, 117
Doyle, Louise 23, 28, 40, 148, 154
Doyle, Mary Foley 7, 187, 201
Doyle, Richard 166-167
Dreiser, Theodore 154
du Chaillu, Paul 63-64, 77, 187
Du Maurier, George 79
Dunraven, Lord 141
Duval, Horace C. 88, 121

East Lynne 126
Edinburgh 91, 118, 136, 138, 156, 160, 214
Edison electric works 132
Edison Phonograph Works 25
Edison, Thomas Alva 26, 108
Edwardes, George 113
Eggleston, Edward 151
Ehlers, E. M. L. (Colonel) 121
Eider (steamship) 24
Elbe (steamship) 24, 27, 62, 169-170
Electricians 34, 151
Eliot, Charles 86

Eliot, Samuel A. 86
Ellis Island 27
Ellsworth, J. W. 53
Ellsworth, William Webster 21, 88, 92, 197
Elmira, New York 129-130, 147
Elmira College 24
Emerson, Ralph Waldo 30, 92, 125
English-Speaking Union 155
Ericson, Leif 77
Erie Canal 45, 47
Etruria (steamship) 151-153, 221
Evans, W. T. 121
Exposition Universelle, Paris 53
Express robbery 56, 183

"Facts about Fiction" (lecture) 20, 49-50, 77, 180
Fawcett, Edgar 36
Feibleman, Isidore 56
Field, Eugene 21, 24, 36, 49, 53, 77, 78-79, 81, 98, 181, 192-193
Field, Marshall, department store 51
Fine, Henry Burchard 118
Fingerprints 140
Firm of Girdlestone, The 166
Fisher, William A., Jr. 119
Fitzgerald, Cissy 146
Flournoy, Theodore 69
Flushing, New York 132, 146-147
Football 109-111
Ford, Clara, *see* Westwood, Frank
Fordham, New York 103
"Foreign Office Romance, A" 36, 109
Fox, Margaret and Kate 68
France 17
Frank Leslie's 106, 153
Frederic, Harold 36
Freeman, Mary Wilkins, *see* Wilkins, Mary
French, Alice 79
Frohman, Charles 30, 55, 182
Frost, President 150
Froude, James Anthony 85
Fulton, Chandos 34, 121

Gaiety Girl, A 113, 146

Garland, Hamlin 36, 53, 59, 63, 81, 98, 182
Garman, Charles Edward 95
Garnet, Henry Highland 114
Garrett, John Work 119, 208
Gates, Merrill E. 95, 101, 199
General Electric 133
Genowine, George 78
George V 133, 213
Gerard, Brigadier 36, 109, 118, 127, 144-146, 154
Ghost 133
Gibbons, James (Cardinal) 102
Gibbs, Montgomery P. 144
Gibson, Charles Dana 114
Gibson, W. Hamilton 44
Gilbert and Sullivan 66, 82, 120
Gillette, William 55, 88, 139, 182
Gladstone, William E. 78
Glens Falls, New York 37, 130-132
Goethe, Johann Wolfgang von 44
Goff, John W. 121
"Golden Pince-Nez, The" 142
Goldsmid, F. J. (Sir) 169
Golf 116, 141-142, 218
Gollywog 115, 206
Goodwin, A. T. 121
Goodwin, J. Cheever 55
Gorringe, Commander 120
Gosse, Edmund 78
Governesses 173
Grahame, Kenneth 81
Gramophone 25, 170
Grant, Ulysses S. 58
Graphophone 25, 170
Gray, Ada 126
Gray, T. A. & Co. 78
"Great Keinplatz Experiment, The" 36
Great Shadow, The 144, 164-165
"Great Thoughts" 39
"Greek Interpreter, The" 45, 162
Green Flag, The 117, 124, 154
Greusel, John Hubert 66, 188, 198
Grolier Club 52, 171
Gubbins, Helen (Brodie) 25
Gubbins, John Harington 25, 170
Guggenheimer, Randolph 121

Gunnison, Herbert F. 88
Gunsaulus, Frank W. 78
Gutsch, Geheimrath und Frau 25, 170

Haas, Ernest 119
Haggard, H. Rider 36, 220
Haldeman, J. A. (General) 121
Halstead, Murat 85, 87
Hamilton, Alexander 87, 143
Hardy, Thomas 50
Harper, E. B. 121
Harper & Brothers 43, 79, 101, 114, 127, 154
Harper's Weekly 36, 43, 114, 123, 154
Harrison, Benjamin 144
Harte, Bret 29
Harvard College 32, 49, 52, 53, 54, 69, 86, 125
Harvest home 61-64
Hatch, Cora L. V. 69
Hatch, Richard D. 119
Hawaii 100
Hawkins, Anthony Hope 114
Hawthorne, Nathaniel 30, 149, 165
Hayes, Rutherford B. 121
Hayman, Al 55, 182
Hays, Franklin W. 56-57
Hayt, H. C. 130
Head, Elizabeth 78, 95
Head, Franklin H. 52, 63, 78, 81, 89, 181
Heap, David Porter 34
Hearn, Lafcadio 59, 185
Henderson, David 54
Herrick, Gerardus Post 119
Hewitt, Abram S. 121
Hickman, Major 25, 168
Higginson, Thomas Wentworth 49, 179
Higinbotham, Harlow and Rachel 48-49, 51, 81
Hill, David Bennett 32
Hinrichs, Frederick W. 88
"His First Operation" 105
"His Last Bow" 112
Hitchcock, Charles H. 91
Hitchcock, Ripley 116, 150

Hobbs, J. Howard (Rev.) 148
Hobson, Maud 146
Hole, Reynolds (Rev.) 44, 49, 96, 111, 117, 121
Holmes, H. H. 126
Holmes, Oliver Wendell 39, 91-92, 103,104, 120-121, 125, 131, 147, 209
Holmes, Sherlock, death and resurrection 28, 66-67, 127, 143-144, 154, 188, 190
Hopkins, Gerard Manley 24, 170
Hopkins, William Swinton Bennett 95
Hornung, Willie 116, 169
Houghton, A. J., brewers 93
Hound of the Baskervilles, The 154, 187
Howard, Bronson 29
Howard, May 58
Howells, William Dean 24, 36, 43-44, 57, 82 , 98, 105, 132, 134, 150, 151, 176
Hudson River 27, 37, 46, 122, 131, 149, 151
Hudson, Thomas Jay 70
Hudson's Bay Company 152
Hugo, Comtesse 22
Hume, William H. 121
Hunting 40-41
Hutchinson, Charles L. 49

Idler, The 35, 36, 70, 91, 105, 140, 149, 153, 174, 189, 191
Immigration 27
Imperial and Arion quartettes 77
Indian wars 37-38, 50, 122, 132, 165
Indianapolis, Indiana 55-57, 59, 60, 67
Inter-Ocean (Chicago newspaper) 19, 62, 83, 109, 180
Irving, Henry (Sir) 62, 86, 90, 145, 186
Irving, Washington 158, 165
Isaacs, David (Colonel) 133

"J. Habakuk Jephson's Statement" 166
Jamaica, New York 146, 148
James, Alice 125
James, E. C. (Colonel) 121
James, Henry 36, 125
James, William 69, 125
Janet, Pierre 69
Japan 25, 26, 148, 170, 185
"Japanned Box, The" 26
Jefferson, Joseph 64, 78, 88, 90
Jeffreys, Judge 117, 126
Jennie on the streetcar 18
Jennings, George B. 60
Jerome, Jerome K. 35, 36, 50, 82, 105, 190
Jerome, Thomas 70, 190
Jesuits 34, 38, 101, 165
Jews in New York 31, 44, 111
Jex-Blake, Sophia 136
Johnson, Arthur J. 138

Kaye, Fred 146
Keek, Robert P. 98
Kehoe, Jack 112-113
Kelvin, William Thomson (Lord) 22
Kendall, Lydia W. 90, 196
Kendrick, D. H. 97
Kennan, George 19, 148
Kensington, Hotel 28
Key, Francis Scott 102
Kimball, Ingalls 53, 193
King, Charles 203
King, Katie 69
Kingsley, Charles 120
Kinsley, H. M. 61
Kipling, Caroline 140-142, 217
Kipling, Rudyard 36, 42, 48, 50, 71, 84, 116, 139-142, 154
Kohlsaat, H. H. 62, 186
Korea 17

Ladies' Home Journal 149
"Lady or the Tiger, The" 28
Lake George, New York 37-38
Lambdin, A. C. 111
Lang, Andrew 164
Langtry, Lillie 97, 132, 142
Larned, W. C. 53
Lathes, Richard (Colonel) 121
Latrobe, Benjamin Henry 102

Lawrence, Frank R. 121-122, 150
Leadville, Colorado 82
Leckie, Malcolm 84
Lecture circuit 18-19, 34-35, 124-125, 169
Lee, William H. 93, 198
Leo XIII, Pope 102
Leslie, Frank 106
Letters, Doyle's during trip 7, 97, 187
Liberty, statue 27, 148
"Life on a Greenland Whaler" 124
Lily Dale, New York 69, 189
Lincoln, Abraham 30
Lineff, Madam 148
"Lion's Mane, The" 166
Lippincott, Craige 107, 203
Lippincott, J. B. & Co. 80, 107, 144, 192, 194
Lippincott, J. Dundas 107
Lippincott's Magazine 33, 79, 107
Little, Robert Forsyth, Jr. 119
Little Jack Sheppard 152
Little Room 80
Liverpool 153
London, sights 153
Longfellow, Henry Wadsworth 125
Longmans 164
"Lord of Chateau Noir, The" 45, 84, 94-95, 130, 165, 167, 177
Lord, Chester S. 121
"Los Amigos Fiasco, The" 120
Lotos Club 33, 120-122, 131, 150, 209
Love, Doyle's comments 50
Lovell, Coryell (publishers) 79
Lovell, John W. 43
Low, Edward H. 121
Low, Seth 87, 121
Lowell, James Russell 125, 150, 209
Lyceum circuit 19, 169

Mabie, Hamilton Wright 45, 89, 149, 150, 177, 221
Macdonald, John A. (Sir) 135
Machetti, Filberto 55
MacArthur, Robert Stuart 44
MacManus, Theodore F. 65-66

Mahany, Rowland H. 139
Mallarmé, Stephane 81
Maltby, Elizabeth 89
Mann, Dr. 70
Marbot, Jean Baptiste de 145-146
Marlowe, Julia 88
Marquette, Jacques 76
Marriage, Doyle's comments 50
"Marriage of the Brigadier, The" 145
Marshall, John 89
Martinot, Sadie 139
Massor, Frederic 144
Matthews, Brander 126
Matz, Mary and Otto 51
Mauch Chunk, Pennsylvania 112
"Mazarin Stone, The" 26, 170
Maznenet, D. 132
McAlpin, Edwin A., Jr. 119
McCarthy, Francis F. 101
McCay, Leroy W. 118
McClure, Robert 194
McClure, Samuel S. 123-124, 150, 194
McClure's magazine 36, 84, 91, 123-124, 191, 194
McCormick, Stanley R. 119
McCosh, James 119
McCulloch, Oscar Carleton 56
McElroy, William H. 96, 121, 131
McKeen, James 87
McMichael, Clayton 107
McMillan, James 70
McNair, Mary Wilson 130
"Medal of Brigadier Gerard, The" 109, 127
"Meeting of the Sweethearts, The" 36
Memoirs of Sherlock Holmes, The 20, 22, 53, 127, 154
Meredith, George 20, 29, 43, 50, 56, 71-75, 77, 198
Meyers, J. W. 65
Micah Clarke 19, 22, 28, 36, 93, 117, 126, 138, 139, 164, 167, 168
Micawber Club 66, 188
Millard, George M. 53
Miller, Joaquin 54
Miller, Lewis 46

Millham, Josephine 130
Mills, Luther Laflin 64
Milwaukee, Wisconsin 64, 76-78, 82
Minor Prophets, club 66
Mitchell, Silas Weir 107, 203-204
Monkhouse, Harry 146
Monroe, Frederick Mitchell 88
Montréal, Québec 152
Moody, William Vaughn 54
Moore, Decima 146
Mora, Helena 58
Moran, Edward 121
Moriarty, James, see Reichenbach Falls
Mormons 47
Morristown, New Jersey 142
Morse, Jerome E. 121
Mount Holyoke College 91
Muirhead, James F. 41
Munsey's Magazine 123
Murillo, Bartolomé (painter) 60
Murray, David Christie 121
Murray, F. T. 121
Murray, James Ormsbee 118
Murray, Rosa 144
"My First Book" 84, 194
Myers, F. W. H. 69
Mystery of Cloomber, The 166
Mystery of Sasassa Valley, The 166

Napoleon Bonaparte 40, 74, 84, 118, 144-146
Napoleon Bonaparte (play) 144
National Capital Press Club 104
New Age magazine 35
New Jersey, College of, see Princeton
New Orleans, Louisiana 56, 183
New Rochelle, New York 119-120
New York, docks 27, 171
—— lectures in 44, 114, 117, 119, 221
—— sights 29-31, 111-113
Newark, New Jersey 108-109
Newport, Rhode Island 32
Niagara Falls 133-135, 213-214
Nicoll, William Robertson 89
Nightingale, Florence 136
Nixon, Elizabeth (Mrs. William) 51

Nixon, William Penn 52
Nordica (Lillian Norton) 51, 148
North American Review 34
North American, The 107
North-German Lloyd Line 24
Northampton, Massachusetts 88-91, 93, 95
Northrop, A. L. (Dr.) 121
Norwich, Connecticut 97-98
"Norwood Builder, The" 140, 183
Nye, Edgar (Bill) 21, 151, 221

O'Brien, Charles 66
O'Brien, M. J. (Judge) 121
Ogden, Utah 82
Oglesby, Richard James 63, 186-187
Orange, New Jersey 116-117
Ormsbee, Agnes Bailey 151
Ottoman Empire 148
Outlook magazine 45
Oxford, Bishop of 22

Paderewski, Ignace 88, 121, 142
Page, Thomas Nelson 51, 150
Palmyra, New York 47
Parasite, The 36, 69, 109, 128, 154
Paris (steamship) 97
Parker, Gilbert 36, 50
Parkman, Francis 37-38, 91, 125, 131, 165, 174
Passport, The 139
Patch, Sam 129
Paterson, New Jersey 143
Patterson, Edward 121
Patton, Francis Landey 118
Peary, Robert 87, 88
Pease, Lewis F. 119
Peck, Clarence L. 49
Pelton, Charles 60
Penn, William 106
Pennsylvania, University of 109-111
Perry, Bliss 118, 140
Pfatischer, Mathias 25
Philadelphia 92, 106-108, 111-112, 117
Phonograph 25
Photography 57, 151, 184

Physicians 56-57, 105, 111, 127-128, 136-138, 203-204, 214-216
Pickering, Annie (Dr.) 136-138, 214-216
Pickering, Latimer (Dr.) 130, 136-138, 214-216
Pierce, James F. 121
Pinkerton, Allan 112
Piracy in publishing 80, 147, 192-193
Pittsburgh, Pennsylvania 106, 203
Plymouth 25
Pocket University, The 45, 177
Poe, Edgar Allan 29, 56, 90, 102-104, 105, 149, 160, 202
Poindexter, Philip 106
Police 32, 56, 60, 87, 112
Political affairs 17, 31, 42, 100, 103-104, 121, 147, 202
Pollock, Frederick (Sir) 22
Pond, James B. (Major) 7, 8, 18, 21, 27, 29, 33, 44, 45, 70, 77, 81, 97, 121, 125, 126, 146, 168, 169, 198
Pond, W. A. & Co. 44
Porter, Horace (General) 121
Portsmouth, England 72, 109
Portsmouth Literary and Scientific Society 71, 190-191
Potter, Henry Codman (Rt. Rev.) 150
Pratt, Enoch 102
Pratt, William Fenno 90
Presbyterianism 91, 118-119, 133, 148, 150
Preston, Jessie and Georgina 152, 222
Princeton, lecture at 117-119
Princeton University 109-111, 117-120
Printing, quality 79
Prisons 129, 147, 212 – *see also* Sing Sing
Pullman cars 21, 75-76
Pullman strike 76, 117
Punch (magazine) 167

Queens County, New York 30, 86, 146
Queenstown 153
Quiller-Couch, Arthur 36, 71, 74

Raffles 116
Railways 45-46, 75-76, 130, 152, 191
Rand McNally 80
Raymond, Andrew Van Vranken 133
Raymond, Frankie M. 54
Reade, Charles 164, 167
Reade, Winwood 167
"Red Circle, The" 112
"Red-Headed League, The" 167
Redpath Lyceum Bureau 19
Refugees, The 19, 20, 22, 36, 38, 117, 126, 142, 165, 167, 180, 199
Reichenbach Falls 131, 134, 214
Reid, Mayne 30, 157, 166
Remington, Frederic 33, 107, 121
"Resident Patient, The" 127, 211
Rice, F. Willis 63
Richards, George and Mrs. 116-117
Richards, J. Havens 101
Richmond County, New York 30, 32
Riddle, George 96
Riley, James Whitcomb 19, 55-57, 59, 98, 151, 183, 198
Roberts, Algernon B. 119
Robinson, John R. 97
Robinson, Nugent 34
Rochester, New York 127-129, 211-212
Rockefeller, John D. 44
Rodney Stone 109
Roessle, T. E. 100
Roherer, A. L. 132
Roman Catholic Church 102, 105, 147, 180
Rosebery, Lord 17
Ross, Robert E. 119
Rossetti, Dante Gabriel 194
Round the Fire Stories 154
Round the Red Lamp 36, 71, 95, 104-106, 127, 146, 154, 199, 203
Royal Artillery 25
Rubinstein, Anton 126
Ruspoli, Prince 32
Russell, Alice M. 78-79
Russell, Clark 36, 50

Russell, Sol Smith 64, 78, 89
Rutgers Female Institute 26
Rutherford, William 136
Ryan, Paddy 108
Ryerson, Egerton 138
Ryerson, George Sterling 138, 216
Ryerson, Martin 49
Ryley, Charles 146

Sage, O. V. 126
Saltus, Edgar 33-34, 173
Salvation Army 100
Santayana, George 54, 125
Saunt-Gaudens-Augustus 113
Savage, Ephraim 165
Savage, William 70
"Scandal in Bohemia, A" 117, 125, 192
Scheinert, Hans 25
Schenectady, New York 122, 132-133
Schreiner, Olive 50, 56, 198
Scott, James W. W. 52, 63, 78, 81
Scott, Walter 44, 91, 158, 163, 166
Scribner, Charles 32
Scribner's magazine 123, 141
Seelye, President 89
"Selecting a Ghost" 116
Shakespeare, William 32, 53, 88
Shaw, George Bernard 126
Shaw, John M. 57
Shea, Daniel T. 98
Shearer, J. L. 60
Shenandoah Valley 112-113
Shenandoah (play) 29, 48, 172
Sheridan, Philip 29
Sherlock Holmes (play) 55, 139
Sherman, William Tecumseh 58
Sicard, George S. 101
Sign of the Four, The 21, 34, 61, 80, 107, 160, 192-193, 220
Sing Sing 46, 126
Sino-Japanese War 148
"Six Napoleons, The" 145
Skeat, W. W. (Prof.) 169
Skinner, Otis 88
Skis 142, 154
Skyscrapers 48

"'Slapping Sal', The" 120
Slavery 114
Sloane, William Milligan 118, 144
Smith College 88-89, 95, 196
Smith, Alfred E. 121
Smith, Charles Emory 107
Smith, Donald (Sir) 152
Smith, Edgar W. 142, 219
Smith, F. Hopkinson 150
Smith, Goldwin 130, 137
Smith, Greenhough 22
Smith, Joseph 47
Smith, Ralph Dusenbury 119
Socialist style 74
Society for Psychical Research 69, 84, 189
Songs of the Road 81, 194
Sonn, George Y. 108
South African War 25
Southampton 24
"Speckled Band, The" 166
Speer, Fitzhugh Coyle 119
Spiritualism 13, 23, 34, 35, 68-70, 81, 84, 126, 129, 173, 182, 183, 185, 211-212
Splaine, Cyprian (Rev.) 24, 170
Springfield, Massachusetts 89, 91, 92, 93
Staigen, Minna 25
Stark Munro Letters, The 35, 36, 54, 106, 140, 153, 193, 210
State University of New York 26, 121
Staten Island, New York 30, 32
Stead, William T. 51
Steamships 24, 62, 97, 151, 186
Stein, Gertrude 125
Steiner, Harry L. 66
Steinmetz, Charles 133
Stephen, Harriet 23
Stephen, James Fitzjames (Sir) 23
Stephen, Leslie (Sir) 23, 73
Stevens, George W. 65-66
Stevenson, Eugene 144, 219
Stevenson, Robert Louis 50, 54, 56, 72-73, 95, 153, 222
Stires, E. M. 64
Stockton, Frank 28

Stoddard, John Lawson 34
Stoddart, J. M. 34
Stoker, Bram 186
Stone, Herbert S. 53, 78, 79, 81, 181, 193
Stone, Melville E. 51-52, 64, 77, 78, 81, 104
Stone, Melville E., Jr. 52
Stonyhurst College 24
Story of Waterloo, The 29, 62, 105, 186
Stowe-Gullen, Augusta 215-216
"Straggler of '15, A" 105, 126, 145
Strand magazine 22, 23, 123, 144
Streetcar 18
Strong, William L. 103
Stubbs, William 22
Study in Scarlet, A 72, 80, 107, 193
Suckling, J. E. 137
Sullivan, John L. 108-109, 139
"Sweethearts" 84
Swenson, Eric Pierson 40
Swift, Jonathan 50
Swing, David 32, 54, 78
Sydell, Rose 58
Syphilis 111
Syracuse, New York 198

Taft, William Howard 60
Tainter, Charles Sumner and Lila 25
Tammany Hall 103-104, 121, 147
Tarbell, Ida 84
Taylor, John A. 88
Tennyson, Alfred (Lord) 39, 209
Terry, Ellen 86, 133
Thackeray, William Makepeace 23, 45, 72-73, 124-125, 156-157, 159, 191
Thanet, Octave 79
Thanksgiving Day 140
Theatre 29, 48, 54-55, 88, 113, 144, 152
Thelen, Walker 79
Theosophy 34, 173
Thiers, Louis Adolphe 144
"Third Generation, The" 105
Thompson, John (Sir) 135, 153
"Three Gables, The" 43
"Three Garridebs, The" 112

"Three Harlots, The" 81, 193-194
"Three Students, The" 172
Through the Magic Door 174, 202
Ticonderoga, New York 37
Titsworth, Judson 77
Todd, David 95
Todd, Mabel Loomis 95, 200
Toledo, Ohio 64-66
Too Much Johnson 88
Torbett, Ollie 148
Toronto, Ontario 64, 82, 98, 118, 130 135-139, 187
Townsend, George W. (Mrs.) 139
Transportation 45-56 – *see also* Railways, Steamships
Trenton, New Jersey 109
Troy, New York 132
Trudeau, Edward Livingston 40
Tuberculosis 22, 23, 40, 154
Twain, Mark 19, 29, 33, 121, 129, 134, 139-140, 142, 151, 217
Twentieth Century Club, Chicago 48-51
Typhoid 154

Uncle Bernac 145
Uncle Remus 150
Under the Gaslight 113
Union College 132-133, 171
Union Jack 25, 42, 134-135, 137
Unitarianism 86-87, 91, 114
United Press 52
United States, description 41-42, 97-98
——, food 59
——, in Doyle's works 98, 111-113
——, newspapers 90
——, slang 70-71
United States Book Company 79-80, 192
University of the City of New York 30, 172
Upper Norwood Scientific and Literary Society 50
Utica, New York 47, 93, 198

Vaccination 146
Valley of Fear, The 112-113

Van Dyke, Henry 89, 150
van Heese, C. M. and C. T. 60
Venezuela 155
Verne, Jules 103
Victoria Regina 17, 153
Villiers, Frederick 71, 197
Vincent, John 46
Violet (spirit) 69
Voltaire 127
von Gössel, F., Captain 24
von Holst, Hermann 63
Vrooman, J. W. 121

Waldorf Hotel 113
Walery, photographer 79
Walker, Henry (Capt.) 151
Walker, John Brisben 34, 123, 150
Walker, Roberts 96
Walker, W. W. 121
Wall Street 29
Wallace, Elizabeth 78
Wallace, Lew 44, 96, 111, 133
Wantagh, New York 147
Ward, Frederick A. 87
Warner, Charles Dudley 150
Washington Court House, Ohio 61
Washington, D.C. 100-101
Washington, George 30, 47
Waterloo 29, 40, 62, 105, 145
Watt, A. P. 154
Way, W. Irving 52
Weber and Fields 58
Weeks, B. S. 121
West Point, New York 34, 46
West, Charles E. 26, 87, 171
Westwood, Frank 64, 136, 138, 187
Weyman, Stanley 154
Wheat, price of 63, 186
Whelpley, A. W. 60
White Company, The 22, 28, 36, 43, 52, 67, 71, 123, 143, 154, 164, 167
White, J. William 107, 111
White, Stanford 113
Whittier, John Greenleaf 125, 131
Wilde, Oscar 19, 82, 166
Wilkins, Mary 29, 36, 150, 172
Williams, Chauncey L. 52

Williams, Sherman L. 131-132
Williams, William Carlos 143
Willson, J. S. 138
Wilson, William R. 119
Windsor, Ontario 66
Winslow, Erving (Mrs.) 198
Winton, Alexander 75
Wister, Owen 107, 151
Woolf, Leonard and Virginia 23
Woolley, C. J. 65
Wooster, George H. 121
Worcester, Massachusetts 94-95, 101
World Building 29, 172
World War I 25, 111, 205

Yale University 82, 96, 137
"Yellow Face, The" 198
Yonkers, New York 101, 114-116, 167

Zangwill, Israel 22, 50
Zola, Emile 33, 149